The Aerospace Business

This textbook provides a detailed overview of industry-specific business management and technology management practices in aerospace for relevant bachelors and MBA programs.

The Aerospace Business: Management and Technology sequentially addresses familiar management disciplines such as production management, labor relations, program management, business law, quality assurance, engineering management, supply-chain management, marketing, and finance, among others. In this context it analyzes and discusses the distinctive perspective and requirements of the aerospace industry. The book also includes subjects of special interest such as government intervention in the sector and strategies to deal with the environmental impact of aircraft. As each chapter deals with a separate management discipline, the material reviews the historical background, technical peculiarities, and financial factors that led the aerospace industry to evolve its own distinct practices and tradition. Theoretical bases of the practices are explained, and the chapters provide actual examples from the industry to illustrate application of the theories. The material is compiled, organized, and analyzed in ways that often provide original perspectives on the subject matter.

University students, particularly in programs oriented towards aviation and aerospace management, will find the book to be directly applicable to their studies. It is also extremely appropriate for aerospace MBA and executive MBA programs, and would suit specialized corporate or government training programs related to aerospace.

Wesley Spreen's professional career in the aerospace industry includes executive and managerial jobs at Boeing, Lockheed, General Dynamics, Textron, and the US Air Force. At Lockheed he was managing director of the F-16 international coproduction consortium, which at the time was the largest cooperative industrial program in the history of the aerospace industry. At Boeing he was Director of International Marketing and Sales for the company's helicopter division.

The Aerospace Business

Management and Technology

Wesley Spreen

Routledge
Taylor & Francis Group

LONDON AND NEW YORK

First published 2020
by Routledge
2 Park Square, Milton Park, Abingdon, Oxon OX14 4RN

and by Routledge
52 Vanderbilt Avenue, New York, NY 10017

Routledge is an imprint of the Taylor & Francis Group, an informa business

British Library Cataloguing-in-Publication Data
A catalogue record for this book is available from the British Library

Library of Congress Cataloging-in-Publication Data
A catalog record has been requested for this book

ISBN: 978-0-367-28059-8 (hbk)
ISBN: 978-0-367-28058-1 (pbk)
ISBN: 978-0-429-29945-2 (ebk)

Typeset in Bembo
by Deanta Global Publishing Services, Chennai, India

Printed and bound by CPI Group (UK) Ltd, Croydon, CR0 4YY

To my daughters Janette and Elizabeth, perfectly described by
John Milton in *Paradise Lost*:

Grace was in all her steps, heaven in her eye, in every gesture dignity and love.

Full disclosure

In any book of this scope there is often insight to be gained by comparing history and management practices at different companies and in different geographical regions. The author has made every attempt to be objective and impartial in these comparisons. However, he is a former executive of Lockheed and Boeing, and his views have no doubt been influenced by those experiences. Geography is destiny. On the other hand, he has spent more than 11 years in residence in Europe, working closely with European aerospace entities that were often Airbus members, and he has vast respect for the ideals, the accomplishments, and the managerial competence of that undertaking.

In Canada, Brazil, Japan, China, India, Russia, Korea, and elsewhere in the world we are all colleagues in the industry, and we have much to learn from each other.

Contents

Abbreviations and acronyms

A&D	Aerospace and Defense
AAQG	American Aerospace Quality Group
AC3B	Airworthiness Certification Criteria Control Board
ACARE	Advisory Council for Aviation Research and Innovation in Europe
ACWP	actual cost of work performed
AD	airworthiness directive
AECA	Arms Export Control Act
AFP	automatic fiber placement
AFPD	Air Force Policy Directive
AHM	aircraft health monitoring
AIA	Aerospace Industries Association
AIG	American International Group
APT	automatically programmed tool
APU	auxiliary power unit
ASB	alert service bulletin
ASD	Aerospace and Defence Industries Association of Europe
ASTM	American Society for Testing and Materials
ASU	Aircraft Sector Understanding
ATE	automated test equipment
ATR	Avions de Transport Régional
AVIC	Aviation Industries of China
AWACS	Airborne Warning and Control System
AWJ	abrasive water jet
BAFO	Best and Final Offer
BCWP	budgeted cost of work performed
BCWS	budgeted cost of work scheduled
BGA	business and general aviation
BIS	Bureau of Industry and Security
BLS	Bureau of Labor Statistics
BNDES	Banco Nacional de Desenvolvimento Econômico e Social
BWB	blended wing and body
BXA	Bureau of Export Administration
CAA	Civil Aeronautics Authority

CAA	Civil Airworthiness Authority
CAA	Civil Aviation Authority
CAAFI	Commercial Aviation Alternative Fuels Initiative
CAB	Civil Aeronautics Board
CAEP	Committee on Aviation Environmental Protection
CAPEX	capital expenditure
CAST	China Aerospace Science and Technology Corporation
CATIA	computer-aided three-dimensional interactive application
CCB	change control board
CCL	Commerce Control List
CDR	Critical Design Review
CDRL	contract data requirements list
CER	cost estimating relationships
CFE	customer-furnished equipment
CFE–CGC	Confédération Française de l'Encadrement – Confédération Générale des Cadres
CFIUS	Committee on Foreign Investment in the United States
CI	configuration item
CIEEMG	Commission interministérielle pour l'étude des exportations de matériel de guerre
CIP	component improvement program
CIS	Commonwealth of Independent States
CNC	computerized numerically controlled
CO$_2$	carbon dioxide
COFACE	Compagnie Française d'Assurance pour le Commerce Extérieur
COMAC	Commercial Aircraft Corporation of China
CORSIA	Carbon Offsetting and Reduction Scheme for International Aviation
COTS	commercial off-the-shelf
CPM	Critical Path Method
CPMIEC	China Precision Machinery Import Export Corporation
CR	change request
CTC	cost-to-complete
DCAA	Defense Contract Audit Agency
DFARS	Defense Federal Acquisition Regulation Supplement
DOC	Department of Commerce
DoD	Department of Defense
DPD	digital product definition
DSCA	Defense Security Cooperation Agency
DSU	Dispute Settlement Understanding
DTI	Department of Trade and Industry
EADS	European Aeronautics, Defence and Space Company
EAQG	European Aerospace Quality Group
EAR	Export Administration Regulations
EASA	European Union Aviation Safety Agency

ECA	export credit agency
ECAC	European Civil Aviation Conference
ECN	engineering change notice
ECO	engineering change order
ECO	export controls organization
ECP	engineering change proposal
ECR	engineering change request
EDC	Export Development Canada
EETC	enhanced equipment trust certificates
EPNdB	effective perceived noise in decibels
EPROM	erasable programmable read-only memory
ESA	European Space Agency
ETS	emissions trading system
EU-ETS	European Emissions Trading System
EVM	earned value management
FAA	Federal Aviation Administration
FACE	Future Airborne Capability Environment
FAR	Federal Acquisition Regulation
FAR	Federal Airworthiness Regulation
FASB	Financial Accounting Standards Board
FIRRMA	Foreign Investment Risk Review Modernization Act
FMS	foreign military sales
FO	*force ouvrière*
FRR	Flight Readiness Review
FT	Fischer–Tropsch
GA	General Aviation
GAMA	General Aviation Manufacturers Association
GAO	Government Accountability Office
GARA	General Aviation Revitalization Act
GATT	General Agreement on Tariffs and Trade
GDP	Gross Domestic Product
GE	General Electric
GFE	government-furnished equipment
GHG	greenhouse gas
GOCO	government-owned contractor-operated
GPA	Guinness Peat Aviation
HALE	high altitude long endurance
HEFA	Hydroprocessed Esters and Fatty Acids
HSM	high-speed machining
IAE	International Aero Engines
IAI	Israel Aerospace Industries
IAM	International Association of Machinists
IAQG	International Aerospace Quality Group
IASB	International Accounting Standards Board
ICA	instructions for continued airworthiness

ICAO	International Civil Aviation Organization
ICD	interface control documentation
IFE	in-flight entertainment
ILFC	International Lease Finance Corporation
IMP	integrated master plan
IMS	integrated master schedule
IPCC	Intergovernmental Panel on Climate Change
IPS	integrated product support
IPT	integrated product team
ISO	Organization for Standardization
ITAR	International Traffic in Arms Regulation
ITC	International Trade Commission
ITT	invitation to tender
JAA	Joint Aviation Authorities
JSF	Joint Strike Fighter
KAI	Korean Aerospace Industries
KIS	keep-it-sold
LASU	Large Aircraft Sector Understanding
LCA	large civil aircraft
LLP	life-limited parts
LRU	line replaceable unit
MALE	medium altitude long endurance
MBD	model-based definition
MCR	Mission Concept Review
MDR	Mission Definition Review
MRB	material review board
MRCA	Multi-Role Combat Aircraft
MRO	maintenance, repair, and overhaul
MTT	Moscow Institute of Thermal Technology
MWI	manufacturing work instruction
NAICS	North American Industrial Classification System
NAMMA	NATO Multi-Role Combat Aircraft Development and Production Management Agency
NAMMO	NATO MRCA Management and Production Organization
NASA	National Aeronautics and Space Administration
NATO	North Atlantic Treaty Organization
NC	numerically controlled
NCR	non-conformance report
NDI	non-destructive inspection
NDIA	National Defense Industrial Association
NEC	nowhere else classified
NETMA	NATO Eurofighter and Tornado Management Agency
NextGen	Next Generation Air Transportation System
NLRB	National Labor Relations Board
NORC	Naval Ordnance Research Calculator

NORINCO	China North Industries Corporation
NOx	Generic Nitrogen Oxide Pollutants
NRCC	Nuclear Regulatory Commission Controls
NTSB	National Transport Safety Board
OBS	organizational breakdown structure
OCCAR	Organisation Conjointe de Coopération en matière d'Armement
ODTC	Office of Defense Trade Controls
OECD	Organization for Economic Cooperation and Development
OEM	original equipment manufacturer
OMS	Open Mission Systems
ORR	Operational Readiness Review
OT&E	Operational Test and Evaluation
P&W	Pratt and Whitney
P2F	passenger to freighter
PBP	performance-based payments
PDP	predelivery payments
PDR	Preliminary Design Review
PERT	Program Evaluation Review Technique
$\mathbf{P_{go}}$	probability that the program will occur
PM	program manager
PMA	Part Manufacturer Approval
PMP	program management plan
ppm	parts per million
PRR	Production Readiness Review
$\mathbf{P_{win}}$	probability of win
QEC	quick engine change
QMS	quality management system
RFI	request for information
RFP	request for proposal
RFQ	request for quotation
RFT	request for tender
RMA	reliability, maintainability, availability
RNAV	area navigation
RNP	required performance navigation
RPV	remotely piloted vehicle
SADI	Strategic Aerospace and Defense Initiative
SAE	Society of Automotive Engineers
SAR	System Acceptance Review
SARPs	Standards and Recommended Practices
SB	service bulletin
SCM	subcontract management
SCM	Subsidies and Countervailing Measures
SDR	System Design Review
SECBAT	Société d'Étude et de Construction de Breguet Atlantic

SEMP	systems engineering management plan
SEP	systems engineering plan
SIC	Standard Industrial Code
SIP	Synthesized Iso-Paraffins
SJAC	Society of Japanese Aerospace Companies
SM	Single Manager
SMP	subcontract management plan
SOO	statement of objectives
SOPs	standard operating procedures
SOW	statement of work
SPEEA	Society of Engineering Employees in Aerospace
SPF	superplastic forming
SRD	system requirements document
SRR	System Requirements Review
SRU	shop replaceable unit
STOVL	short takeoff vertical landing
TC	Type Certificate
TCTO	time compliance technical order
TO	technical order
TRR	Test Readiness Review
UAC	United Aircraft Corporation (Russia)
UAS	unmanned aerospace system
UAV	unmanned aerospace vehicle
UAW	United Auto Workers
UCAV	unmanned combat aerospace vehicle
UCI	Unmanned Aircraft Systems Control Initiative
UNFCCC	United Nations Framework Convention on Climate Change
UTAS	United Technologies Aerospace Systems
VOC	volatile Organic compounds
VTOL	vertical takeoff and landing
WBS	work breakdown structure
WIP	work-in-process
WTO	World Trade Organization
WTW	well-to-wake

1 Introduction

Figure 1.1 The beginning of a new industry.

It put a man on the moon. The aerospace industry is exceptional in many respects. It is a technological crown jewel that synthesizes much of the most advanced scientific and engineering knowledge of modern civilizations. It produces products that, even to technologically jaded citizens of the twenty-first century, are breathtaking in their appearance and capabilities.

The structure and characteristics of the industry are described in detail in Chapter 2, but a few summary statistics published by the Aerospace Industries Association (AIA) provide insight into the economic importance of the industry in the USA:

- The US Aerospace & Defense (A&D) industry supports 2.4 million jobs in the USA in 2016, representing approximately 2% of the nation's total employment base and 13% of the nation's manufacturing workforce.

- End-use manufacturers of A&D systems accounted for 35% (845,000) of the industry's total jobs, while the supply chain accounted for the remaining 65%, or 1.6 million jobs.
- In 2016, the US Aerospace & Defense industry generated $872 billion in sales revenue.
- End-use manufacturers of A&D systems accounted for 52% of total sales, while the industry's supply chain accounted for the remaining 48% of sales.
- A&D generated $307 billion in value-added products and services, which accounted for 1.8% of US Gross Domestic Product.
- A&D is the nation's leading net exporting industry and generated a record trade balance of $90 billion in 2016.
- A&D accounts for 10% of total US exports in goods, and is the nation's second-largest exporting industry.

The Aerospace and Defence Industries Association of Europe (ASD), the European equivalent of AIA, publishes some similar data:

- Total turnover for the A&D industry in Europe for 2016 was €220.2 billion.
- Total employment in 2016 was 843,400.
- The industry generated €20 billion in research & development (R&D) in 2016.
- European A&D exports in 2016 were €123 billion.

Distinguishing characteristics of the aerospace industry

This book will look in detail at some of the fundamental ways in which the aerospace industry is managed differently from other industries. Before proceeding to that detailed study, it is worthwhile to consider a few of the **intangible** characteristics that differentiate aerospace from its industrial peers:

- Aircraft and space vehicles are perhaps the ultimate technological icons of our civilization. The industry represents a single-point confluence of many of the most advanced technical achievements of our species.
- Aircraft and rockets are big, visible, noisy, and in the aesthetic of some observers, awesome to behold.
- They are extremely expensive to acquire and to operate.
- The complexity of aerospace design and manufacture is probably unmatched by any other industry.
- Since its advent, the industry has been a symbol of national prestige and military hegemony.
- The industry is intrinsically international in outlook and structure. In many ways it represents the most sophisticated manifestation of large-scale technological cooperation among nations.

- The industry and its products are inherently exposed to risk of large-scale catastrophic occurrences, resulting in application of rigorous international and national safety standards and regulations.
- The products of the industry are characterized by a dichotomy of civil or military applications. The two segments often overlap, eliciting the attention and direct involvement of governments and international organizations.
- The increasing volume of air transportation combined with public concern about rising emissions seem to be leading to an environmental dilemma that will eventually have to be resolved by government involvement, technological improvements, and societal change.

The structure of this volume

In many respects, the aerospace industry is managed in the same ways as other manufacturing industries. In other ways, aerospace management methods have evolved in ways that are distinctly different. The objective of this book is to identify the distinct management methods of the industry, to understand how they came to evolve, and to study how they are applied.

To accomplish this, we will proceed by sequentially focusing on the traditional disciplines familiar to any student of management.

In Chapter 2 we will examine the **general structure of the aerospace industry**, starting by studying its historical evolution. We will survey the many specialized products and industry sectors that make up its horizontal segmentation, and will pay special attention to the military–civil dichotomy that divides the industry into halves of roughly equivalent size. We will see how the industry is distributed geographically within Europe, the USA, and elsewhere, and will discuss the industry's vertical stratification and its value chain, beginning with raw material suppliers and proceeding to the giant integrated aircraft manufacturers at the top of the pyramid.

Chapter 3 deals with the **aerospace workforce and labor relations**. It analyzes the geographical distribution of the workforce in North America, Europe, and Asia, and looks at government initiatives to foster its growth. It follows the history of organized labor in the industry, and considers political controversies caused by redistribution of aerospace jobs as a result of international collaborative ventures.

Chapter 4, on **aerospace law, international accords, and contracting procedures**, is a summary of the context and application of laws and international agreements applying to the aerospace industry, including government airworthiness regulations and agencies, civil liabilities and tort law governing civil and military aircraft, export control licensing, and international limitations on government subsidies. A section on aerospace contracting methods is also included.

Chapter 5 addresses **government financial support of aerospace**. It reviews the history of government nationalization and subsequent privatization of aerospace industries, international agreements intended to curtail market distortions caused by government loans and subsidies, and an overview of the long-term Euro–American dispute involving perceived unfair subsidies to Boeing, Airbus, Bombardier, and Embraer.

Chapter 6 covers the unique history of **international cooperation in aerospace**, including **joint ventures, teaming, and industrial offsets**. It analyzes the motivation for international cooperation and the structural arrangements that aerospace firms use to work together internationally, and includes a study of economic benefits and political controversy surrounding industrial offsets.

Chapter 7 explores **aerospace accounting and financial management**, and contains explanation and analysis of unconventional financial methods and accounting treatments used in the industry. These practices are often a result of inordinately large capital investments and extended time intervals between program launch and breakeven. The chapter studies financing strategies used in the industry, including arrangements with risk-sharing partners. Financial practices in both the civil and military sectors are discussed and accounting concepts used by Airbus and Boeing are compared and contrasted.

Chapter 8 is a treatment of **aerospace systems engineering and technology management**. It is a detailed review of how the aerospace industry developed the concept of systems engineering, what the concept accomplishes, and how the discipline has been defined and applied to control technology during the phases of design, production, and post-delivery. Procedures used for change management and configuration control are described in detail.

Chapter 9 describes practices the industry has developed for **management of aerospace programs**. Beginning with a definition of an aerospace program, the chapter recounts the early history of the need for a management system to control the growing design and production complexity in the industry. Basic tenets of the program management concept are explored, and standard aerospace program management practices are explained. Illustrative examples are provided, including management structures of major joint international programs.

Chapter 10 addresses **aerospace production management**, and traces the evolution of aerospace production methods, including innovative technologies originally developed specifically for aerospace applications. Recent aggressive initiatives to improve efficiencies by introducing lean manufacturing methods are described. Concepts for scheduling and control are discussed, including the use of work breakdown structures. The flow of planning, control, and implementation in the factory are traced in detail.

Chapter 11, on the subject of **management of aerospace quality assurance**, includes a discussion of the concept of cost of quality in the aerospace industry, and follows the historical development of international aerospace quality standards. A detailed explanation is provided of AS/EN 9100, the principal quality standard that currently defines industry requirements. Procedures for managing the disposition of non-conforming material are defined.

Chapter 12 studies **aerospace supply chain management**, and looks at the aerospace supplier network that accounts for the majority of the value of new aircraft. Alternative methods for organizing the supply chain are analyzed and compared. Historical experiences by Boeing and Airbus are described and discussed. Subcontract management and control practices are surveyed.

Chapter 13 explores the distinctive practices involved in **aerospace marketing**. The entire sales process is traced from beginning to end, with a discussion of unique circumstances that characterize the product and the industry. Different processes for civil and military markets are compared. Considerations for international marketing are surveyed, including industrial offsets and international alliances.

Chapter 14 is an overview of **maintenance, repair, and overhaul (MRO)** of aircraft. This sector involves services performed on aircraft in service, and thus differs from much of the other material in this book, which principally addresses activities related to management, design, and production of aerospace products. The chapter describes the principal categories of MRO work, classifications of aerospace parts inventories, management of technical data, maintenance of airborne software, and the distinctions between civil and military MRO activities.

Chapter 15 considers **environmental challenges facing the aerospace industry** in the context of rising global concern over greenhouse gasses and other emissions. Aviation is currently a relatively small contributor to gasses, but increasing air travel and decreasing emissions from other sources may result in a dramatic rise in aviation's future share of the total. The chapter studies trend data and international environmental conventions addressing aviation and surveys solutions being developed by the aerospace industry, including alternative biofuels, electric and hybrid aircraft, hydrogen fuel, aerodynamic improvements, and carbon trading schemes. Noise emissions and sound-reduction technologies are also discussed.

2 Structure of the aerospace industry

Overview of the industry structure

Classification systems are inherently arbitrary, but the aerospace industry lends itself to division into major segments based upon the types of products produced. The firms in these segments share common affinities, and governments and economic observers use the segments as practical means of classifying firms and measuring market activity.

The US Department of Commerce (DoC) uses Standard Industrial Classification (SIC) codes to categorize the industrial activity of all firms in the USA. In this system, the SIC codes are four-digit classifications that are subcategories of three-digit industry groups of a broader nature. The DoC considers most aerospace activity to fall within industry groups 372, **Aircraft and Parts**, and 376, **Guided Missiles and Space Vehicles and Parts**. The specific SIC codes are shown in Table 2.1. Also shown are corresponding North American Industrial Classification System (NAICS) codes that have recently come into use by the US Office of Management and Budget.

These broad categories are further refined in other systems of classification, notably by the industry itself. The following breakdown by major product categories and subcategories is typical of efforts to identify specific segments.

Note that this particular classification includes engines, but does not include aerospace electronics, commonly called avionics, or other items of aerospace equipment such as landing gear, hydraulics, control systems, electrical systems, environmental control systems, and aircraft interiors. The value of

Table 2.1 US Department of Commerce and US Office of Management and Budget codes for aerospace industry segments

SIC	Industry sector	NAICS
3721	Aircraft	336411
3724	Aircraft engines	336412
3728	Aircraft parts	336413
3761	Guided missiles and space vehicles	336414
3764	Space vehicle propulsion units	336415
3769	Guided missile and space vehicle parts	336419

Table 2.2 Aerospace market segments identified by *Aviation Week & Space Technology*

Aerospace industry product categories	
Category	Products
Military fixed wing aircraft	Attack
	Bombers
	Cargo/transport/refueling
	Early warning
	Electronic warfare
	Fighters
	Observation
	Patrol anti-submarine
	Reconnaissance
	Research/test Bed
	Training
	Utility
Commercial fixed wing aircraft	Narrow body turbofans
	Wide body turbofans
	Turboprops
Rotary wing aircraft	Naval
	Scout/attack
	Tiltrotor
	Training
	Transport
	Utility
Business and general aviation aircraft	Turbofan
	Turboprop
	Reciprocating engine powered
Gas turbine engines	
Unmanned aerial vehicles and drones	
Space launch vehicles	Manned systems
	Unmanned systems
Missiles	Air-to-air
	Air-to-surface
	Anti-armor
	Anti-ballistic
	Anti-ship
	Anti-submarine
	Surface-to-air
	Surface-to-surface

these product lines is a significant part of the overall aerospace market, and although the firms sometimes classify themselves as members of other sectors such as the electronics industry, they also have a strong identity as part of the aerospace market.

In addition to the manufacturing sectors described above, the aerospace industry is generally considered to encompass a broad range of services that are substantial in terms of revenue and numbers of people employed.

Table 2.3 Aerospace industry segments as classified by the US Office of Management and Budget

Standard Industrial Classifications Applicable to the Aerospace Industry

3721 Aircraft
37211 Military aircraft
37215 Civilian aircraft
37217 Modification, conversion, and overhaul of previously accepted aircraft
37218 Aeronautical services on complete aircraft, NEC

3724 Aircraft engines and engine parts
37241 Aircraft engines for military aircraft
37242 Aircraft engines for civilian aircraft
37243 Aeronautical services on aircraft engines
37244 Aircraft engine parts and accessories

3728 Aircraft parts and auxiliary equipment, NEC
37281 Aircraft parts and auxiliary equipment, NEC
37282 Aircraft propellers and helicopter rotors
37283 Research and development on aircraft parts

3761 Guided missiles and space vehicles
37611 Complete guided missiles (excluding propulsion systems)
37612 Complete space vehicles (excluding propulsion systems)
37613 Research and development on complete guided missiles
37614 Research and development on complete space vehicles
37615 All other services on complete guided missiles and space vehicles

3663 Radio and television communications equipment
36631 Communication systems and equipment, except broadcast

3764 Space propulsion units and parts
37645 Complete missile or space vehicle engines and/or propulsion units
37646 Research and development on complete missile or space vehicle engines and/or propulsion units
37647 Services on complete guided missile or space vehicle engines and/or propulsion units, NEC
37648 Missile and space vehicle engine and/or propulsion unit parts and accessories

3769 Space vehicle equipment, NEC
37692 Missile and space vehicle engine and/or propulsion unit parts and accessories
37694 Research and development on missile and space vehicle parts and components, NEC

3669 Communications equipment, NEC
36691 Alarm systems
36692 Traffic control equipment
36693 Intercommunication equipment

3812 Search, detection, navigation, guidance, aeronautical and nautical systems, instruments, and equipment
38121 Aeronautical, nautical, and navigational instruments, not sending or receiving radio signals
38122 Search, detection, navigation, and guidance systems and equipment

3829 Measuring and controlling devices, NEC
38291 Aircraft engine instruments, except flight

Note: NEC = Not elsewhere classified.

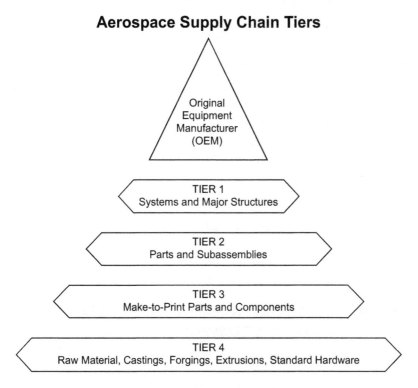

Figure 2.1 The hierarchical structure of the aerospace industry.

Examples are the aircraft maintenance, repair, and overhaul sector, known as MRO, and the satellite services component of the space sector. These service activities will be included in our broader overview.

Another means of describing market segments involves stratifying the market into vertical tiers. With this approach, the **original equipment manufacturer (OEM)**, or **prime contractor**, who contracts to deliver the completed aerospace product to the final customer, is at the top of the hierarchy. Below the OEM are subordinate tiers of suppliers that feed intermediate products into the manufacturing process. Buying and selling activities occur at each transition from one tier to the next. The industry's supply chain is discussed in detail in Chapter 12.

This chapter will attempt to identify and describe principal segments of the aerospace market, considering the natural delineations of the technical differences between products, such as airliners, missiles, and spacecraft. At the same time, the major market dichotomy between military aerospace and civil aerospace will be considered. Aerospace activities by geographical regions will also be noted.

Chapter 3, which addresses the aerospace workforce, will show that the industry worldwide currently creates jobs for more than a million direct

Table 2.4 Aerospace production is concentrated
in a small number of countries

Aerospace industry revenue ($ billions)

Country	2017 Revenue
USA	408
France	69
China	61
UK	49
Germany	46
Russia	27
Canada	24
Japan	21
Spain	14
India	11
Brazil	9

Source: Statistica.

Global Aerospace Revenue Projection 2020
Civil-Military Dichotomy

Billions of 2010 Constant Dollars

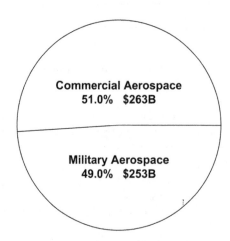

**Commercial Aerospace
51.0% $263B**

**Military Aerospace
49.0% $253B**

Total 2020 value: $516 Billion

Figure 2.2 The approximately equal shares of military and commercial aerospace.

Note: this total value is less than shown in Table 2.4 due to exclusion of some industry activities.
Source: Deloitte & Touche LLP.

employees. If jobs indirectly created by the industry are included, this number increases by several multiples.

Measurements of revenue of the industry vary according to composition of statistical data, but the credible economic reporting firm Statistica showed revenue of $739 billion in 2017 for the 11 largest aerospace producing countries.

How do the various market segments compare in terms of size and economic importance?

At the top level, the biggest dichotomy in the industry is the division between civil and military equipment. The relative proportions of this dichotomy vary from country to country and from subsector to subsector, but for aggregate worldwide aerospace production we find that roughly half of annual revenues are military in nature.

For the important subsector of completed aircraft deliveries, approximately 75% of annual sales are civil aircraft, and the largest component of civil aircraft production consists of large airliners and mid-sized regional transports. Business aircraft is the category with the second-biggest revenue total.

From the perspective of the value chain that produces the finished products, the largest revenue shares belong to the large prime contractors or OEMs. The indicated shares vary according to how the data is compiled, but the OEM revenue share is approximately 60% of total industry output. Looking farther down the value chain, the propulsion industry has the largest share among subcontractors at about 10%, followed by other contributors.

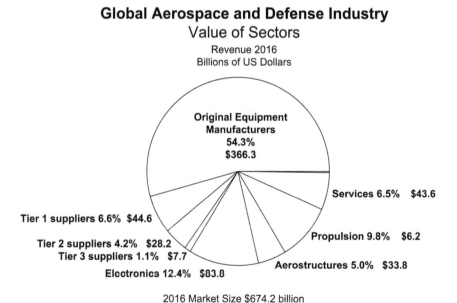

Global Aerospace and Defense Industry
Value of Sectors
Revenue 2016
Billions of US Dollars

Original Equipment Manufacturers 54.3% $366.3

Services 6.5% $43.6

Propulsion 9.8% $6.2

Aerostructures 5.0% $33.8

Electronics 12.4% $83.0

Tier 3 suppliers 1.1% $7.7

Tier 2 suppliers 4.2% $28.2

Tier 1 suppliers 6.6% $44.6

2016 Market Size $674.2 billion

Figure 2.3 Original equipment manufacturers' domination of defense aerospace.

Source: Deloitte.

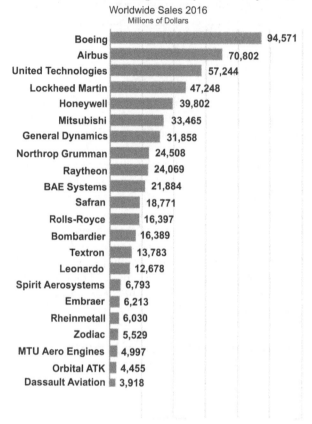

Revenues of Leading Aerospace Companies

Worldwide Sales 2016
Millions of Dollars

Boeing	94,571
Airbus	70,802
United Technologies	57,244
Lockheed Martin	47,248
Honeywell	39,802
Mitsubishi	33,465
General Dynamics	31,858
Northrop Grumman	24,508
Raytheon	24,069
BAE Systems	21,884
Safran	18,771
Rolls-Royce	16,397
Bombardier	16,389
Textron	13,783
Leonardo	12,678
Spirit Aerosystems	6,793
Embraer	6,213
Rheinmetall	6,030
Zodiac	5,529
MTU Aero Engines	4,997
Orbital ATK	4,455
Dassault Aviation	3,918

Figure 2.4 A few very large producers control a big share of the industry.

Source: Statistica.

Military aircraft

The military aircraft segment of the aerospace market has several striking characteristics. First, in terms of value it is highly concentrated among a few countries, principally the USA, the European Union, Russia, Japan, and China. Secondly, it is highly diverse, encompassing a vast array of specialized systems.

The general category of military aircraft is very broad and somewhat imprecise. Some military types, particularly transports and utility helicopters, have been certified by civil airworthiness authorities and are sold in commercial markets in slightly modified configuration.

The mix of military aircraft types varies dramatically among countries, reflecting their military threats and requirements. Some specialized military aircraft types are typically limited to countries with diverse requirements and large defense budgets.

Virtually all nations of significant size operate fighters, generally defined as armed fixed wing aircraft with combat capability. For comparative purposes, Table 2.5 is a snapshot of international fighter aircraft inventories during the last decade. Although the highest numbers are in large, economically important countries, we also see large fleets in nations located in historic conflict zones. The numbers do not reflect qualitative differences in aircraft. Most of the North Korean aircraft, for example, are obsolete models from the 1950s and 1960s.

The mix of military aircraft types operated by national armed forces varies dramatically from country to country. At one extreme are the small number of countries with strategic military roles, notably the USA, Russia, and China, who possess heavy bombers, intercontinental ballistic missiles, aerial refueling tankers, airborne early warning radars, and other strategic aeronautic systems. Typical more-or-less industrialized nations generally operate a more limited variety of aircraft, principally limited to fighters, medium transports, trainers, and helicopters. The poorest nations likewise attempt to maintain small inventories of fighters, transports, trainers, and helicopters, but they are often out of date and of limited quantity.

Table 2.5 Estimated international inventories of fighter aircraft during the last decade

National inventories of fighter aircraft

Fixed wing aircraft with combat capability

Country	Quantity	Date
1 USA	3,318	2011
2 Russia	1,900	2008
3 China	1,500	2014
4 India	1,080	2011
5 Egypt	900	2011
6 North Korea	661	2011
7 Pakistan	502	2006
8 Turkey	465	2014
9 South Korea	458	2012
10 Germany	423	2014
11 Israel	420	2011
12 Iran	407	2006
13 Libya	385	2014
14 Japan	374	2011
15 Taiwan	360	2014
16 Syria	335	2005
17 Italy	320	2011
18 Greece	308	1999
19 France	306	2009
20 Saudi Arabia	287	2006

Source: Forecast International.

Of the many companies that constitute the aerospace industry, a relatively small number have the technical and financial resources necessary to design and manufacture modern military aircraft. Figures 2.5, 2.6, and 2.7 identify these companies and the types of aircraft they make.

Figure 2.5 conveys the impression that the Russian and Chinese aerospace industries are negligible presences in the international market for combat aircraft. However, Russia has a long and impressive history of designing and building highly capable aircraft of the type. Following the near-collapse of the Russian aerospace industry after the disintegration of the Soviet Union, the industry has been reorganized and refinanced, and is once again starting to emerge in international markets. China also has reorganized its military aerospace industry and is experimenting with indigenously designed advanced fighters.

The large and important military transport market is dominated by Lockheed Martin, Airbus, and Boeing, who historically have built heavy commercial transports. The less valuable market for smaller transports is more diversified.

The military helicopter market consists primarily of transports of various sizes, but also includes armed attack helicopters and specialized types for missions such as reconnaissance, search and rescue, minesweeping, antisubmarine warfare, and so on. The supply side of the market is characterized by many international suppliers and is highly competitive. This is a segment of the military aerospace market in which Russian industry has retained a formidable presence.

Worldwide Fighter/Attack Aircraft Market Share

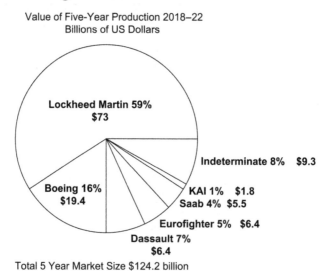

Value of Five-Year Production 2018–22
Billions of US Dollars

Total 5 Year Market Size $124.2 billion

Figure 2.5 The limited field of combat aircraft manufacturers.

Source: *Aviation Week & Space Technology.*

Military Transport Aircraft Market Share

Value of Five-Year Production 2018–22
Billions of US Dollars

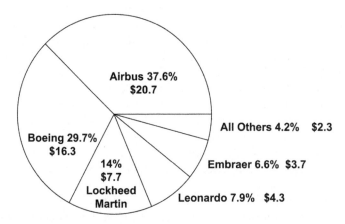

Total 5 Year Market Size $55.1 billion

Figure 2.6 Airbus, Boeing, and Lockheed Martin dominate the market for military transports.

Source: *Aviation Week & Space Technology.*

Military Rotorcraft Market Share

Active Units 2010

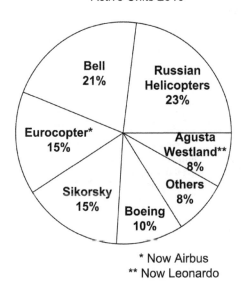

* Now Airbus
** Now Leonardo

Figure 2.7 Military helicopters: manufacturers' market shares.

Source: Frost and Sullivan.

Large civil transport aircraft

This is the most concentrated segment of the aerospace industry, dominated entirely by Boeing and Airbus. In terms of value it is also by far the most important component of the civil aerospace industry. The historical Soviet manufacturers of civil airliners, Tupolev, Antonov, and Ilyushin, have struggled to compete in the post-Cold War-free markets, but perhaps will eventually recreate themselves and reemerge. Likewise, the Chinese civil aircraft industry, which historically has been absent from international markets, has been targeted by the Chinese government for development, and has launched several airliner programs intended to compete in international markets.

In recent years the competition between Boeing and Airbus has been intense as the companies have battled for domination throughout the world. This competition has been an unqualified benefit to aircraft buyers, who enjoy the advantages of highly competitive markets: lower prices, improved products, and improved service.

In recent years, total deliveries of these large aircraft have exceeded 1,200 units. The market is notoriously cyclical, and demand is derived entirely from passenger demand for airline transportation and by air freight requirements, which in turn are largely driven by cyclical economic factors. Rates of retirements of older aircraft also affect demand for new aircraft. In spite of the cyclical nature of orders, both companies commonly have backlogs of several years of undelivered aircraft, so recent delivery trends have tended to be stable.

Commercial Aircraft Market Share

Value of Five-Year Production 2018–22
Billions of US Dollars

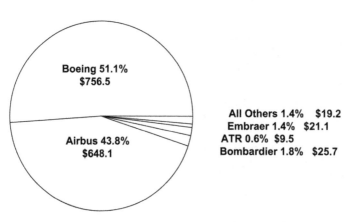

Total 5 Year Market Size $1,480 billion

Figure 2.8 The duopoly of large commercial aircraft manufacturers.

Source: *Aviation Week & Space Technology.*

Geographical Market Distribution 2017–2036
Passenger Aircraft Above 100 Seats
& Freighter Aircraft Above 10 Tons
Aircraft Units Delivered

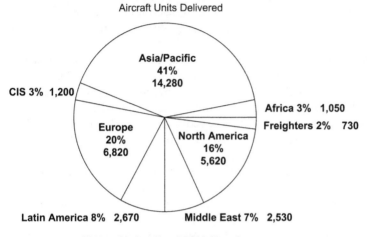

20 Year Market Size 34,900 Aircraft

Figure 2.9 Most airliners are delivered to Asia, Europe, and North America.

Source: Airbus.

The market for large commercial aircraft is quintessentially international, reflecting the geographically dispersed nature of the airline industry. Forecasts of market demand for the next 30 years indicate that almost 80% of purchases will come from Asia, Europe, and North America.

Twenty-year forecasts indicate that the market will continue to grow substantially, as demand increases and approximately 13,000 older aircraft are retired from service. Airbus estimates that the overall market will absorb approximately 35,000 new aircraft deliveries. Boeing estimates are similar.

Regional airliners

One of the most dramatic developments in the civil airline industry in recent decades has been the growth and evolution of regional airlines, sometimes called commuter airlines. Regional airlines are generally defined as operators that provide scheduled air service over relatively short distances between smaller cities, in aircraft of fewer than 100 seats. The growth of these airlines has resulted in burgeoning demand for suitable aircraft.

Initially regional airliners were exclusively turboprops, which are cheaper to produce and are highly efficient over short-range, low-altitude routes. In the 1980s, more than 95% of regional airliners in service were turboprops. Subsequently larger jets displaced turboprops in much of the regional market.

The rapid transition to jets from turboprops appeared to end by 2002, by which time approximately half the regional airliners in service were jets. Of the illustrious historical producers of regional turboprops such as Fokker, British Aerospace, Fairchild, and Dornier, the only remaining major producers are Bombardier and the European consortium Avions de Transport Régional, or ATR.

Contributing to the overall health of the market, the average size of regional aircraft has grown, adding value for producers. Paradoxically, in spite of the strong growth of the market, the number of major suppliers has diminished. Three long-time suppliers of regional jets, Fokker, BAE Systems, and Fairchild Dornier, have either withdrawn from the market or have ceased operations. The regional jet market is now dominated by Embraer and Bombardier.

However, new competitive entrants are emerging in the form of Russia's Sukhoi, Japan's Mitsubishi, and Commercial Aircraft Corporation of China, Ltd. (Comac). Sukhoi and Comac have introduced the Russian Regional Jet and the ARJ21, respectively, both of which are in limited initial service. Mitsubishi is close to introduction of its Mitsubishi Regional Jet, and Comac is also in final development of the C919.

Market projections by Embraer and Bombardier vary somewhat, but are consistent in their conclusion that the market will continue to experience strong growth. The consensus is that sales for the next 20 years will approach $200 billion.

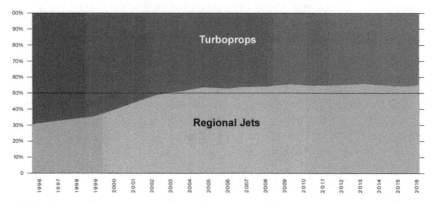

Large Regional Aircraft
Mix of Turboprops and Regional Jets

Figure 2.10 Market shares of regional jets and turboprops have stabilized in recent years.

Source: Flightglobal Fleets Analyzer.

Regional Transport Aircraft

Projected Unit Production % Market Share by Manufacturer
2017–2031

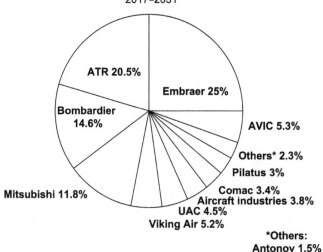

ATR 20.5%

Embraer 25%

Bombardier
14.6%

AVIC 5.3%

Others* 2.3%

Pilatus 3%

Mitsubishi 11.8%

Comac 3.4%

Aircraft industries 3.8%

UAC 4.5%

Viking Air 5.2%

*Others:
Antonov 1.5%
RUAG 0.5%
Indonesian Aero 0.3%

Figure 2.11 Current domination by ATR, Bombardier, and Embraer is threatened by emerging entrants.

Note: Sukhoi is part of UAC.
Source: Forecast International.

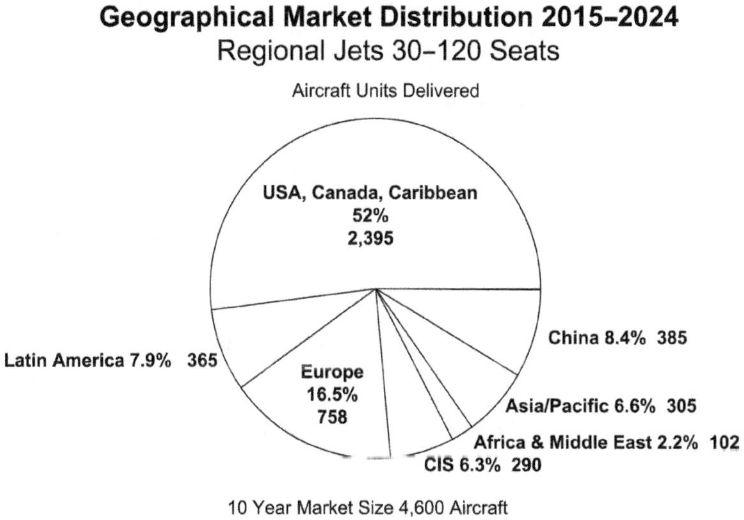

Geographical Market Distribution 2015–2024
Regional Jets 30–120 Seats

Aircraft Units Delivered

USA, Canada, Caribbean
52%
2,395

China 8.4% 385

Latin America 7.9% 365

Europe
16.5%
758

Asia/Pacific 6.6% 305

Africa & Middle East 2.2% 102

CIS 6.3% 290

10 Year Market Size 4,600 Aircraft

Figure 2.12 North America is by far the largest geographical market for regional jets.

Source: Embraer.

Business aircraft

Business aircraft are generally defined as aircraft of modest size, typically 6–20 seats, owned by companies for the purpose of providing transport for business reasons. New models recently introduced by Boeing, Airbus, Bombardier, and Embraer are significantly larger and are essentially airliners outfitted for the purpose of corporate travel. The FAA defines business transportation as 'any use of an aircraft (not for compensation or hire) by an individual for transportation required by the business in which the individual is engaged'. The FAA defines corporate/executive transportation as 'any use of an aircraft by a corporation, company or other organization (not for compensation or hire) for the purposes of transporting its employees and/or property, and employing professional pilots for the operation of the aircraft.'

In terms of value, the market is dominated by jets, but approximately 20% of business aircraft sold are turboprops, primarily at the lower end of the price range. It is a highly diverse and competitive market.

As Figures 2.13 and 2.16 show, major players on the supply side of the market are Raytheon (USA), Cessna (USA), Learjet (USA), Pilatus (Switzerland), Dassault (France), Gulfstream (USA), and Bombardier (Canada).

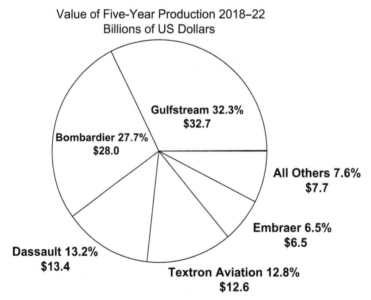

Business Jets Market Shares
Value of Five-Year Production 2018–22
Billions of US Dollars

Gulfstream 32.3%
$32.7

Bombardier 27.7%
$28.0

All Others 7.6%
$7.7

Embraer 6.5%
$6.5

Dassault 13.2%
$13.4

Textron Aviation 12.8%
$12.6

Total 5 Year Market Size $101.1 billion

Figure 2.13 The business aircraft market is characterized by many competitors.

Source: *Aviation Week & Space Technology*.

An important development in this market in the 1990s was the advent of fractional ownership, which became a common alternative to the historical practice of company ownership of individual aircraft for their exclusive use. Under fractional ownership schemes, the aircraft is owned by intermediary companies that guarantee to provide aircraft and crews immediately upon request by participating subscriber companies or individuals. The subscribers, in turn, make large up-front payments to acquire equity shares in the aircraft, and pay hourly charges for aircraft use. Fractional ownership arrangements are viewed as advantageous by many companies because aircraft utilization rates are higher (thus diminishing the cost of ownership) and because the individual subscriber companies do not have to incur the significant expense of maintaining their own flight crews and flight operations departments.

Both Honeywell and Rolls-Royce, major suppliers of turbine engines to business aircraft, issue annual projections of future aircraft sales in the market segment. According to Honeywell's projections, 7,700 new business jets worth $251 billion will be delivered internationally from 2019 to 2028.

A conspicuous characteristic of the market for business aircraft is that the share of the USA is disproportionately large. For geographical and historical reasons, American businesses utilize business aircraft to a greater extent than enterprises in other countries. The US market is more than double the rest of the world combined. The European and South American markets are the second and third largest markets, respectively.

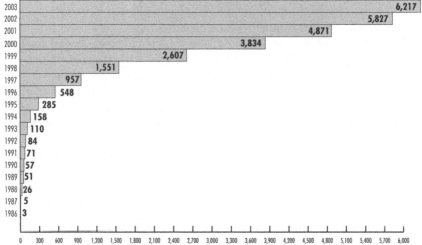

Figure 2.14 The rise in fractional ownership of business aircraft has had a major impact on the market.

Source: AvData Inc.

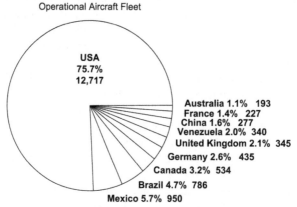

Business Jets Geographical Distribution 2016
Top Ten Operating Countries

Operational Aircraft Fleet

USA
75.7%
12,717

Australia 1.1%   193
France 1.4%   227
China 1.6%   277
Venezuela 2.0%   340
United Kingdom 2.1% 345
Germany 2.6%   435
Canada 3.2% 534
Brazil 4.7% 786
Mexico 5.7% 950

Fleet Size for Ten Major Operating Countries 16,804 Aircraft

Figure 2.15 The USA is the primary market for business aircraft.

Source: Statistica.

General aviation

The general aviation (GA) segment is normally considered to consist of smaller, privately owned aircraft. However, the distinction between general aviation and business aviation is sometimes blurred, and often, data pertaining to general aviation also includes some business aircraft.

The USA has historically been the dominant supplier of general aviation aircraft, but a pattern of disastrous product liability lawsuits against the manufacturers in the 1970s and 1980s caused many of them to cease production, and international producers, notably in France, expanded to fill the void. Annual American production of general aviation aircraft plunged from over 17,000 in 1979 to only 2,600 in 1983. Cessna, the largest manufacturer of general aviation aircraft, stopped production of piston–engine aircraft in 1986. Many aircraft that had been the subject of product liability lawsuits were more than 40 years old. The tendency of general aviation owners to maintain and operate their aircraft indefinitely created an almost never-ending 'liability tail' for the manufacturers. With close to 400,000 general aviation aircraft in use by 1994, GA manufacturers faced enormous product liability exposure.

Faced with a precipitous decline of the industry segment, Congress passed the General Aviation Revitalization Act of 1994 (GARA), which immunized general aviation aircraft manufacturers against lawsuits for defects in products older than 18 years. Since the advent of GARA, the industry in the USA has experienced a resurgence, and international manufacturers have in

General Aviation Sales 2017

Fixed Wing Sales by 12 Largest Producers

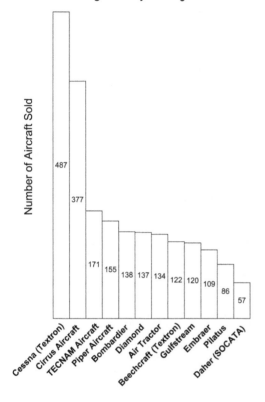

Figure 2.16 A characteristic of the general aviation sector is the large number of producers.
Source: The General Aviation Manufacturers Association.

many cases managed to survive and prosper. GARA is discussed in detail in Chapter 4.

An earmark of the general aviation segment is its diversity. It is a vestige of the earliest days of aviation, when technology was relatively simple, and when a relatively modest investment was sufficient to enable new manufacturers to enter the field. Today, major general aviation manufacturers are large-scale, capital-intensive producers of highly complex aircraft, but the segment also includes smaller family-owned companies that produce cheap, simple designs.

The General Aviation Manufacturers Association (GAMA), the principal international trade group of the market segment and the authoritative source of data pertaining to the category, defines general aviation as all aviation other than military and scheduled commercial airlines. Accordingly, GAMA data

Table 2.6 North America is the biggest market for all three categories of general aviation

General aviation airplane shipments by type of airplane 2016

Worldwide delivery regions (% of total)

Piston					Turboprop					Business jet				
North America	Europe	Asia Pacific	Latin America	Middle East and Africa	North America	Europe	Asia Pacific	Latin America	Middle East and Africa	North America	Europe	Asia Pacific	Latin America	Middle East and Africa
69.6	10.1	10.2	5.8	4.3	57.8	10.6	13.2	9.9	8.4	62.0	18.8	7.7	6.2	5.3

Source: The General Aviation Manufacturers Association.

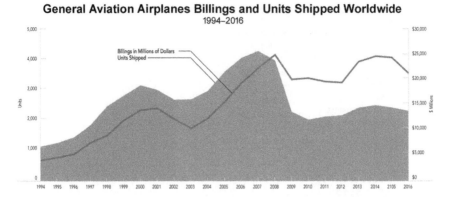

Figure 2.17 According to the General Aviation Manufacturers Association trade group, the 2016 value of the general aviation segment was $21 billion.

Source: The General Aviation Manufacturers Association.

include aircraft that are separately reported by the National Business Aviation Association, the principal industry group for the business aviation subsector.

In terms of value, approximately two-thirds of general aviation manufacturing are based in the USA, with the remainder based primarily in Europe, Canada, and South America.

Helicopters

Recent worldwide annual helicopter sales have exceeded $15 billion and are projected to increase substantially. As is the case with other segments, the market is characterized by a distinct dichotomy between civil and military buyers, although some transport helicopter types have found applications in both military and civil roles.

The market for military helicopters is significantly larger than its civil counterpart. Since the war in Vietnam the helicopter has assumed a fundamental role in moving ground forces and in providing fire support. Military forces buy helicopters in large numbers, and military configurations on the average are larger and more expensive than civil types. Military helicopters are almost always multiengine turbine designs, the costliest technical configuration.

In terms of value, the preponderance of civil helicopters is also multiengine turbine types, but the lower-cost piston-powered helicopters and single-turbine types are the largest sellers in terms of units sold. Robinson Helicopters of the USA, a manufacturer of small, low-cost piston-powered helicopters, delivers at higher rates than any other manufacturer in the industry. Measured by gross sales of civil helicopters, the market leader is Airbus (formerly Eurocopter), a manufacturer of single-engine and multiengine turbine helicopters.

Worldwide Helicopters Market Share
Combined Military and Civilian

Value of Five-Year Production 2013–17
Billions of US Dollars

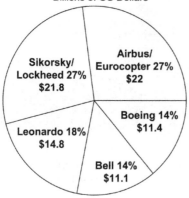

Total 5 Year Market Size $81.1 billion

Figure 2.18 The helicopter segment is dominated by five major producers.

Source: *Aviation Week & Space Technology.*

Military Rotorcraft Market Share
Active Units 2010

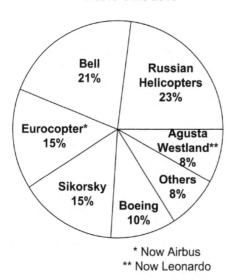

* Now Airbus
** Now Leonardo

Figure 2.19 Military helicopters are the segment of the aerospace market where Russian manufacturers have the largest presence.

Source: Frost & Sullivan.

Table 2.7 Units by size class

Projected civil helicopter sales by size class (2018 data)	
Size class	Market percentage by units
Light single engine	41
Light twin engine	25
Intermediate and medium twin engine	33
Heavy multiengine	2

Source: Honeywell.

Civil Rotorcraft Market Share

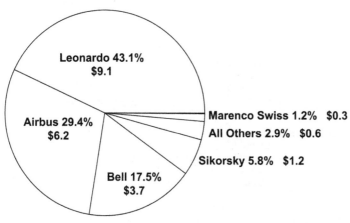

Value of Five-Year Production 2018–22
Billions of US Dollars

Total 5 Year Market Size $21.1 billion

Figure 2.20 European manufacturers dominate the civil helicopter market.

Source: *Aviation Week & Space Technology.*

Engines

Historically, engines have been the single most expensive component of most aircraft, with the exception of the airframe itself. This relationship holds less true in the modern era, particularly in the case of specialized military aircraft that perform as airborne platforms for advanced electronics and weapons systems. Nevertheless, engines retain their primordial importance. The industry is highly competitive. Small differences in reliability, power, or fuel consumption can have a dramatic impact in the marketplace, and the major engine manufacturers are locked in a continuing struggle for technological superiority and market leadership.

A special aspect of the aero engine sector is that much of the industry's revenues and profits are derived from follow-on support of delivered engines. Because engines typically remain in service for decades, this revenue stream is a predictable and stabilizing influence on the industry, but it also accentuates the importance of making the initial engine sales that generate the aftermarket business. Consequently, competitions for engine sales tend to be exceptionally aggressive.

In terms of value turbine engines constitute an overwhelming share of the aero engine market. Piston engines continue to be produced for small aircraft,

Aviation Gas Turbines Market Share

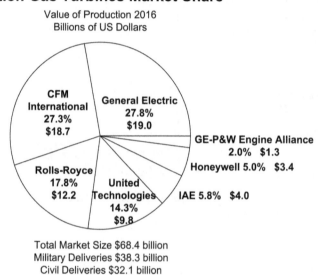

Value of Production 2016
Billions of US Dollars

Total Market Size $68.4 billion
Military Deliveries $38.3 billion
Civil Deliveries $32.1 billion

Figure 2.21 Both Europe and the USA have important shares of the engine sector.

Source: Forecast International.

Table 2.8 Categories of jet engines for aircraft

Aviation gas turbines	
Unit production % market share by type (projection 2018–2032)	
Type	*Market percentage by units*
Turbofan	48.9
Turbojet	6.2
Turboprop	9.3
Turboshaft	16.7
Auxiliary power unit	19.0

Source: Forecast International.

but this subsegment is essentially a fringe activity within the overall market. The main turbine market can be divided into segments according to power ratings of the engines (which correlates with the type of aircraft for which they are intended), or by technical categories of fan jets, turboprops, or turboshafts. A further dichotomy is the inevitable classification by military or civil applications.

The international market for large turbine engines is dominated by four major producers: General Electric (USA), Pratt & Whitney (USA), Rolls-Royce (UK), and Safran (France), formerly named Snecma. Because of the large costs and financial risks of introducing new engines, cooperation among the companies has become commonplace. Noteworthy among the cooperative ventures have been the alliance between GE and Safran-Snecma to produce the CFM-56 engine, and the International Aero Engines consortium formed by Pratt & Whitney of the USA, the Japanese Aero Engines Corporation, MTU Aero Engines of Germany, and Rolls-Royce to develop and build the V2500. In addition to the major producers, the industry includes a few smaller firms that have historically produced engines for smaller sectors such as helicopters, general aviation aircraft, cruise missiles, regional transports, and business jets. Most significant among these second-echelon players are Honeywell of the USA, serving the regional transport market, and Turbomeca (recently acquired by Safran) of France, serving the helicopter market. In addition, the former Soviet engine manufacturers located in Russia and Ukraine continue to produce for their domestic markets within the CIS.

The major players have an overwhelming presence in both the civil and military international markets, although Safran's presence in the military market is comparatively small.

A practice of the aerospace industry is that aircraft OEMs typically offer their aircraft to customers with a choice of several engine options. The customer chooses among various engine–aircraft combinations that have been approved and certified by government airworthiness authorities. Often major aircraft sales competitions are accompanied by parallel competitions for the engines that will be installed on the aircraft. The engine suppliers compete on the basis of performance, economy, aftermarket support history, economics, and compatibility with engines installed in aircraft already in the buyer's fleet. Frequently the final customer contracts directly with the engine manufacturer and arranges for the engines to be delivered directly to the aircraft manufacturer's assembly line.

Engine and aircraft manufacturers work together very closely on a technical level. The engines must meet fundamental criteria such as power output and maximum weight limits, but they must also be fully integrated with the aircraft in terms of engine controls, fuel line connections, bleed air volume and connections, gearbox connections, engine mount locations, cooling and fire suppressions systems, nacelle aerodynamics design, and so on. Aircraft buyers welcome the possibility to choose among several engine suppliers because they feel it gives them negotiating leverage in the procurement of this very expensive component.

As an industry practice, the initial costs of integrating and certifying engine–aircraft combinations are shared between the engine supplier and the aircraft prime contractor.

Avionics and airborne electronics

As in other aerospace market segments, exact definitions and categorization are elusive in the avionics segment. Historically avionics have been construed to mean airborne electronic equipment, principally including instruments, displays, and systems for communication, navigation, and pilotage. However, as electronic applications have expanded, particularly for military aircraft, to include radars, weapons guidance systems, synthetic imaging, electronic countermeasures, command and control systems, and control systems for unmanned aircraft, the delineations between avionics and weapons systems have lost much of their meaning.

The market segment is typically divided into commercial and military subsegments. Although military and civil avionics perform many of the same functions, they have generally been separate product lines for suppliers. The explanation for this apparently illogical situation is that civil avionics are subject to compliance with technical standards promulgated by civil airworthiness authorities such as the FAA, whereas military avionics must comply with military specifications such as MILSPECs promulgated by military authorities. Until fairly recently the civil and international authorities made no serious attempts to rationalize their parallel sets of standards. However, in the face of rising costs of specially designed military avionics, and in recognition that approved civil avionics were perfectly adequate for many military requirements, in the 1990s military procurement authorities began initiatives to use commercial off-the-shelf, or COTS, equipment in military aircraft. As a consequence, past rigid divisions between the two subsegments of the market have begun to disappear for some categories of avionics equipment.

For the narrower historical definition of avionics (instruments, displays, communications, navigation, and pilotage systems), the commercial segment of the market is larger, reflecting the larger overall quantity of civil aircraft.

Table 2.9 The diverse and growing sector of airborne electronics

Categories of airborne electronics and avionics
Communication and navigation systems
Data processing equipment
Displays and instruments
Electronic warfare systems
Integrated avionics systems
Radars and sensors
Weapons control and targeting systems
Air traffic control radar

Table 2.10 Major military airborne electronics suppliers

Military airborne electronics leading producers

Projected 2020 revenues ($ billions)

Company	Revenues
Northrop Grumman	6.4
Rockwell Collins	5.4
Lockheed Martin	4.8
Honeywell	4.4
Raytheon	2.7
Thales	1.3

Source: Forecast International.

Table 2.11 Civil avionics producers

Leading civil avionics producers

2013 revenues ($ billions)

Company	Revenues
Thales Group	17.9
Honeywell Aerospace	13.5
Parker-Hannifin	12.8
Rockwell Collins	4.4
Garmin	2.4

Source: Sai Anand.

According to various sources, the total 2020 market for airborne electronics is projected to reach approximately $90 billion, divided roughly equally between commercial and military sales.

As flight deck avionics become fully digital, and as the integration of processors and displays advances, the importance of software has greatly increased. The major avionics suppliers furnish fully integrated avionics suites that are linked with standardized data busses utilized by avionics software to exchange information among system modules. The systems display information on various multifunctional screens at the choice of the pilot or navigator. In this fully integrated world, the value of the software component of avionics continues to rise.

Space

In its most fundamental aspects, the business of the space industry has changed little since the Sputnik era: the basic tasks consist of preparing ground launch stations, manufacturing satellites, utilizing rockets to launch them into orbit, and managing the satellites while they are in orbit.

Although activities involving earth-orbiting satellites are the core of the space business, a relatively minor adjunct involves government-funded exploration missions outside the Earth's gravitational field. The most spectacular of these missions were the manned expeditions to the moon as part of the Apollo program from 1969 to 1972. Equally fruitful from a scientific perspective have been earth observation satellites, orbiting telescopes, and unmanned probes sent to the other planets and moons of the solar system.

In spite of the decades that have passed since man's earliest successes in reaching outer space, the space industry remains the exclusive domain of a limited number of major countries that have the financial resources and technological capabilities to design, manufacture, and manage the advanced equipment characteristic of the industry. Nations or international consortia that have successfully launched earth-orbiting satellites of some sort include the USSR, USA, France, Australia, China, Japan, United Kingdom, European Space Agency, Italy, India, Israel, Iran, and Iraq. Many nations not included on this list have significant involvement in space. Pakistan, for example, has designed and manufactured a series of satellites that have been launched by China because Pakistan itself does not have an indigenous launch capability. Brazil has extensively funded a space program, including development of launch rockets and a launch pad, and the country appears destined to eventually become a competitor in the space industry. As satellites decrease in size,

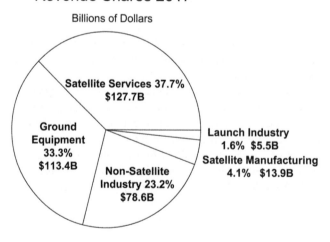

Commercial Space Industry Segments
Revenue Shares 2017

Billions of Dollars

Satellite Services 37.7%
$127.7B

Ground Equipment 33.3% $113.4B

Launch Industry 1.6% $5.5B

Satellite Manufacturing 4.1% $13.9B

Non-Satellite Industry 23.2% $78.6B

Total 2017 Revenues: $339.1 Billion

Figure 2.22 In terms of value, ground-based activities of the space industry are the largest part.

Source: Satellite Industry Association.

numerous small companies and universities worldwide have produced small cubesats for specialized commercial or scientific applications.

The space industry, which is neatly divided into four major segments according to products and business activities (ground stations, launchers, satellites, and satellite management), can also be divided into three comprehensive categories according to the nature of its customers: military space activities, private commercial space activities, and government civil space activities. Military space includes spy satellites, military communications, military navigation aids, and other secret applications. Commercial satellites generally involve communications, television and radio broadcasts, and imaging. Government civil space satellites encompass weather satellites, civil navigation aids, and communications.

Historically, the military component of the space market has been the largest, followed by government-owned civil activities, followed by the private commercial component. More recently, however, as commercialization of space has expanded and become a routine part of daily life for much of the world's population, the privately owned civil component of the space industry has grown to become by far the largest part.

A significant recent development in the industry has been the privatization of launch services and vehicles. In economic terms launch services are a relatively small part of the overall industry, but are obviously essential. New start-ups have entered the field, offering new technologies, more price competition, and greater choice for satellite operators.

The Global Space Economy 2015
Government and Commercial

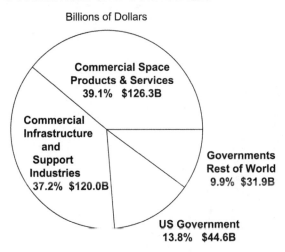

Billions of Dollars

Commercial Space
Products & Services
39.1% $126.3B

Commercial
Infrastructure
and
Support
Industries
37.2% $120.0B

Governments
Rest of World
9.9% $31.9B

US Government
13.8% $44.6B

Total 2015 value: $322.9 Billion

Figure 2.23 The commercial share of the market overshadows the government share.

Source: The Space Foundation – *Space Report 2016.*

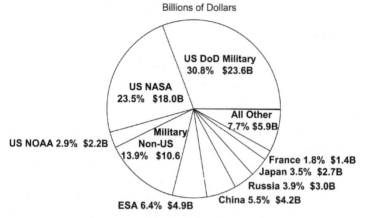

Worldwide Government Space Activity 2015

Billions of Dollars

- US DoD Military 30.8% $23.6B
- US NASA 23.5% $18.0B
- All Other 7.7% $5.9B
- US NOAA 2.9% $2.2B
- Military Non-US 13.9% $10.6
- France 1.8% $1.4B
- Japan 3.5% $2.7B
- Russia 3.9% $3.0B
- China 5.5% $4.2B
- ESA 6.4% $4.9B

Total 2015 value: $76.5 Billion

DoD: Department of Defense
NASA: National Aeronautics and Space Administration
NOAA: National Oceanic and Atmospheric Administration
ESA: European Space Agency

Figure 2.24 Government space activities are split between military and civil.

Source: The Space Foundation – *Space Report 2016*.

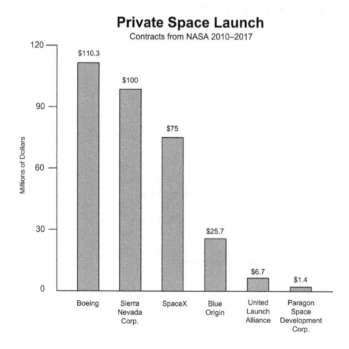

Private Space Launch

Contracts from NASA 2010–2017

Millions of Dollars

- Boeing: $110.3
- Sierra Nevada Corp.: $100
- SpaceX: $75
- Blue Origin: $25.7
- United Launch Alliance: $6.7
- Paragon Space Development Corp.: $1.4

Figure 2.25 A recent phenomenon in the industry is the emergence of private launch services.

Source: NASA.

Missiles

Guided tactical missiles began to emerge as a significant segment of the aerospace industry in the 1950s, when technologies for seekers, guidance systems, and rocket engines had matured sufficiently to assure that the weapons could hit their targets with some degree of reliability. The guided missiles replaced earlier unguided military rockets dating from World War II. These earlier rockets had taken the form of tactical battlefield multilaunch systems (such as Russian 'Stalin organs'), ballistic missiles (German V–2s), unguided cruise missiles (German V–1s), and air-launched line-of-sight anti-armor rockets.

As guided missiles began to emerge to take advantage of advancing technology, essentially the same classifications of rockets remained, with the notable additions of ground-launched anti-aircraft missiles, air-to-air missiles, anti-shipping missiles, and anti-radiation missiles intended to destroy enemy radar sites.

In the earliest days of guided missiles, access to the relatively advanced technology was limited to NATO countries and the Soviet Union, and a small number of suppliers produced the missiles that were available. Later, however,

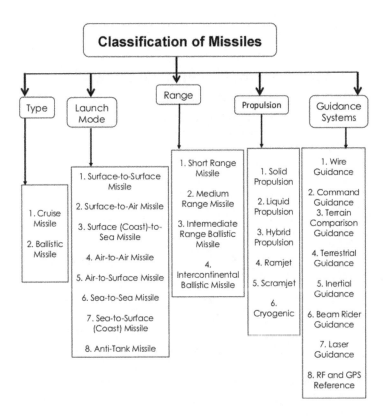

Figure 2.26 Missiles can be classified according to various criteria.

Source: HMR Institute of Technology and Management.

Missiles Market Shares
Production Units

Percentage of Market Share 2018–22

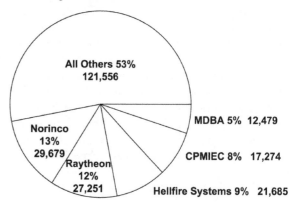

Norinco: North Industries Co.

CPMIEC: China Precision Machinery Import-Export

All Others 53%
121,556

Norinco 13% 29,679

Raytheon 12% 27,251

MDBA 5% 12,479

CPMIEC 8% 17,274

Hellfire Systems 9% 21,685

Total Five Year Production: 229,924 units

Figure 2.27 A multitude of international companies is involved in missile production.

Source: *Aviation Week & Space Technology.*

Missiles Production Market Shares
Production Value

Percentage of Market Share 2018–22
Billions of US 2018 Dollars

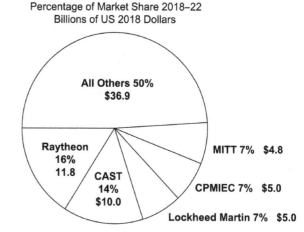

CAST: China Aerospace Science and Technology Corp.

CPMIEC: China Precision Machinery Import-Export

MITT: Moscow Institute of Thermal Technology

All Others 50%
$36.9

Raytheon 16% 11.8

CAST 14% $10.0

MITT 7% $4.8

CPMIEC 7% $5.0

Lockheed Martin 7% $5.0

Total Value of Five Year Production $73.5 billion

Figure 2.28 In terms of value, the missile sector is characterized by a few major producers and many smaller ones.

Source: *Aviation Week & Space Technology.*

as the technology became widely disseminated and better understood, design and manufacturing capability spread to Asia and the Middle East. The sales market for the equipment has also spread internationally, and at present virtually every national military force is equipped with some kind of guided missiles, however rudimentary.

Because of the diversity of the missiles and their manufacturing sources, data concerning the size of the international market tends to be somewhat imprecise, but the total market for tactical guided missiles is valued at roughly $15 billion per year. Part of the explanation for the lack of the precision of this evaluation is the difficulty of separating the value of the missiles themselves from the value of related equipment, such as launchers, ground control stations, radars, etc., that are often part of the value of sales contracts.

Unmanned aerial vehicles

The emergence of drones, also known as unmanned aerospace vehicles or UAVs, as an identifiable discrete market segment is a phenomenon that demonstrates how the convergence of technology, economics, and user requirements can result in widespread adoption of new products.

Although UAVs themselves are not new, their utilization was relatively limited until the 1990s. Early UAVs were often target drones that carried self-contained guidance systems to direct them over a fixed course that did not involve a return to base. The conventional modern definition of a UAV is an aircraft capable of returning from its mission intact, either by landing on a surface or being snared in some fashion. UAVs can have self-contained guidance systems that are programmed prior to launch, or they can be controlled by pilots on the ground, who communicate with them via wireless data links. This latter subcategory of UAVs is known as remotely piloted vehicles, or RPVs.

The basic technologies necessary to pilot RPVs from the ground has existed for decades, as witnessed by the widespread hobby of radio-controlled model aircraft. However, these early remote-control systems were essentially three-channel radios governing actuators that controlled flight in the xyz axes, and the remote pilot needed to keep the aircraft within sight in order to guide it. The true military usefulness of RPVs could not be exploited until vast volumes of data could be transmitted between the aircraft and the base station over long distances. In other words, the limiting factor was the lack of mature technology to permit broadband wireless data compression and modems. Until the advent of broadband capability, the UAVs were primarily limited to rudimentary tasks such as simple photo reconnaissance, which required the aircraft to return to base before the data could be downloaded or the film removed from the camera. Complex flight missions were not possible because of the inability of the aircraft and ground station to exchange sufficient data.

The development of reliable broadband wireless modems and data links in the 1990s, combined with continuing miniaturization of mission equipment such as cameras, laser illuminators, and digital flight control systems, finally gave UAV designers the tools to create RPVs that could be flown by pilots at remote ground stations, who had access to all the aircraft information that a pilot in the cockpit would have, including high-definition synthetic images. At the same time, the aircraft could transmit large volumes of data, such as digital images, and could respond to complex mission commands from its operators.

Ironically, the advent of operational RPVs was delayed somewhat by the resistance of the military establishment in the major industrialized countries. RPV missions did not fit well with conventional military organization and operational doctrine, and air forces in particular often viewed RPVs as a threat to their traditional roles and responsibilities. This institutionalized resistance was gradually overcome as the obvious operational advantages of RPVs became evident to all. RPVs are generally cheaper than their manned counterparts, can be built on much smaller scales, are capable of greater endurance, and avoid putting the life of a pilot at risk.

Because UAVs often utilize relatively unsophisticated airframes as platforms for advanced guidance, control, communications, and targeting systems, many of the aircraft are designed and sold by smaller companies, including start-ups. Some of the early small operational UAVs such as Predator, ScanEagle, and Pioneer were introduced by little-known firms General Atomics, Insitu, and Pioneer. However, as UAV operational concepts become more ambitious and as the airframes become larger and more complex, traditional major aerospace companies such as Boeing, Northrop Grumman, Bell Helicopter, and BAE Systems have become heavily engaged.

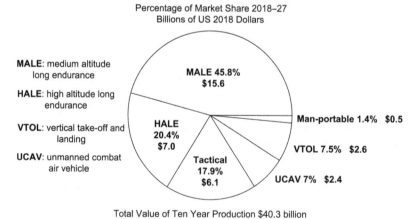

Figure 2.29 Diverse missions for military drones.

Source: *Aviation Week & Space Technology.*

Major Unmanned Aircraft Manufacturers
Percentage of Market Share 2018–22
Billions of US 2018 Dollars

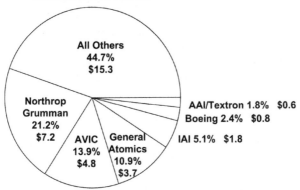

All Others
44.7%
$15.3

Northrop Grumman
21.2%
$7.2

AVIC
13.9%
$4.8

General Atomics
10.9%
$3.7

AAI/Textron 1.8% $0.6
Boeing 2.4% $0.8

IAI 5.1% $1.8

Total Value of Five Year Production $34.2

Figure 2.30 The biggest drone manufacturers are involved with military applications.

Source: *Aviation Week & Space Technology.*

Commercial Drone Market
Business and Civil Government
2016–20 Addressable Market by Industry or Function

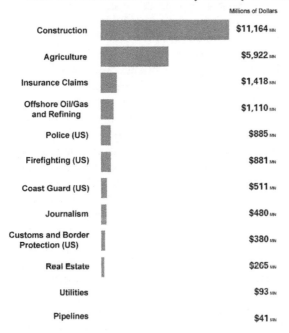

Millions of Dollars

Construction	$11,164 MN
Agriculture	$5,922 MN
Insurance Claims	$1,418 MN
Offshore Oil/Gas and Refining	$1,110 MN
Police (US)	$885 MN
Firefighting (US)	$881 MN
Coast Guard (US)	$511 MN
Journalism	$480 MN
Customs and Border Protection (US)	$380 MN
Real Estate	$265 MN
Utilities	$93 MN
Pipelines	$41 MN

Figure 2.31 Commercial applications of drones.

Source: Goldman Sachs.

This new market segment is difficult to quantify because it is diverse and relatively unstructured, and because much activity is in the form of research and development rather than in the delivery of competed aircraft.

Although the technological development of this new aerospace sector has been led by military applications, drones have been widely adopted by commercial industry for diverse applications such as agriculture, construction, and miscellaneous ground surveillance purposes. Conceivably, in the future these civil applications will expand to the point that they eclipse military uses.

Maintenance, repair, and overhaul services

The maintenance, repair, and overhaul segment, known as MRO, is fundamentally different from other parts of the aerospace industry because it is overwhelmingly service oriented and because it deals with equipment in service rather than with new production. In addition to maintenance activities, it is also heavily involved in aircraft modifications and upgrades, such as conversion of passenger aircraft to freighter configurations.

Aircraft are major items of capital investment that are expected by their owners to have economic lifetimes spanning many years. They are complex machines that require intensive maintenance and periodic inspections and overhaul. This work involves highly trained technicians, specialized facilities, and expensive equipment. Over the lifetime of the aircraft, these maintenance costs typically exceed the original equipment purchase price. In the aggregate, it is an enormous business that generates a predictable cash flow over a long period of time. In the case of individual companies, it often involves continuous aggressive competition for short-term contracts.

Maintenance of aircraft requires access to numerous heterogeneous technologies. This diversity is reflected by the nature of the work performed and the characteristics of the firms involved. The work can be categorized in various ways. A convenient breakdown is by flight-line maintenance, heavy depot-level airframe maintenance, modifications, engine maintenance, and component maintenance.

As in other parts of the aerospace industry, this segment is divided into civil and military components. Some firms do work on both civil and military aircraft, but significant differences in security, airworthiness regulations, and technology tend to discourage simultaneous involvement in both subsegments. Both military and civil aircraft owners perform some of their maintenance work themselves and subcontract some of the work to qualified third parties.

The MRO market is international, with national market sizes reflecting aircraft populations in geographical regions. The largest MRO spending is from North America, followed by Europe and Asia. The overall percentage of spending from Asia is expected to grow dramatically as aircraft fleets grow proportionately with economic development in the region.

The geographical diversity of the MRO firms is commensurate with the geographical diversity of aircraft ownership. Major firms operate in North America, Europe, and Asia. Because of the inherent mobility of the aircraft,

Worldwide Civil MRO Market
Distribution by Type of Work Performed
2023 Projection

Billions of US Dollars

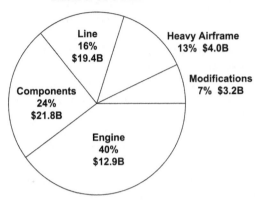

Total Civil Market Size $80.9 billion

Figure 2.32 Breakdown of MRO work by type.

Source: ICF International and *Aviation Week & Space Technology*.

Worldwide Military MRO Market

2013 Expenditures
Billions of US Dollars

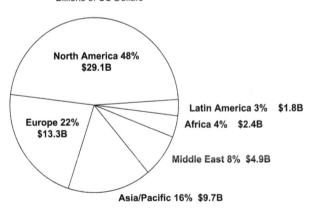

Total Military Market Size $60.7 billion

Figure 2.33 Geographical distribution of military MRO work reflects the size of national
military forces.

Source: ICF International.

there is considerable international competition for MRO work, particularly involving tasks such as heavy airframe maintenance that do not have to be performed close to the owner's center of operations.

Civil MRO activities are regulated by national airworthiness authorities, and facilities are required to possess certifications appropriate for the type of work they perform. They often operate under certifications delegated by the original aircraft manufacturers, who have the complete technical information and expertise to assure that maintenance, repairs, and modifications are done safely. In the case of such delegations, the OEMs are responsible for ensuring that the MROs adhere to airworthiness standards imposed upon the OEMs. The MROs are routinely audited by both the OEMs and airworthiness authorities to ensure compliance with these standards.

A major recent trend in the industry has been the outsourcing of MRO work traditionally performed by the large operators themselves. Historically most large airlines and large military forces maintained their own aircraft, using facilities and personnel internal to their operations. However, in recent years there has been a tendency to consider that aircraft maintenance and modifications are not necessarily core competencies of aircraft operators, and that MRO work can be performed more efficiently and at lower cost by specialist firms.

As maintenance outsourcing has increased, the OEMs have recognized an opportunity to expand their own businesses and profits, and have created subsidiaries devoted to MRO work. Although maintenance and modification

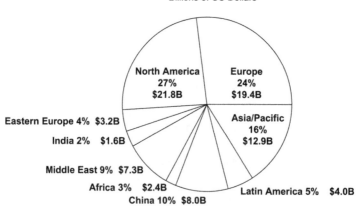

**Worldwide Civil MRO Market
2023 Projection**

Billions of US Dollars

Total Civil Market Size $80.9 billion

Figure 2.34 The major MRO market is North America, followed closely by Europe and Asia.

Source: ICF International and *Aviation Week & Space Technology*.

Original Equipment Manufacturers

Typical Revenue Mix From MRO Business

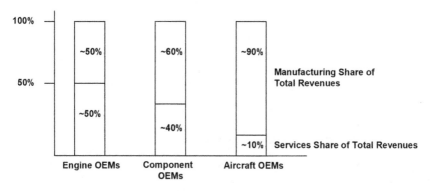

Figure 2.35 OEMs recognize MRO business as a profitable opportunity for expansion.
Source: ICF International.

work is different from production-line manufacturing, many of the procedures, technologies, and skills are the same, and the OEMs consider that these obvious synergies give them a competitive advantage in the business. The OEM share of the market continues to grow, but the smaller MRO firms have often been able to remain effective competitors by often offering lower costs and greater responsiveness to customer requirements.

All forecasts of the future of the MRO market indicate continued revenue growth. As the operational fleet of aircraft expands, as the average age of aircraft increases, and as aircraft parts and skilled technical manpower become more expensive, the business is expected to sustain constant expansion.

3 The aerospace workforce and labor relations

The nature of the aerospace workforce

The Aerospace Industries Association, or AIA, the American trade group representing the aerospace and defense industries, reported that total employment in the combined industries in 2016 was 2.4 million workers in the USA, representing 2% of the country's overall employment and 13% of the nation's manufacturing workforce. The AIA numbers included 1.6 million workers in the industry's supply chain.

However, the reported size of the aerospace industry workforce depends on the source of the information and the methodology used to calculate it.

AIA's counterpart in Europe, the Aerospace and Defence Industries Association of Europe, or ASD, reported US aerospace employment in 2015 as 487,600. This number excluded defense industry output that was not specifically related to aerospace, and also excluded workers in the supply chain.

In this chapter, we will mostly use the narrow definition of aerospace industry employment, focusing on workers at companies directly involved in the aerospace manufacturing business. This is consistent with our definition of the industry in Chapter 2, in which we described the industry as consisting of firms involved in producing aircraft, engines, missiles, spacecraft, and aerospace-specific subsystems and structures. In this definition, we also included the MRO service sector, involved in maintenance, repair, and overhaul.

As Figure 3.1 shows, most aerospace workers are located in the USA and the European Union. Canada, Japan, and Brazil also are major contributors. Russia has a large aerospace workforce and a history of technical capability, but the value of its output is disproportionately small. China and India are not shown on the map. The Chinese workforce was estimated to be 350,000 in 2012. India's aerospace employment was officially estimated at 200,000 in 2014, of which 32,108 worked at government-owned Hindustan Aeronautics Ltd.

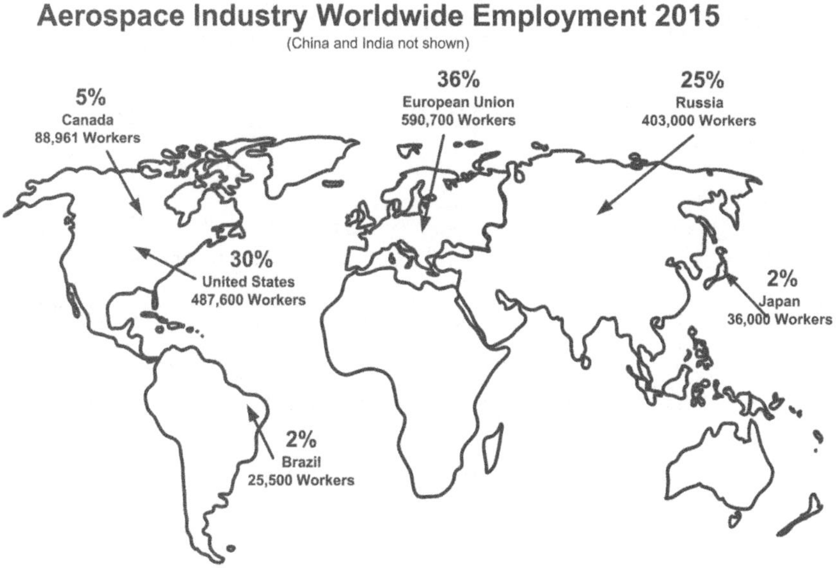

Aerospace Industry Worldwide Employment 2015

(China and India not shown)

5%
Canada
88,961 Workers

36%
European Union
590,700 Workers

25%
Russia
403,000 Workers

30%
United States
487,600 Workers

2%
Japan
36,000 Workers

2%
Brazil
25,500 Workers

Figure 3.1 The aerospace workforce worldwide.

Source: Members of the International Coordinating Council of Aerospace Industries Associations (ICCAIA).

Cyclical employment

Employment in the industry is cyclical in nature due to several factors, of which the most significant are normal economic cycles, changes in international geopolitical climate, and technological progress.

Economic cycles affect investment decisions by major corporations, including commercial airlines. The volume of airline passengers tends to increase in times of economic prosperity, as the traveling public has more disposable income to spend on vacations and discretionary travel, and increased levels of business activity result in more work-related travel. In response to this increased demand for their services, airlines expand capacity by placing orders for more aircraft. In periods of economic contraction, aircraft purchases decline, resulting in reduced production and ensuing layoffs.

The **international geopolitical climate** directly affects the size of national defense budgets, of which an important component is the procurement of military aircraft. In times of peace and reduced perceived overseas military threats, defense budgets tend to decline, and less money is spent to buy military aircraft. Aircraft production declines accordingly.

Technological progress has historically resulted in fluctuations in employment levels, particularly at individual factories. Especially during the first century of aviation, the rapid rate of technological progress ensured that new aircraft designs would be obsolete within a few years of their introduction.

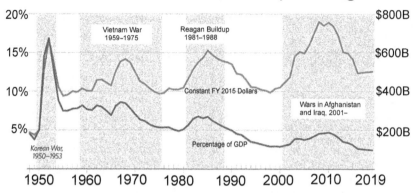

Historical US Defense Spending

Figure 3.2 Declining defense spending as a percentage of GDP.

Source: The Heritage Foundation.

By today's standards the new designs at the time were relatively simple and could be brought to market quickly. Thus the paradigm for new aircraft programs became rapid design, immediate launch of high-volume series manufacturing, and an abrupt end to the program as newer and better designs came to market. In the aggregate, long-term employment levels continued to grow, but workers were frequently displaced and compelled to relocate to find new jobs on other programs that were starting up. More recently, the life span of aircraft programs has become much longer as the cost and complexity of aircraft have increased exponentially, resulting in longer development phases and financial barriers to launching new programs. In the modern aerospace industry, workers sometimes spend entire careers working on a single program spanning multiple decades, a phenomenon that virtually never occurred prior to the 1970s.

The longer life span of aircraft programs benefits employees in terms of job security, but has negative effects in terms of diversity of experience of the workforce. Whereas, for example, a design engineer beginning work in the 1940s could expect to be involved in the design of multiple new aircraft over the course of his career, an engineer starting work in 2010 might be lucky to be involved in a single new design program. Although new engineers certainly gain technical expertise by working closely on existing designs, there is concern within the industry of a loss of competence in the process of designing new and better aircraft.

Longer-term employment trends in individual countries vary. In general, employment levels in traditional aerospace manufacturing countries have declined over time as new manufacturing technologies have enabled less labor-intensive production, even as delivery rates have increased. In less advanced economies that have more recently become involved in aerospace as part of their development strategies, employment levels have increased. In 2006, aerospace employment in the USA reached its lowest post-World War II level, and has increased modestly since then.

Table 3.1 Declining frequency of new aircraft programs

Postwar US military aircraft programs

Decade						
1950s		*1960s*	*1970s*	*1980s*	*1990s*	*2000s*
XP-5Y	XF-Y	A-6	F-14	F-117	F22EMD	JSFEMD
A-20	F-8U	SR-71	S-8	F-20	YF-22	UCAV
XC-120	F-6M1	SC-4A	YA-99	X-29	YF-23	
F-4D	U-2	X-21	A-10	T-46	JSF X36	
F-3H	SY-3	X-19	F-15	T-45	JSF X37	
B-52	F-105	C-141	F-16	B-2	C-17	
A-3D	X-13	B-70	YF-17	V-22		
X-3	C-133	XC-142	B-1			
S-2F	F-107	F-111	YC-15			
X-2	B-58	A-7	YC_14			
F-10F	F-106	DV-10	AV-8B			
F-2Y	F-5D	X-22	F/A-18			
F-100	X-14	X-26B				
B-57	C-140	X-5A				
F-102	T-2	X-24				
R-3Y1	F-4					
F-104	A-5					
A-4D	T-39					
B-66	T-38					
F-11F	AQ-1					
C-130	X-15					
F-101	F-5A					
T-37	X-1B					

Source: RAND Corporation.

Aerospace Industry Employment in the United States

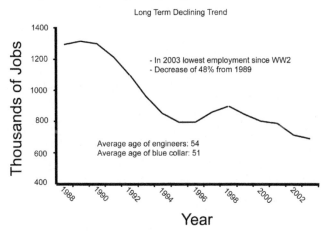

Figure 3.3 Declining aerospace employment in the USA.

Source: US Bureau of Labor Statistics and Aerospace Industries Association.

General characteristics of the aerospace workforce

Aerospace industry employees differ in significant ways from their counterparts in other industries. Aerospace workers tend to be older, better educated, better paid, and less likely to voluntarily leave their jobs.

Although aerospace is a manufacturing industry, its products are heavily weighted with design and engineering content. Approximately half its workforce consists of production employees, with the remainder engaged in non-production activities requiring higher education, often relating to engineering, design, and other forms of technology management.

Aerospace production involves a broad spectrum of advanced technologies, complex equipment, and special materials. The industry's production workers are highly trained, and are paid accordingly. According to the US Bureau of Labor Statistics, aerospace production workers receive approximately double the average wages of their counterparts in other industries.

In aerospace, the rate of employees who voluntarily quit their jobs is lower than most other major industries. Perhaps this is because they are well paid, working conditions are relatively good, the work itself tends to be interesting, and the final product is often inspirational.

Partly as a consequence of the propensity of aerospace employees to remain with their employers, the industry has an unusually high percentage of older and more experienced workers. This is an advantage in terms of retention of skills and collective knowledge. The potential downside is the prospect of abrupt loss of that collective knowledge as large numbers of employees reach retirement age.

Share of Production Workers in the US Aerospace Industry

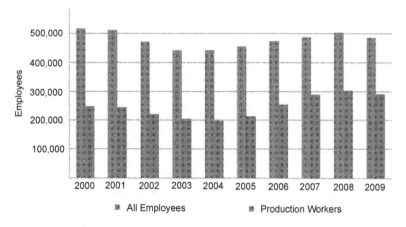

Figure 3.4 The share of production workers is declining in the overall aerospace workforce.

Source: Bureau of Labor Statistics.

US Aerospace Production Workers – Earnings per Week

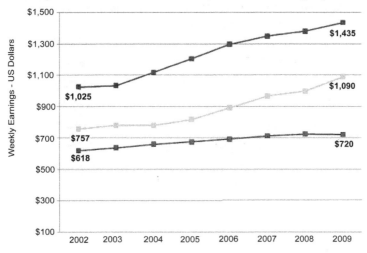

Figure 3.5 Aerospace production workers are well paid compared to other industries.

Source: Bureau of Labor Statistics.

Employee Voluntary Separation Rates
Selected Industries

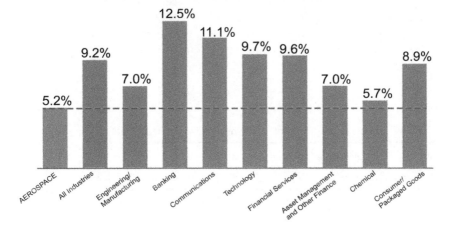

Figure 3.6 Aerospace workers tend to remain in their jobs.

Source: *Aviation Week & Space Technology*; Saratoga Industry Benchmarks.

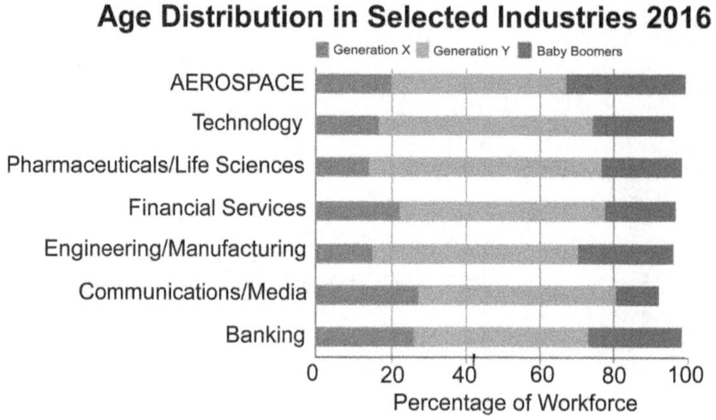

Age Distribution in Selected Industries 2016

Figure 3.7 Baby Boomers constitute a disproportionate share of the aerospace workforce.
Source: *Aviation Week & Space Technology.*

In terms of gender and ethnicity of the workforce, the industry in the USA has historically been dominated by white males, but this characteristic is changing, as is true of American industry in general. A comprehensive 2017 survey determined that 24% of the aerospace workforce was female, down from 26% in a similar survey undertaken in 2007. However, in engineering jobs, 15% of employees were women versus 12% in 2007. Data reflecting race and ethnicity show that racial composition is somewhat related to size of company, with the percentage of Hispanic and black employees being higher for companies with headcounts between 1,000 and 10,000, while companies with fewer than 1,000 employees tend to have the least diversity and more commonly reflect local demographics.

Table 3.2 The aerospace workforce overwhelmingly consists of white men

Aircraft and parts manufacturing employment (2017)

Race or gender category	Percentage of total employed
Women	21.6
White	79.2
Black or African American	8.1
Asian	9.2
Hispanic or Latino	13.1
Total reported category employment: 753,000	

Note: Percentages exceed 100 because of self-identification in multiple categories.
Source: US Bureau of Labor Statistics.

As the industry addresses the challenges posed by its need to find new technically trained employees to replace large numbers of older workers who are eligible for retirement, executives have come to recognize that the aerospace industry is competing directly against Silicon Valley for new recruits. Multiple internal studies assessing the competitiveness of aerospace salaries and benefits have found them to be roughly equivalent, but in some cases initiatives have been launched to adjust compensation packages to eliminate pay gaps. Researchers have also addressed the question of whether young technical workers are inordinately attracted to the youth-oriented information technology industry rather than the more traditional aerospace industry. The good news for the aerospace industry is that surveys indicate that young technicians are attracted by the prospect of designing, building, and operating tangible flying machines, in contrast to many Silicon Valley jobs that are perceived to be abstract exercises in gathering and manipulating data for retail purposes.

Aerospace clusters and employment

Because the structure and business practices of the aerospace industry involve widespread subcontracting of structural components and subsystems, production activity is typically fragmented and geographically dispersed. In the USA, virtually every state in the union has some level of aerospace manufacturing, often involving relatively small third-tier subcontractors. Nonetheless, the preponderance of aerospace employment is concentrated in a small number of geographical clusters of larger firms. The nature of aerospace manufacturing entails heavy capital investments and other economic barriers to entry, so the firms tend to be large, and the majority of aerospace workers are employed by companies with more than 1,000 workers.

Aerospace Employment and Size of Firm – 2009

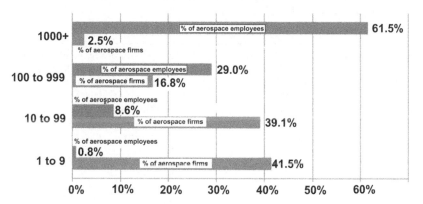

Figure 3.8 Large firms are the source of most aerospace jobs.

Source: Bureau of Labor Statistics.

Table 3.3 Aerospace firms and employment are clustered geographically in the USA

Top ten US metro markets for aerospace employment (2016)

North American Industry Classification System (NAICS) codes 3364, 481, 4881

Metro area	Number in employment	Number of entities
Seattle, Tacoma, Belleview, WA	105,560	319
Los Angeles, Long Beach, Anaheim, CA	86,482	755
Dallas, Fort Worth, Arlington, TX	76,123	486
New York, Newark, Jersey City, NY/NJ	67,053	609
Atlanta, Sandy Springs, Roswell, GA	49,133	301
Chicago, Napierville, Elgin, IL/IN/WI	41,925	345
Miami, Ft Lauderdale, West Palm Beach, FL	40,418	898
Phoenix, Mesa, Scottsdale, AZ	32,318	292
Wichita, KS	29,098	204
Houston, The Woodlands, Sugarland, TX	26,313	251

Source: EMSI, Garner Economics.

The aerospace clusters have developed over time because of various factors including historical connections with aviation, availability of experienced aerospace workers, suitable infrastructure, presence of technical universities and research institutes, and government policies.

The same phenomenon of geographical aerospace clusters occurs in Europe, Russia, India, Japan, and elsewhere.

Politicians and local community leaders have generally considered the aerospace industry to be desirable and have tried to attract it to their regions. Economists specializing in economic development have observed that economic growth results when resources such as capital and labor are reallocated

Table 3.4 European aerospace activity is also clustered geographically

European aerospace clusters (2005)

Country	Number of aerospace jobs	Main clusters
United Kingdom	150,000	Bristol, Lancashire, Farnborough
France	101,000	Toulouse, Bordeaux, Île-de-France
Germany	70,000	Bavaria, Hamburg/Bremen
Italy	39,000	Turin, Milan, Naples
Spain	18,000	Madrid, Bilbao
Sweden	13,000	Linkoping, Göteborg
Netherlands	11,000	Amsterdam
Belgium	7,000	Gosselies
Ireland	4,000	Dublin
Portugal	4,000	Lisbon
Austria	4,000	Vienna
Greece	4,000	Athens

Source: Niosi, J and Zhegu, M 2005, 'Aerospace Clusters: Local or Global Knowledge Spillovers?', *Industry and Innovation*.

from declining traditional industries to technically innovative industries. Applying this theory to the contemporary case of South Carolina in the USA, for example, the regional economy has benefited as resources have been reallocated from textiles to aerospace.

Such a strategy seems obvious. Average annual salaries for textile workers in the USA in 2017 were $26,670 according to the US Bureau of Labor Statistics, whereas production-line workers in the aerospace industry made an average of $51,240. Aerospace engineers averaged $113,970.

So, as political leaders became aware of the benefits of aerospace employment, and as the concept of regional aerospace clusters gained currency, geographical regions began to compete against each other to attract aerospace jobs. Local economic development agencies offered inducements to aerospace companies to relocate to their areas, including benefits such as favorable tax treatment, infrastructure improvements, establishment of technical training schools, and rent-free use of industrial land. Inevitably, a major consideration of manufacturing companies was the nature of labor laws in the localities. Most of the aerospace companies in the USA and Europe had originated in areas with histories of strong union organization and occasional disruptive strikes. In the USA, labor laws and practices vary from state to state depending upon attitudes and legislation imposed by state governments.

The development of the Mexican aerospace industry demonstrates a classic template for the establishment of manufacturing clusters and the creation of jobs. Beginning in the late 1960s, a few California aerospace firms tentatively set up simple manufacturing operations in Mexico in order to benefit from low Mexican labor costs. These initial factories were located in the Mexican state

Aerospace Industry Clusters in Mexico

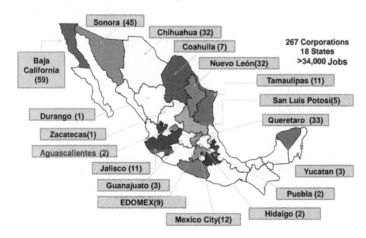

Figure 3.9 Mexico has followed a classic pattern of developing aerospace clusters.

Source: FEMIA (La Federación Mexicana de la Industria Aeroespacial, A.C.).

of Baja California, in close proximity to the Southern Californian aerospace manufacturers. As production in Baja California grew, in 2000 the Mexican government formulated a strategic plan to foster expansion of the industry, and North American trade agreements facilitated cross-border economic relations. Additional manufacturing facilities were established in the Mexican border states of Sonora and Chihuahua, close to the American aerospace clusters in Arizona and Texas. As capability grew, with the development of a skilled workforce and physical infrastructure, the aerospace industry in Europe, Canada, and Brazil also began to place subcontracts in Mexico to benefit from low costs. By 2015, 300 facilities employing more than 43,000 workers had been established in Mexico, primarily in the cluster along the US border.

Government inducements

Government inducements to industry are fraught with political risk. Although organized labor has generally been supportive of government initiatives to attract or protect local aerospace industry, unintended consequences sometimes result. Large subsidies or tax credits to the companies are often criticized as corporate welfare, and some taxpayers consider that the magnitude of government giveaways is disproportionate to the number of jobs created or protected. And, inevitably, hard feelings result if one party or the other believes that the terms of the deal have not been met. In 2003, the Washington State legislature approved tax benefits for Boeing that saved the company an estimated $1 billion between 2006 and 2013. A declared objective of the tax concessions was to encourage aerospace employment in Washington State. In 2013 a bipartisan review committee determined that that the objective had been met, although the causal link between tax concessions and jobs was impossible to definitively establish.

In 2013 the state legislature passed another set of concessions for Boeing estimated to be worth $8.7 billion through 2040, including tax cuts, measures to streamline the permitting process, and state investment in transportation infrastructure requested by Boeing. As was the case with the 2003 law, a declared purpose of this new legislation was to encourage aerospace employment in the state.

However, by 2015 Boeing employment in Washington State had declined by 3,000, and the 2 principal Boeing unions had organized demonstrations demanding that the terms of the state's financial concessions be revised or withdrawn. Workforce numbers continued to decline moderately for several years thereafter, but the state's financial inducements remained in place.

Regional government support of aerospace companies takes forms other than tax relief. The governor and Congressional delegation from Kansas were particularly aggressive in lobbying for Boeing during a US Air Force competition for 179 aerial refueling tankers that began in 2007 and lasted until contract award in 2011. The competition initially resulted in the selection of a tanker based on an Airbus design, but the selection was overturned after widespread political uproar, and eventually the contract was awarded to Boeing. Kansas officials were particularly active throughout the political process, in order to protect workers at a Boeing defense plant in Wichita designated for production of the tanker and employing 2,160 workers. However, in 2012, after the award of the tanker contract, Boeing announced that tanker production would be concentrated at Puget Sound in Washington, and the Wichita plant would be closed. Accusations of treachery from Kansas politicians and workers ensued. In its defense, Boeing claimed that despite closure of the Wichita plant, the tanker program would add 7,500 new jobs elsewhere in Kansas.

The organized labor movement and aerospace

As is the case with most traditional manufacturing industries in Europe and the USA, aerospace is heavily unionized and the industry has a colorful legacy of labor strife and extended strikes. Adding to workforce unrest is the cyclical nature of the industry, resulting in abrupt and massive layoffs.

The aerospace industry's relationship with organized labor has historically been thorny. Boeing workers originally unionized as part of the International Association of Machinists, Lodge 751, in 1935. In the same year, Consolidated Aircraft, a major producer in the mid-century decades, relocated from Chicago to San Diego after a strike shut down its Chicago manufacturing operations for 50 days. San Diego's attractions were tax concessions offered by the government, more sunny weather for flight operations, and, most importantly, a low level of organized labor.

The 1930s were a fertile period for union expansion in the USA, as depression-era labor laws were enacted to protect workers from employer abuses.

A particularly nefarious aspect of union history at Boeing and other aerospace companies was the IAM's policy relating to racial minorities in the workforce. Non-whites were specifically excluded from the union until 1948, at which time exclusionary language was removed from the union's charter, partly at the behest of Boeing's Lodge 751 membership.

Strikes were rare during the period of World War II as labor and industry united behind the effort to win the war, but labor–management tensions continued nonetheless. In 1943, 20,000 machinists demonstrated in Seattle to protest a wage freeze imposed by Boeing. And in 1944, Boeing engineers began to organize the Society of Professional Engineering Employees in Aerospace, or SPEEA. SPEEA was an anomaly in the American labor movement because it represented relatively well-paid and well-educated professional workers, in an era before mass unionization of professional government and office workers.

Immediately after the war Boeing laid off more than 50,000 workers as military production was curtailed, and in 1948 the machinists went on strike for almost 5 months. The aerospace industry generally prospered in the 1950s and 1960s, but in the late 1960s Boeing reacted to a major business downturn by laying off more than 80,000 workers. The remaining workers, recognizing that the survival of the company was at stake, declined to strike at the time, and employment levels gradually rose again.

Boeing Employment in Washington State

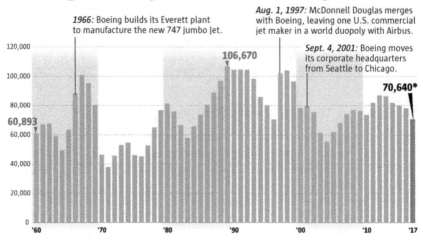

1966: Boeing builds its Everett plant to manufacture the new 747 jumbo Jet.

Aug. 1, 1997: McDonnell Douglas merges with Boeing, leaving one U.S. commercial jet maker in a world duopoly with Airbus.

Sept. 4, 2001: Boeing moves its corporate headquarters from Seattle to Chicago.

106,670

70,640*

60,893

Figure 3.10 By 2017 employment levels in Washington State had fallen by nearly 16,400 jobs from its most recent peak of 87,023 in 2012.

Source: *The Seattle Times.*

However, relations between Boeing management and workers were generally perceived to deteriorate during the 1980s, and in 1989 more than 57,000 workers went on strike for 44 days over issues primarily related to pay.

An historical characteristic of aerospace industry unions has been competition and occasional antagonism among separate unions as they jockey against each other to obtain certification to officially represent work units, and as the goals and objectives of the individual unions and work units inevitably diverge. Because aerospace factories are large and encompass workers with diverse skills and specialties, frequently the workforces of single factories are represented by multiple unions, each of which represent specific trades or work specialties. This potentially causes conflict. Likewise, individual factories of the same company may be represented by different unions in different geographical areas, and subcontractors' workers may be represented by other unions again. The unions with the greatest membership among aerospace production workers in the USA are the International Association of Machinists and Aerospace Workers (IAM), the United Auto Workers (UAW), and the Teamsters.

An illustrative example of the consequences of interunion acrimony occurred during a 1975 strike by the IAM at McDonnell Douglas factories in Long Beach, Torrance, and Santa Monica, California. At the Long Beach factory approximately 12,000 workers were represented by the UAW and 155 by the IAM. The Torrance and Santa Monica factories, which supplied parts and assemblies to the DC-9 airliner final assembly line at Long Beach, were primarily represented by the IAM. IAM workers in all three plants went on strike in February 1975, but UAW workers in Long Beach, who were the overwhelming majority of that facility's workforce, continued working and did not observe the IAM picket lines. As parts supplies from Torrance and Santa Monica ceased, by March aircraft production essentially halted, and most of the non-striking UAW workers at Long Beach received involuntary layoffs. The strike ended in April with minimal gains for the IAM workers, but the forced layoffs in Long Beach resulted in long-term antagonistic relationships between the unions.

The Boeing merger with McDonnell Douglas in August 1997 created the world's largest aerospace company, but also disrupted labor relations as the new company attempted to deal with unfamiliar union bargaining units and to reconcile and standardize conflicting union contracts governing wages and benefits at different business units. Inevitably, the expanded company also implemented plans to streamline operations by reorganizing and shedding redundant resources, resulting in layoffs. In reaction to these management initiatives and dissatisfaction over pay, more than 17,000 SPEEA members walked off the job in February 2000, and remained on strike for 40 days.

In recent years the industry has pursued a strategy of establishing new production operations outside traditional geographic clusters, with the result that new smaller clusters have come into existence and have grown. In the USA, these new clusters have overwhelmingly been in so-called 'right-to-work states', where rates of union membership are lower, industrial wages and the

Figure 3.11 A protest poster from the Boeing engineers' strike in 2000.

Source: Society of Professional Engineering Employees in Aerospace.

cost of living tend to be somewhat lower, and social attitudes are generally less supportive of unions. In the parlance of labor law, right-to-work states specifically prohibit union contracts from requiring that union dues be collected from workers who are not union members. Differences among state labor laws is a result of provisions of the Federal Taft-Hartley Act of 1947, which empowered unions nationwide to collect union dues from all employees within unionized workforces. However, Taft-Hartley gave individual state governments the prerogative to pass laws that exempted them from this mandatory collection of union dues from non-members. As of 2018, 28 states had passed laws with this dues-collection exemption.

Predictably, entrenched unions in traditional aerospace clusters have resisted migration of industrial activity to non-union facilities in right-to-work states. In a particularly noteworthy case in 2009, Boeing announced that it would create a second production line for its new 787 Dreamliner in Charleston, South Carolina, a right-to-work state, instead of at the Puget Sound plants in the state of Washington that were already building the plane. The announcement was made shortly after Boeing signature of a labor contract renewal with the International Association of Machinists and Aerospace workers, which represented Boeing employees in Washington, and which had gone on strike five times since 1975.

Immediately after the Boeing announcement that the new production line would be located in South Carolina, the machinists union protested to the US National Labor Relations Board, alleging that the Boeing choice of Charleston was intended to intimidate union members and prevent them from exercising their right to strike. Shortly thereafter, an NLRB lawyer filed a complaint against Boeing supporting the machinists' claims, and implying potential remedies including reversal of plans to establish the Charleston production line.

Boeing mounted a legal defense against the NLRB complaint, which was eventually dropped by the government, and Boeing proceeded with plans to expand 787 manufacturing operations in Charleston. Major attempts by the machinists to gain representation of the Charleston workforce failed in 2015 and 2017. In general, growth of aerospace manufacturing in right-to-work states has continued. In March 2017 Lockheed announced that it would move the F-16 fighter assembly line to Greenville, South Carolina from Fort Worth, Texas, where the aircraft had been built since its introduction in the 1970s. The ostensible justification for the move was that dwindling F-16 production rates did not require a facility the size of Lockheed's Fort Worth factory, where all available space was required for the production of Lockheed's new F-35 fighter. However, the movement of manufacturing work to the non-unionized South Carolina factory was a clear message to the heavily unionized Texas workforce. Likewise, when in 2012 Airbus announced plans to establish a factory in the USA for assembly of A320s, the location it chose was Mobile, Alabama. Inducements from the state and local governments included $158.5 million in tax credits and benefits, but certainly a major factor in the Airbus choice of location was the non-union workforce in Mobile.

The aerospace industry workforce in Western Europe is almost universally unionized. Compared with US labor laws, European laws in general impose greater restrictions upon employers when they lay off workers. Consequently, companies strive to avoid layoffs whenever possible, and fluctuations in levels of employment tend to be less abrupt than in the USA.

In Germany, organized labor has historically been less militant than in France. Union representatives are often included as members of German works councils that make important management decisions. Management and labor have often been able to reach a degree of consensus, sometimes on a nation-wide scale, that contrasts with confrontational labor relations in other countries.

In response to the inherently cyclical nature of the market for commercial aircraft, unionized workers and management in Airbus factories in Germany began in the 1990s to develop new arrangements for securing employment for workers and increasing flexibility of production. In order to eliminate cycles of layoffs and rehiring, the experimental model allowed workers to bank over-time hours in periods of high-rate production. In periods of declining production, employees would work less but would remain on the payroll at full pay as the company decremented their banked overtime. This system was tested in a four-year pilot study at the Nordenham Airbus plant. Following the initial pilot phase, the working time model was modified to include three working accounts, and the arrangement was eventually introduced in all German Airbus factories following other modifications in 2002. The working time model eventually instituted company-wide consisted of three accounts: a normal overtime account (*Arbeitszeitkonto*), a security account (*Sicherheitskonto*), and a working-life account (*Lebensarbeitszeitkonto*). The overtime account is used to deposit overtime hours that can be used by employees for more leisure time, subject to management approval depending upon factory workload. The security

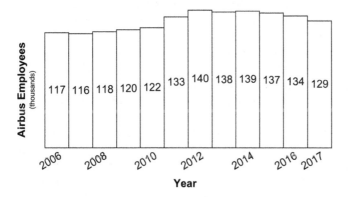

Airbus Employees Worldwide 2006–2017

Figure 3.12 Airbus employment has been relatively stable.

Source: Statistica.

account is intended to increase job security and allows the company to take hours out of the employee accounts when factory workload is insufficient, instead of laying off workers. The working-life account enables employees to invest in financial funds that yield earnings over time and potentially enable employees to retire early.

In recent years the most extensive layoffs by Airbus were in 2007, when the enterprise was experiencing financial losses on the A380 program. At the same time, Airbus was saddled with structural inefficiencies that were relics of political compromises made in the past to placate national governments that had provided financial resources for successive aircraft programs. Under the national framework agreements, Airbus member country governments had agreed to provide funding for new programs in return for Airbus assurances that specific industrial work would be performed in the contributing countries. Over time Airbus management began to rankle under the terms of these political arrangements, which were intended to provide regional jobs rather than maximize production efficiencies or lower costs.

In October 2006 Airbus CEO Christian Streiff resigned after three months in the job, during which time he had developed a detailed plan to streamline and rationalize international operations, entailing prospective layoffs of approximately 10,000 workers in France, Germany, the UK, and Spain. Streiff met strong resistance from the Airbus board of directors and government representatives when he aggressively insisted that the enterprise should be managed to maximize production efficiency rather than to accommodate legacy political compromises intended to protect jobs.

Months after Streiff's departure his plan for cost reduction and reorganization was implemented essentially intact, following much political agonizing and under the leadership of a new and more conciliatory CEO. The initiative entailed the sale and closure of several plants, and elimination of 4,300 jobs in France, 3,700 jobs in Germany, 1,250 jobs in the UK, and 400 in Spain.

In February and March 2007, in reaction to the announced layoffs, 4,850 German and 4,300 French workers participated in wildcat and political strikes. German workers, who were not legally permitted to engage in political strikes, nonetheless struck at three German plants. In European labor concepts, a political strike aims to influence a change in the behavior of the government, whereas an economic strike seeks to alter the employers' conduct in labor negotiations. The Airbus conflict quickly became a combination of political and economic strikes, largely because of the convoluted and unwieldy organizational structure of the enterprise.

Airbus was initially an amalgamation of public and private ownership. It had originally been created in 1970 by technocrats in France, Germany, the UK, and Spain as a consortium under French law, in the form of a *groupement d'intérêt économique*, with various ownership shares in the hands of European governments, private companies, and nationalized companies. Ownership structure evolved over the years, and by the time of the 2006 crisis Airbus ownership had taken the form of a quasi-corporate structure, 80% owned by

European Aeronautic Defence & Space Co., or EADS. In the midst of the crisis EADS bought the 20% of Airbus it did not own from British defense giant BAE Systems PLC. The French government maintained a 15% share of EADS ownership. The German auto manufacturer Daimler-Chrysler, as well as a number of German regional state governments, also had sizable shares in the entity, and at the time of the restructuring Daimler sold a 7.5% ownership share to a group of banks including public institutions controlled by German regional authorities. To counter this German influence, the French region of Midi-Pyrenees announced a plan to acquire a significant ownership share, with the political support of the Picardie and Aquitaine regions, homes of other French Airbus operations.

The Airbus restructuring plan eventually received lukewarm endorsement from the political leadership in Germany, France, and the UK, but sporadic labor action continued, led by the IG Metall union in Germany and in France by CFE-CGC and FO, the primary unions representing French Airbus workers. However, internal conflicts among the unionized workforce arose in reaction to elements of the restructuring plan that envisioned transferring work between France and Germany. Local union leadership began to make chauvinistic statements critical of other Airbus work units, and protest slogans were sometimes directed against other production facilities across national borders, rather than against Airbus management.

Occasional industrial action continued through 2007 and had another flare-up in 2011, but for the most part the restructuring was implemented as originally planned. An important legacy of the restructuring and associated labor strife was that Airbus management was subsequently freed to some extent from government policies that imposed rigid allocation of Airbus jobs among member countries in compliance with government framework agreements established when government funding had been allocated for new programs. In addition to the movement of production tasks from France to Germany, the British factories that had historically received a 20% share of Airbus work prior to BAE's sale of its 20% Airbus ownership sale to EADS in 2006 found that their share of the new A350 aircraft to fallen to less than 14% by 2018. In the final analysis, Airbus management gained more latitude to operate as a conventional business, allocating resources based upon efficiency rather than following arbitrary political work-sharing agreements.

Airbus continued to experience turmoil related to political issues following the UK declaration in 2017 of its intent to withdraw from the European Union. At the time, 16% of the value of Airbus aircraft was made in the United Kingdom, supporting 100,000 aerospace jobs, of which 14,000 were direct Airbus employees. By 2018, as exit negotiations between the UK and the EU remained inconclusive, Airbus senior management declared that the uncertainty was potentially disruptive to the Airbus supply chain and jeopardized the future role of the UK with Airbus.

Separate from the aerospace industry's relationships with its own unionized workforce, the industry occasionally suffers consequences of union disputes involving aircraft customers. In June 2006, for example, Air Canada canceled a $6 billion purchase contract for 32 new Boeing 777 and 787 aircraft after the airline's pilots refused to ratify a labor agreement that Canadian management had insisted was essential for operation of the new aircraft. At the time, Air Canada was emerging from bankruptcy and had recently merged with Canadian Airlines, which caused internal union disputes concerning pilot seniority among membership. Eventually the union turmoil was resolved and the airlines signed a new purchase agreement with Boeing, but several of the new aircraft earmarked for Air Canada had meanwhile been reallocated to other customers. Initial deliveries were delayed, but the program was finally executed more or less according to original plans.

A smaller but equally messy labor relations disagreement involving a Boeing customer occurred in 2018, when four US union entities representing airline pilots challenged Boeing action to send pilots to Colombia to fly 787s to partially replace approximately 100 Avianca pilots who were fired after participating in a 7-week strike in 2017 that a Colombian court had ruled to be illegal. The replacement pilots were employees of an overseas third-party agency under contract to Boeing. A chapter of the US Airline Pilots Association accused Boeing of strikebreaking, but the affair passed without further business impact.

International work sharing and industrial offsets

Industrial offsets are a business practice of the postwar aerospace defense industry that has been controversial in terms of effects upon the workforce. Simply stated, offsets are production work that the prime contractor or his domestic subcontractors place with subcontractors in the home country of the foreign customer. Often sales contracts require that a specific percentage of the total value of the sales contract be subcontracted as offsets.

As early as 1950 the increasing prevalence of offsets began to generate concern by the US government that the practice was causing loss of jobs within American industry. The Defense Production Act of 1950 mandated that the Bureau of Industry and Security (BIS) of the US Department of Commerce prepare recurring reports on the impact of offsets on US trade in defense articles and services.

In compliance with the law, BIS collects data annually from US firms involved in defense exports with associated offset agreements in order to assess their impact. The 22nd BIS study on the subject, published in 2016, reported that US defense contractors entered into 33 new offset agreements with 14 countries valued at $1.5 billion. The value of these agreements equaled 34.26% of the $4.4 billion in reported contracts for sales to foreign entities of defense articles and services with associated offset agreements. In 2016, US firms also reported 508 offset transactions conducted to fulfill prior offset agreement obligations with 26 countries at an actual value of $2.6 billion, with an offset credit value of $3.1 billion.

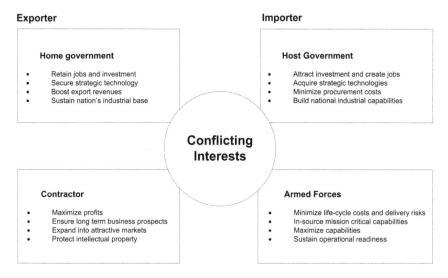

Inherent Conflicts in Offset Arrangements

Exporter

Importer

Home government

- Retain jobs and investment
- Secure strategic technology
- Boost export revenues
- Sustain nation's industrial base

Host Government

- Attract investment and create jobs
- Acquire strategic technologies
- Minimize procurement costs
- Build national industrial capabilities

Conflicting Interests

Contractor

- Maximize profits
- Ensure long term business prospects
- Expand into attractive markets
- Protect intellectual property

Armed Forces

- Minimize life-cycle costs and delivery risks
- In-source mission critical capabilities
- Maximize capabilities
- Sustain operational readiness

Figure 3.13 Offset arrangements entail conflicts among different interests.

Source: AT Kearney.

The US aerospace industry has experienced a long-term trend of declining employment since 1989 for a variety of reasons, including periods of decreased government spending for defense goods and space exploration; rising imports of aircraft, engines, and components; and increasing productivity and structural changes in the defense and commercial aerospace industries, including widespread mergers and consolidations. Some industry observers and stakeholders have contended that declining employment is partly attributable to offset agreements. Industry management, on the other hand, emphasizes that offset requirements are a standard feature of aerospace and defense sales to foreign governments, often legally mandated by national laws of customer countries. Thus, if sellers refuse to comply with offset requirements, sales will be lost, with the net result that more US employment would be lost. Over time, offset agreements have come to be recognized as a standard aspect of defense aerospace business, and even unions generally accept that international sales result in net job creation in the USA, despite some of the production work being allocated to the customers' home industries.

The benefits of offset programs to national workforces of customer countries arc illustrated by a survey of British industry to assess the employment impact of the offset agreement related to the 1987 British purchase of seven airborne warning and control system (AWACS) aircraft from the USA. Although data was incomplete, the survey confirmed that hundreds of jobs in the UK were created or preserved as a direct result of the offsets.

Table 3.5 A study by the UK government indicates that offsets are effective in creating and sustaining jobs

Employment impacts of AWACS offsets

Period	No. of companies consulted	No. of non-responses	No. of companies claiming no effect	No. of companies saying job sustained	No. of companies saying job created	Total no. of jobs sustained	Total no. of jobs created
July–Dec 1988	107	25	30	45	7	790	12
Jan–June 1989	108	28	33	40	7	536	6
July–Dec 1989	106	22	34	42	8	698	97
Jan–June 1990	67	10	17	35	5	573	4
July–Dec 1990	56	9	19	27	1	706	0
Overall Response	444	21%	38%	54%	8%	1279	113

Source: HCP 218, Statement on the Defence Estimates 1992, House of Commons, Defence Committee, London: HMSO, 1992, pg. 19.

But this general acceptance of offsets has not always prevailed. As total employment in the US aerospace industry decreased by 545,000 workers between 1989 and 1995, growing concern about perceived harmful effects of offset arrangements began to attract attention in the USA.

The international decline in aircraft demand due to market factors caused employment to fall in all major aircraft-producing nations. Aggregate aerospace employment in the three main producers (the USA, Europe, and Japan) fell by more than 550,000 workers during the period, according to data published by the European Commission. However, American producers experienced a disproportionate share of the workforce losses, a reduction of approximately 40% from 1989 levels, whereas employment in continental Europe dropped about 20% and Japan remained almost unchanged.

Although some commentators, analysts, and labor leaders at the time attributed the US losses to effects of international offsets, there was insufficient verifiable data to support these claims. In any case, economic health in the industry improved after 1995, and employment levels rose significantly from 1996 through 1998, before gradually declining again thereafter.

In 1995, an early academic study on the effect of international offsets on the US aerospace industry (Barber R., and Scott R 1995. *Jobs on the Wing: Trading Away the Future of the US Aerospace Industry*, Economic Policy Institute, Washington, DC) concluded that 469,000 US aerospace jobs would be lost between 1995 and 2013 as a result of offsets and ensuing increased foreign competition. The study was a serious attempt to address the subject, but in fact the authors faced insurmountable obstacles as they tried to isolate and analyze the numerous variables that affected industry employment trends, and their final conclusions were to some extent based upon hypotheses and assumptions.

Even prior to the advent of mandatory offset agreements as part of defense contracts, industrialized nations routinely sought to participate in the manufacture

Table 3.6 A pessimistic scenario of US aerospace job losses attributable to international offsets

Potential job losses attributable to increased foreign content of aircraft made in the USA and total jobs at risk due to foreign competition (1994–2013)

	Revenues ($ billions)		Total job losses		
Period	Peak annual lost revenue	Cumulative lost revenue	Total jobs	Direct jobs	Indirect jobs
1994–1998	1.6	4.0	17,863	10,219	7,644
1999–2003	3.5	17.8	39,498	22,596	15,902
2004–2008	5.4	41.1	60,386	34,546	25,840
2009–2013	7.2	73.5	80,553	46,083	34,470
Projected losses due to declining US market share					
1994–1998	2.1	10.7	23,933	13,692	10,241
1999–2003	4.2	31.8	47,194	26,999	20,195
2004–2008	7.3	68.4	81,863	46,833	35,031
2009–2013	12.0	128.6	134,650	77,031	57,619
Total jobs at risk due to increased foreign competition					
1994–1998	3.7	14.7	41,796	23,911	17,885
1999–2003	7.8	49.6	86,692	49,595	37,097
2004–2008	12.7	109.5	142,249	81,378	60,871
2009–2013	19.2	202.1	215,202	123,114	92,089

Source: Scott, R 1999, 'The Effects of Offsets, Outsourcing, and Foreign Competition on Output and Employment in the US Aerospace Industry', *Trends and Challenges in Aerospace Offsets*, The National Academies Press, Washington, DC.

of military aircraft from overseas sources. This is understandable. Governments spending large amounts of taxpayer money for foreign aircraft types prefer that the domestic economy benefits in terms of technology acquisition and jobs. As jet fighters entered air force inventories in the postwar period, numerous licensed production arrangements were established between American aerospace companies and aerospace industries in allied countries. These production licenses, which had the full support of the US government, sometimes involved slightly older designs that were no longer front-line equipment in the US military and which were not considered to be technically sensitive. North American Aviation, for example, licensed Canadair to produce the F-86 Sabre for the Canadian market and other selected overseas customers. The first flight of a Canadian-built version was in 1950, and a total of 1,815 were eventually delivered. Australia's Commonwealth Aircraft Corporation also obtained manufacturing rights for the F-86 for its national military forces, and began deliveries of a modified version in 1954. Mitsubishi Heavy Industries was licensed to produce the F-86 for Japan, and delivered 300 aircraft between 1956 and 1961.

Another major postwar licensed production program entailed production of Lockheed's F-104 Starfighter by a consortium of manufacturers in Germany, Italy, Belgium, The Netherlands, and Turkey. Production began

in 1960. A total of 996 aircraft were built by the consortium, creating an estimated 100,000 jobs in the struggling European aerospace industry of the time.
Lockheed also sold an F-104 manufacturing license to Canadair, with first
delivery in 1962, and a total production of 200 aircraft.

Similarly, the British aerospace industry licensed some of its postwar designs
to European industry. Hawker Aircraft licensed its Hunter design to Belgium
and The Netherlands. Beginning in 1956, production lines in the two countries
delivered 64 and 48 aircraft, respectively. In 1951 the US Air Force signed a contract under which the Glenn L. Martin Company would build English Electric
Canberra bombers in the USA, eventually including 403 American-built aircraft.

The future of the aerospace industry workforce

The characteristics of the aerospace workforce have changed continually over
time, sometimes abruptly. Historically, major drivers of these changes have
been changes in market forces, introduction of new technologies, emergence
of new industry sectors, and geopolitical factors such as wars. We can expect
that these same forces will continue to affect the industry, but that additional
factors will also be felt.

Ethnic and gender diversity

In the USA and Europe, historically aerospace workers have overwhelmingly
been white males, except during the period of World War II, when women
went to work in large numbers at aircraft factories. As ethnic compositions in
both regions evolve, and as more women gravitate to jobs in technology and
management, the aerospace industry will increasingly reflect the composition
of the general population.

Intellectual content and skill levels will rise

Although aircraft manufacturing will always require a degree of hands-on
human intervention, increasing factory automation will continue to eliminate
simple manual tasks that have historically occupied much of the workforce.
Shop-floor jobs such as drilling holes, applying sealant, installing rivets, and
loading assembly fixtures will continue to disappear in large numbers. As jobs
diminish on the shop floor, the proportion of workers involved in design, software development, and production management will increase. As a result of
these changes, the workforce will be more highly trained and educated, with
commensurate higher pay.

Less short-term cyclical impact on employment

As the lifecycles of new aircraft designs lengthen, and as backlogs of undelivered aircraft extend years into the future, the industry's historic pattern of

massive layoffs and workforce fluctuations will diminish. Another factor affecting this change is the increase in skill levels of aerospace workers, which makes them harder to replace, and consequently makes their employers less willing to terminate them.

Emergence of workforces in Japan, China, India, and Russia, and participation by smaller economies

Inevitably, the sustained efforts of Russia, China, India, and Japan to become significant participants in the international aerospace industry will show results, and the aerospace workers from those countries will acquire levels of knowledge and skills that reduce the gap between them and their counterparts in Europe and the USA. Japan has recently introduced internationally competitive commercial transport aircraft, and Russia and China strive to do so. India has actively targeted aerospace as a strategically important industry. Japan, China, and India continue to grow in importance as major elements of the international aerospace supply chain. Small nations such as Singapore, Malaysia, Indonesia, Taiwan, and Morocco will not be major aerospace powers in the foreseeable future, but will develop the industry as technology leaders in their national economies. In the relatively labor-intensive sector of maintenance, repair, and overhaul, employment will increase, particularly in Asia, as rapidly growing air transportation on the continent creates demand for regional MRO facilities and the workforces to operate them.

Continuing international collaboration

As the industry and its workforce continue to spread around the planet, leaders of aerospace programs will take advantage of available international resources. Almost all important aircraft today are the result of some degree of international collaboration, and this trend will certainly continue. As a reflection of the industrial activity of today's world in general, aerospace globalization will continue and expand.

Reallocation of employment among aerospace sectors

The aerospace industry is large, complex, and constantly changing. The jobs of the future will reflect the demand for evolving aerospace products and services in the years to come. Employment in some subsectors such as MRO will certainly grow as operational fleets of aircraft continue to expand. Manual factory labor will shrink. New technologies will create jobs in domains such as remotely piloted aircraft, airborne Wi-Fi systems, ground management of microsatellites, and in market segments yet to be conceived.

4   Aerospace law, international accords, and contracting procedures

The first legislation pertaining to manned flight was an ordinance enacted in Paris in 1784 to restrict the use of hot air balloons over the city, shortly after the Montgolfier brothers became the world's first known aviators. The initial international treaty addressing aviation was the First Hague Conference of 1899, which attempted to limit the use of balloons in combat after they were successfully deployed for military purposes during the Franco-Prussian War of 1870–1871.

From the very earliest days of aviation it became evident that legacy legal codes did not adequately address new issues that accompanied the arrival of the age of flight. People began to dispute ownership of the air above their property. The populace wanted laws to ensure safety and tranquility as big noisy machines began to pass overhead. Aircraft owners wanted assurances that they could expect consistent operating rules as they traveled from one locality to the next. And when accidents happened, the parties involved wanted clarity of how responsibility and liability would be assigned.

New issues emerged as aircraft improved and began to fly internationally. Aviators wanted standardization of regulations governing flight, safety, and financial matters relating to aircraft.

Thus, as the size and importance of aviation and the aerospace industry grew, bodies of national law governing the sector also grew, accompanied by numerous aviation-specific international accords and treaties.

This chapter is a general survey of the legal framework that governs the aerospace industry. It will initially look at some of the key national laws and regulations that pertain to aerospace and will examine a few important international agreements applicable to the industry. It will then review standard contracting practices used by aerospace companies and their customers.

Early aviation legislation and federal regulatory agencies in the USA

Aviation in the USA was largely unregulated by the Federal government until the Air Commerce Act was passed by Congress in 1926. The Act created an Aeronautics Branch within the US Department of Commerce with regulatory powers over civil aviation. The Aeronautics Branch was assigned responsibility for pilot testing and licensing, issuing aircraft airworthiness certificates, and establishing and enforcing safety regulations. The agency also became responsible for organizing the nation's airways, operating and maintaining aids to air navigation, and investigating aircraft accidents.

In 1934, the Aeronautics Branch was renamed the Bureau of Air Commerce. In 1936, the Bureau assumed authority over a national air traffic control system, replacing fragmented air traffic control centers formerly operated by commercial airlines, and expanding it dramatically.

In 1938, the Civil Aeronautics Act moved oversight of non-military aviation into a new independent agency, the Civil Aeronautics Authority. The new CAA was empowered to regulate fares and routes for commercial airlines. In 1940 the Civil Aeronautics Board was established and given the CAA's former responsibilities for accident investigation, regulation of safety of civil aviation, and pricing of commercial aviation.

In response to technological changes and remarkable increases in commercial aircraft traffic in the 1940s and 1950s, Congress and the Eisenhower administration passed the Federal Aviation Act of 1958, which reorganized and combined the responsibilities of the CAA and CAB into a new entity, the Federal Aviation Agency, subsequently renamed the Federal Aviation Administration (FAA).

The FAA continues to have purview over air traffic control and management of commercial airports, but it is the agency's broad regulatory authority over aircraft safety that is of primary interest to the aerospace industry.

National airworthiness institutions and practices

To protect its citizens from the inherent dangers of flying machines, almost every nation has a national airworthiness authority, known generically as a Civil Airworthiness Authority, or CAA (not to be confused with the UK's Civil Aviation Authority, the counterpart of the FAA), that regulates matters involving air safety. In most countries, regulation of civil aviation safety consists primarily of controlling five critical aspects of aircraft and their operation:

- Design of aircraft, airborne equipment, and ground-based equipment affecting flight safety
- Conditions of manufacture and test of aircraft and equipment
- Standards of maintenance of aircraft and equipment
- Standards of operation of aircraft and equipment
- Control of air traffic

Historically, airworthiness standards have been imposed by national laws that varied from one country to the next, creating an international web of inconsistent and often incompatible regulations. In recent decades the major aerospace nations have undertaken initiatives to harmonize their airworthiness rules, and

Table 4.1 National authorities with similar authority and responsibilities

National civil airworthiness authorities

Country	National civil airworthiness authority
USA	Federal Aviation Administration
France	Direction Générale de l'Aviation Civile
Germany	Luftfahrt-Bundesamt
United Kingdom	Civil Aviation Authority
Japan	Japan Civil Aviation Bureau
Russia	State Civil Aviation Authority of Russia
China	Civil Aviation Administration of China
India	Directorate General of Civil Aviation
Australia	Civil Aviation Authority – Australia
European Community	Joint Aviation Authorities, EASA*

Note: *European Union Aviation Safety Agency.
Source: European Union Aviation Safety Agency.

the countries of the European Union have established an international agency empowered to manage airworthiness for their national territories. However, the process of standardization is far from complete, and sales of aircraft across international borders generally entail complex regulatory issues that must be dealt with.

The Type Certificate

The Type Certificate, or TC, is the official document issued by a national airworthiness authority attesting that the design of an aircraft or item of equipment complies with the standards of the authority. The airworthiness standards themselves are contained in voluminous technical references that regulate every aspect of aircraft design, much as building codes regulate design of office buildings and residences. In the USA, FAA technical standards are contained in the Federal Airworthiness Regulations, or FAR. Different volumes of the FAR pertain to different types of aircraft. FAR part 29, for example, controls large transport helicopters. FAR part 25 applies to large fixed wing transport airliners. Other national CAAs maintain their own airworthiness standards.

Airworthiness standards are fundamental to aircraft design. Consequently, when aerospace manufacturers develop concepts for new aircraft that they intend to design and manufacture, the design engineers and the airworthiness authorities begin collaboration from the outset of the project. This process of collaboration continues until the aircraft has been manufactured and tested and the type certificate has been issued. In peculiar aerospace industry parlance, an aircraft that receives a type certification is said to be 'certificated'.

The process of obtaining type certification for aircraft or equipment is complex, detail-oriented, and time-consuming. Responsibility for managing the certification process is normally assigned to the program manager and the engineering department.

Aerospace products are widely exported and imported. Government airworthiness authorities have historically been limited to national jurisdictions. Standards and regulations have varied from one country to the next, and the industry must deal with the issues involved with aircraft crossing national frontiers.

In the early days of aviation, each national airworthiness authority individually performed recertification for every type of foreign aircraft prior to allowing the aircraft to operate in the national airspace. To eliminate the waste of time and resources required to perform redundant type certifications in each country, the international community has established a body of cooperative agreements to streamline the certification process.

The FAA procedure for issuing type certification is to require the applicant to prove complete compliance with Federal Airworthiness Regulations. Almost always, any aircraft that is proposed for international export has a type certificate from the airworthiness authority in the manufacturer's home country. The FAA process for certifying imported aircraft allows the applicant to use the home-country certification process to show compliance with some FAR requirements. In the case of differences between requirements of the home-country CAA and the FAA, the applicant is required to demonstrate to the FAA that the equipment to be imported does indeed meet the additional requirements of the FAA. This is a laborious and time-consuming process that essentially requires the aircraft to be recertified. As a result of this daunting problem, national airworthiness standards in most of the world have converged over the years. Until 1990, the obvious major exceptions to this historical convergence were the countries of the former Soviet Bloc, which since the end of the Cold War have been making rapid progress to rewrite their national airworthiness standards to be compatible with those of the rest of the world.

The most prevalent modern solution to reconciling national airworthiness standards is the concept of reciprocal agreements, also known as bilateral agreements, between national governments. Bilateral agreements between national airworthiness authorities result from painstaking efforts by the authorities to harmonize their standards and to confirm that the verification processes in both countries are satisfactory to both parties. Implementation of such standardization demands a major investment in time and resources, but when it is complete the airworthiness authorities in the two countries agree to accept each other's type certificates. The export-import process is greatly simplified.

This movement towards internationalization of airworthiness standards has gathered enormous momentum in recent years. Within Europe, the Joint Aviation Authorities, or JAA, has been a very visible symbol of this movement.

The JAA is an associated body of the European Civil Aviation Conference, or ECAC, which represents civil aviation regulatory authorities of the European governments who have agreed to cooperate in developing and implementing common safety regulatory standards and procedures. The JAA also has placed much emphasis on harmonizing the JAA regulations with those of the USA. The JAA was created in 1990, when the founding members signed the 'JAA Arrangements' in Cyprus. Founding members were Austria, Belgium, Cyprus, Denmark, Finland, France, Germany, Greece, Hungary, Iceland, Ireland, Italy, Luxembourg, Malta, Monaco, The Netherlands, Norway, Poland, Portugal, Spain, Sweden, Switzerland, Turkey, and the United Kingdom. Membership has continually grown since 1990.

Signatory countries have implemented the terms of the JAA Arrangements, and national airworthiness authorities in the member countries now issue type certifications based upon technical verification, testing, and investigation performed by the JAA.

Building upon the success of the JAA, the European transport ministers agreed in June 2001 to create the European Union Aviation Safety Agency, or EASA, which has become a true pan-national European equivalent of the FAA for certification matters. The agency was formally chartered in 2003. EASA effectively takes over responsibility for many important functions of the national airworthiness agencies of European Union countries. It has significantly simplified the way aircraft and their systems are certified, replacing diverse national processes with a common system and a single certificate. EASA makes access to external markets easier by ensuring agreements can be swiftly reached on harmonization and the mutual recognition of certificates. It facilitates and promotes the free movement of engineers with common qualifications within the EU.

At the same time that the JAA has been harmonizing standards within Europe, the FAA has been working to reconcile American standards with Europe, Asia, and the rest of the world. To this end, the FAA has formalized numerous international bilateral agreements. Harmonization efforts of the JAA have greatly facilitated this process.

Exporting and importing aircraft and equipment

The actual mechanics of exporting an aircraft vary from country to country, but most of the major aerospace manufacturing countries require a document called an export airworthiness approval before a civil aircraft or major piece of aerospace equipment can be exported. In the case of the USA, an export airworthiness approval is issued by the FAA for aircraft, engines, propellers, appliances, and other major items. Prior to issuance of an export airworthiness approval, a determination is made that these items conform to their FAA-approved design, are in a condition for safe operation, and meet all special requirements established by the importing country's Civil Aviation Authority.

Note that in the USA civil aircraft and major equipment are not normally exportable unless they are certified by the FAA and obtain an FAA determination that they are certifiable in their country of destination. This practice

Table 4.2 The extent of FAA bilateral agreements with national CAAs continues to grow

Bilateral Agreements Between FAA and International Airworthiness Authorities (Summary of Products Eligible for US Import - October 2000)

Bilateral Countries (Revised 2000)	Aircraft		Aircraft Engines		Propellers		Appliances		Conformity Inspection			Third Country Provisions	Maintenance	Agreement Date
	New	Replacement/Modification parts For Exported Aircraft	New	Replacement/Modification Parts for Exported Engines	New	Replacement/Modification Parts for Exported Propellers	New	Replacement/Modification Parts for Exported Appliances	Materials	Parts	Subassemblies			
Argentina	X	X	X	X	X	X	X	X	X	X	X			1991
Australia	X	X	X	X	X	X	X	X	X	X	X	X		1975
Austria	X	X	X	X	X	X								1959
Belgium	X	X	X	X	X	X	X	X	X	X	X	X		1973
Brazil	X	X	X	X	X	X	X	X	X	X	X	X		1976
Canada	X	X	X	X	X	X	X	X	X	X	X	X	X	1984, 2000
China	X	X					X		X	X	X			1991, 1995
Czech Republic	X	X	X	X	X	X	X	X						1970
Denmark	X	X	X	X	X	X	X	X	X	X	X	X		1982
Finland	X	X					X	X	X					1974
France	X	X	X	X	X	X	X	X	X	X	X	X	X	1973, 1999
Germany	X	X	X	X	X	X	X	X	X	X	X	X	X	1997, 1999
Indonesia														1992

(Continued)

Table 4.2 Continued

Country											Year
Israel	X	X	X	X	X	X	X	X			1968, 1974
Italy	X	X	X	X	X	X	X	X	X	X	1973
Japan	X	X	X	X	X	X	X	X	X	X	1977
Malaysia	X		X	X	X	X	X	X	X		1997
Netherlands	X	X	X	X	X	X	X	X			1974
New Zealand	X	X	X	X	X	X	X	X	X		1970, 1979
Norway	X	X			X		X	X			1957, 1978
Poland											1976, 1980
Romania	X	X			X						1976
Russia	X	X			X		X	X	X		1998
Singapore											1981
South Africa	X	X	X	X	X	X	X	X	X	X	1955, 1984
Spain											1984
Sweden	X	X	X	X	X	X	X	X	X	X	1978
Switzerland	X	X	X	X	X	X	X	X	X		1973
United Kingdom	X	X	X	X	X	X	X	X	X	X	1977
											1972

Source: FAA.

also prevails in other major aerospace producing countries. When potential customers are located in countries that are not parties to any of the major multinational certification agreements and do not have bilateral agreements with the FAA or JAA, it may be problematic to obtain an export certificate. Fortunately, as airworthiness standards and management practices become progressively standardized this problem has become uncommon except for customers in a small number of particularly isolated countries.

Most countries are signatories to the Convention on International Recognition of Rights in Aircraft, known as the 'Mortgage Convention', which defines procedures for deregistration of aircraft in one country and reregistration in another. Before an imported aircraft can be registered in the USA, for example, the FAA must receive written notification from the government of the former country of registry, confirming that the aircraft's registry in the original country has been canceled. Under the terms of the Mortgage Convention, the government agencies must confirm that the exported aircraft has no outstanding financial liens against it before the written notification of deregistration is sent. In the case of aircraft to be exported, the home airworthiness authority will be requested to send confirmation of deregistration to the airworthiness authority in the receiving country. The confirmation will contain all known information concerning ownership and financial encumbrances against the aircraft.

Airworthiness control of military aircraft

Civil airworthiness authorities, as their names imply, have responsibility for matters involving civil aircraft. Military aircraft are generally not included in their purview. Standards for designing and maintaining military aircraft are customarily the responsibility of the military owners. In the USA, for example, military aircraft and engine parts are certified under the provisions of Air Force Policy Directive 62-6 as 'public aircraft'. AFPD 62-6 designates the Single Manager (SM) for each aircraft as the airworthiness certification official and establishes the Airworthiness Certification Criteria Control Board (AC3B). The SM sets the technical specifications for each separate program, establishing requirements for the system program engineering offices, the OEMs, part manufacturers, and repair facilities.

The special needs of commercial and military aerospace dictate some degree of difference between civil and military certification processes. However, the existence of parallel standards often requires that maintenance, repair, and overhaul operations, or MROs, have completely separate facilities for civil and military activities, with the obvious cost penalties and redundancies that such an arrangement entails. Labor costs and efficiency of mechanics are impaired by the proliferation of different technical standards. Commercial mechanics are generally required to be certified by the civil airworthiness authorities, whereas mechanics working on military aircraft are subject to different qualification requirements.

The International Civil Aviation Organization (ICAO)

In concert with the national and regional airworthiness authorities, ICAO is the principal international organization with the mission of coordinating the activities of the national authorities. ICAO, whose activities extend well beyond the narrowly defined subject of airworthiness, is chartered with the responsibility for the following aims and objectives related to the development of the principles and techniques of international air navigation and to fostering planning and development of international air transport:

- Ensure the safe and orderly growth of international civil aviation throughout the world
- Encourage the development of aircraft design and operation for peaceful purposes
- Encourage the development of airways, airports, and air navigation facilities for international civil aviation
- Meet international needs for safe, regular, efficient, and economical air transport
- Prevent economic waste caused by unreasonable competition
- Ensure that the rights of member states are fully respected and that every member has a fair opportunity to operate international airlines
- Avoid discrimination between member states
- Promote safety of flight in international air navigation
- Generally promote the development of all aspects of international civil aeronautics

ICAO is a specialized agency of the United Nations, created with the signing in Chicago on 7 December 1944 of the Convention on International Civil Aviation, universally referred to as the Chicago Convention. ICAO is the permanent body charged with the administration of the principles laid out in the convention.

The 96 articles of the Chicago Convention establish the privileges and restrictions of all signatory states and provide for the adoption of International Standards and Recommended Practices (SARPs) regulating international air transport. The convention accepted the principle that every state has complete and exclusive sovereignty over the airspace above its territory and provided that no scheduled international air service may operate over or into the territory of a signatory state without its previous consent.

Standards and practices established by ICAO have no legal force until they are formally adopted by national governments. Incorporation of ICAO's recommendations is strictly voluntary on the part of member states. However, ICAO's exceptional international credibility and moral force, combined with the interest of the members in maintaining international standards of behavior, have the result that the organization's recommendations are almost always incorporated into national regulations.

ICAO's activities impact aerospace manufacturers because the body's rulings pertaining to aircraft operations often directly affect aircraft design and sometimes establish technical factors that put competitors to relative advantage or disadvantage. ICAO is, for example, the primary international arbiter for noise standards governing civil aircraft. Because all aircraft have different noise characteristics, relatively minor differences in noise standards can impose major compliance issues for some aircraft. ICAO technical staff and engineers from the aerospace manufacturers work closely during the process of writing standards to ensure that the standards accomplish their objectives without unfairly imposing arbitrary terms.

International conventions to limit government-sponsored export financing

As will be discussed in Chapter 5, all the major aircraft producing nations operate export credit agencies, or ECAs, that support their national aerospace industries by making credit available for foreign buyers of aircraft produced domestically. Because their objective is to support national industry, ECAs have sometimes distorted markets by using their financing power as a competitive tool, departing radically from commercial lending practices in order to promote sales efforts.

In recognition that such market distortions are undesirable, in 1986 the aircraft producing countries established the Large Aircraft Sector Understanding, or LASU, under the aegis of the Organization for Economic Cooperation and Development. It essentially placed limits on ECA lending offered in support of Airbus and Boeing. Controversies arose later because of financing conditions offered by Canada and Brazil in support of their domestically produced aircraft, and in 2011 LASU was expanded and modified, becoming the Aircraft Sector Understanding, or ASU. It was signed by Australia, Brazil, Canada, the European Union, Japan, Korea, New Zealand, Norway, Switzerland, and the USA.

Restrictions on foreign ownership of aerospace entities

As will be discussed in Chapter 6, the Committee on Foreign Investment in the United States (CFIUS) is a powerful interagency panel with the responsibility to review impending foreign takeovers of American firms considered to have strategic value. The committee's power was increased by the Foreign Investment Risk Review Modernization Act (FIRRMA) of 2018. CFIUS has blocked a number of proposed foreign investments in US businesses related to aerospace, notably by Chinese entities.

Issues of civil liability

Related to laws and regulations promulgated by governments is the subject of legal liability to which aircraft manufacturers are exposed in civil suits.

Civil actions against the manufacturers generally involve tort law. A tort, in common law jurisprudence, is a civil wrong that causes someone else to suffer loss or harm, resulting in legal liability for the person or entity who commits the tortuous act.

In a courtroom, the question of what exactly constitutes a 'civil wrong' is often ambiguous, and particularly so in the field of aviation. Certainly, an aircraft maker is culpable if an accident occurs because of a manufacturing defect where the aircraft was built of shoddy parts that did not conform to the engineering design. Likewise, the manufacturer is to blame in the case of a design defect that renders the aircraft incapable of performing the primary functions for which it was designed and sold.

However, tort law in some jurisdictions includes the doctrine of strict liability, which is the imposition of liability on a party without a finding of fault such as negligence. The claimant need only prove that the tort occurred and that the defendant was responsible. Legal jurisdictions that observe strict liability generally permit it to be applied in situations considered inherently dangerous, and aircraft manufacturers have been repeatedly sued in this context by plaintiffs claiming that flying in heavier-than-air machines is inherently dangerous. Of course, the aerospace and aviation industries make the point that air travel is by far the safest means of transportation on the planet.

Another relevant concept in torts is the crashworthiness doctrine, which posits that manufacturers have a responsibility to design and build aircraft so that passengers will survive crashes without injury. This doctrine, also described interchangeably with the terms 'enhanced injury' and 'second collision', holds that manufacturers can be held liable for injuries even if a crash occurs because of misuse of an aircraft perfectly capable of performing within the envelope for which it was designed and sold.

Many of the tort concepts applied to aircraft were originally developed in the last century to address issues that arose as automobiles came into widespread use. A landmark decision of modern product liability law, and ultimately crashworthiness law, was *MacPherson v. Buick Motor Co.*, a 1916 personal injury action brought by the owner of a new car with a defective steering wheel that resulted in an accident. The New York Court of Appeals ruled that a vehicle maker had a duty to make its products reasonably safe for intended use:

> If the nature of a thing is such that it is reasonably certain to place life and limb in peril when negligently made, it is then a thing of danger. Its nature gives warning of the consequences to be expected. If to the element of danger there is added knowledge that the thing will be used by persons other than the purchaser, and used without new tests, then, irrespective of contract, the manufacturer of this thing of danger is under a duty to make it carefully.

In the decades following the MacPherson ruling plaintiffs' lawyers began to advance the proposition that a manufacturer has a duty to produce a vehicle that is not only safe to operate, but is safe when it crashes, which is clearly outside the scope of its intended use. This is the heart of the crashworthiness doctrine. The landmark case in this area of product liability law is the 1966 decision in *Evans v. General Motors Corp.*, in which the plaintiff claimed that General Motors was liable because it produced a car that did not prevent injury to passengers in a collision. The Seventh Circuit Court of Appeals held that a manufacturer is not under a duty to make his vehicle 'accident-proof or fool-proof; nor must he render the vehicle more safe when the danger to be avoided is obvious to all'.

The court clearly recognized that the intended purpose of a motor vehicle does not include its participation in collisions with other objects, despite the manufacturer's ability to foresee the possibility that such collisions may occur. As defendant argued, the defendant often knows that its automobiles may be driven into bodies of water, but it is not suggested that defendant has the duty to equip them with pontoons.

A key element of the Evans ruling was a statement by the court that if it is desirable to build automobiles to survive collisions without injury to occupants, direction should be promulgated through legislation rather than through court decisions:

> Perhaps it would be desirable to require manufacturers to construct automobiles in which it would be safe to collide, but that would be a legislative function, not an aspect of judicial interpretation of existing law.

The obvious extrapolation of the Evans ruling to the aerospace industry is that aircraft must be designed and built to fly safely under the conditions for which they were intended and sold, but do not have to assure the survival of passengers in the event of a crash.

However, at about the same time as the Evans decision, the question of vehicle safety was receiving much public scrutiny, partly as a result of Ralph Nader's 1965 book *Unsafe at Any Speed*, which concluded that the automobile industry had ignored passenger safety to the extent that passengers were placed at unnecessary risk.

A change in social attitudes towards passenger safety was reflected in the landmark decision *Larsen v. General Motors Corp.* of 1968. In that ruling, the duty of a vehicle maker to deliver a product reasonably safe for its intended use was greatly expanded. The 'intended' use of automobiles was expanded to 'foreseeable' use, thereby including crashes. The Eighth Circuit Court of Appeals clearly broadened manufacturers' liability:

> We perceive of no sound reason, either in logic or experience, nor any command in precedent, why the manufacturer should not be held to a reasonable duty of care in the design of its vehicle consonant with the state of the art to minimize the effect of accidents.

While automobiles are not made for the purpose of colliding with each other, a frequent and inevitable contingency of normal automobile use will result in collisions and injury producing impacts … Where the injuries or enhanced injuries are due to the manufacturer's failure to use reasonable care to avoid subjecting the user of its products to an unreasonable risk of injury, general negligence principles should be applicable. The sole function of an automobile is not just to provide a means of transportation, it is to provide a means of safe transportation or as safe as is reasonably possible under the present state of the art.

Implications for the aerospace industry are clear. Although the manufacturer may be completely free of any responsibility for the circumstances that cause a crash, he nonetheless has a duty to ensure that the aircraft is designed with state-of-the-art features to enable passenger survival.

Of course, there remains enormous ambiguity concerning the definition of 'state-of-the-art' safety features, and herein lies the potential for continuing plaintiffs' suits against aircraft manufacturers. In court, an often-effective defense invariably used by aircraft manufacturers is that the state of the art regarding design features for aircraft safety is specifically defined by the voluminous rules of the Federal Aviation Administration. Because compliance with FAA standards is mandatory for all commercial aircraft, the manufacturers have fulfilled their duty to the flying public. Juries sometimes see it otherwise.

The potential impact of civil lawsuits on the aerospace industry was illustrated dramatically by the fate of manufacturers of light general aviation aircraft during the period from the late 1970s through the 1980s. During that period, manufacturers in the industry segment became the target of a wave of liability lawsuits that far exceeded historical levels. For example, in the four years from 1983 through 1986 alone, Beech Aircraft defended itself against 203 lawsuits, incurring substantial legal expenses. Most of the cases were related to accidents that plaintiffs' lawyers claimed were caused by design and manufacturing defects. All the accidents were investigated by the National Transportation Safety Board, or NTSB, an independent US Government agency charged with determining the probable cause of transportation accidents and promoting transportation safety. In their investigations of the Beechcraft accidents, the NTSB overwhelmingly concluded that manufacturing or design defects did not cause the crashes, which were most commonly attributed to pilot error. However, plaintiffs' lawyers were often able to convince juries composed of laypersons that the NTSB was biased because it relied heavily on analysis performed by the aircraft manufacturers.

The general aviation sector was financially vulnerable to legal attacks because it was less heavily capitalized than the giant corporations producing large commercial transports, and because privately owned general aviation airplanes tend to have much longer lifetimes than their airliner counterparts. Modern designs have progressively incorporated advanced features that tend to make them safer than older aircraft, exposing the old aircraft to a higher risk of lawsuits.

And because they are often flown by less experienced amateur pilots, small aircraft historically have a higher accident rate.

The effect of the onslaught of lawsuits was that manufacturers in the general aviation sector were driven to the brink of collapse. Annual aircraft deliveries dropped from 18,000 in 1978 to approximately 1,000 in 1987. Piper Aircraft declared bankruptcy and suspended production of most of its most popular light models. Cessna, which had been producing aircraft since 1927, declared its first annual loss in 1983 and by 1986 stopped production of all single-engine aircraft. Beech Aircraft ceased production of all piston-engine propeller models except the Bonanza and Baron. Massive factory layoffs ensued.

To address the devastating effects of the lawsuits, in the 1980s stakeholders in the general aviation sector organized an aggressive political lobbying campaign, seeking some degree of legislative protection from liability lawsuits. The campaign was led by the CEO of Cessna Aircraft and the president of the General Aviation Manufacturers Association, the trade group representing the sector. The effort was also strongly backed by the Aircraft Owners and Pilots Association, the largest American organization of private pilots and general aviation aircraft owners, and by the International Association of Machinists and Aerospace Workers, the union representing many of the workers whose jobs had been lost or were in jeopardy. Because much general aviation manufacturing activity is physically located in the state of Kansas, a group of Kansas politicians led by Senator Nancy Kassebaum initiated efforts in Washington to protect the industry. They were opposed by interest groups representing trial lawyers.

The lobbying efforts were successful, and in 1994 Congress passed the General Aviation Revitalization Act, known as GARA, a three-page bill that amended the Federal Aviation Act of 1958. The essence of GARA was to exempt general aviation manufacturers from liability for any of their products that were at least 18 years old at the time of an accident. General aviation aircraft were defined as having less than 20 passenger seats and not being operated in scheduled commercial service.

Following the passage of GARA, the general aviation sector experienced an immediate and striking resurgence in terms of revenues, profits, and employment levels. Quantities of aircraft produced also rose, but less dramatically. The relatively subdued growth in quantities reflected a change in the mix of aircraft produced by the factories. During the liability crisis the manufacturers had ceased production of many of their simpler, cheaper classic designs, and apparently were loath to reintroduce these aircraft, which lacked many safety features of modern designs. Thus the shape of the new general aviation sector changed to reflect a new era. The companies were producing fewer aircraft, sold at higher prices and of more recent design, incorporating recent technology to reduce risk to fliers.

Exposure to legal liability for manufacturers of military aircraft is different in significant ways from exposure faced by civil manufacturers. In essence, a doctrine of 'government contractor defense' generally protects government

US-Manufactured General Aviation Aircraft
Net Factory Billings and Units Shipped

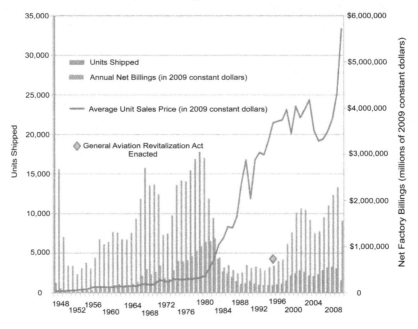

Figure 4.1 Effect of GARA on aircraft sales.

Source: General Aviation Manufacturers Association (GAMA).

contractors from liability for deaths or injuries resulting from design defects in products manufactured in strict accordance with government specifications. Some courts have drawn a distinction between the government contractor defense and the 'contract specification defense'. The two defenses are related, and differences are primarily a matter of scope. The contract specification defense does not apply to a design so obviously defective and dangerous that a competent contractor of ordinary prudence would decline to follow the design. In contrast, the government contractor defense protects the contractor even when the government specifications are obviously defective and dangerous. This defense was originally developed in cases involving public works projects such as road and sewer construction or the dredging of rivers. More recent cases have demonstrated the effectiveness of the government contractor defense in design defect actions brought under theories of negligence, strict tort liability, and breach of warranty for military products. Unsurprisingly, public policy issues relating to the defense industry today are broader and more complex than they were during the days of the early public works cases. In the public works cases, the underlying rationale for the defense was the inherent inequity of refusing to permit the contractor to share in the government's immunity from lawsuits. As applied to military product liability cases, the defense involves additional considerations of separation of powers and national defense. That is, the judiciary has recognized that it should generally defer to the executive branch of government in matters pertaining to technical specifications of equipment purchased by government agencies.

This attitude was confirmed in 1976 by a New Jersey Superior Court in *Sanner v. Ford Motor Co.* The court ruled that a passenger injured in an accident involving an Army vehicle could not recover damages from the vehicle manufacturer, even though the vehicle was manufactured without seatbelts, which were common safety equipment aboard passenger cars at the time. Ford had built the military vehicle in strict compliance with Army plans and specifications that did not require seatbelts. The court found it significant that Ford had prepared a vehicle design including seatbelts but that the Army rejected installation of the seatbelts due to a concern that they might interfere with operation of the vehicle in its military role. Ford was contractually constrained from installing seat belts, roll bars, or other restraints without approval of the Army. The court granted a summary judgment in Ford's favor, stating:

> To impose liability on a governmental contractor who strictly complies with the plans and specifications provided to it by the Army in a situation such as this would seriously impair the Government's ability to formulate policy and make judgments pursuant to its war powers. The Government is the agency charged with the responsibility of deciding the nature and type of military equipment that best suits its needs, not a manufacturer such as Ford. A manufacturer is bound to comply with plans and specifications provided to it by the Government in the production of military equipment. If it does it is insulated from liability.

Additional clarification of the government contractor defense was provided as a result of a consolidated class action before the US District Court of the Eastern District of New York in 1979. The class action sought damages from a number of independent contractors who had supplied the chemical defoliant Agent Orange to the US military for use in Vietnam. The plaintiffs were US servicemen who claimed they were injured by contact with the chemical. They also claimed that the dangerous characteristics of Agent Orange were well known to contractors. In 1982 the court set forth three elements that a defendant must prove in order to prevail on the government contractor defense:

- The government must have established the specifications for the product.
- The product manufactured by the defendant must have met the government's specifications in all material respects.
- The government must have known as much or more than the defendant about the hazards associated with the product.

The court in the Agent Orange case specifically emphasized that if these three elements were demonstrated in a satisfactory way, the manufacturer was shielded against all claims, whether framed as negligence, strict liability, or breach of warranty.

The 1987 case *Harduval v. General Dynamics* illustrates the principles and complexities of the government contractor defense. It involved legal action brought by the widow of a US Air Force pilot killed when his F-16 fighter crashed into a mountain shrouded by clouds in Korea in 1982. Two other aircraft flying in close proximity observed the fatal aircraft to be flying normally when it entered the cloud bank. No definitive cause of the crash was ever established. The widow brought suit against the manufacturer of the aircraft, General Dynamics, claiming defective design of the aircraft.

The civil trial, which took place in the Harduval home state of Florida, was tried in Federal district court under the state laws of Florida. This arrangement was because the circumstances of the case qualified under Federal law for 'diversity jurisdiction', which pertains when the contested dollar amount exceeds a specific threshold and when the plaintiff and defendant are from different states.

At the trial various theoretical explanations for the crash were presented by experts testifying on behalf of the plaintiff and defendant. Plaintiff theorized that the crash was caused by chafing of electrical wires, which caused loss of control of the aircraft. The defendant presented a theory that pilot error and disorientation were the most likely cause. The evidence was far from conclusive for either position, but the jury found for the plaintiff and awarded $3.1 million in damages. Defendant requested that the judge overrule the findings of the jury. The district court denied the defendant's request and issued a written opinion concluding that the defendant had failed to demonstrate conditions necessary to support the government contractor defense. General Dynamics appealed.

In 1988, nine months after the Florida district court issued its memorandum decision in the Harduval case, the US Supreme Court decided *Boyle v. United Technologies Corp.* The Boyle case involved the death of a US Marine Corps pilot killed in a helicopter crash. His estate sued the helicopter manufacturer, maintaining that the emergency escape hatch was defectively designed. Like the Harduval case, the Boyle case was a diversity action tried in Federal court under state law. In this case the law of Virginia applied. The local jury in Virginia, apparently relying upon aspects of state law that allowed government contractors to be held liable for design defects, issued a verdict favoring the plaintiff. The manufacturer appealed, and the Federal Court of Appeals found that the manufacturer could not be held liable under Virginia tort law for any design flaws since it met the requirements of the government contractor defense. Boyle appealed, but the Court of Appeals ruling was subsequently upheld by the US Supreme Court. The emphatic message of the Boyle ruling was that protection provided to contractors under the government contractor defense could not be diminished by state laws. The Court recognized that in certain areas of 'uniquely federal interests', state law must be preempted by federal common law. One such area of uniquely federal interest is the government's procurement of military equipment.

In 1989, the US Court of Appeals for the Eleventh Circuit, taking into account the Boyle decision, concluded that the original lower court verdict in the Harduval case was partly based upon a finding that defective manufacturing under state law was sufficient to remove the government contractor defense from the case. Because the legal basis of that argument had been recently been invalidated by the Boyle ruling, the appeals court reversed the lower court ruling in the Harduval case, and entered a judgment in favor of General Dynamics:

> We conclude that plaintiff's claims are subject to the government contractor defense, and that the record before us establishes the conditions of the defense. Accordingly, we reverse the judgment of the district court and remand for entry of judgment in favor of General Dynamics.

Thus, in the aftermath of legal precedents such as Sanner, Agent Orange, Boyle, and Harduval, the government contractor defense emerges more than ever as a robust defense against product liability claims. To reiterate, the conditions that must be met in order for the defense to be successfully invoked are:

- The government must have established the specifications for the product.
- The product manufactured by the defendant must have met the government's specifications in all material respects.
- The government must have known as much or more than the defendant about the hazards associated with the product.

The commercial contracting process

To facilitate business transactions in the culturally diverse international aerospace industry, standardized contracting processes are generally used. Standardization has been the evolutionary result of buyers and sellers gradually adapting to each other's processes to facilitate business relationships. Buyers and sellers of virtually every nationality are able to communicate in contractual terms and transact aerospace business relatively smoothly within the framework of these standard processes. Because of the historical dominance of the USA and the United Kingdom in aerospace, many of the business practices are derived from those countries.

The contract is a legal agreement consisting of an offer by the seller and an acceptance by the buyer, defining all pertinent conditions relating to the sale.

Reduced to its basic elements, the contracting process is straightforward and easy to understand. The customer identifies a requirement. Based on the requirement, he or she invites suppliers to submit offers to sell. The buyer analyzes the offers, selects a winning supplier, and negotiates a contract with the seller.

Each of the major steps can have numerous subsidiary steps, and additional steps can be added by the buyer or the seller if circumstances warrant. The buyer, particularly in the case of private-sector enterprises, ultimately has the flexibility to make the process as simple or as complicated as he or she wants.

The Aerospace Contracting Process

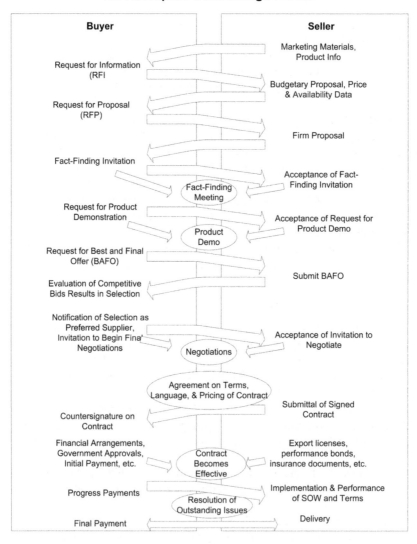

Figure 4.2 The aerospace contracting process.

Recognizing that every aerospace contract reflects circumstances and developments that are unique in some ways, the following sequence describes typical contracting events and the activities associated with them.

The customer issues a solicitation

The customer has several alternative ways to request sales information from the seller. All of these diverse forms of request fall within the general terminology of solicitation.

He or she can issue a document generally known as a request for information, or RFI, which requests non-binding preliminary data concerning prices, delivery schedules, and product performance. The RFI asks for preliminary selling data, but does not ask for a contractually binding offer to sell. If the buyer later wants to obtain a complete formal sales offer, he or she must request it from the seller. Usually the RFI is utilized when the customer wants to

Typical Request for Information

REQUEST FOR INFORMATION
MEDIUM LIFT HELICOPTERS

1.   The Indian Air Force (IAF) is considering the acquisition of Medium Lift Helicopters in the 8-15 ton class along with simulators. The approximate number required is 80. The major requirements that have to be met are as follows:-

   a) The Helicopter should be in the 8-15 ton class. The helicopter should be capable of all weather, day and night operations. The helicopters would be utilized in the troop transport, cargo helicopter, armed helicopter and utility helicopter roles.

   b) The helicopter should be capable of carrying all contemporary weaponry that are fitted on helicopters including anti armour and air-to-air missiles.

   c) The helicopter should be equipped with all required avionics and a comprehensive suite of sensors as determined by the role of the helicopter. It should also be equipped with a comprehensive self protection suite.

   d) The helicopter should have high serviceability and the maintainability requirement should be minimum.

2.   In addition to the above, information regarding service ceiling, hover IGE, payload and max AUW at sea level may kindly be provided.

3.   In case your company is interested it is requested that ROM costs for working out the financial implications be indicated for the Govt. of India to make an assessment.

4.   You may send your replies to this office for onward submission to Air HQ, New Delhi, India.

Figure 4.3 An RFI can be a very general solicitation for information to enable preliminary planning and budgeting.

Source: Indian Air Force.

obtain planning and budgetary information prior to engaging in the actual purchasing process.

If the purchase will involve a commodity item or a product with which the buyer already has technical familiarity, the purchaser may issue a request for quotation, or RFQ, which is sometimes nothing more than a request for a price.

When the customer wants to purchase a complex aerospace product that entails broad program aspects such as training, logistics support, documentation, technical integration, and so on, a request for proposal, or RFP, is issued. Equivalent terminologies are the request for tender, or RFT, and the invitation to tender, or ITT. The requests specify the customer's essential needs, such as the number of aircraft required or the indispensable operational requirements, but give the seller considerable latitude to formulate a comprehensive program that he or she believes will best meet the customer's parameters.

The fundamental difference between a response to an RFI and a full-scale proposal is that the RFI response contains less detail and is generally not a contractually binding offer to sell. In theory, the pricing data provided in the RFI response is an approximate preliminary estimate. In fact, most sellers recognize that preliminary estimates sent to the customer will eventually have an effect upon final pricing negotiations, so the estimates are often prepared with the same precision and level of effort involved in formal proposals.

Although either an RFI or an RFP is normally the formal kickoff for contractual activities, sometimes the seller will proceed in the absence of a written request from the buyer. If the seller considers it important to provide the buyer with formal pricing data for the product, but if the buyer is not ready to issue a request, the seller has the option to offer an unsolicited proposal. More detail of the composition of proposals is below. The only significant difference between a conventional proposal and an unsolicited proposal is that the customer requests the former, whereas the latter is submitted at the seller's initiative.

Formal face-to-face discussions between the buyer and suppliers occur

When major contracts are involved, at some point prior to submission of the formal proposal the buyer and the competing suppliers meet to clarify the terms of the RFI or RFP. In the case of government purchases in industrialized countries with well-defined procurement systems, this meeting usually takes the form of a bidders' conference that is conducted within a framework of formal rules to ensure that all bidders are treated equally and are provided with exactly the same information. At the conference, a representative of the buyer will review the terms of the solicitation and will publicly answer any questions posed by the audience of bidders.

In the case of non–governmental commercial sales that are less rigidly regulated, the buyer may elect to meet privately with competitors to explain the conditions of the solicitation.

The seller makes the decision to bid or no-bid

Preparing a proposal or response to inquiries by the customer is expensive and consumes resources. Consequently, if the customer request is perceived to be very unlikely to lead to a sale, the seller has the option of responding to the customer inquiry with a no-bid letter. This brief letter acknowledges receipt of the customer's inquiry and informs the customer that the seller does not intend to pursue the opportunity. Reasons for a no-bid decision may be that the customer is not considered to be qualified, that the required aircraft does not correspond with the seller's product line, that another competitor is considered to have an insurmountable advantage, or any number of other considerations.

The seller manages internal resources to prepare information for the customer

Because the response to the customer inquiry will eventually be provided to the customer in a formal contractual document, the information must be prepared in accordance with approved processes, and must be appropriately reviewed and approved within the seller's organization. To organize the effort of preparing the information, a proposal manager is appointed. He or she defines the proposal tasks, establishes schedules for completion, and monitors interim status. The proposal manager is also responsible for overseeing the physical preparation of the proposal, including text editing, preparation of artwork and exhibits, and printing.

As soon as the formal RFI or RFP is received, the proposal team undertakes a systematic detailed analysis of the document. Paragraph by paragraph, the team notes the customer requirements contained in the document. Each of these requirements is listed, and responsibility for preparing individual responses is assigned to specific team members. As responses are submitted to the proposal manager by the team members, they are assigned paragraph numbers and are incorporated into the proposal document. This detailed list of data requirements and responses is known as a compliance matrix. It is a scorecard that tracks the completion of all data items requested by the customer. In cases in which the seller cannot or does not want to supply specific elements of data requested by the customer, non-compliance is noted in the matrix. In addition to serving as a management tool for the proposal manager, the compliance matrix is also attached as part of the proposal to the customer, so that he or she can readily locate specific data within the overall document.

The proposal is reviewed internally and approved for release

When the work of compiling input for the proposal is complete, the content of the proposal is reviewed by senior management, including representatives of program management and all functional departments that will be involved in the performance of an eventual contract. The rigorousness and level of detail of the management review will depend to some extent on the nature of the

Sample Compliance Matrix

RFP Pg #	RFP Sec #	RFP Requirement	Prop Sec #	Section Title
72	6.2	Proposal Documentations:		
		The proposal shall include:		
72		* Technical configuration/specification document	6.2.1	Technical Configuration/ Specification Document
73		* Optional features listing/document	6.2.2	Optional Features Listing/Document
74		* Logistics support package	6.2.3	Logistics Support Package
76		* Separate commercial proposal	6.2.4	Commercial Proposal
78	6.3	Certifications:		
78		Aircraft must hold a current and valid Airworthiness Certificate.	6.3.1	Certifications
79		In addition, all Supplement Type Certificates (STC) for modified equipment, applicable AD's and Mandatory and Recommended Service Bulletins must be accomplished prior to the date of inspection and Technical Acceptance for the first aircraft.	6.3.2	Certifications, Supplemental
80		The manufacturer shall supply aircraft certification and documentations required to meet the registration requirements requested by Buyer.	6.3.4	Registration
81	6.4	Maintenance Inspection Program:		
83		The proposal should include a detailed manufacturer maintenance program.	6.4.1	Maintenance Inspection Program
85		It should also include a commitment for the development of a customized maintenance inspection program, if required, at no additional cost.	6.4.2	Maintenance Inspection Program
87	6.5	In-Service Technical and Logistical Support:		Maintenance Inspection Program
88		Bidders shall quote for a long term In-Service Technical and Logistical Support program.	6.5.1	Maintenance Inspection Program

Figure 4.4 A compliance matrix from an RFP for military equipment.

Source: Canadian Ministry of Defence.

proposal. High-value firm proposals for major programs will, of course, receive greater scrutiny than non-binding budgetary estimates for minor tasks.

The proposal is submitted to the customer

The manner of physical submission of the proposal depends upon circumstances surrounding the purchase. For minor purchases, the proposal is simply mailed or electronically transmitted to the customer. For major competitive purchases, the customer sometimes organizes formal ceremonies in which all competitors appear in person to officially present their proposals to a designated representative of the buyer.

A common practice is for the buyer to request or require that the proposal be submitted by a specific date, followed by an invitation to the seller to travel to the buyer to explain the proposal after the buyer's representatives have had sufficient time to evaluate and analyze the proposal. If the proposal is physically delivered by the seller to the buyer, it is not usually necessary to have a large team participate in the delivery, because the buyer will not be prepared for detailed discussions until he or she has had sufficient time to read and digest the proposal.

Every contractual offer should specify the period of its validity. Pricing information is perishable, and cannot normally be expected to remain valid without recalculation for a period for more than six months. The total proposed price to the customer is based upon lower-tier proposals from subcontractors, and these lower-tier proposals have expiration dates.

The negotiating team is established and the fact-finding process begins

Generally, the negotiating team consists of many of the same members who constituted the proposal team. Negotiations should be led by the representative from the contracts department, but the program manager should have primary decision-making authority.

After the customer has received the proposal, and as his or her specialists begin to study and evaluate it, the specialists will inevitably need additional information and explanation of material in the proposal. The fact-finding process is intended to provide the clarification desired by the customer. Ideally, the customer will prepare a list of principal questions concerning the proposal and will send the list to the seller in advance of the fact-finding meeting. The seller will then prepare requested explanations. As the fact-finding meeting takes place, discussions will prompt further questions from the customer.

Although fact-finding is theoretically not the same as negotiation, in fact all information and statements provided by either side become part of the negotiation process. Fact-finding is a rich source of information and can potentially have a profound impact upon the outcome of the negotiations that occur later.

Product demonstration is provided

Sometimes, but not always, the customer will insist on a product demonstration, which may consist of fully fledged flight tests. Such demonstrations can be expensive undertakings, particularly in the case of military aircraft that must be tested over a wide range of operational scenarios. In the case of competitive procurements, the customer normally defines a specific profile of performance characteristics that he or she wants to witness, and all competitors are asked to arrange identical demonstrations of these characteristics. The customer then scores the competing products based on their performance against the parameters.

Best and Final Offer is submitted

Following review and discussion of the initial proposal, competitors are often invited to submit their Best and Final Offer, or BAFO.

Competitive selection is made

The customer evaluation team generally has enough information to select a winner of the competition after the proposals have been reviewed, fact-finding has occurred, and a flight evaluation or product demonstration has taken place. Sometimes, especially when many competitors are involved, the customers will take the intermediate step of selecting a limited number of finalists for the competition, known as the short list. If a short list is selected, the customer then proceeds to a more rigorous evaluation to identify the overall winner.

The selection of the winner of the competition is conditional upon satisfactory completion of negotiations. In recognition of this conditional status, the winner is often declared to be the preferred supplier. If negotiations with the preferred supplier break down, the customer may return to other competitors to negotiate a satisfactory deal.

Negotiations commence, proposal revisions occur, final language is agreed, contract is signed

After the preferred supplier is identified, he or she is invited to begin negotiations. Almost always the central focus of negotiations is pricing, although it is likely that the parties will also have differences concerning other elements of the RFP, notably payment terms, delivery schedules, technical factors, and any of the various terms and conditions.

At the completion of the successful negotiating process, which may involve multiple negotiating sessions and may require direct personal involvement by senior representatives from both sides, the lead negotiators initial an agreement between the parties. This agreement is prepared in final format, and is subsequently signed by officials designated by both parties to make binding contractual commitments on their behalf.

Modalities (export license, bank guarantees, performance bonds, etc.) are completed

The contract should provide a very clear definition of the conditions that have to be met before the contract becomes effective. These conditions depend upon relevant circumstances, but generally include the requirement for the seller to obtain government export licenses, that financial arrangements be finalized, and that performance bonds, if required, be issued. In cases of major government purchases, legal approval by parliament or by the treasury prior to the expenditure of funds is often required.

Initial payment is made

The single most significant event in the implementation of a new contract is the initial payment by the customer.

The contract is implemented

Once the necessary conditions for the implementation of the contract are met, the seller's contracts department issues an internal work authorization notice within the company to notify other departments that the contract is officially in effect. The program office, which has primary authority for performing the terms of the contract and for spending the money necessary to do so, then issues a program directive, internally announcing the nature of the program and appointing a program manager. The program manager is given authority and control over the budget for the program. Control of the budget is accomplished by establishing individual budgetary accounts and work orders for the specific tasks that are part of the program plan and program master schedule. Program management processes are described in detail in Chapter 9.

The contracts department has responsibility for formally communicating a list of contractual obligations to the program office, monitoring accomplishment of these obligations, and initiating action to collect payments as they become due from the customer.

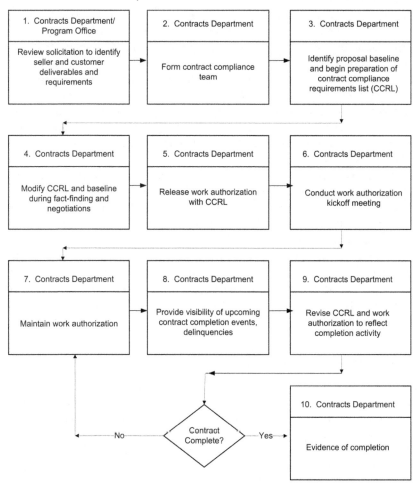

Contract Compliance and Work Authorization Process

Figure 4.5 Contract compliance and the work authorization process.

Export controls

Throughout the modern era, governments and their citizens have wrestled with the issue of control of exports of military and 'dual-use' equipment. Dual-use items are goods and technology developed for civilian uses, but which can be used for military applications or to produce weapons. On one side of the issue, manufacturers of equipment generally want to sell their products and therefore do not support unreasonable controls on exports. On the other side, many diplomats and concerned citizens recognize that armaments provide power to their owners, and believe that governments should prevent domestically produced armaments from being furnished to regimes that will misuse them.

Modern aircraft are particularly potent instruments of military power, and are often the focus of international debates concerning government control over exports.

An obvious problem facing efforts to regulate exports is that, because multiple sources exist for most types of aircraft and other armaments, controls imposed upon exporters from a single country will be ineffective unless similar controls are imposed upon exporters of similar material from other countries.

In recent years there has been a major movement by most industrialized nations, the principal suppliers of military aircraft and other armaments, to band together to prevent exports of military equipment to countries that might misuse it. In a noble effort, these producer countries have agreed on moral standards for armament exports, and have fashioned international treaties that formally govern their behavior.

Noteworthy among these international agreements is the European Community Common Export Control Policy, superseded in 2009 by the EU Export Control Regime, discussed later in this chapter, which regulates exports of dual-use material and technology from all members of the European Union under a common standard.

Of broader scope, but less specific, is the Wassenaar Arrangement, an ambitious undertaking that attempts to codify international standards for military exports, to standardize national laws regulating these exports, and to share information among member countries concerning their efforts to implement the terms of the Arrangement.

The Wassenaar Arrangement

The Wassenaar Arrangement, the first global multilateral agreement on export controls for conventional weapons and sensitive dual-use goods and technologies, received final approval by 33 co-founding countries in July 1996 and became effective in September 1996.

The Wassenaar Arrangement is of monumental significance because it represents the first worldwide effort by major weapons-producing nations to unite to establish a common policy for control of military exports. In fact, national rivalries, business interests, and conflicting national diplomatic objectives often prevent the member countries from maintaining common policy. Nevertheless, Wassenaar remains an essential symbolic step towards establishing effective worldwide control of armaments and military technology.

Wassenaar was designed to promote transparency, exchanges of information, and greater responsibility in transfers of conventional arms and dual-use goods and technologies. It complements and reinforces the existing international accords for non-proliferation of weapons of mass destruction and their delivery systems by focusing on control of transfers of armaments and sensitive dual-use goods and technologies where risks are judged greatest.

The participating states seek through their national policies to ensure that transfers of arms and dual-use goods and technologies do not contribute to the development or enhancement of military capabilities that undermine international and regional security and stability. The arrangement does not intend to impede legitimate civil transactions and is not directed against any state or group of states. All measures undertaken with respect to the arrangement are in accordance with member countries' national legislation and policies.

Wassenaar countries are expected to maintain effective export controls for the items on the agreed lists, which are reviewed periodically to take into account technological developments and political factors.

Membership of the Wassenaar Arrangement is open on a global and non-discriminatory basis to prospective adherents that comply with the agreed criteria. To be admitted, a state must be an exporter of arms or industrial equipment; maintain non-proliferation policies and appropriate national policies including adherence to relevant non-proliferation regimes and treaties; and maintain fully effective export controls.

In 2018 the participating states of the Wassenaar Arrangement were: Argentina, Australia, Austria, Belgium, Bulgaria, Canada, Croatia, Czech Republic, Denmark, Estonia, Finland, France, Germany, Greece, Hungary, India, Ireland, Italy, Japan, Latvia, Lithuania, Luxembourg, Malta, Mexico, The Netherlands, New Zealand, Norway, Poland, Portugal, Republic of Korea, Romania, Russian Federation, Slovakia, Slovenia, South Africa, Spain, Sweden, Switzerland, Turkey, Ukraine, the United Kingdom and the USA.

US Export Control

The Arms Export Control Act (AECA) is the cornerstone of US munitions export control law. The International Traffic in Arms Regulations (ITAR) implements the dictates of the AECA statute. All persons or entities that engage in the manufacture, export, or brokering of defense articles and services must be registered with the US government. The ITAR sets out the requirements for licenses or other authorizations for specific exports of defense articles and services. The AECA requires the State Department to provide annual and quarterly reports of export authorizations to Congress. Certain proposed export approvals and reports of unauthorized retransfers also require Congressional notification. Within the State Department, the agency responsible for management of military export controls is the Office of Defense Trade Controls, or DTC.

The Export Administration Act of 1979, as amended, authorizes the US Department of Commerce, in consultation with other appropriate agencies, to regulate the export or reexport of US-origin dual-use goods, software, and technology. The Department of Commerce implements this authority through the Export Administration Regulations (EAR). In addition to export controls agreed in the multilateral regimes, the Department of Commerce also imposes certain export and reexport controls for national security, foreign policy, and other reasons, most notably against countries designated by the US Secretary of State as state sponsors of international terrorism, as well as certain countries, entities, and individuals subject to sanctions. Additionally, the Department of Commerce administers and enforces regulations that prohibit transactions by US entities with certain countries under the Trading with the Enemy Act and the International Emergency Economic Powers Act. The entity within the Commerce Department with authority for control of exports of commercial goods, services, and data is the Bureau of Export Administration, or BXA.

Various other US agencies have licensing authority for sensitive exports of a specialized nature. Exports related to nuclear technology are controlled by the Nuclear Regulatory Commission, which reports to the Departments of Energy and Commerce. Any exports that are the subject of official US government embargoes and sanctions are controlled by the Department of the Treasury.

US lists of controlled exports correspond directly with the lists maintained by the various multinational nonproliferation regimes, but are augmented by unilateral controls deemed necessary by the US government to ensure national security and foreign policy imperatives. The three major lists of controlled items are the Commerce Control List (CCL), the United States Munitions List (USML), and the Nuclear Regulatory Commission Controls (NRCC).

Common European Union Export Control Policy

As part of the movement by the member states of the European Union towards economic and political integration, the EU has progressively instituted a body of policies that have greatly reduced differences and incompatibilities between the national rules of the individual members pertaining to controls of exports of military and dual-use material, services, and technology.

Standardization of export control policy has been effected particularly as a result of three particular initiatives involving the EU membership:

- European Community (EC) Common Regime for Export of Dual-Use Material and Technology
- Wassenaar Arrangement
- European Union Code of Conduct for Arms Exports

EC Common Regime for Export of Dual-Use Material and Technology. Under the terms of the Treaty of Rome, the fundamental document that is the basis for the European Union, member states retain control over their own national defense, including control over exports of military equipment. However, the member states agree that the EU should have regulatory control over dual-use material and technology. As described above, dual-use items are goods and technology developed for civilian uses, but which can be used for military applications or to produce weapons.

The European dual-use Regulation 1334/2000, which set up a Community regime for the control of exports of dual use items and technology, was adopted by the Council in June 2000. This regulation was an update of a series of earlier versions of export control rules, and the 2000 version has been updated several times subsequently.

The major innovation in the 2000 regulation was the creation of the Community General Export Authorisation, which liberalized most of the trade with close trading partners and created a level playing field for EU exporters. For ten specific countries of destination, export controls were greatly relaxed in order to reduce unnecessary administrative obstacles to trade. The ten countries on the preferential list were: Australia, Canada, Czech Republic, Hungary, Japan, New Zealand, Norway, Poland, Switzerland, and the USA. The Community General Export Authorisation applied to nearly all goods that could be traded freely in intra-Community trade.

As for intra-Community trade, the new regulation harmonizes the list of dual-use items that had required an authorization to circulate within the EU. It focuses on most sensitive items in the ballistic, nuclear, and chemical fields. Encryption controls are liberalized in order to facilitate the development of the European computer and software industries.

The last innovation was the introduction of controls of intangible transfers of technology for exports outside the European Community. The new regulations defined technology transfer via fax, telephone, and electronic media transmission, and dealt with the control of technical assistance related to certain military end uses, including oral transfers.

EU bureaucrats were given authority to introduce changes to the Council regulation in order to update the lists of items to be controlled by the EU. The EU was also empowered to participate in information exchanges and administrative cooperation with licensing authorities of member states. A representative of the European Commission was designated to chair the Coordination Group responsible for establishing best practices among national licensing authorities.

Wassenaar Arrangement. The countries of the European Union have acted to incorporate the terms of the Wassenaar Arrangement, described above, into the binding regulations of the Union.

European Union Code of Conduct for Arms Export. The individual countries of the European Union control arms exports by means of their own unique legislation covering the subject. However, the EU member states exchange information on all issues relating to conventional arms exports, ranging from customs rules in force and control of the arms trade in third countries to the member states' policies with regard to specific countries or regions. One of the first steps in this coordination of arms export policy among the member states was the adoption of the Luxembourg and Lisbon Common Criteria in 1991 and 1992. In 1997, the UK and France proposed that the members of the European Union draft an EU Code of Conduct for Arms Exports. This Code was adopted by the 15 foreign affairs ministers in the form of a Council declaration on 8 June 1998.

The Code of Conduct defines a list of criteria that all member states agree to observe. The national legislation of each of the member states has been revised to ensure compliance with the criteria, which define principles of responsible behavior for international arms exports.

In addition to the EC Common Regime for export controls, the individual nations continue, at least for the time being, to regulate national exports that may have military application. German export control laws are administered

Export License International Interfaces

Greek Airborne Early Warning System

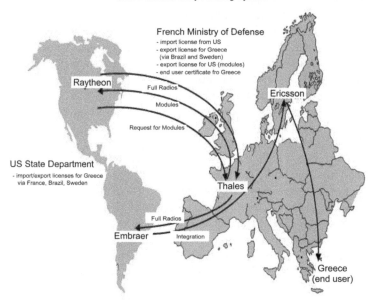

Figure 4.6 Export licenses always have added administrative complexities, but international cooperative programs such as Thales' proposal for the Greek Airborne Early Warning system are particularly daunting. The program involved Swedish radars, French electronic modules, American radios, and Brazilian airframes.

Source: Thales.

by the Federal Office of Economics and Export Control, known as BAFA, an acronym for Bundesamt für Wirtschaft und Ausfuhrkontrolle. In the United Kingdom, licenses to export arms and other goods controlled for strategic reasons, including many types of aircraft, are issued by the Secretary of State for Trade and Industry acting through the Export Control Organisation (ECO). All relevant individual license applications are circulated by the Department of Trade and Industry (DTI) to other government departments whose responsibilities involve controls of certain materials and technologies. In France, normal procedure for issuance of licenses is that approval is given by the Minister of Defense, acting on behalf of the Prime Minister, upon advice from the Interministerial Commission for the Study of Military Equipment Exports, known as CIEEMG (*Commission Interministérielle pour l'Étude des Exportations de Matériels de Guerre*). However, in cases where the Prime Minister authorizes it, the Minister of Defense can deliver the authorization of prior consent directly, without consultation with the CIEEMG.

Emerging legal issues

Over time, new legal considerations relating to aerospace continue to emerge as technology and society change. A subject of particular attention is the legal status and implications of data created by the operation of aircraft.

As digital sensors, processors, and data links have improved over time, modern aircraft systems produce vast amounts of data and distribute it widely for purposes such as air traffic management, technical diagnostics, maintenance planning, navigation, passenger identification, and operations planning. As vast amounts of aircraft-related data is created, questions arise concerning ownership of the data, liability for errors or misuse, and control of distribution of data.

Because the OEMs have developed the systems to generate and capture data, concern has been expressed within the maintenance, repair, and overhaul sector that the OEMs will abuse their privileged access to data in order to dominate the aftermarket by unfairly taking business from other MRO businesses. This consideration potentially raises anti-trust concerns.

Other issues relating to data are intellectual property rights and confidentiality laws. Business agreements involving aircraft operators are beginning to contain contractual language addressing control and use of data, attempting to manage data access and applications. Contractual limits to data use continue to evolve.

Security of aircraft-related data systems is not a legal issue as such, but potential consequences of an insecure system open numerous legal issues. Negative consequences for an MRO business if its data is lost or hacked could be severe. New EU laws authorize fines to 'essential service operators' and 'digital service providers' up to 4% of global revenue if they fail to adequately manage cyber-risk attacks. Aircraft manufacturers and operators have clear legal liability in the case of failure to adequately address data system security.

As digital systems permeate aircraft design and take a greater role in actual control of aircraft in flight, numerous questions of product liability arise. The two Boeing 737 MAX crashes in 2018 and 2019 abruptly brought to public attention the role of digital autopilots and raised issues surrounding the critical question of delineation of responsibility between the human pilot and the airborne aircraft software.

These questions remain the subject of animated discussion by regulators, in courts, and within the industry, yet to be resolved.

5 Government economic support of the aerospace industry

The subject of government financial assistance to the commercial aerospace industry is rife with controversy. Acrimonious international disputes, sometimes personally involving heads of state, are commonplace. Numerous legal complaints and countersuits valued in billions of dollars have been brought to international tribunals empowered to enforce trade agreements. Thousands of workers have protested in fear of losing their jobs because of unfair subsidies to competitors. It is an emotional subject with contrasting points of view.

In its earliest days, the aerospace industry was a model of the purest form of capitalism. Flying machines were simple and cheap to make. Start-up investment required was small, and entrepreneurs throughout the USA and Europe were designing and building prototypes in sheds. Barriers to entry were minimal, and competition was unconstrained among the hundreds of small firms that entered the market.

Within a few decades, that original period of entrepreneurial exuberance had passed. As aircraft technology expanded exponentially, the aircraft themselves became bigger, vastly more complex, and expensive to produce. The original workshops in sheds were supplanted by enormous factories equipped with expensive capital equipment. Many of the original entrepreneurs had failed and left the industry, and substantial financial barriers to entry discouraged new competitors from entering. The remaining companies were generally corporations or their international equivalents.

By the 1930s there were still dozens of robust privately owned aerospace firms in continental Europe and in the UK, the USA, and Japan. However, by that time the capitalistic owners were growing increasingly dependent upon government business, particularly in the continually expanding sector of military aircraft.

The ambiguous relationship between private owners and their government benefactors has remained important to the industry and has sometimes been difficult. Governments have almost universally recognized that their domestic aerospace industries are important to their national economies and are an important factor in their national defense. Historically, governments have been willing to provide their domestic aerospace industries with financial support, often including preferential contracts and subsidies.

Government ownership of aerospace

As an indication of government recognition of the importance of the aerospace industry and the extent to which the industry's finances are dependent upon government money, numerous aerospace firms have been nationalized, notably in France and the UK. In 1936, approximately 80% of the existing French aircraft industry was nationalized by the newly elected left-wing Front Populaire government and combined into seven separate state-owned companies. The industry was reorganized many times over the years following, and now has been largely privatized in incremental steps, although the French government maintains ownership shares of 11% in Airbus, 30% of Safran, and indirectly of 13% of Dassault.

In the UK, the Conservative government of Edward Heath had reluctantly acquired ownership of aircraft engine manufacturer Rolls-Royce in 1971 when the company was liquidated in bankruptcy. The subsequent Labour government of Prime Minister Harold Wilson nationalized most of the remainder of the British aerospace industry in 1977. The four companies nationalized, British Aircraft Corporation, Hawker Siddeley Aviation, Hawker Siddeley Dynamics, and Scottish Aviation, were estimated to represent approximately 80% of the British aerospace industry in terms of both annual sales and number of employees. The companies were combined into the new state-owned entity British Aerospace. The government's motivation for the nationalization was largely a matter of political ideology, but part of the publicly announced

Table 5.1 Government ownership shares in European defense and aerospace firms is commonplace

Top European defense firms with major aerospace activities

Nation	Company	Defense revenues (2011)		State ownership	
		€ M	*% Total*	*Direct*	*Total*
UK	BAE Systems	21,498	97%	0%	0%
EU	EADS	12,526	25%	28%	28%
IT	Finnmeccanica	9,525	55%	30%	30%
FR	Thales	6,819	52%	27%	30%
UK	Rolls-Royce	3,518	27%	0%	0%
FR	Safran	2,362	20%	30%	30%
SE	Saab	2,186	84%	0%	0%
UK	Cobham	1,389	65%	<3%	<3%
FR	Dassault Aviation	890	27%	0%	13%
UK	GKN	803	11%	0%	0%
CH	RUAG	750	52%	100%	100%
UK	Ultra Electronics	674	80%	0%	0%
UK	Meggitt	674	40%	0%	0%
FIN	Patri	557	90%	73%	81%
DE	MTU Aero Engines	446	15%	0%	0%
E	Indra Sistema	403	15%	<3%	<3%

Source: Avascent.

justification was the goal of securing long-term viability for the industry. The Secretary for Industry noted that government support to the airframe segment of the industry had amounted to the equivalent of about $820 million in the prior decade, while about $1 billion had been spent on military research and development (R&D) and about $2.6 billion more had been spent on military aircraft-related procurement over the same period. The industry returned to private ownership in 1981, when the Conservative government of Margaret Thatcher sold a majority share of British Aerospace to private investors. The remaining 48% ownership stake in the company was sold to investors in 1985.

In Brazil, the principal national aerospace company Empresa Brasileira de Aeronáutica (Embraer) was created as a government-owned corporation in 1969. Embraer acquired Aerotec, another Brazilian state-owned aerospace company, in 1987. In 1994, as Embraer faced bankruptcy, it was privatized. In 2000 it underwent an initial public offering and was listed on the New York Stock Exchange and the major Brazilian securities exchange. The Brazilian government retains an interest through possession of golden shares, giving it veto power over major corporate decisions.

The Canadian aerospace industry traces its roots to subsidiaries of private British aircraft manufacturers that were nationalized by the Canadian government during World War II. De Havilland Canada, of Toronto, formerly the Canadian unit of the British parent de Havilland, was converted into a crown corporation of the Government of Canada during the war. In 1980 the company was privatized by the government and in 1986 was sold to Boeing, which in turn sold it in 1992 to Bombardier Aerospace of Montreal.

Canadair was created in 1944 as a separate entity by the government of Canada, absorbing the operations of Canadian Vickers Ltd., formerly a subsidiary of its parent in the UK. In 1946 a corporate antecedent of General Dynamics Corp. of the USA bought the company, but in 1976 it returned to Canadian government ownership. It remained a crown corporation until 1986, at which time it was facing insolvency because of financial problems with its new Challenger business jet and was sold to Bombardier, becoming the core of Bombardier Aerospace.

The USA does not have a history of nationalized industry, but at the beginning of World War II, before the USA had yet become a belligerent, President Roosevelt asked Congress to provide funds for the expansion of the aviation industry. In 1940, Congress passed 'An Act to Expedite the Strengthening of the National Defense', which gave the Secretary of War broad powers to boost war equipment production. Immediately thereafter the government began construction of dozens of defense plants that were made available to private industry to produce military equipment. Many of the vast numbers of warplanes delivered in the ensuing war years were produced in these plants by Lockheed, Douglas, Curtiss, North American, Consolidated, and others.

After the war, the government-owned plants, which were known as government-owned/contractor-operated (GOCO) facilities, either remained under government ownership or were conveyed free of charge to local municipalities

Table 5.2 GOCO facilities are a vestige of World War II

Government-owned/contractor-operated production facilities

GOCO facility of note	Production history	Current status
Air Force Plant No. 4 Fort Worth, TX	Produced the B-24 Liberator bomber in WW2, later produced the B-36, B-57, F-111, and F-16	Currently operated by Lockheed Martin for production of F-35
Air Force Plant No. 77 Ogden, UT	Production of Minuteman ICBM and Short Range Attack Missile by Boeing	Remains a facility of Hill Air Force Base
Air Force Plant No. 85 Columbus, OH	Produced Curtiss-SB2C-5 Helldiver for the Navy during WW2, later occupied by North American Rockwell for production of F-100, A-5, T-2, T-28, and OV-10 aircraft, and B-1 components	Conveyed to Columbus Municipal Airport Authority
Air Force Plant No. 42 Palmdale, CA	Used for early development of jet aircraft at Edwards AFB in Korean War period. Used by Lockheed and Rockwell for production of U-2, XB-70 Valkyrie X-15, B-1 Lancer Bomber, SR-71 Blackbird, F-117A Nighthawk, B-2 bomber, and Space Shuttle	Currently site of production line for Northrop B-21 stealth bomber and home of Lockheed Skunk Works and other experimental aircraft operations
Air Force Plant No. 6 Marietta, GA	In WW2 Bell Aircraft produced B-29 bombers under license from Boeing. Lockheed produced the B-47 under license from Boeing, later produced the C-130, C-141, C-5, and F-22	Continues to be occupied by Lockheed Martin
Air Force Plant No. 19 San Diego, CA	Consolidated Aircraft produced B-24 bombers during WW2, and later produced F-102 and F-106 fighters. Lockheed-Martin produced rocket boosters for Atlas and Titan rockets	Now houses US Navy's Space and Naval Warfare Systems Command
Air Force Plant No. 44 Tucson, AZ	Hughes Aircraft and Raytheon for production of various missile types	Continues to be occupied by Raytheon
Air Force Plant No. 3 Tulsa, OK	Initially occupied by Douglas Aviation, in WW2 produced A-24 Dauntless dive bombers, B-24 Liberator strategic bombers, and A-26 Invader medium bombers. Later produced B-47 Stratojet strategic bombers and B-66 Destroyer medium bombers	McDonnell Douglas closed its Tulsa operations in 1994. The plant was conveyed to the city of Tulsa and converted to a factory to produce school busses

Source: US Department of Defense.

and converted to other uses. In 1970 the Secretary of Defense ordered the sale or transfer of many government facilities, and by 1980 only 147 were still owned by the government. Many others have been sold since. The plants that remain in government ownership include Air Force Plant No. 4 in Fort Worth Texas, where the Lockheed F-35 fighter is currently built, Air Force Plant No. 6 in Georgia, where the Lockheed C-130 production line is located, and Air Force Plant No. 42 in Palmdale, California (at Edwards Air Force Base), site of the production line for the Northrop B-21 bomber.

Government ownership of corporations is incompatible with the capitalistic ethos in the USA, but American politicians have intervened on occasion to rescue major companies threatened with failure. In the aerospace industry, the most notable example was the government bailout of Lockheed in 1971.

In that year Lockheed was in a precarious financial position as it incurred losses on its contract to produce the C-5A transport for the US Air Force, and simultaneously struggled to introduce its L-1011 Tristar airliner for the commercial market. Rolls-Royce, which was developing the new RB-211 engine for the Tristar, encountered technical problems with the engine and declared bankruptcy in early 1971. Lockheed was heavily indebted and financially vulnerable, without adequate financial resources to survive program delays and additional costs caused by the Rolls-Royce difficulties.

The British government agreed to finance a successor corporation to Rolls-Royce to build the engines only if Lockheed obtained additional credit of up to $250 million required for its own survival. Private creditors declined to extend further credit to Lockheed, but in August 1971 Congress passed the Emergency Loan Guarantee Act, which established a mechanism for providing funds to any major business enterprise in crisis. Lockheed was the first recipient. Public justification for the aid, supported by President Nixon, was that Lockheed's failure would have meant significant job losses in California, a reduction of GDP, and a negative impact on national defense.

Lockheed was granted a line of credit of $250 million under the provisions of the Emergency Loan Guarantee Act and the British government rescued Rolls-Royce. The Tristar program was eventually launched and began to generate positive cash flow, and by 1979 Lockheed had repaid the full amount of its government-sponsored loans.

Regardless of whether aerospace industry ownership has been public or private, governments everywhere have nurtured the industry and have provided financial support, be it direct or indirect. In the USA and Japan, in keeping with the capitalistic traditions of the countries, direct government ownership has generally been avoided and financial support has been indirect in nature. In Europe and elsewhere direct government ownership has occasionally been embraced and outright subsidies and loans are common.

In China, which has not yet become a significant competitor in the international aerospace market, the domestic aerospace industry is overwhelmingly government-owned. Aviation Industry Corporation of China (AVIC) is the predominant state-owned aerospace and defense conglomerate. It consists of over 100 subsidiaries, 27 listed companies, and has an estimated 500,000 employees. AVIC has announced its intention to become a top international competitor in the commercial aircraft market, and is actively working to develop aircraft models for international sales. When the Chinese aircraft enter the international market, the government ownership and financial support of the industry will certainly become an issue with western competitors.

In Russia, the United Aircraft Corporation (UAC), created in 2006, is the majority state-owned aerospace and defense corporation that consolidates most of the country's legacy companies dating from the Soviet era. Much of its activity involves military aircraft, but it has launched an airliner program targeted at the international market. As is the case with China, government ownership and financial support of UAC will predictably elicit protests from privately owned international competitors if Russian aircraft enter the market in a significant way.

International accords limiting government financial support

In the present era of globalization, characterized by international treaties governing worldwide commerce and establishing rules of fair play, national subsidies and government financial support of the aerospace industry are restricted or banned altogether, in recognition that unfettered government subsidies would result in harmful distortions to international markets. The international agreements are more permissive of government support for national industries of developing countries with nascent aerospace production activity.

Three principal international agreements have established rules for government financial assistance to the international large civil aircraft (LCA) industry. The first of these, the General Agreement on Tariffs and Trade (GATT) Tokyo Round in 1979 resulted in an agreement addressing trade in civil aircraft and a subsidies code. The second, a 1992 bilateral agreement between the USA and the EC on trade in large civil aircraft, supplemented the GATT agreement but was later suspended when the USA withdrew. The third, which was part of the Uruguay Round of the GATT in 1994 that created the World Trade Organization (WTO), included the Agreement on Subsidies and Countervailing Measures (SCM Agreement) and the Dispute Settlement Understanding (DSU). The SCM Agreement and the DSU were significant because earlier agreements had provided no provisions for penalties or remedies in the case of violation of the terms.

The agreements curtailed direct subsidies by prohibiting all future production subsidies and limiting development subsidies to 33% of a new plane's total development costs. These development subsidies were allowable only in the form of loans to the companies that were required to be repaid within 17 years. Interest on the loans was required to be at least as high as the rate paid by government debt. Indirect subsidies were limited to 3% of the industry-wide revenue and 4% of the revenue for each individual manufacturer. These indirect subsidies were defined as any 'identifiable reduction in costs of large civil aircraft resulting from government-funded research and development in the aeronautical area'.

Methods of government financial support

All four of the major Western commercial aircraft manufacturers (Airbus, Boeing, Bombardier, and Embraer) receive financial support from their governments. The nature of support varies from country to country.

From the very inception of Airbus, the home governments of the firms involved in production have provided 'launch aid' in the form of loans with soft repayment conditions. In the mid-1960s, when the Airbus concept was formulated by leading aerospace firms in France, Germany, and the UK, the European aerospace industry was fragmented, consisting of numerous mid-sized firms that did not collectively have the financial resources to launch a major new aircraft program. By 1966 the participating firms approached their

Government Launch Aid Arrangement
Airbus A330/A340

As soon as each Associated Manufacturer has undertaken to ensure that its share of the development work specified in Annex 2 to these Arrangements is carried out and to defray its share of expenditure of non-attributable development work, each of the Signatory Governments will take the necessary measures, according to appropriate national procedures, to enable its Associated Manufacturer to complete its part of the AIRBUS A 330 / A 340 development programme. This duty relates to the AIRBUS A 330 / A 340 aircraft as defined in Annex 1 to these Arrangements, and, without prejudice to the relevant national arrangements, shall be deemed to be fulfilled by the granting of reimbursable advances to the respective Associated Manufacturers up to the following maximum amounts :

French Republic :
> FF 7 800 000 000 (seven thousand eight hundred million French Francs)
> applied to the initial phase of the programme ;

Federal Republic of Germany :
> DM 2 996 000 000 (two thousand nine hundred and ninety six million Deutsche Mark)
> applied to both phases of the programme ;

United Kingdom of Great Britain and Northern Ireland :
> £ 450 000 000 (four hundred and fifty million Pounds Sterling)
> applied to the initial phase of the programme ;

Kingdom of Spain :
> PTAS 29 356 000 000 (twenty nine thousand three hundred and fifty six million Pesetas)
> applied to both phases of the programme ;

Kingdom of Belgium :
> BFR 1 908 000 000 (one thousand nine hundred and eight million Belgian Francs)
> applied to the initial phase of the programme.

Figure 5.1 An extract from the government arrangements to fund the Airbus A330 and A340 programs.

governments to ask for loans to launch the initial A300B program, and in 1967 the three governments agreed to provide the loans.

The European aerospace industry is no longer the fragmented and financially frail group of companies it was in the 1960s, but the European governments have continued the practice of providing loans to participating firms to finance up-front launch costs as Airbus has introduced new aircraft.

Terms of government loans to Airbus have varied from program to program, but they have certain common features:

- Repayment to be accomplished over a fixed number of aircraft deliveries
- Pro-rata installment payments to be made at the time of individual aircraft deliveries
- Interest rates below commercial market rates
- Forgiveness of outstanding balance if targeted aircraft sales quantity is not met

Two Airbus programs have ended after relatively short production runs, before the balances of their government launch aid was repaid. The A340 program ended in 2012 after 377 deliveries, and the A380 was terminated in 2019, with the final 251st aircraft to be delivered in 2021. In both cases, the substantial unpaid government loan balances were forgiven.

The flow of government financial benefits to Boeing takes entirely different forms. A large minority component of the company's business involves direct government contracting, notably with the Department of Defense (DoD) and the National Aeronautics and Space Administration (NASA). The company contracts to provide military equipment, satellites, rockets, maintenance, and other goods and services to the government. Some of these contracts involve aeronautical research that is directly or indirectly applicable to its commercial aircraft business.

There is no doubt that Boeing's commercial aircraft have benefited from technology derived directly from the military programs. The 707 airliner, for example, which secured Boeing's position as a dominant producer of commercial jet transport aircraft, was a derivative of the KC-135 aerial refueling tanker that Boeing developed for the US Air Force.

Of course, the principal European commercial aerospace companies have historically also been heavily involved in government contracts, and as recently as 2015 almost a quarter of Airbus revenues came from defense and space business.

Another form of financial benefit that Boeing receives from governments is preferential tax treatment by state and local governments. Following common business practice in the USA, when the company is considering locations for new production sites it routinely attempts to obtain concessions including forgiveness of taxes, low-cost land leases, infrastructure improvements, and other advantages. Because of the significant economic benefits that a new Boeing manufacturing site is perceived to bring, localities often compete with each

Table 5.3 US Government estimates of European government launch aid to Airbus

Launch aid for Airbus members ($ billions)

	A300 and A310			A320			A330 and A340		
	France	UK	Germany	France	UK	Germany	France	UK	Germany
Commitments	1.2	0.1	3.0	0.7	0.4	0.9	0.8	0.7	1.6
Disbursements	1.1	0.1	1.5	0.7	0.4	1.0	0.3	0.3	0.3
Value at Government	3.3	0.3	3.1	1.2	0.6	1.1	0.3	0.4	0.3
Value at Corporation	7.5	0.3	5.7	1.8	0.7	1.2	0.4	0.4	0.3

	Program totals			Country totals			All Airbus
	A300 & A310	A320	A330 & A340	France	UK	Germany	
Commitments	4.3	2.0	3.2	2.7	1.2	5.5	9.5
Disbursements	2.7	2.1	0.8	2.1	0.8	2.8	5.6
Value at Government	6.7	2.6	1.1	4.8	1.3	4.7	10.7
Value at Corporation	13.3	3.7	1.0	9.6	1.3	7.1	18.0

Source: US Department of Commerce.

Table 5.4 Airbus revenue breakdown: civil aircraft, helicopters, defense and space

Airbus revenue breakdown by operating division – 2015–2017 (€ millions)			
	Year ended 30 December 2017	*Year ended 30 December 2016*	*Year ended 30 December 2015*
Airbus Commercial Aircraft	50,958	49,237	45,854
Airbus Helicopters	6,450	6,652	6,786
Airbus Defence and Space	10,804	11,854	13,080
Total Divisional Revenues	**68,212**	**67,743**	**65,720**
Other Items	(1,445)	(1,162)	(1,270)
Total	66,767	66,581	64,450

Source: Airbus.

other to offer attractive financial incentives. The aggregate value of these local incentives can be substantial. For example, as an inducement for Boeing to retain production of new aircraft models in Washington State, in 2013 the governor signed a bill that nominally granted Boeing $9 billion in tax relief through 2040, subject to certain conditions.

The Canadian aerospace industry receives direct and indirect financial support from its national and provincial governments. In recent years Bombardier has been the major beneficiary of this support. The federal government has allocated more than C$750 million for support of the CSeries airliner program through vehicles such as the Strategic Aerospace and Defense Initiative (SADI), which supports research and development in the sector. Additional government support for the CSeries included C$117 million from Quebec and £123 million from the UK government related to CSeries work being performed at the Shorts Brothers facility in Belfast, Northern Ireland, a Bombardier unit.

The Canadian government also supports Bombardier by providing export financing. When Bombardier was competing against Embraer to sell approximately 75 midsized passenger jets for approximately $2 billion to Air Wisconsin in 2001, the Canadian government agreed to provide the buyer with up to $1.1 billion in low-interest financing to facilitate the sale. Although governments are commonly involved with aircraft export financing, usually through guarantees, the Air Wisconsin financing was considered exceptional because of the below-market rate offered.

Among the nations home to significant commercial aerospace industries, the Brazilian government appears to disburse the least direct financial aid. However, a significant share of Embraer's revenues has historically come from sales to its government for military aircraft and services.

International legal disputes through the World Trade Organization

Because of the large direct and indirect monetary flows from governments in support of their domestic aerospace industries through ambiguous and sometimes opaque channels, and in light of rigorous WTO rules regulating these flows, it is inevitable that disputes arise concerning perceived violations of the rules.

In fact, disputes on the subject of illicit government financial aid are probably the single most acrimonious aspect of the otherwise fraternal relationships among the world's aerospace companies. All four of the large commercial aircraft producers have filed WTO complaints and countercomplaints against their competitors. Industry lobbyists work closely with their governments in support of the complaints, and public relations departments issue incessant announcements attacking purported violators and describing damages inflicted on national industries.

Complaints against Airbus

In support of Boeing, the USA filed its principal complaint against Airbus in 2006, claiming that European governments had provided approximately $22 billion in prohibited aid. In 2010 the WTO ruled in favor of the USA on 80% of the total alleged subsidy amounts. The ruling was upheld under appeal in May of 2011. The WTO ruled that Airbus had received $18 billion of illegal subsidies, including $15 billion of launch aid. The ruling directed the European governments to remove the harmful effects of all illegal subsidies by December of 2011. On September 22, 2016, the WTO determined that the European governments had failed to meet the compliance deadline to remedy $17 billion worth of past subsidies to Airbus. The WTO also noted that since the time of the earlier ruling, an additional $5 billion in prohibited launch aid had been provided by the European governments to support the new A350. The Europeans once again appealed, and a final judgment in favor of Boeing was upheld in 2018.

Complaints against Boeing

In 2004 the European Union filed a WTO complaint against Boeing, alleging that Boeing had received US federal, state, and local subsidies of a total value of $23.7 billion. Of this amount, the EU maintained that $16.6 billion was in the form of research and development support to the company provided by NASA and the Department of Defense. This support involved NASA and DoD sharing technical data with Boeing and paying Boeing to perform R&D work on behalf of the two entities. The EU complaint also claimed that Boeing had received $2.2 billion in prohibited federal income tax breaks under the Foreign Sales Corporation legislation. The complaint also cited benefits provided to Boeing by state and local governments in the form of tax relief and infrastructure improvements.

In 2012 the WTO issued a ruling upholding the EU complaint of subsidized research and development funding and income tax cuts from the federal government, but reduced the claimed amounts to $3.2–$4.3 billion. In response, the USA agreed to remedies including modifying the R&D funding and eliminating the tax benefits. The EU in 2012 filed a follow-on complaint that the American corrective measures did not comply with the WTO directions. In 2017 the WTO issued a ruling rejecting 28 of the 29 claims in the 2012 EU complaint.

Complaints against Canada

The WTO issued rulings in 1999 and 2002 that the Canadian government had provided prohibited subsidies to Bombardier, primarily in the form of loan assistance for foreign aircraft customers from Export Development Canada (EDC), which is Canada's export credit agency. EDC supports Canadian industry by providing trade finance, export credit insurance, bonding services, and other services to exporters. The violations cited by the WTO involved loan arrangements at below-market pricing, notably to Bombardier customers Comair, Air Wisconsin, and Air Nostrum.

Brazil filed another WTO complaint in 2016, saying that the CSeries had received $3 billion in federal, provincial, and local subsidies. In 2017 the WTO ruled that the specific subjects of the complaint were within WTO jurisdiction, and agreed to assess arguments and issue a decision in the future.

In another completely different venue, in 2017 Boeing protested to the US Commerce Department and the US International Trade Commission (ITC), a US government agency empowered to act against unfair trade practices by foreign entities. Boeing claimed that it had been harmed because Canadian government subsidies to Bombardier had resulted in sales of its CSeries airliner to Delta Airlines in 2016. Boeing maintained that the Delta sale unfairly harmed sales of its rival 737-700 aircraft.

In late 2017, the Commerce Department sided with Boeing in the complaint and imposed a 292% tariff on all CSeries aircraft imported into the USA. However, a few weeks later the ITC reversed the Commerce Department decision and canceled the tariff. In its unanimous ruling dismissing the Boeing complaint, the ITC noted that Boeing was not harmed because the 737-700 was a significantly larger aircraft than the CSeries aircraft ordered by Delta, and thus did not compete in the same market segment. In fact, Boeing had not submitted a proposal in response to the Delta solicitation that resulted in the CSeries order in 2016.

Complaints against Brazil

In 1996 Canada filed a complaint with the WTO, alleging that the Brazilian government export financing program (Programa de Financiamento às Exportações, or PROEX) had offered loans to foreign purchasers of Embraer aircraft at rates and terms that were more attractive than commercially available loans. Brazil restructured the loan program into a format known as PROEX III, which the WTO declared to be compliant in 2000.

A TEACHABLE MOMENT?

There is perhaps a lesson to be learned from Boeing's handling of its complaints against the Bombardier CSeries, entirely aside from the central issue of government subsidies.

At the time of the complaint, Bombardier and the CSeries program were in a precarious financial position, and the order from Delta was the aircraft's largest sale by far. Bombardier was pursuing other vital sales in the USA. The 292% tariff imposed by the Commerce Department at the behest of Boeing could conceivably have caused the collapse of the CSeries program, and possibly threatened the continued existence of Bombardier Aerospace.

Canadian Prime Minister Justin Trudeau was visibly angry at Boeing when the tariff was imposed, and immediately canceled a pending Canadian order for 18 F/A-18 fighter aircraft produced by Boeing. According to the US Department of Defense, the estimated total value of the F/A-18 sale was $5.23 billion.

British Prime Minister Theresa May also expressed displeasure with the Boeing action against Bombardier, which threatened the jobs of approximately 4,000 workers in the Bombardier-owned factory in Belfast, where the CSeries wings were made. May noted the long relationship between Boeing and the UK and commented, 'this is not the sort of behavior we expect from a long-term partner. It undermines that partnership'.

After the US tariff on the CSeries was nullified by the International Trade Commission, the planned F/A-18 procurement was not reinstated. Canada bought fighters from another source.

In summary, throughout the history of the modern international aerospace industry national governments have demonstrated that they will take whatever steps are necessary to protect and develop their national industries. Although government ownership of aerospace companies has decreased among the major Western aerospace producers, state-owned companies remain common in developing countries that aspire to expand their aerospace activities.

A formalized body of international agreements and understandings restricting financial support of commercial aircraft development and production has been ratified by the significant aerospace countries. The terms of the agreements are complex and sometimes ambiguous. The agreements allow government assistance to companies within restrictions, and disagreement over the exact limits of those restrictions has resulted in continuous long-running legal disputes among the signatories. The system is imperfect. Nevertheless, the World Trade Organization appears to have been an important factor in reducing the extent of market distortions caused by government subsidies. As usual the future is unpredictable, and the market entry of heavily subsidized Chinese and Russian aircraft threatens to cause further perturbation.

6 International cooperation, joint ventures, teaming, and industrial offsets

International cooperation on aerospace programs is almost as old as the industry itself. At the onset of World War I, barely 11 years after the first manned flight, domestic American legal squabbles over aviation patent rights had suppressed technical innovation and caused the national industry to fall behind its European counterparts in design technology. Since the American military had no aircraft capable of credibly doing battle with German designs, US pilots initially flew aircraft built in French or British factories. To address the lack of American aircraft, in May 1917 the War Department sent an official commission to Europe to survey the industry and select an aircraft to produce domestically. They selected the British DH-4, designed by Geoffrey de Havilland. Reportedly they chose the De Havilland partly because the British government agreed to provide a free manufacturing license to the Americans, whereas French manufacturers insisted upon purchase of a license and payment of production royalties. American production of the de Havilland aircraft began, but by the end of the war the USA had not produced any aircraft of domestic design for action at the front. In late 1918, the nascent US aerospace industry employed more than 200,000 workers, mostly engaged in the production of the DH-4, aircraft engines, and domestically designed light trainer aircraft.

In spite of the early advent of international cooperation, after World War I international programs among companies or governments became uncommon until the 1950s. A notable exception during World War II was the Rolls-Royce Merlin V-12 aircraft engine, of which 5,523 units were produced under license by Packard in the USA to power the P-51 Mustang fighter. Joint programs were not often necessary because aircraft technology was accessible to many medium-sized companies, and development costs of new aircraft and equipment were low enough to be affordable by independent business entities. The pan-nationalism trend of the late twentieth century had not yet taken hold, and cooperative international industrial programs had not emerged as a familiar way of doing business.

By the final decades of the twentieth century, however, technological content of new aircraft had increased geometrically and development costs had risen to levels beyond the financial resources of most companies. Only a comparatively small number of major aerospace firms were still in business, and

Table 6.1 Development cost of new aircraft is commensurate with size and technological content

Aircraft development costs (1991 constant $ millions)

Aircraft type	Entered service	Development cost	Development cost per seat
DC-3	1936	3	0.1
DC-8	1959	600	3.75
B-747	1970	3,300	7.3
B-777	1995	4,300*	14.0*

Note: *estimated.
Source: Talalay, M, Farrands, C, and Tooze, R, eds. 1996, 'Aviation's Technology Imperative and the Transformation of the Global Political Economy', *Technology, Culture and Competitiveness: Change and the World Political Economy*, Routledge Publishers, London.

governments actively promoted joint programs involving multiple firms, often of multiple nationalities. Economic and political factors had evolved in directions that created circumstances favorable for the emergence of the joint program as a dominant business structure.

Types of international cooperation

International cooperative programs take many forms. The strongest form of international commitment is the acquisition or creation of a **wholly owned subsidiary** overseas. Partially owned subsidiaries are another alternative. However, ownership of foreign aerospace firms is often impractical because of legal obstacles. Historically, government ownership of aerospace firms has discouraged acquisitions by foreign entities. Even in cases in which ownership is private, national governments generally consider the industry to be of strategic importance and impose formidable obstacles to foreign ownership. In the USA, for example, the Committee on Foreign Investment in the United States (CFIUS) is a powerful interagency panel that screens foreign transactions with US firms for potential security risks. Established in 1975, CFIUS powers have been increased over the years as the US government's perception of risk has become more acute. In 2018 the Foreign Investment Risk Review Modernization Act (FIRRMA) was enacted, enhancing the board's powers and allowing CFIUS to review a wider range of transactions, including any 'non-passive' investment in US firms involved in critical technology or other sensitive sectors. It also lengthened the review period, gave CFIUS greater leeway to suspend transactions, increased funding and staffing for the agency, and mandated a separate process to review the export of sensitive US technologies. CFIUS has blocked a number of proposed foreign investments in US businesses related to aerospace, notably by Chinese entities. On the other hand, CFIUS has approved major acquisitions by BAE Systems, a British company, of US firms involved in defense and aerospace. BAE Systems employment in the USA in 2018 totaled 32,000.

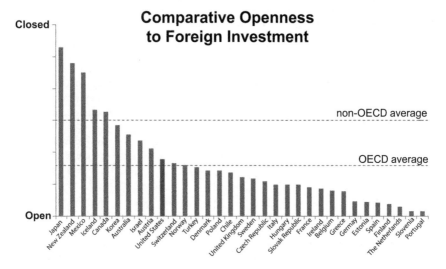

Figure 6.1 Not all national governments are receptive to foreign ownership of domestic industry.

Source: Organization for Economic Cooperation and Development (OECD).

Other nations with well-developed aerospace industries have equally stringent controls governing foreign takeover of ownership.

International **joint ventures** are another option for cooperative business arrangements. Often the joint ventures are based in countries with less developed aerospace industries. The foreign partner is customarily an established aerospace company that provides technology and management expertise. The local partner generally provides facilities, local labor, government support for the project, and access to the market. JVs are particularly favored by political authorities in China and India.

In addition to international equity ventures, firms have the option of working together within cooperative frameworks that do not involve equity participation or joint ownership. **Licensed production** arrangements provide for owners of design technology or production technology to license foreign firms to use the technology in exchange for payments of some sort. Often these technology licenses are accompanied by contracts requiring the licensor to provide training or services related to the physical technology transfer.

Looser forms of international cooperation, often involving multiple partners, also exist. **International consortia** are formed by groups of firms that work together within contractual frameworks to accomplish multinational programs. Sometimes these consortia are led by a single dominant prime contractor who directs the operations of the consortium by means of subcontracts. At other times, administrative organizations are created by the consortium members for the express purpose of managing the business activities and internal

Table 6.2 Chinese government policy strongly encourages aerospace joint ventures

Key international joint ventures in the Chinese A&D sector 2014–2016

Announcement or signing date	Chinese entity	Foreign partner	Foreign partner country	Focus of joint venture
June 2016	Commercial Aircraft Corp. of China (COMAC)	United Aircraft Corp.	Russia	Design and develop new wide body aircraft
April 2016	China Eastern Air Holding Co.	MTU Aero Engines AG	Germany	Provide a high-tech machine pool and modern test cell accommodating engines up to 150,000 pounds of thrust
January 2016	Lingyun Group Co. Ltd.	Israel Aerospace Industries, Ltd. (IAI)	Israel	Expand civil maintenance services and cargo conversion, laying groundwork for additional business
July 2014	Aviation Industry Corp. of China (AVIC)	Safran	France	Research, design, and manufacture core components of turbine engines for civil service in China
July 2014	Aviation Industry Corp. of China (AVIC)	Parker Aerospace Group	USA	Develop fuel, inerting, and hydraulic systems for COMAC C919, assembling and testing MA700 hydraulic systems
April 2014	CETCA	Rockwell Collins	USA	Develop communications and navigation solutions for C919

Source: Deloitte.

coordination of the consortium. These administrative entities can be large, permanent organizations such as Airbus Industrie and Eurofighter GmbH, or smaller ad hoc organizations such as SECBAT (Société Européenne pour la Construction du Breguet Atlantic), which essentially functioned as a steering committee to oversee production of the Atlantic marine patrol aircraft by the aerospace industries of France, The Netherlands, Germany, Belgium, and Italy.

More recently European governments have created OCCAR (Organisation Conjointe de Coopération en matière d'Armement/Organisation for Joint Armament Co-operation), intended to be a permanent intergovernmental structure for managing collaborative European armament programs. OCCAR notably provides management oversight of the Airbus A400M transport and Airbus Tiger helicopter programs.

The least permanent cooperative arrangements are commonly called **teaming agreements**, an imprecise categorization that includes joint efforts ranging from cooperative marketing teams to international manufacturing networks.

Factors driving international cooperation

Although pooling of financial resources is a major impetus for the creation of cooperative international programs, other considerations are sometimes important in the decision-making process leading to the launch of new programs:

International diplomatic factors. Governments have repeatedly attempted to use cooperative aerospace projects as symbols of friendship and common economic interests. In many respects, aerospace projects are suitable for this symbolic role due to their monumental nature in terms of size, visibility, and cost. Joint projects entail close, long-term relationships among industries of the participating countries. Concorde, as an example, is generally viewed as the consequence of a desire by the French and British governments of the 1960s to demonstrate Franco-British unity in the early days of the European Community.

Military standardization. In an age of international military alliances that involve joint operations by armed forces of different nationalities, standardization of equipment has become a necessity. A motive behind NATO government efforts to establish cooperative production of military aircraft is to increase joint effectiveness by standardizing warplanes, thus theoretically lowering unit production costs and rationalizing logistical arrangements necessary to support the aircraft. Standardization was widely cited as a driving force in the creation of the Atlantic marine patrol aircraft of the late 1950s, a joint production of France, Germany, Italy, The Netherlands, and Belgium. Establishment of the F-16 coproduction program among NATO allies was also partly motivated by military standardization.

Suppression of competition. Prior to the advent of Airbus Industrie, a major barrier to the success of the European civil aircraft industry was that many small firms chronically introduced multiple similar aircraft that competed with each other for a limited market. One of the reasons for the success of Airbus was that it provided a means for European manufacturers to work together rather than compete against each other. Likewise, international military programs are often viewed as a means of avoiding harmful internecine competition.

Economic advantages from longer production runs. As Chapter 7 describes, the learning curve effect results in a lower cost of production for each successive aircraft over the life cycle of the production program, so average unit cost decreases for larger production programs. In addition, larger programs allow initial development costs to be spread over a larger number of aircraft, reducing the pro-rata share per aircraft and lowering the unit price. Large collaborative international programs enable participants to benefit from these cost advantages.

Enlargement of prospective markets. Marketing prospects for aircraft are improved if they are manufactured within the national boundaries of the target market. A preference to purchase locally manufactured aircraft is especially strong in the case of military aircraft. Competitive advantage for domestic firms is often institutionalized by law or government regulations such as the Buy American Act in the USA. Consequently, manufacturers of military aircraft recognize that their prospects of selling to foreign customers will improve if they have a local industrial partner.

Technology transfer. International government customers who seek to gain access to technology for their national industries often encourage coproduction as a means of acquiring the technology. Technology transfer associated with cooperative aircraft programs can usually be categorized as either production technology or aerospace design technology. Sharing of design technology tends to be limited unless the partnership is initiated during the preliminary design phase of the aircraft's life cycle. Production technology, on the other hand, is shared whenever joint manufacturing is undertaken. European coproduction of the F-16 fighter, for example, was initiated after design had been mostly completed by General Dynamics in the USA. European firms were

Table 6.3 The US-led Joint Strike Fighter program offered international partners access to technology in direct proportion to their financial contributions to the program

Joint strike fighter partner financial contributions and estimated aircraft purchases

| Partner country | Partner level | System development and demonstration | | Production | |
		Financial contributions ($ millions)	Percentage of total costs	Projected quantities	Percentage of total quantities
United Kingdom	Level I	$2,056	6.2	150	4.7
Italy	Level II	$1,028	3.1	131	4.1
Netherlands	Level II	$800	2.4	85	2.7
Turkey	Level III	$175	0.5	100	3.2
Australia	Level III	$144	0.4	100	3.2
Norway	Level III	$122	0.4	48	1.5
Denmark	Level III	$110	0.3	48	1.5
Canada	Level III	$100	0.3	60	1.9
Total Partner		$4,535	13.7	722	22.8
USA		$28,565	86.3	2,443	77.2

Note: Chart values do not reflect non-financial contributions from partners. Percentages do not add due to rounding.
Source: US Government Accountability Office 2003, 'Joint Strike Fighter Acquisition'.

generally satisfied with production technology the F-16 program gave them in fields such as electronics fabrication, miniaturization, gas turbines, gyroscopes, automatic test equipment, forging of high-strength aluminum, five-axis numerically controlled milling, and so on. However, some participating firms were dissatisfied with their lack of access to F-16 design technology. Later, when European governments considered the Joint Strike Fighter (JSF) as a replacement for the F-16, they successfully insisted on meaningful participation by their national aerospace industries in the JSF design process.

Government emphasis of aerospace as a leading technology sector. An article of faith among government economic planners is that high-technology industrial activities should be encouraged for economic reasons. The landmark Plowden Report issued by the British Ministry of Aviation in 1965 cited numerous examples of technologies that had been developed by the aerospace industry and had subsequently found important applications in other industries. The conclusion was that the national economy as a whole benefited from technological leadership of sectors such as aerospace. This credo has been widely accepted, for better or worse, by government leaders internationally. The Suharto government of Indonesia in the 1980s and 1990s attempted a particularly aggressive national experiment in technology leadership by the aerospace sector. Indonesia engaged in multiple international coproduction programs to develop a significant aerospace industry intended to

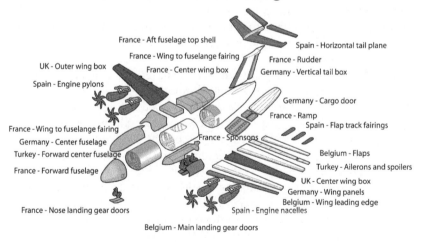

Airbus A400M Work Sharing Partners

Figure 6.2 The Airbus A400M is in many ways a typical contemporary joint international program, involving a pooling of resources of many risk-sharing partners.

Source: Airbus.

promote technology development for the rest of the country. Unfortunately, the effort was ultimately unsuccessful as the industry collapsed following widespread political and economic turmoil in the late 1990s.

The objectives and motivations cited previously are by no means mutually exclusive, and often customers or firms are influenced by a combination of factors. A firm that aspires to penetrate a new foreign market may seek a local partner who can provide an insider's access to the market, but who can also contribute financial resources and specialized technology. A government customer is likely to insist upon international collaboration involving local industry in order to secure jobs, technology, and prestige for his national aerospace sector.

Organizational structures of cooperative international aerospace programs

International cooperative ventures take many forms, and the individual ventures tend to adopt special organizational structures that are most suitable to the circumstances of each program. In the 1970s and 1980s, a period of mass international consolidation of the aerospace industry, governments and industry began to experiment with new large-scale cooperative programs. The organizational structures of the programs were diverse, reflecting the prevailing political and economic environments and the priorities of the cooperating parties. Political scientists and students of management of different nationalities began to analyze the organizational architectures, and concluded that they could be grouped into three principal categories of organizational models. The categories were given different terminology by different observers, but came to be known as the **pilot-role model**, the **cooperative model**, and the **integrated model**.

The pilot-role model was most similar to management structures of modern civil aircraft programs in which a single dominant original equipment manufacturer (OEM) subcontracts internationally, sometimes enlisting risk-sharing partners. Details of this approach are discussed at length in Chapter 12. The pilot-role model was utilized, for example, on the F–16 European cooperative program, in which the USA, Belgium, Denmark, The Netherlands, and Norway jointly built more than 1,000 aircraft, of which 500 were delivered from European production lines. Because of the disproportionately large US share of the program, and because the aircraft had been designed by the American firm General Dynamics (later partially acquired by Lockheed), management of the program at the government level was led by the US Department of Defense, with provisions for continuous consultation with the defense ministries of the participating European countries. At the industrial level it was led by General Dynamics, which served as the prime contractor, placing subcontracts with the European aerospace firms involved in production. Compared to other organizational models of the time, it was a relatively simple, direct, and responsive structure.

Table 6.4 An international consensus on categorization of organization of cooperative programs

Alternative organization models – consensus among knowledgeable observers

Comptroller General[1]	Robert Gessert[2]	Mark Lorell[3]	Georges Ville[4]	EEC[5]
'Pilot Approach'	'French Model'	'Pilot Firm'	'Maîtrise d'oeuvre confiée à un partenaire'	'Maîtrise d'oeuvre'
'Cooperative Approach'	'Panavia Model'	'Bilateral Organization'	'Association des partenaires'	'Dédoublement des tâches'
'Integrated Approach'	n.a.	'Transparent Firm'	'Maîtrise d'oeuvre confiée à l'entreprise commune'	'Groupement Multinational'

Sources:
[1] US General Accounting Office, Transatlantic Cooperation in Developing Weapon Systems for NATO: A European Perspective, Washington, D.C., 21 March 1979, pp. 15–19.
[2] Robert A. Gessert, et al., The Impact on the Rationalization of European Defense Industry of Alternative US Approaches to Transatlantic Defense Cooperation, (McLean, Virginia: General Research Corporation), April 1979, vol. 2, pp. 40–41.
[3] Mark A. Lorell, Multinational Development of Large Aircraft: The European Experience, (Santa Monica, California: The Rand Corporation), July 1980.
[4] Georges Ville, 'Airbus Industrie' (Paper presented at the Colloque Intérnational sur la Gestion des Grands Projets, at Lyon, France.
[5] Commission des Communautés Européenes, Programme d'action pour l'aéronautique européene, (Luxembourg: Office des publications officielles des communautés européenes), 1975, pp. 31–33.

The cooperative organizational model was used for joint European military programs in which the participating governments provided roughly equivalent funding and their national industries received roughly equivalent production workshares. The Tornado program, also known as the Multi-Role Combat Aircraft (MRCA), was the eminent example of an application of this model. The national aerospace industries of the participating countries were also equally involved in design, development, and testing of the new aircraft. Because the cooperative architecture of the program entailed a high degree of continuing coordination and decision-making among the partners at the levels of government and consortium management, the organizational structure included numerous joint committees at different levels. The NATO MRCA (Multi-Role Combat Aircraft) Management and Production Organisation (NAMMO) was established at the government level and endowed with legal status and authority to conclude contracts and international agreements on behalf of the participating nations. NAMMO delegated partial authority to NATO MRCA Management Agency (NAMMA), based in Munich. NAMMA was the government entity with primary responsibility for direct oversight of the consortium. Panavia Aircraft GmbH was a German company established by the three industrial partners for the purpose of jointly managing

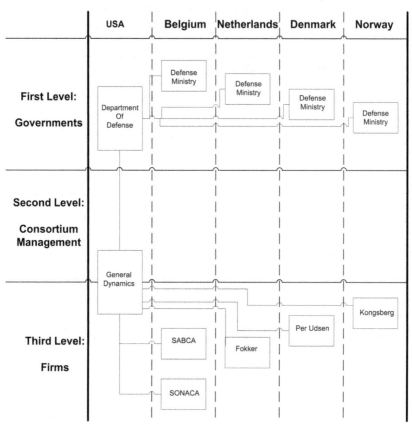

Figure 6.3 A representative pilot-role model international organizational structure.

the industrial work. Thus, decision-making passed from the three defense ministries to NAMMO, to NAMMA, to Panavia, to the firms. The joint entities were generally expected to reach unanimous decisions on important issues.

The integrated model, of which the Airbus A-300B was the primary example, dispensed with the many multinational entities of the cooperative model, and leadership of the consortium relied on a single organization consisting of industry professionals drawn from the aerospace firms. Although Airbus Industrie was ultimately responsible to the national governments that provided political and financial support, the organizational structure enabled the enterprise to be managed in a relatively efficient and agile manner.

Analytical studies of the three organizational models and the outcomes of the cooperative programs associated with them have been performed, yielding

Tornado: Example of Cooperative Model Organization

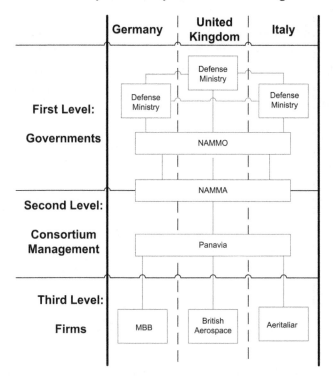

Figure 6.4 A representative cooperative model international organizational structure.

tentative conclusions concerning their relative benefits and drawbacks. The results are unsurprising:

- The cooperative model assures that political interests of all international partners are fully considered in the decision-making process, with no single partner gaining ascendancy over the others. A downside of this collegial process is that leadership can be indecisive, decisions can be delayed, suboptimal industrial decisions are sometimes made in order to enable political compromise, and the programs in general can be subject to delay.
- Advantages of the integrated model are that consortium leadership consists of industry professions who have the flexibility to respond to contingencies relatively quickly, and the structure is flexible enough to accommodate the addition of new members of the joint program. Disadvantages are that, in reality, unbalanced political influence may accrue to the national governments who provide the greatest share of financial support, and inefficient distortions to the industrial structure may result as a consequence.

Airbus A-300B: Example of Integrated Model Organization

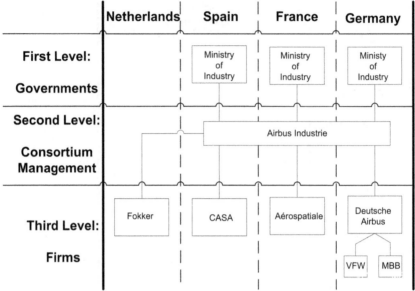

Figure 6.5 A representative integrated model international organizational structure.

- The pilot-role model benefits from the efficiencies and agility of a single dominant manager, but this dominance is also its biggest potential downside. Governments and industrial partners may be uncomfortable or unwilling to accept a subordinate role.

As the industry has progressed into its second generation of cooperative programs, their organizational models have evolved somewhat. Airbus, for example, has morphed from a consortium management entity into a conventional company that owns its manufacturing assets, and now operates more in the nature of Boeing's role as a standard OEM. On the other hand, the Eurofighter Typhoon that succeeded the Tornado has inherited an organizational structure similar to Tornado's, with Eurofighter Jagdflugzeug GmbH replacing Panavia as the industrial consortium, and NATO Eurofighter and Tornado Management Agency (NETMA) replacing NAMMO and NAMMA. For other European cooperative undertakings such as the A400M transport and the Tiger helicopter, the joint government agency exercising oversight is OCCAR (Organisation Conjointe de Coopération en matière d'Armement/ Organisation for Joint Armament Co-operation), an international organization created for the express purpose of management of cooperative defense programs. As mentioned earlier in this chapter, OCCAR is unlike many of

Table 6.5 Each of the three organizational models has distinct advantages and disadvantages

International aerospace cooperative program organizational models

Organizational model	Advantages	Disadvantages
Cooperative (example: Tornado)	Admits political considerations to the decision-making process	Economic inefficiencies often result from interjection of political factors
	Popular with politicians because it allows them to retain control of consortia decisions	As a result of political control, decisions are frequently delayed or incorporate compromises that are harmful to consortia interests
	Because decisions are made on the basis of consensus, no governments lose prestige vis a vis the other participants	No single strong leader
Integrated (example: original Airbus structure)	Decision-making by professional managers	Selection of managers may be based upon political factors
	Board of directors structure is flexible enough to allow weighting of participants' managerial influence according to actual contribution, thus avoiding perceived loss of prestige	In practice, single firms and governments may dominate
		Working relationships among firms are subject to change
	Board of directors structure readily accommodates addition of new member firms	
Pilot-role (example: F-16)	Decision-making by professional managers	Many politicians are unwilling to relinquish control of the project
	Economic considerations are given high priority	Loss of opportunity for politicians to pursue political objectives
	Single strong leader makes rapid decisions	Perceived loss of prestige for firms and governments that follow leadership of pilot
		Potential for abuse of power by pilot role firm and government

Source: Spreen, W 1986, *International Cooperation in the Aerospace Industry: Objectives, Structure, Performance* (doctoral dissertation), Université Catholique de Louvain

its predecessors because it is conceived as a permanent organization whose lifetime is not limited by the individual programs with which it is involved.

As cooperative international programs continue to become a prominent feature of the aerospace landscape, organizational tools to manage them will certainly evolve and improve. The third generation of cooperative programs will include participation by Chinese and Russian industry in leadership roles. It will be interesting to see the structures that are developed to handle the unique exigencies of those programs.

Government regulatory involvement

Early obstacles to international aerospace cooperation were the disparate body of national airworthiness standards and procedures that compelled makers of civil aircraft to certify their products individually in multiple national jurisdictions. In recent decades, however, the advent of the European Union Aviation Safety Agency (EASA) has consolidated and standardized airworthiness regulations among EU members. At the same time, EASA and the Federal Aviation Administration (FAA) have largely standardized American and European procedures and technical requirements. Both EASA and the FAA have established reciprocal agreements with third-country airworthiness authorities, further simplifying the process of international certification. The problem of diverse military airworthiness standards has been resolved somewhat by the widespread implementation by Europe and the USA of NATO standards based upon legacy US military standards. The NATO standards, in turn, have been replaced to some extent by standards such as AS/EN 9100, published by independent agencies. This subject was studied in more depth in Chapter 4.

Export licenses required for military and dual-use aircraft have also been an historic barrier for joint international programs. Differing national political attitudes towards exports of military aircraft continue to complicate business operations of multinational undertakings, but a number of international agreements such as the European Community Common Export Control Policy and the Wassenaar Arrangement have simplified the process somewhat. This subject was also discussed in Chapter 4.

Industrial offsets

In addition to the highly structured forms of international cooperation described previously, **industrial offsets** have emerged as a routine framework for international business relationships among aerospace firms.

In large-scale international aerospace sales, the customer may insist that the aircraft seller provide the buyer's country with certain kinds of industrial benefits as a condition of sale. Commitments to provide these compensatory industrial benefits, known as offsets, are often a condition of sale.

The involvement of **offset agreements** is particularly common in sales of military aircraft, where the buyer is almost always a sovereign government that has an interest in promoting the interests of its domestic industry.

The use of offsets came into widespread practice in the aerospace industry in Western Europe in the period following World War II, when the shattered European aerospace industry was struggling to rebuild but was often dependent upon American industry for military aircraft. European governments wanted to acquire work for their domestic aerospace industries, and at the same time wanted to offset the enormous negative balance-of-payments effects of importing foreign aircraft. To compensate for the loss of financial reserves and aerospace jobs that resulted from aircraft imports, European governments began to insist that part of the work involved in aircraft manufacture be transferred to Europe. As time passed, the concept of offsets became more complex and spread to other parts of the world. As the modern fully developed European aerospace industry began to export military aircraft to international markets, it also began to include offset commitments in its sales contracts.

In industry parlance, the term **offset** is generally taken to mean the entire range of industrial and commercial benefits provided to foreign governments as an inducement or condition to purchase military goods or services. Benefits take the form of coproduction, licensed production, subcontracting, technology transfer, in-country procurement, marketing and financial assistance, joint ventures, and many other arrangements. Offsets sometimes become involved in purchases of civil aircraft, particularly when government-owned airlines are the purchaser, but offsets are primarily a characteristic of military sales.

A defining feature of both defense and commercial offsets per the previous definition is that the foreign government plays a role (either directly or through state-controlled companies) in obtaining the benefits from the exporter.

Large amounts of money are involved in international sales of aircraft, and the value of offsets is commensurate. The US Department of Commerce compiles data on offsets provided by American firms, and reports that during the decade of the 1990s, total defense-related offsets, most of which involved the aerospace industry, consistently exceeded $2 billion per year, and sometimes exceeded $3 billion. Comprehensive data applying to offsets offered by the European aerospace industry is less readily available, but it is safe to assume that European-source offsets are proportional to the volume of European exports of military aerospace equipment.

Figure 6.6 shows the value of US defense offset transactions each year from 2007 to 2016. 'Value' in this context means the amount of offset credit awarded to US exporters by offset-receiving nations.

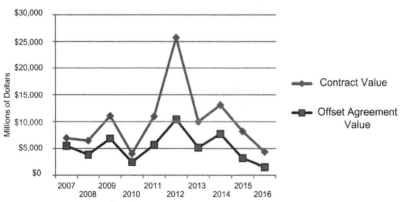

**Summary of US Defense Export Sales Contract Values
With Related Offset Agreements (2007–2016)**

Figure 6.6 The value of industrial offsets is enormous, and is expected to grow as offset practices become institutionalized throughout the world.

Source: US Department of Commerce, Bureau of Industry and Security.

Data compiled by the US government shows that the defense aerospace industry is particularly prone to become involved in transactions that entail offset commitments. From 1993 to 1998, 89% of defense offsets (measured by value) were associated with the export of aerospace goods or services by US firms. During the same period, US defense aerospace exports accounted for approximately 70% of all US defense exports, indicating that aerospace was disproportionately represented in defense offset transactions.

Categories of offsets

Offset arrangements appear in many forms, dictated primarily by the industrial policy needs of the buyer country and the imagination of the parties to each transaction. Although new forms are constantly evolving, they fall into two principal categories, **direct** and **indirect** offsets. Direct offsets are arrangements in which the benefit provided to the buyer country is directly related to the aerospace system sold in the underlying transaction. For example, in a sale of military aircraft, the seller might be required to assemble part of the aircraft structure in the buyer country instead of in the prime contractor's facility in his home country. Because this side agreement is directly related to the underlying aircraft sale, it would be considered a direct offset.

Indirect offsets, by contrast, involve activities unrelated to the system sold in the underlying transaction. In the example of an aircraft sale, an indirect offset arrangement might require the vendor to purchase its office furniture from a company within the buyer country. This would be considered an indirect offset because office furniture is not related to the aircraft.

The US Government Accountability Office (GAO), one of several US government institutions that have studied the impact of aerospace offset practices

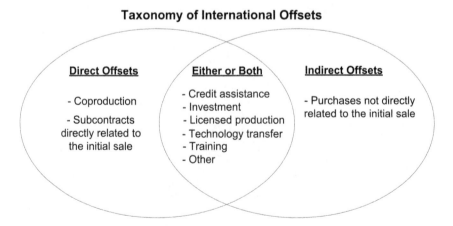

Figure 6.7 The imprecise classification of direct and indirect offsets.

Source: US Department of Commerce, Bureau of Industry and Security.

on the American economy, has identified a number of subcategories of offset arrangements:

Coproduction and subcontracting

In the coproduction arrangements studied by GAO, US vendors contracted with one or more companies in the buyer country to assemble, build, or produce articles related to the underlying sale. In the subcontracting arrangements, US vendors agreed to buy goods or services related to the underlying sale from suppliers in the buyer country. Coproduction and subcontracting offsets appeared in 20% of the transactions reviewed by GAO.

An example of a coproduction offset program was the 1991 Korean Fighter Program, in which the government of South Korea and General Dynamics (later partially acquired by Lockheed) concluded a $5.2 billion transaction involving the purchase of F-16 fighter aircraft. The parties structured the deal so that the government of South Korea purchased 12 of the aircraft off the shelf and bought 36 in the form of aircraft kits to be assembled in Korea. In addition, South Korea obtained the right to manufacture an additional 72 F-16s under license.

An example of an offset program involving subcontracting was the sale of Apache attack helicopters to the United Kingdom in the 1990s. As part of the sales agreement, valued at nearly $4 billion, McDonnell Douglas agreed to purchase from British firms $350 million worth of equipment for the helicopters.

Other procurement

In this type of indirect offset arrangement, the prime contractor agrees to purchase goods and services unrelated to the actual aerospace system sold. According to GAO, this form of offset was present in 9% of the transactions reviewed.

An example of procurement involving indirect offset was Lockheed Martin's agreement as part of its sale of C-130 aircraft to Canada to purchase assemblies and avionics from Canadian industry for Lockheed's C-5 transport plane.

Technology transfer

In these cases, US vendors transfer technology, technical assistance, or training to the buyer country. The technology is in some cases unrelated to the underlying aerospace item sold. In the GAO review, this form of offset appeared in 48% of the transactions studied.

An example was Lockheed's agreement, as part of its sale of F-16 fighter aircraft to South Korea, to transfer manufacturing and assembly expertise, enabling South Korea to assemble from kits and manufacture many of the aircraft sold as part of the deal.

Marketing assistance

In this form of offset, aerospace contractors help foreign companies market their products overseas. The basis of this type of offset arrangement is the assumption that the firm with the offset obligation has greater marketing expertise or market access than the foreign firm that benefits from the agreement. Such offsets were present in 23% of the transactions reviewed by GAO.

An example was McDonnell Douglas' agreement, as part of its $3 billion sale of F/A-18 fighters to Finland, to provide international marketing assistance for the REDIGO training aircraft produced by the Finnish company Valmet Aviation, Inc.

Financial assistance, investment, and joint ventures

In this form of offset arrangement, US contractors took equity positions, provided start-up financing, or provided other services to support a new or existing business entity in the buyer country. According to GAO, such offsets appeared in 13% of the transactions reviewed.

An example was McDonnell Douglas Helicopter Company's initiative to enter into several joint ventures in the United Arab Emirates as part of its sale of Apache attack helicopters to that country. The joint ventures, mostly unrelated to aerospace, developed products to clean up oil spills and recycle printer cartridges used in photocopiers and laser printers.

The main types of offset transactions, by value, are: 1) the counterpurchase of goods from the offset-receiving country, which is usually a type of indirect offset; 2) subcontracts provided to companies in the offset-receiving nation for items used in the product being exported, which are direct offsets; and 3) direct transfers or licensing of technology, which may be either direct or indirect offsets.

The political importance of offsets in Western Europe was succinctly described by Bernard Udis of the University of Colorado in his 1994 study *Offsets in Defense Trade: Costs and Benefits*:

> Defense ministry officials in all countries were quick to observe a major political issue – to keep the Parliament contented which, in turn, requires that public opinion be willing to support the expenditure of public funds to buy weapons and equipment from abroad with ostensible benefits to foreign workers and industry. To counter the impression that such foreign gains come at the expense of domestic interests, offsets are presented to show a longer term gain to the national economy, national defense and the Alliance, and to indicate that such gains are spread to the general economy as well as to the domestic defense sector.

In the year 2000, the US Department of Commerce surveyed major American defense firms that had recently made international defense sales to gauge the importance of offset in international sales of military aircraft. The survey asked the firms to guess the hypothetical outcome that would have befallen them if

Table 6.6 A depiction of the mixture of indirect offset projects executed by McDonnell Douglas as offsets associated with its sale of the F-18 fighter to Spain in the 1980s

Distribution of F-18 offsets by sector through 31 March 1994

Sector	Share of offsets
Defense	28.42%
Chemicals and pharmaceuticals	17.54%
Iron and steel	12.46%
Foodstuffs and consumer goods	8.75%
Electronics and civil IT	8.07%
Investment and civil technology	4.55%
Shipbuilding	3.90%
Capital goods	3.80%
Other	12.51%

Source: Gerencia de Cooperación Industrial.

they had not offered an offset package as part of their sales proposal. Results of the survey were:

- In 11% of the responses, the surveyed firms believed that they would have won the competition anyway.
- In 22% of the responses, the firm believed that it would have lost the competition, but that the sale would have been awarded to a rival American firm that had offered an offset package.
- In none of the responses did the firm believe that the international customer would have procured the equipment from an internal domestic source.
- In 59% of the responses, the firm believed that it would have lost the competition, and that the contract would have been awarded to a non-US firm that had offered an offset package.
- In 8% of the responses, the firm believed that the customer would have canceled the requirement and bought nothing.

Offsets and commercial programs

In international sales of civil aircraft, offsets are less pervasive than in the military aircraft market, and are certainly much less formalized. Perhaps this is because of the increasing body of international agreements that greatly restrict the practice. Another important factor is that the advent of Airbus has enabled the European civil aerospace industry to reach approximate parity with its American counterpart, thereby eliminating the need for transatlantic civil offsets. A third factor is that, as the trend towards privatization of national airlines has accelerated, government ownership has diminished accordingly, and private owners of airlines are generally not enthusiastic about interjecting offset requirements into their aircraft purchase contracts.

Three international agreements restrict the use of offsets in commercial trade. The first of these is the General Agreement on Tariffs and Trade's (GATT) 1979 Government Procurement Code, now known as the World Trade Organization's (WTO) Agreement on Government Procurement. Article XVI of the Agreement provides that signatories 'shall not, in the qualification and selection of suppliers, products or services, or in the evaluation of tenders and award of contracts, impose, seek or consider offsets'. This prohibition on offsets does not apply to the procurement of defense goods or services which involve essential security interests.

The agreement was most recently revised in 2012, and 46 countries had become signatories by 2016, including the USA, the European Union and most of its member countries, Japan, and other countries with significant aerospace activities. Developing countries signing the agreement are allowed to negotiate conditions under which they may use offsets, and these signatory countries have in some cases negotiated exemptions for their procurements of transportation products including aircraft.

The second international agreement limiting offsets is GATT's 1979 Agreement on Trade in Civil Aircraft, signed by the USA, the EC and its member countries, and other countries. Article 4.3 of this Agreement states that 'Signatories agree that the purchase of products covered by the Agreement should be made only on a competitive price, quality and delivery basis', which implicitly proscribes purchases requiring offsets. Responsibility for enforcement of the GATT agreement has more recently been transferred to the World Trade Organization. Thirty countries had signed the agreement by 2018.

The third applicable agreement is the bilateral 1992 US–EC Agreement on Trade in Large Civil Aircraft. This Agreement interprets Article 4.3 of GATT Agreement on Trade in Civil Aircraft (discussed in the previous paragraph) as prohibiting offsets by stating that:

> the signatories agree that Article 4.3 does not permit Government-mandated offsets. Further, they will not require that other factors, such as subcontracting, be made a condition or consideration of sale. Specifically, a signatory may not require that a vendor must provide offset, specific types or volumes of business opportunities, or other types of industrial compensation. Signatories shall not therefore impose conditions requiring subcontractors or suppliers to be of a particular national origin.

Apart from official international agreement that prohibit offsets related to civil aircraft sales, the offsets continue to occur under various guises, although they are rarely referred to as offsets. Aerospace firms recognize the importance of nurturing beneficial long-term relationships with the countries in which they aspire to sell, and they often use industrial cooperation as a way to gain local recognition and governmental support. Boeing Commercial Aircraft, which has experience in developing broad long-term international relationships, has manufacturing subcontracts on the national territory of most of its major international customers, notably Japan and China. Airbus endeavors to do likewise.

China in particular has been the beneficiary of industrial work transferred by Airbus and Boeing. China is the largest civil aircraft export customer for both companies, and the Chinese national airlines have strong political connections with the central government, which strongly encourages industrial collaboration in the aerospace industry.

In 2018, Boeing claimed that its activity in China contributed $800 million to $1 billion annually in direct support of China's economy, including procurement from Chinese suppliers, joint venture revenues, operations, training, and research and development investment.

Airbus is equally aggressive in its strategy of industrial cooperation with China. In 2008 it opened a final assembly facility in Tianjin, which is projected to increase production to six aircraft per month by 2020. The Airbus H135 helicopter is assembled in Qingdao, and Airbus is working with the Chinese firm Avicopter to codevelop the H175 medium utility helicopter, which will be assembled at Harbin in northeast China.

The controversial nature of industrial offsets

Understandably, the practice of transferring industrial work overseas by means of offset agreements is controversial. Organized labor in particular has often expressed the view that offsets are detrimental to the interests of domestic industry because they result in jobs lost in the selling country. Likewise, government critics have registered concern that offsets of technology transfer result in loss of indigenously developed technical advantages of the exporting country. American unions sometimes contend that the resulting shift of the nation's jobs overseas constitutes a permanent economic loss that outweighs the business and competitive rewards reaped by individual US aerospace contractors, subcontractors, and shareholders from foreign weapons and aircraft contracts. Aerospace industry representatives, on the other hand, have generally expressed the view that international aerospace exports are net creators of many thousands of jobs in the home country, and that manufacturing tasks transferred overseas are typically a small part of the overall export contract. Industry also maintains that technology transfers overseas generally involve technology that is available through other channels, and rarely involves highly advanced, state-of-the-art technical knowledge.

It is noteworthy that the major industrial nations placing offset work overseas are sometimes themselves beneficiaries of incoming offsets. In the USA, for example, the official position of the Department of Defense is that it does not demand offsets. In practice, foreign companies that want to sell military equipment to the USA often have to grant a license to a US prime contractor for the production of their aircraft and weapons. Examples include the British Harrier jet and the Swiss Pilatus trainer aircraft, both of which were purchased by the DoD but manufactured in the USA. To European suppliers, such requirements were considered to be pure offset obligations.

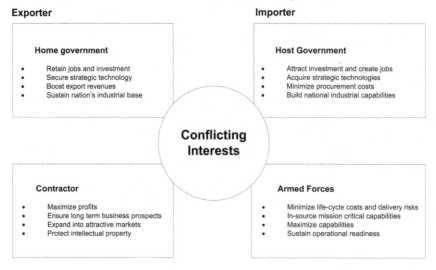

Figure 6.8 Industrial offsets elicit conflicting points of view from parties affected by them.

Source: AT Kearney.

Offset parameters and qualifying conditions

The nature of the formal contractual commitment depends upon specific national regulations, local industrial capability, and the circumstances of the sale, but it generally includes a combination of specific firm commitments and expressions of intent. At a minimum, the agreement includes the following elements:

- **Amount of obligation**, expressed as either an absolute amount or as a percentage of contract value
- **Qualifying types of offset**, which may include some or all of a wide variety:
  - Direct procurements
  - Coproduction
  - Marketing assistance
  - Investments
  - Export sales
  - Import substitutions
  - Transfer of technology
  - Joint ventures
  - Licensing agreements
  - Training
  - Credit assistance

Table 6.7 Industrial offsets have become a standard business practice for defense exports

Offset percentages by country and region (1993–2004)

Europe			Middle East and Africa		
Country	% Offsets	Country %	Country	% Offsets	Country %
Austria	174.2%	200%	Egypt	W	case basis
Belgium	80.1%	case basis	Israel	48.6%	50%
Czech Republic	W	100%	Kuwait	31.4%	35%
Denmark	100.0%	100%	Saudi Arabia	W	35%
EPG	27.8%	NA	South Africa	W	30%
Finland	100.0%	100%	Turkey	46.6%	min 50%
France	84.6%	100%	UAE	56.1%	min 50%
Germany	100.0%	up to 100%	**Regional Total**	55.7%	
Greece	113.4%	80 to 300%			
Italy	93.8%	min 70%	*Asia*		
Lithuania	W	100%	Country	% Offsets	Country %
NATO	55.8%	NA			
Netherlands	119.3%	up to 150%	Australia	45.8%	60%
Norway	104.8%	100%	Indonesia	W	100%
Poland	W	100%	Malaysia	37.3%	100%
Portugal	27.9%	100%	New Zealand	W	30
Romania	W	80%	Philippines	100.0%	80–100%
Slovenia	W	100%	Singapore	W	case basis
Spain	88.5%	up to 100%	South Korea	61.9%	30%
Sweden	103.9%	100%	Taiwan	20.0%	40%
Switzerland	78.5%	100%	Thailand	26.6%	50%
United Kingdom	84.6%	100%	**Regional Total**	45.7%	
Regional Total	89.3%				

North and South America

Country	% Offsets	Country %
Brazil	W	100%
Canada	96.9%	100%
Chile	W	100%
Regional Total	99.0%	

Note:
EPG = F-16 European participating governments.
NA = Not available.
W = Data withheld.
Source: US Department of Commerce, Bureau of Industrial Security, Offsets Database and Country Policy Research.

- **Definition of parties eligible to qualify for offset credit**

  This definition is an enumeration of the specific parties who will be considered by the offset administration authority to be acting on behalf of the prime contractor to fulfill offset obligations in the customer country. Examples are:
  - The company committing to the offset obligation (usually the prime contractor)
  - Subsidiaries
  - Subcontractors
  - Suppliers
  - Other parties directly influenced by the prime contractor

- **Causality**

  Causality is the definition of the circumstances under which the prime contractor can claim to have caused a specific transaction to occur, so that it can qualify for offset credit. In some cases, for example, corporate subsidiaries of the prime contractor might place manufacturing work in the customer country, but the work may not qualify for credit. This would be the case if the subsidiary were engaged in a long-standing production arrangement with the customer country that predated the prime contractor's aircraft sale. Logically, the offset administration authority can claim that the subsidiary's work would have taken place in the customer country regardless of the prime contractor's aircraft sale to the customer.

- **Valuation of transactions**

  Agreement between the parties must be defined concerning how much of each transaction can be counted as offset credit. Examples of questions to be resolved are: whether offset credit will be based upon the total value of delivered goods, or upon the value added in local factories; whether training will be counted in the total; and whether implicit technology transfer will have additional value.

- **Multipliers**

  Individual offset transactions have big qualitative differences that have to be recognized in the offset accounting methodology. Multipliers are commonly used to adjust for these differences. Normally, in-country purchases of locally produced products are considered basic transactions without multipliers. Direct investment into local industry is considered more desirable, and will receive a multiplier of, for example, ten. In other words, $1 million of direct investment will garner $10 million of offset credit. Other, more desirable, transactions such as an outright grant of modern production equipment or technology can earn higher multipliers still. In all cases, guidelines for multipliers should be clearly defined in advance, and all transactions involving multipliers should be approved on a case-by-case basis before their individual implementation.

- **Period of performance**

  The offset administration authority will require that the offset obligation be completed within a specified interval. This period should be clearly defined, and should include start date (or milestone event that will begin the period), length of the period, grace period for extension, and methods for mutually agreeing to changes in the period. The parties should also define the conditions that will formally complete the offset obligation. At fulfillment of the obligation, the authority should be required to issue a formal statement declaring that the prime contractor has met the conditions of his obligation.

- **Termination**

    Because the offset agreement is often separate from the contractual sales document, the agreement needs to specify the conditions under which the offset program will be terminated. If the aircraft program is terminated or significantly curtailed, the offset program should be adjusted accordingly. The parties should agree in advance concerning disposition of offset credits in the event of termination of the offset program. The authority should be required to issue a contractual declaration of any termination-related changes to the offset agreement.

- **Performance milestones**

    Offset agreements generally include intermediate milestones, often in the form of percentage-of-completion requirements. Such milestones ensure that the prime contractor immediately demonstrates good faith efforts to fulfill his obligation. Because of the time required to get organized and to begin production, offset accomplishments begin slowly and accelerate geometrically later in the program. However, the offset administration authority will prefer to see immediate accomplishments so that it can satisfy expectations of national politicians and industry. Another consideration for the authority is that it has greater leverage over the prime contractor earlier in the program, before the prime contractor has received the bulk of payments for the fulfillment of the aircraft delivery program. From the point of view of the contractor, it is important to avoid the establishment of aggressive milestones for unrealistic early accomplishment of the offset program.

- **Penalties and performance guarantees**

    The offset agreement will provide for penalties to be incurred in the event that the prime contractor fails to fulfill his offset commitment in accordance with the conditions to which he has agreed. The most common form of penalty, and the easiest to administer, takes the form of liquidated damages. Liquidated damages are specific cash payments paid to the customer country. The size of the payment will depend on the magnitude of the offset shortfall, and the agreement should specify a formula for calculating the amount and establish timing for payment of the penalty. The agreement should specify that payment of liquidated damages relieves the contractor from all further offset obligations, and that no further contractual remedy is required.

    Customarily, the customer country will insist on financial guarantees that the offset obligation will be fulfilled. In its simplest form, a guarantee can take the form of a written corporate commitment to pay contractual penalties if commitments are not met. More common are third-party guarantees, in the form of letters of credit or surety bonds, provided by banks or insurance companies paid by the contractor.

* **Escalation factors**

   Offset obligations are multiyear commitments, and sometimes the offset administration authority will suggest annual escalation of the obligation based on economic indices.

* **Force majeure**

   Events beyond the reasonable control of the prime contractor are subject to occur, and agreements commonly have force majeure provisions that give relief to the contractor, often in the form of an extension of the grace period for completion of the commitment. Natural disasters, strikes, acts of war, and terrorism are typical examples of force majeure factors.

* **Reporting requirements**

   It is in the interest of both parties that status of the offset program be summarized in frequent reports submitted by the contractor and approved by the authority. The format, intervals, and reporting periods should be defined in advance, as well as procedures for negotiating and arbitrating disputed items.

* **Confidentiality**

   Within reasonable limits, the contractor is entitled to protect information about her offset program. Government transparency will require that most transactions be publicly reported, and that summary financial information about performance towards the offset obligation be disclosed. However, the contractor has a right to confidentiality when she is engaged in conceptual exploratory talks with potential partners, or when she is performing due diligence in view of local investment possibilities.

* **Banked credits**

   Once the offset program is under way and begins to gather momentum, there is a real possibility that the amount of offset realized within the period of performance will exceed the contractual commitments of the contractor. If there is any possibility that the prime contractor will compete for other business in the customer country, and will possibly incur future offset obligations, the company will attempt to include language in the offset agreement that will allow it to bank surplus credits to be used in the future. Most countries have policies concerning whether or not they will permit banked credits.

Alternative international contracting methods

International sales of civil aircraft are typically handled in the framework of conventional commercial contracts, tailored to accommodate specific terms pertaining to configuration, payment, financing, postdelivery support, mechanisms for handling disputes, and so on.

Contracting methods for international sales of military aircraft are more complex, and fall into two general categories:

Direct commercial sales are similar to civil sales in that the manufacturer sells directly to the customer, which in this case is a foreign government entity. The government customer normally has a standardized contractual procedure and format that the seller is required to follow. The two parties negotiate detailed terms and pricing. The seller is responsible for obtaining the necessary export licenses from his home government and for ensuring that the sales contract contains the appropriate language of buyer's compliance with the export control laws of the seller's country.

In **government-to-government sales**, as the terminology implies, the purchasing government deals directly with the government of the manufacturer's home country. Nations that are major suppliers of military equipment have established specialized government entities that act as intermediaries between foreign governments and the companies that produce the military equipment. The foreign customer contacts the intermediary agency and specifies the equipment she wants to buy. The intermediary agency then negotiates terms of a conditional procurement contract with the domestic equipment producer, and passes the detailed pricing and terms information to the foreign customer. If the customer is satisfied with the conditions she signs a purchase agreement with the intermediary agency, who then in turn executes its conditional procurement contract with the manufacturer. Over the life of the contract the intermediary agency acts on behalf of the foreign purchaser to manage and enforce the terms of the contract with the supplier. Procedures vary from country to country.

In the USA the intermediary agency handling **foreign military sales (FMS)** is the Defense Security Cooperation Agency (DSCA), part of the US Department of Defense.

7 Aerospace accounting and financial management

Accounting and financial practices within the aerospace industry are idiosyncratic in several significant respects. Most of these peculiarities are directly attributable to a few unavoidable facts of life in the industry:

> Extraordinary amounts of capital investment are required to launch new aircraft programs. Up-front costs include detailed design, production planning, tooling fabrication, prototype testing, certification, and so on.

- Years of negative cash flow elapse from the moment of program launch until the program reaches positive cash flow.
- Enormous working capital is required to sustain manufacturing work-in-process while many very expensive aircraft undergo assembly spanning several months.
- The 'learning curve effect' dictates that early aircraft in the production series will cost significantly more to produce than later units. These early aircraft are thus likely to be sold at a loss because manufacturers set competitive sales prices intended to generate profits over the life of the program, encompassing later production years at lower unit cost.
- The high unit sales prices of commercial aircraft, often in the hundreds of millions of dollars, means that very few airlines have the internal financial resources to purchase sizable aircraft fleets. Consequently, a menu of financial strategies has evolved to provide financing for aircraft sales.

Investment in initial development

The magnitude of investment required to launch new civil aircraft programs is legendary. Within the industry, a decision to introduce a major new airplane is known as 'betting the company' because the company is at real risk of failure if the new product fails to sell well enough to recover the investments. The history of aerospace is littered with examples of unsuccessful aircraft programs that resulted in the financial collapse of the companies that launched them. Notable postwar examples are the Fokker F-100, the Douglas DC-10, and the

Lockheed L-1011 (in which Lockheed had the good fortune to be rescued by financial assistance from the US government).

Financial risk factors pertaining to new military aircraft programs are somewhat different. Normally, military aircraft prime contractors do not launch new programs at their own risk. The standard paradigm is for governments to issue a competitive request for proposal, evaluate proposals submitted by competitors, and choose a winning prime contractor. The execution phase of the contract normally consists of two principal parts: the non-recurring phase, which includes design, development, tooling, testing, and other start-up activities; and the recurring phase, which includes series production of individual aircraft. Because the up-front start-up costs are shouldered overwhelmingly by the government customer rather than the prime contractor, the contractor is exposed to much less financial risk. On rare but notable occasions, aerospace companies launch major military aircraft at their own risk, funding up-front costs with their own money. These are usually cases in which the company leadership believes that it can create a product that the government will buy, in spite of being unable to elicit initial government interest in the product concept. A well-known example is the Predator-B drone, later designated Reaper, the first unmanned hunter-killer aircraft capable of carrying and launching heavy air-to-ground guided munitions. Complete funding of design and manufacture of two prototypes was undertaken by Predator-A manufacturer General Atomics, which had been unable to convince the US Air Force of the usefulness of an armed drone. Until the advent of Predator-B, the military mindset had been that drones were observational devices. Times change. Eventually, the Air Force announced plans to buy hundreds of the model.

For a new civil aircraft program, the cash-flow profile typically involves years of outflow during design, development, preparation for industrialization, and manufacture of the earliest high-cost aircraft. Later, as deliveries continue and unit production costs decrease, individual aircraft begin to yield positive cash flow, and cumulative negative cash flow declines. If all goes well, eventually cumulative cash-flow breakeven occurs and the program continues to generate positive cash flow for years to follow.

The size of the required capital investment for new programs, which of course relates directly to interim net cumulative negative cash flow, depends upon size, complexity, technological risks, and the time span of the program. In 2010, development costs for the Airbus 320neo, a derivative design of the original A320, were estimated by the manufacturer to be approximately $1.3 billion. By industry standards this was a modest sum, reflecting the limited scope of the program, which involved redesign of the existing A320 to incorporate new fuel-efficient engines, aerodynamic improvements to wings, and an upgraded cabin interior. Early estimates of development costs for recent technologically ambitious, completely new aircraft such as the Airbus A380 and the Boeing 787 have been in the neighborhood of $15 billion, although many analysts believe that eventual total costs were closer to twice that amount.

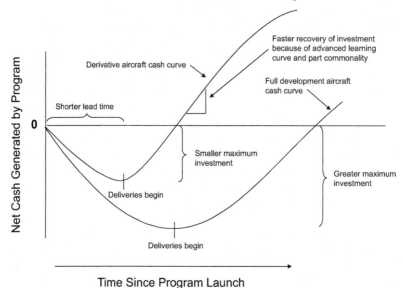

Derivative Aircraft Program
Theoretical Cost and Schedule Advantages

Figure 7.1 Conceptual cash-flow profile of new and derivative aircraft programs.

Table 7.1 Historical development costs of new aircraft programs

Aircraft	Year of first service	Development costs (constant 2004 $)
Historical development costs		
Selected aircraft		
Douglas DC-3	1936	4.3 million
Douglas DC-6	1946	144 million
Boeing 707	1958	1.3 billion
Boeing 747	1970	3.7 billion
Boeing 777	1995	7.0 billion
Airbus A380	2007	14.4 billion
Boeing 787	2012	13.4 billion

Source: Adapted from Bowen, J 2010, *The Economic Geography of Air Transportation: Space, Time, and the Freedom of the Sky*, Routledge, London.

In order to diminish capital requirements and risk, original equipment manufacturers (OEMs) typically structure new aircraft programs to include risk-sharing partners. The most prevalent example of this type of risk sharing involves participation by engine manufacturers. New aircraft are designed to provide optimal performance if powered by engines that meet specific technical parameters of thrust, weight, size, and fuel consumption. If no such engine exists, the aircraft designer meets with engine manufacturers to plan development of a suitable new engine. Although the new engines are often derivatives of existing engines, the development costs are so high that they become a major component of overall investment costs. Standard practice in the industry is that engine manufacturers independently shoulder the cost and risk of new engine development. Pratt & Whitney's estimated development cost for the PW1000G Geared Turbofan engine for the Airbus A320neo and a new generation of mid-sized aircraft was $10 billion.

An additional risk borne by engine suppliers is that often they do not have exclusive rights to supply engines for specific aircraft models. The international industry providing jet engines for large commercial aircraft consists of three major companies: General Electric, Pratt & Whitney, and Rolls-Royce. Another important presence is CFM International, a joint venture of General Electric and France's Safran. Generally more than one of these manufacturers elects to develop an engine for a new aircraft model. The aircraft OEM then offers the aircraft for sale with a choice of engine options. The final customer has the choice of engine to be installed on the aircraft. Often this final customer negotiates separate purchase contracts with the aircraft manufacturer and the engine manufacturer. In this case, the engines are shipped to the aircraft assembly line as buyer-furnished equipment. From the customer's perspective the obvious advantage of multiple engine suppliers is that it ensures competition in the market segment, theoretically resulting in lower prices and higher quality.

Other risk-sharing partners typically include airframe subcontractors and equipment suppliers. These partners, who are normally selected on a competitive basis, are provided with 'interface data' that defines the parameters of the aircraft part that they will provide, including size, weight, available power, and performance requirements. The partners then make the investment to design their product. When the design is approved by the OEM, the partners fund their own production start-up costs and begin manufacture. The various components are then sent to the OEM's site for final assembly of the aircraft.

The risk-sharing partners model has proven to be an effective strategy for reducing the OEM's initial investment, but it introduces other considerations that increase risk. It unquestionably increases overall program complexity and reduces control by the OEM. Instead of building and assembling all parts of the airframe at a single facility, the work is dispersed internationally, controlled by complex schedules and intercompany contracts, subject to complications of exchanging data, shipping material, and assuring quality. A problem at a single partner can result in havoc for the entire program, and may be undetected until it is too late to plan corrective action. This subject is discussed in length in Chapter 12.

An extreme case of control problems and corrective measures was illustrated by Boeing's $1 billion purchase in 2009 of Vought Aircraft Industries, a problematic critical supplier of the aft fuselage section of the 787 airliner. After successive production problems at the Vought facility impacted final

Airbus A320neo
Shares of Engine Suppliers
2017

LEAP
CFM International*
2,179 aircraft
42.5%

Geared Turbofan
Pratt & Whitney
1,463 aircraft
28.3%

Undecided
1,523 aircraft
29.5%

* CFM International is a joint venture between GE and Safran

Figure 7.2 Competition in the engine market.

Source: Flight Ascend Consultancy.

assembly at the Boeing plant in Seattle, Boeing bought Vought and replaced the management team with Boeing veterans. Throughout the early history of 787 production the program was hindered by problems of subcontractors failing to perform. The issues were eventually resolved, but the program was repeatedly delayed, and eventually Boeing and the rest of the industry were left with an acute reminder of the downside risks of sharing development costs among many partners.

Airbus Industrie was originally conceived in 1970 as an international consortium of European aerospace companies with the objective of sharing financial resources and distributing financial risk. Although the Airbus entity has been repeatedly reorganized and legally restructured since its earliest days, it remains a vehicle to enable risk-sharing partners to unite for the purpose of launching and executing aircraft programs.

A characteristic of Airbus financing of new program development is its partial reliance upon loans provided by governments of the countries in which

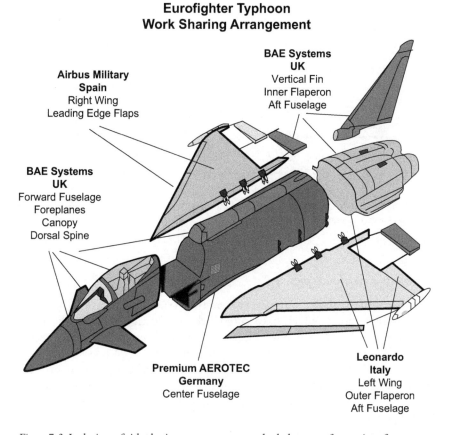

**Eurofighter Typhoon
Work Sharing Arrangement**

**BAE Systems
UK**
Vertical Fin
Inner Flaperon
Aft Fuselage

**Airbus Military
Spain**
Right Wing
Leading Edge Flaps

**BAE Systems
UK**
Forward Fuselage
Foreplanes
Canopy
Dorsal Spine

**Premium AEROTEC
Germany**
Center Fuselage

**Leonardo
Italy**
Left Wing
Outer Flaperon
Aft Fuselage

Figure 7.3 Inclusion of risk-sharing partners as a standard element of new aircraft programs.
Source: Eurofighter GmbH data.

Airbus production operations are located. These government loans, officially called 'repayable launch investment', are nominally reimbursed as Airbus is obligated to repay a fixed amount for each aircraft delivered. The World Trade Organization estimated in 2010 that the amount of these loans exceeded $15 billion. Exact terms of the loans are not public information. In programs where aircraft sales quantities are insufficient to repay the government launch investment, apparently Airbus is not liable for the unpaid balance. As shown next, the standard footnote in Airbus financial statements declares:

> Refundable advances from European Governments are provided to Airbus to finance research and development activities for certain projects on a risk-sharing basis, i.e. they are repaid to the European Governments subject to the success of the project.

Airbus Financial Statement - 'Other Financial Liabilities'

Other Financial Liabilities

	31 December	
(In € million)	2017	2016
Liabilities for derivative financial instruments[1]	1,127	6,544
European Governments refundable advances	5,537	6,340
Others	284	429
Total non-current other financial liabilities	**6,948**	**13,313**
Liabilities for derivative financial instruments[1]	1,144	4,476
European Governments refundable advances[2]	364	730
Liabilities to related companies	334	116
Others	343	439
Total current other financial liabilities	**2,185**	**5,761**
Total	**9,133**	**19,074**
thereof other financial liabilities due within 1 year	*2,126*	*5,761*

(1) See " – Note 36: Information about Financial Instruments".
(2) Refundable advances from European Governments are provided to Airbus to finance research and development activities for certain projects on a risk-sharing basis, i.e. they
are repaid to the European Governments subject to the success of the project.

Figure 7.4 A page from Airbus financial statements depicting refundable advances from governments.

Source: Airbus.

Financing work-in-process

All manufacturing operations have an investment in work-in-process, or WIP: the unfinished goods which have entered the production cycle but have not been completed or delivered to customers. For purposes of financial reporting, WIP is shown on the balance sheet as a current asset.

Because of the high value of aircraft and the unusual length of the production cycle, the total WIP value at aircraft factories can reach amounts unimaginable in other industries. In Boeing's 10-Q filing with the US Securities and Exchange Commission in 2016, the company reported that the current WIP value for the 787 program alone was more than $34 billion.

One obvious strategy for reducing the value of WIP is simply to reduce manufacturing span time. This was part of the 'lean manufacturing' initiative that swept the manufacturing sector worldwide in the 1990s, and by 2003 Boeing was able to claim that the span time for 737 assembly, at the rate of 21 aircraft delivered per month, had been reduced from 6 weeks to 3 weeks, reducing WIP proportionally. Another element of lean manufacturing is the concept of just-in-time parts delivery, which reduces the value of on-hand inventory to support production.

Even with the best of management, WIP remains a major capital requirement for aerospace producers. In recognition of this financial reality, the industry has adopted business practices in which the customer accepts part of the burden by making progress payments to the manufacturer over the course of production. In 2016, Boeing reported that it had received more than $28 billion in progress payments and financial advances for commercial aircraft programs.

A small portion of these financial advances are deposits made by customers at the time purchase contracts are signed. For commercial aircraft programs, the preponderance of advance payments from the customer occur later in the production cycle, and are known as predelivery payments, or PDPs. Terms of PDPs are not standardized in the industry, and are subject to negotiations between buyer and seller. The payments are generally made in increments, beginning at the signing of the purchase agreement and continuing at specified intervals prior to aircraft delivery. The size of the payments customarily ranges between 15 and 30% of the aircraft price. Because PDPs are substantial cash outlays over time, buyers often seek third-party financing. PDP lenders typically fund only a portion of the total, with the buyer paying the remainder.

PDP borrowing is generally short to medium term. The loans are secured by the aircraft to be eventually produced, and lenders typically make payment directly to the seller and require quarterly service payments and balloon repayment upon aircraft delivery.

These arrangements entail obvious risks to the lender. If the initial PDP is made at the time of purchase, often more than four years in advance of delivery of large commercial aircraft, no aircraft physically exists to provide basis for the security. And in a contemporary environment of thinly financed airlines with limited history, the airline customer may no longer be in business when the aircraft is finally delivered. To address this risk, PDP loans are often written with the condition that aircraft ownership is assignable to the lender if the borrower is unable to repay the loan. This provision is subject to approval by the seller. If the borrower fails and aircraft ownership is then reassigned to the lender, the lender theoretically has a reasonable chance of recovering his investment by once again reassigning ownership to a new buyer who is searching for an aircraft and who wants to jump the queue of four or five years for backlogged new orders.

For sales of military aircraft and equipment to the US government, advance payments take the form of either performance-based payments or progress payments based on cost reimbursement. Performance-based payments, or PBPs, are applicable only to fixed-price contracts, and involve milestone payments upon physical verification by the government that specific contractual events have been satisfactorily accomplished. Maximum allowable PBP payments are 90% of the contractual sales price.

Progress payments based upon incurred costs have historically been more commonly used on large military aircraft series production programs. The nominal upper limit of reimbursement is 80% of incurred cost including payments to subcontractors, which is less generous than PBP arrangements, but payment intervals are more frequent, typically biweekly for major contracts.

The administrative framework for cost-based progress payments is more burdensome than for PBPs. The contractor is required to have an accounting system that conforms to Department of Defense guidelines, and the government must be given authorization for routine audits of all financial records of the contractor.

European defense agencies have advance payment arrangements roughly similar to US Department of Defense practices.

Financial reporting strategies

There is no doubt that special financial factors affecting the aerospace industry can potentially lead to financial reports that distort impressions of the financial health of the companies. One example is the issue of whether to expense new aircraft development costs in the year incurred, or to capitalize these costs and amortize the resulting asset over the life of the program. If the multibillion-dollar costs of developing new aircraft were to be reported as expenses in the years incurred, the income statements for the years of development would likely show drastically reduced earnings or even losses. In the years following the development period, after which development costs would already have been expensed, earnings would be extraordinarily high because they would not be reduced by charges for amortization of investment costs of development.

For purposes of financial reporting, the aerospace industry has historically capitalized development costs, including production start-up costs, and then amortized the capital investment over the life of the entire aircraft program. The justification for this concept is that it more fairly represents the year-to-year financial health during periods in which massive cash outlays are being made to position the company's business for future success. This practice of capitalizing development costs is common to some other industries characterized by massive development investments.

Boeing also uses the concept of 'program accounting' to report the cost of aircraft sold. The theoretical basis of program accounting is that unit production costs decline over time due to volume efficiencies and learning effects. This phenomenon of declining aircraft production costs, known as the 'learning curve effect', has been widely studied and is universally recognized within the industry. The concepts underpinning the learning curve were first described in the *Journal of the Aeronautical Sciences* in 1936 by TP Wright. Wright's analysis gained wider recognition during World War II when Army and Air Force scientists noticed that the cost for a given aircraft model declined with increased production in accordance with a fairly predictable formula. Each time the cumulative production doubled, cost declined by a fixed percentage. In the aircraft industry at that time this reduction was about 20%.

Thus, if profits for each unit sold were to be calculated on the actual cost for that unit, aircraft early in the production series would be associated with enormous losses, and aircraft sold later would show enormous profits. To address this distortion, program accounting provides for a nominal estimated cost to be assigned over the entire production series. The excess costs on the first units produced are capitalized and amortized and are later expensed over the units subsequently produced at a lower cost. This approach was formalized by the American Institute of Certified Public Accountants in 1981, but has since been the subject of some controversy and additional scrutiny.

Airbus, on the other hand, follows International Financial Reporting Standards, which requires inventories to be measured at the lower of cost or net realizable value and reports the cost of goods sold on a job order basis for

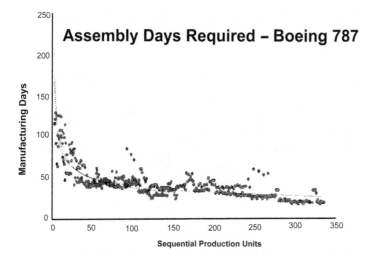

Figure 7.5 Data demonstrating the learning curve effect.

Source: Boeing.

each commercial aircraft manufactured and sold. This difference in accounting methodology between Boeing and Airbus clearly affects the way profits for the two companies are calculated.

To address the confusion pertaining to this aspect of financial reporting, Boeing began declaring financial results on both a program accounting basis and a unit cost basis. In 2018, it issued financial statements for 2017 including the following note:

> This is a non-GAAP measure. Management is providing Commercial Airplanes' Earnings from Operations computed using non-GAAP unit-cost based accounting in response to requests from specific investors. The company does not intend for unit-cost information to be considered in isolation or as a substitute for program accounting. The basic difference between unit-cost based accounting and program accounting is that unit cost accounting determines cost of sales based on a more discrete costing of the individual airplane while program accounting determines cost of sales based on the average profitability over the airplane program accounting quantity. Unit cost accounting records cost of sales based on the cost of specific units delivered, and to the extent that inventoriable costs exceed estimated revenues, a loss is not recognized until delivery is made. Note 1 of the Company's 10-K filing describes program accounting.

Aerospace industry practices for recognizing revenue have received recent scrutiny and are evolving. In 2014 the US Financial Accounting Standards

Boeing Program Accounting versus Unit Cost Accounting
(reported results 2010–2015)

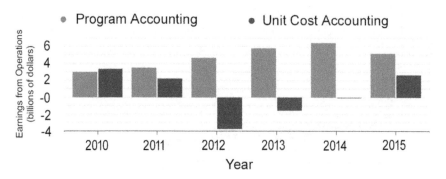

Figure 7.6 Contrasting reported results depending on the accounting method.

Source: Boeing.

Board issued new rules for revenue recognition, to be implemented in 2018. At the same time, the International Accounting Standards Board, or IASB, issued an International Financial Reporting Standard that imposed virtually identical requirements on firms that report results in compliance with international standards. Because of the long time span of many of their contracts, aerospace and defense companies have typically used the percentage-of-completion method to recognize revenue. Under the new FASB and IASB standards, companies would recognize revenue when control of a good or service is effectively transferred to the customer. Because the current percentage-of-completion method recognizes revenue while work-in-process remains under the manufacturer's control, implementation of the new rule is likely to result in delayed revenue recognition, with the consequence that reported earnings will be allocated to different periods. Current contracts that have in the past been stated on the basis of percentage-of-completion will have to be assessed to determine if they continue to qualify for recognition of revenue on that basis. If not, financial statements are required to be restated. In 2017, virtually the entire panoply of major American aerospace firms declared that they intended to make significant restatements of prior years in order to show material effects of the new standard.

Effects of the accounting changes were expected to be particularly felt by jet engine manufacturers, who often sell the engines themselves at no profit, with the expectation of making money over the long term by means of engine overhaul and maintenance contracts. Rolls-Royce, for example, had historically booked revenue at the time of customer signature of its 'Total Care' long-term maintenance contracts. The company announced in 2017 that, beginning in 2018 under the new standards, it would declare revenue only when the actual work was performed, and would restate earlier financial results to reflect the change. In 2017 GE announced that it was examining past practices for recognizing revenue for long-term engine maintenance contracts, and would modify its accounting system to comply with the new FASB rules. In early 2018 the US Securities and Exchange Commission declared that it was conducting an audit of GE's historical accounting treatment of long-term engine maintenance contracts.

US government accounting standards for defense contracts

The US government's voluminous rules governing contracting are codified in the Federal Acquisition Regulation, or FAR. Companies involved in defense contracts are additionally subject to the Defense Federal Acquisition Regulation Supplement, or DFARS.

The FAR and DFARS together define in detail the accounting methodology and principles that must be applied in financial statements prepared by defense contractors selling to the government in the framework of cost-based contracts. The regulations stipulate the types of costs that are allowable or unallowable, standards of reasonableness of costs, supporting documentation required, treatment of specific cost categories, and so on. These Federal rules are significantly different from normal civilian industry practices in many respects. Company marketing expenses, costs of doing international business, royalty fees, and interest payments may be partially unallowable as cost buildup for government contracts, for example.

In cases of companies selling off-the-shelf products to the government at fixed prices and with no government funding of development costs, the companies are generally not required to furnish FAR-compliant financial records. However, because government purchases of military aircraft are typically structured so that the contractor receives reimbursement of costs plus a profit based upon a stipulated percentage of the costs, the government is acutely interested in monitoring the contractor's accumulation of costs for those contract types.

To ensure compliance with FAR and DFARS, companies with cost-based government contracts are subject to periodic audit by the Defense Contract Audit Agency, or DCAA. The most common purpose of DCAA audits is verification of contractor cost reporting for billing purposes, such as progress payment requests or final deliveries. DCAA also audits financial records of companies who have submitted proposals to obtain contracts to be priced on the basis of costs. In cases where the contracts will span several years into the future, DCAA reviews the contractor's projection of future costs and makes a determination of the acceptability of forward bidding rates.

Commercial aircraft purchase financing

In the modern age, a minority of commercial aircraft are bought in cash by the customer. The inordinate cost of the individual aircraft, multiplied by the quantities of most purchases, result in financial demands that are simply beyond the cash resources of many customers.

In a sense, the subject of purchase financing should more properly be considered in the domain of the air transport industry rather than the aerospace industry. After all, it is the operators' ultimate responsibility to put together the money to acquire the aircraft they will be operating. However, as we have seen, financial arrangements interject themselves well in advance of final delivery of the aircraft as the buyer makes up-front deposits, predelivery payments, and pays for major components such as engines delivered to the aircraft manufacturer during the assembly process. Additionally, the aircraft manufacturer often offers technical advice and support to his customers concerning financial modalities. In some cases, the manufacturer operates an in-house financing entity that provides direct loans or leases to customers, but this is a relatively small part of the overall aircraft financing industry.

In many respects, aircraft are financed using methods and instruments common to major purchases of heavy equipment in other industries, but some aspects are peculiar to the aircraft business.

Most aircraft financing arrangements can be grouped into four principal categories:

- **Bank debt** involves loans that are usually secured with the value of the aircraft.
- **Capital markets instruments** are usually secured structured debt transactions such as enhanced equipment trust certificates (EETCs) or unsecured debt raised by an airline, lessor, or parent. Capital markets are both public and private. With an EETC, a trust of investors purchases the aircraft and then nominally leases it to the operator, on condition that the airline will receive title upon full performance of the lease. EETCs blur the line between finance leasing and secured lending, and in recent form have adopted many of the characteristics of securitization arrangements.
- **Export credit agency guaranteed loans** are supported by a guarantee from an export credit agency, including both commercial bank loans and bond transactions funded in the capital markets. Direct export credit lending is also included. Export credit agencies are described below.
- **Financing by aircraft manufacturers** is essentially a subsegment of the capital market. Boeing Capital Corporation and Avion Capital are the financing arms of Boeing and Airbus.

As Table 7.2 shows, in recent years bank debt has been the preferred method of financing commercial aircraft purchases, closely followed by capital markets and customer cash. Financing through government-sponsored export credit agencies, or ECAs, has historically been a primary channel for international sales. It has become a minor factor in the market recently as commercial lending has become cheap and more accessible following recovery from the 2008 financial crisis. Another factor in the decline in ECA use has been the chaos at the US Export-Import Bank resulting from American government indecision.

Table 7.2 Purchase financing alternatives

Sources of industry delivery financing

Historical share of funding by capital provider

	2009	2010	2011	2012	2013	2014	2015	2016	2017	2018
Cash	20%	26%	25%	26%	25%	24%	23%	28%	26%	26%
Capital markets	15%	14%	15%	18%	19%	28%	24%	30%	24%	25%
Bank debt	28%	26%	27%	23%	30%	33%	30%	33%	44%	38%
Export credit	33%	34%	33%	33%	26%	15%	13%	8%	4%	8%
Insurance	—	—	—	—	—	—	—	—	1%	2%
Manufacturer	4%	—	—	—	—	—	—	1%	1%	1%
Total financing ($ billions)	**69**	**62**	**77**	**96**	**104**	**115**	**122**	**122**	**122**	**139**

Source: Boeing.

Governments of all the major Western aircraft-producing economies oper-ate export credit agencies, which either lend money themselves or guarantee loans made by commercial lenders. The purpose of ECAs is to make credit available at reasonable interest rates to potential purchasers with subprime credit ratings. Because interest rates through ECAs are slightly higher than prime rates, they are generally avoided by blue-chip buyers who can borrow at the prime rate.

In addition to the US Export-Import Bank, other important national ECAs are UK Export Finance, France's Coface, Germany's Hermes, Export Development Canada, and Brazil's Banco Nacional de Desenvolvimento Econômico e Social, or BNDES.

ECAs in these countries were created with the objective of supporting export sales by national industries to potential customers with weak finan-cial credibility. However, there is clear opportunity for competitive market distortions if the ECAs are used to provide lending at favorable terms unre-lated to commercial market rates. In this case, ECA loans essentially become government-subsidized financial inducements to customers for the purpose of influencing buying decisions.

To prevent misuse of ECAs, the home countries of Boeing and Airbus col-laborated within the framework of the Organization for Economic Cooperation and Development, or OECD, to establish in 1986 the Large Aircraft Sector Understanding, or LASU, which promulgated rules governing loans, includ-ing minimum down payments, maximum periods, interest rates, creditwor-thiness factors, and so on. For years, LASU was effective in preventing gross abuse of ECA activity, but became outdated as new aircraft manufacturers, notably Embraer and Bombardier, emerged and began to sell regional air-craft in international markets in significant quantities. Aircraft from Mitsubishi and French-Italian cooperative venture ATR also became a presence in the regional aircraft market.

Table 7.3 Virtually every nation involved in aircraft export operates an export credit agency

Comparison of national export credit agency products

| ECA/country | Normal maximum percentage of cover | | Financing products | | | Bond insurance against unfair calling | Bond support for the issuance of bonds | Lines of credit | |
	Political risk	Commercial risk	Unconditional cover	Fixed rate at CIRR available	Foreign currency financing possible			General purpose	Project
CESCE Spain	99	94	N	Y	Y	Y	Y	N	N
COFACE France	95	95	N	Y	Y	Y	N	N	Y
ECGD UK	100	100	Y	CBC	Y	Y	N	Y	Y
EDC Canada*	100 for direct loans, up to 75 for guarantees	100 for direct loans, up to 75 for guarantees	Y	Y – but no interest make-up on guarantees	Y	Y	Y	Y	Y
EKN Sweden	100	90	N	Y	Y	Y	Y**	Y	Y
EXIM Bank USA	100	100	Y	Y – direct Loans N – guarantees	Y – direct Loans N – guarantees	N***	N***	Y	Y
ATRADIUS Netherlands	98	95	N	N	Y	Y	Y	Y	Y

EULER HERMES (KfW*) Germany	95	95	NN	Y (CBC in 2002)	Y	Y	N	Y	Y
NEXI Japan	97.5	95	Y	Y	Y	?	N		Y
SACE Italy	95	95	N	Y	Y	Y	N	Y	Y

Notes:

* Direct lenders

** EKN – In the form of counterguarantees for contract guarantees (bonds)

*** Exim's Working Capital Guarantee Program has permitted that its 'revolving line of credit guarantee' be utilized as a counterguarantee against a commercial bank's stand-by letter of credit on a case-by-case basis.

CIRR = commercial interest reference rate.

Source: UK Export Credits Guarantee Department (ECGD), International Comparison Survey, 2003.

To update LASU, the agreement was expanded in 2007 to include Canada, Japan, and Brazil. The name of the agreement was altered to become the Aircraft Sector Understanding, or ASU, and its scope was expanded to include regional aircraft. The ASU bifurcated the market into large aircraft and smaller aircraft including regional types, and established further detailed lending parameters applying to each category. Prior to ASU, Canada and Brazil had filed repeated separate complaints to the World Trade Organization, alleging that aircraft from Embraer and Bombardier respectively were being heavily subsidized in export sales by means of favorable credit terms offered by the ECAs of the two countries.

In 2011 the ASU was further revised into an updated protocol referred to as 2011 ASU. The impetus for the revision was the aftermath of the 2008

Table 7.4 Changes in international rules pertaining to government-provided export credit

Evolution of export credit rules

Aircraft sector understanding and large aircraft sector understanding

Pre-2007 LASU	*2007 ASU*	*2011 ASU*
LASU among USA, UK, Germany, France, Spain (Boeing, Airbus)	Added Brazil and became relevant for Canada and Japan	Single set of rules apply to all OECD countries plus Brazil
WTO framework between Brazil and Canada (Embraer, Bombardier)	Embraer, Bombardier, MJET, ATR operating under OECD framework	
3% fee (discretionary increases for weaker credits)	Increased premium based on risk classification	Further increased premium based on risk classification plus market adjustments
Market pricing	Spread 16–249 basis points	
No universal risk classification process	Bifurcated system, including pricing (Cat 1 for large aircraft, 5 classes and 12-year term) (Cat 2 for other aircraft, 15 classes and 15-year term)	Single system, including one risk classification process for all borrowers (8 risk classes, 12-year term)
Discretionary structural flexibility – wraps, soars allowed	Mandatory structural risk mitigants of Cat 1 but not Cat 2; no wraps, soars for either	Increased mandatory structural risk mitigants required; no wraps, soars
Only Ex-Im Bank provided discount for Cape Town	Variable max discounts for Cat 1 and Cat 2	10% max discount for Cape Town
Home market rule observed	Same as Pre-2007	Same as 2007, unless CSeries competition (matching contemplated)
Brazil and Canada did not recognize home market rule		
	Long transition	Shorter but significant transition

Source: Organization for Economic Cooperation and Development (OECD).

financial crisis, which made commercial lending unobtainable or very expensive for many customers, thereby greatly increasing the importance and potential market distortions of ECA loans. Another impetus was the advent of the Bombardier CSeries aircraft, which introduced complications because its size spanned the two categories of the original ASU. To deal with these developments, the 2011 ASU eliminated the size bifurcation altogether, and stipulated yet more detailed rules concerning conditions of ECA loans.

Aircraft leasing

Closely intertwined with the subject of aircraft finance is aircraft leasing, an alternative financial strategy for operators to obtain aircraft. As Figure 7.7 shows, almost 40% of large aircraft purchases are made by leasing companies. These aircraft are in turn leased to passenger airlines and air freight operators.

The first dedicated aircraft operating leasing companies were Ireland's Guinness Peat Aviation (GPA) founded by Tony Ryan, who later in his colorful career founded Ryanair, and International Lease Finance Corporation (ILFC), founded in the USA by Steven Udvar-Hazy. Both were launched in the 1970s and established business models for today's multibillion-dollar industry.

Most of the GPA was sold to GE in 1993 and is now part of GE Capital Aviation Services. ILFC was acquired by insurer AIG in 1990 and later sold to AerCap in 2014. Udvar-Hazy left in 2010 to launch Air Lease Corporation.

Many relatively small companies are involved in aircraft leasing, but the top ten lessors comprise more than 50% of business worldwide. Note that the

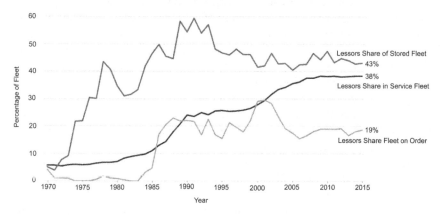

Figure 7.7 Growth in aircraft ownership by leasing companies.

Source: World Leasing Yearbook.

Table 7.5 Major aircraft leasing companies

Aircraft lessors 2015		
Manager	*Total fleet*	*Fleet share (%)*
GECAS	1,518	16.1
AerCap	1,246	13.2
BBAM LLC	405	4.3
SMBC Aviation Capital	397	4.2
CIT Aerospace	327	3.5
BOC Aviation	274	2.9
Air Lease Corporation	268	2.9
ICBC Leasing Co	268	2.9
Aviation Capital Group	257	2.7
AWAS	256	2.7
Boeing Capital Corp.	241	2.6
Avolon Aerospace Leasing	223	2.4
Macquarie AirFinance	200	2.1
Aircastle Advisor LLC	164	1.7
Total	**6,044**	**64.2**

Source: World Leasing Yearbook.

two largest remain GECAS and AerCap, successors to the start-up companies founded by Ryan and Udvar-Hazy.

Leases take many forms, of which the simplest and most conventional is the operating lease, in which the lessor provides an aircraft for the lessee to operate for a period of time. If the leased aircraft are purchased new from the manufacturer, the lessor handles all aspects of the purchase transaction, including financing and predelivery payments.

Operating leases for narrowbody aircraft, which are the most common, typically span from three to seven years, but longer or shorter durations are sometimes arranged. Widebody aircraft, for which transfer of ownership is more difficult to arrange, usually have longer-term leases. Terms of leases vary. Ordinarily, the operator returns the aircraft to the lessor when the lease expires, but often the lessee has an option to extend the lease or to purchase the aircraft from the lessor at fair market value.

Typical financial terms of operating leases provide for up-front security deposits of two or three months of lease payments, followed by monthly payments of 1% of new aircraft cost. Of course, financial terms are negotiable and vary according to market conditions.

Most leases require the lessee to pay into a separate maintenance reserve, which is drawn down as funds are applied to maintain the aircraft.

Because the residual value of the aircraft at the completion of the lease has a major impact upon the lessor's profitability, leases generally contain very specific language defining the physical condition of the aircraft that the lessee is obligated to return to the lessor.

Joint ventures and cross-ownership of aerospace companies

A financial characteristic of the aerospace industry is the extent of cooperative relations among the firms, including joint ventures and cross-ownership. The subject of international cooperation is discussed in more detail in Chapter 6. Generally, the motivation for cooperative undertakings is to pool financial and technical resources. In Europe, cooperation among firms often extends to cross-ownership of shares, and this ownership is reflected in financial statements.

The equity method is the accounting technique commonly used for reporting investments in associate companies. The firm reports the income earned on the investment on its income statement, and the reported value is based on the firm's share of the company assets. Equity accounting is usually applied where an investor entity holds 20 to 50% of the voting stock of the associate company. The investing firm records such investments as an asset on its balance sheet.

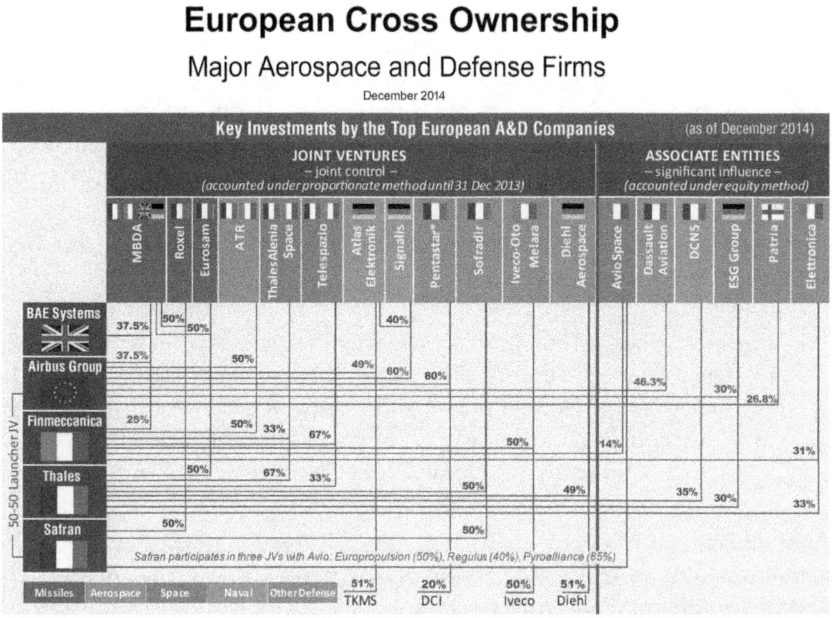

European Cross Ownership
Major Aerospace and Defense Firms
December 2014

	MBDA	Roxel	Eurosam	ATR	ThalesAlenia Space	Telespazio	Atlas Elektronik	Signalis	Pentastar*	Sofzadir	Iveco-Oto Melara	Diehl Aerospace	Avio Space	Dassault Aviation	DCNS	ESG Group	Patria	Elettronica
BAE Systems	37.5%	50%	50%						40%									
Airbus Group	37.5%			50%			49%	60%	80%				46.3%	30%		26.8%		
Finmeccanica	25%			50%	33%	67%				50%		14%						31%
Thales		50%			67%	33%				50%	49%			35%	30%			33%
Safran	50%									50%								

Safran participates in three JVs with Avio: Europropulsion (50%), Regulus (40%), Pyroalliance (65%)

| Missiles | Aerospace | Space | Naval | Other Defense | 51% TKMS | 20% DCI | 50% Iveco | 51% Diehl |

Key Investments by the Top European A&D Companies (as of December 2014)

JOINT VENTURES — joint control — (accounted under proportionate method until 31 Dec 2013)

ASSOCIATE ENTITIES — significant influence — (accounted under equity method)

50-50 Launcher JV

Figure 7.8 Cross-ownership of aerospace and defense firms.

Source: Avascent.

8　Aerospace systems engineering and technology management

Aerospace design is a synthesis of trade-offs among competing priorities: cost, weight, size, performance, safety, power, payload, range, radar signature, noise, reliability, and so on.

Aerospace design engineers have state-of-the-art knowledge of the diverse technical specialties required to create the extraordinarily complex elements of a modern aircraft. There is no doubt that the industry has command of the technology. A separate question is how this technology is integrated and optimized into a product representing the best trade-offs among the infinite design alternatives, recognizing that each subsystem poses conflicts with every other subsystem, and that they all conflict with constraints of cost, risk, and schedule.

The dilemma of trade-offs in the design process is not new, and has been eloquently described over the ages:

> When we mean to build, we first survey the plot, then draw the model; and when we see the figure of the house, then we must rate the cost of the erection: which if we find outweights ability, what do we then but draw anew the model in fewer offices, or at last desist to build at all?
>
> William Shakespeare, *King Henry IV*, Part 2, Act 1, Scene 3

Another icon of Western civilization, the National Aeronautics and Space Administration, struggles daily with design trade-offs, and has defined the **systems engineers' dilemma** as follows.

At each cost-effective solution:

- To reduce cost at constant risk, performance must be reduced.
- To reduce risk at constant cost, performance must be reduced.
- To reduce cost at constant performance, higher risks must be accepted.
- To reduce risk at constant performance, higher costs must be accepted.
- In this context, time in the schedule is often a critical resource, so that schedule behaves like a kind of cost.

In early days of the industrial revolution, when designs of machinery and civil engineering projects were relatively simple by today's standards, it was possible for a single enlightened overseer to independently weigh trade-offs and make configuration decisions. This management approach generally worked well, but in some early cases of complex design, traditional management methods produced outcomes that were not completely favorable. The Fidenae Amphitheatre, which collapsed in Rome in 27 CE killing more than 20,000 people, was apparently an example of suboptimal engineering trade-offs, as were the collapses of the Tower of Siloam in Jerusalem, Beauvais Cathedral in France (which collapsed twice, in 1284 and again in 1573 after it was rebuilt), and Malmesbury Abbey in 1500 in England.

The basis and origin of systems engineering

By the mid-twentieth century, as aircraft designs became overwhelmingly complex, the aerospace industry and associated government agencies began to realize that technological progress would reach a choking point unless strategies could be developed to manage technology flowing into new products. Aircraft are large and complex, and their component parts interact so extensively that a change in one part is likely to affect many others.

Military weapons development problems at the end of World War II provided an impetus for the creation of a concept that would later be called **systems engineering**. In 1945, when development of the Nike Ajax air defense missile system was initiated, available rocket propulsion was barely sufficient to give the missile an adequate tactical range. Engineers recognized that maximum range depended on several parameters, such as the weight and size of the warhead, efficiency of aerodynamic design, degree of maneuverability provided by the control system, and shape of the trajectory and average speed along it. An effort that was an innovative precursor of systems engineering was undertaken. The engineers explored a variety of combinations of the missile's properties, with the objective of achieving the best balance between range and other tactical characteristics. The analysts were working to derive what would become the same type of optimization equation used by later generations of systems engineers.

Control and feedback variables were important aspects of the overall Nike missile systems problem. Conceptually, the whole system was a feedback loop. The missile was controlled by guidance transmitted from a rudimentary ground computer. Guidance from the computer was in turn based upon information from tracking radar that was observing the missile flight. The closed feedback loop went from the missile to the computer and back to the missile again. There were also secondary feedback loops, such as that of the autopilot controlling the attitude of the missile. The analysis of elaborate systems involving interlaced feedback paths is an important element of modern systems engineering.

The term **systems engineering** was apparently first used by Bell Telephone Laboratories in the course of their innovative work on electronics and data processing in the 1940s. Early concepts were expanded by the RAND Corporation, which was created in 1946 at the impetus of the US Air Force for the purpose of studying the interplay of complex technologies with military systems and missions.

In essence, systems engineering is the design of the whole rather than simply the design of the parts. The first priority of systems engineers is to retain an absolute focus on the objectives of the overall system that is being designed. They then attempt to gain a comprehensive understanding of how individual parts and subsystems perform and how they interact and affect each other as an ensemble during operation. The goal of the systems engineer is to adjust the component parts so that together they will maximize the objectives of the complete top-level system.

Designers of many mundane objects deal with the complete finished product and have to deal with systems engineering considerations. But in cases where that whole has many components and many complicated interactions occurring when they are connected, real systems engineering is required and becomes a demanding intellectual exercise.

In complex systems, the large and predictable interactions often dominate, but frequently a large accumulation of small individual factors will collectively exert tremendous unexpected influence on performance. A large system of many parts that individually appear to be sufficiently accurate may collectively produce unacceptably inaccurate results. Likewise, a system of many apparently reliable individual parts may add up to an unreliable complete system. These and other system characteristics make systems engineering a challenge.

The application of systems engineering is indispensable in the design of complex machines such as aircraft. Consider a relatively simple example such as the installation of an antenna to enable satellite-based Wi-Fi internet capability on a passenger airliner. Engineers have to identify a location on the aircraft that has a clear view of the satellites that will be sending signals. An external antenna that can receive the signals withstand the forces of high-speed flight has to be designed, tested, and qualified. Because the aircraft structure will support the antenna, it has to be analyzed to ensure that it can withstand the additional local loads, including effects on the overall structural integrity of the airframe introduced by new forces and new penetrations in structure to accommodate fasteners and wire routing. Because the antenna is in the airstream, the changes to aerodynamic performance of the aircraft must be analyzed to determine effects upon individual variables such as fuel consumption, noise, buffeting, flight characteristics, and the aircraft control system. The weight of the antenna must be introduced into weight-and-balance calculations for the aircraft, possibly resulting in changes to software that manages the automatic transfer of fuel during flight to optimize weight distribution. Because the antenna requires electrical power, impact to the aircraft's overall power system must be analyzed and possibly modified. Because additional wiring will penetrate the structure and potentially emit electromagnetic interference, the routing must be analyzed by structural engineers and electronics specialists. The impact of Wi-Fi signals associated with the new antenna must be tested for all critical systems aboard the aircraft. New software to support the antenna must be integrated with other on-board software, verified for integrity, and analyzed to ensure protection from hacking. And so on.

Not only must all of these variables be analyzed separately, but they must also be analyzed in terms of how they interact with each other, and an optimal design solution that fully considers the trade-offs must be found.

As the systems approach was embraced in aerospace engineering, its basic tenets were adopted in broader management functions. Systems engineering techniques of analysis of variables and search for optimization came to be used in both the initial planning of projects and management of the subsequent execution phases. So-called planning, programming, and budgeting, or PPB, techniques were developed to include financial factors into the overall management of the system.

Because of the high degree of integration of systems design and project management functions, borderlines between the two sometimes become blurred.

Systems Engineering as a Part of Program Management

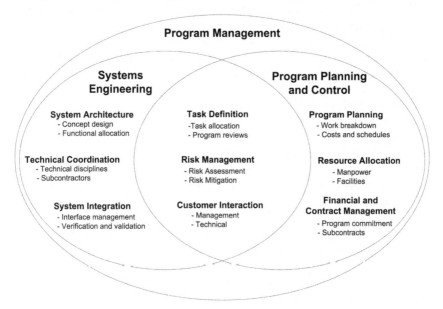

Figure 8.1 Systems engineering and program management are essential complementary elements of aerospace programs.

Systems engineering processes

Conceptually, the systems engineering process begins when **customer requirements** are provided to the organization that will be doing the technical work, and the system design processes begin. In this phase, the system designers attempt to understand the customer expectations and to interpret these expectations into detailed technical definitions. Alternative design concepts are identified and compared, and a preferred concept is selected. An initial design solution is then developed, and preliminary detailed design requirements are flowed down to the lower-level engineering groups that will carry out the detailed design of the subsystems and components.

Then the **system design processes** begin, in which the specialized engineering groups use the detailed requirements to develop actual designs of the hardware and software to be created, and submit these designs for higher-level review. To reduce costs, whenever possible the design requirements should be met by existing designs or by off-the-shelf items that can be purchased.

During this phase, working groups of engineers develop **interface control documentation (ICD)**, which includes interface control drawings, interface control specifications, and other documentation that depict physical and functional interfaces of systems or components that have interdependencies or which function together, and which therefore must be compatible in all respects.

As the product realization process continues, systems engineers work to ensure the complete integration of the separate subsystems, perform formal validation of the overall design, and submit the product for approval to higher levels of management review.

At this point the **technical management processes** commence. Specific plans for the project are developed to manage technical subjects and to ensure that communications are established across interfaces between various work groups. Processes are defined to assess progress against top-level requirements, and decision analysis methods are defined.

Throughout these sequential processes, openness and flexibility are encouraged so that at any point the sequence can be short-circuited if unexpected technical developments arise that necessitate corrections or revalidation of plans that have earlier been reviewed and approved. Back-and-forth flows of communication among all the steps of the sequence are supported at all times.

Throughout the design and management process, **trade studies** are used to identify desirable and feasible alternatives among requirements, technical objectives, design, program schedule, performance, and cost. Choices among the alternatives are then made, based upon defined criteria. Formal trade studies are conducted at multiple levels in the design process. The conclusions of the studies are documented as part of the decision-making process that leads to a balanced technical solution.

Both formal and informal trade studies are conducted in any systems engineering activity. Formal trade studies tend to be conducted in support of major milestone decision forums. In a more informal context, engineering choices at every level involve assessments of trade-offs that are essentially informal trade studies. Generally, the conclusions of these informal assessments are documented in summary detail only, recording the design process as it evolves.

The design process is by no means linear. Throughout the process new information and concepts come to light, sometimes resulting in a need to reassess earlier decisions. **Validation of design** is conducted continuously at all levels, culminating in a formal system verification and validation review. However, validation continues even after the baseline design is formally established and manufacturing begins. Conspicuous examples are airframe static strength test analysis and fatigue life analysis, in which early production units of structural components are tested until failure in large jigs where hydraulic rams exert forces that replicate stresses anticipated in flight. Fatigue life testing, in particular, involves months of testing in which the structure is repeatedly deformed to simulate repetitive flexing that will occur over the aircraft's life cycle. If this rigorous testing results in premature structural failure, the deficient structure must be redesigned and strengthened, with renewed testing and validation of the new design.

Early in the program, when structure and timing of all supporting activities are under study, a **systems engineering management plan (SEMP)** is prepared and distributed. The SEMP, which is subsidiary to the overall **program management plan (PMP)**, contains detailed direction stipulating how systems engineering responsibilities will be performed to achieve system development. It typically consists of three principal sections:

- **Development program planning and control**, which includes statements of work, organizational structure, schedules, risk management, and measurement of technical performance
- **Systems engineering processes**, which include operational requirements, functional analysis, system analysis and trade-off strategy, and system test and evaluation strategy
- **Engineering specialty integration**, which includes human factors engineering, safety engineering, producibility engineering, and **reliability, maintainability, availability (RMA) engineering**

For major US Department of Defense acquisition programs, the SEMP is a specific contractual requirement. Normally the request for proposal issued by the government customer will contain a **systems engineering plan (SEP)**, which is a general description of the systems engineering effort expected by the customer. The SEP includes general statements of requirements and contractual expectations pertaining to technical staffing and organization, technical review planning, and integration with program management. The SEP, prepared by the customer, essentially becomes the guideline for the SEMP, prepared and executed by the contractor.

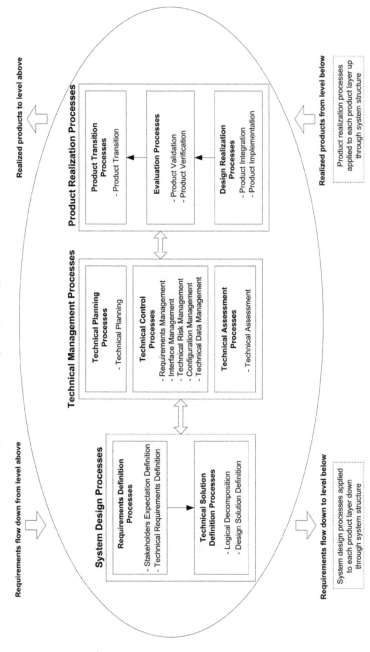

Figure 8.2 The systems engineering processes advance from design to technical management to product realization.

The review process

A key aspect of systems engineering is the concept of regular reviews convened for the purpose of exposing all interested parties to the current status of the project, allowing them to verify that their areas of responsibility are being adequately addressed and to encourage exchanges of ideas in the spirit of improving the final outcome. The reviews typically result in lists of action items intended to address potential problems or opportunities for improvement.

Obviously, the types, frequencies, and intensities of reviews vary according to the nature of the project at hand. Reviews typical of major aircraft design programs are described next. Note that the individual reviews may be repeated if new developments warrant or if the review board concludes that the program is not ready to advance to the next step.

The **Mission Concept Review (MCR)** is an initial discussion to address the new program at its highest conceptual level. It confirms the mission need and scrutinizes objectives and the concepts and strategies for realizing those objectives.

The **System Requirements Review (SRR)** examines the functional requirements and performance requirements that have been defined for the system. A preliminary program plan is presented and is reviewed to ensure that it complies with the program concept and will satisfy mission requirements.

The **Mission Definition Review (MDR)** examines the proposed requirements to ensure that the overall concept is complete, feasible, and consistent with available resources, including allotted time.

The **System Design Review (SDR)** examines the proposed system architecture and design and the flowdown to all functional elements of the system.

The **Preliminary Design Review (PDR)** is a particularly important milestone intended to demonstrate that the preliminary design meets all system requirements with acceptable risk and within the cost and schedule constraints. Its purpose is to provide assurance that optimal design choices have been selected, interfaces have been identified, and verification methods have been described. Satisfactory completion of the PDR is a mandatory prerequisite for proceeding with detailed design.

The following are typical objectives of a PDR:

- Ensure that all system requirements have been validated, the requirements are complete, and the flowdown is adequate to verify system performance.
- Show that the proposed design is expected to meet the functional and performance requirements.
- Show sufficient maturity in the proposed design approach to proceed to final design.
- Show that the design is verifiable and that the risks have been identified, characterized, and mitigated where appropriate.

The **Critical Design Review (CDR)** demonstrates that the maturity of the design is appropriate to support advancing to the manufacturing phase of the program, and that the design will yield a product that will meet performance requirements within the identified cost and schedule constraints.

The following are typical objectives of a CDR:

- Ensure that the system design contains detailed hardware and software specifications that can meet functional and performance requirements.
- Ensure that the design has been satisfactorily audited by production, verification, operations, and other specialty engineering organizations.
- Ensure that the production processes and controls are sufficient to proceed to the fabrication stage.
- Establish that planned quality assurance activities will establish measurable verification and screening processes for producing a product that complies with specifications.
- Verify that the final design fulfills the specifications established at PDR.

The **Production Readiness Review (PRR)** is held for programs involving a production phase. The PRR determines the readiness of the system developers to start efficient production. It focuses on the quality of production engineering, production planning, tooling, material availability, configuration control, quality control, and availability of trained manpower.

The **Test Readiness Review (TRR)** ensures that the test article, test facility, support personnel, and test procedures are ready for testing and data acquisition, reduction, and control.

The **System Acceptance Review (SAR)** verifies the adequacy of the specific end products in terms of their expected maturity level and assures compliance with customer expectations. The SAR examines the system, end products, documentation, and test data. It is the final review to determine that the system is ready to be moved from the lab or factory to its intended operational environment.

The **Flight Readiness Review (FRR)** examines all available data pertaining to design, testing, and safety to confirm that the aircraft is ready for initial flight operations. It also ensures that all flight and ground hardware, software, personnel, and procedures are operationally ready.

The **Operational Readiness Review (ORR)** examines the entire system to determine that documentation, procedures, and trained manpower comply with requirements and are ready to enter service.

The following are typical objectives of an ORR:

- Determine that the system is ready to transition into an operational mode through examination of available ground and flight test results, analyses, and operational demonstrations.
- Confirm that the system is operationally and logistically supported in a satisfactory manner considering all modes of operation and support.

Typical Program Reviews

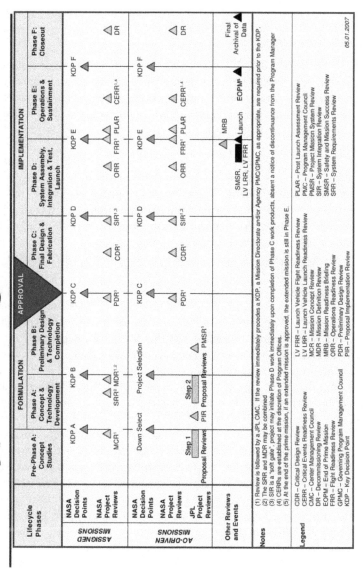

Figure 8.3 A NASA conceptual depiction of program phases and reviews.

Source: NASA.

- Ensure that operational documentation is complete and represents the system configuration and its planned modes of operation.
- Establish that the training function is in place and has demonstrated capability to support all aspects of system maintenance, preparation, operation, and recovery.

Configuration definition

Over time the systems design process advances through progressive phases that depend upon the nature of the product, but which often include design concepts, testing, preliminary design, more testing, detailed design, prototyping, flight testing, and production design. In each phase, as more knowledge is acquired, technical refinements and improvements are incorporated and problems are eliminated.

As the final design eventually emerges, it is painstakingly documented in a body of records known as the **configuration definition**, also known as the **configuration identification**. These records consist of engineering drawings associated with specific part numbers, supplemented by a bill of material and parts list, specification control drawings, process specifications, material specifications, notation of next higher assembly, and so on.

In the modern age of computer-aided design and integrated databases, the task of managing this vast amount of divergent data is easier than it was in the days of hand-drafted drawings and typewritten lists. Now, design drawings for physical structure are generated on three-dimensional models such as Dassault Système's computer-aided three-dimensional interactive application (CATIA) and stored in digital files that are fully integrated with other databases containing the various technical information included in the configuration definition, as noted previously. Thus, engineering definition is now commonly referred to as **model-based definition (MBD)** or **digital product definition (DPD)**, and is characterized by complete datasets that contain all relevant information. However, some traditional design practices persist. Original drawings for older aircraft have mostly been converted to 3D datasets, but some pen-and-ink drawings remain in active engineering data repositories. Likewise, other anachronisms persist, such as masterforms, which are metallic blocks that define complex external skin curvatures. To avoid ambiguities and confusion arising from multiple forms of technical media that possibly do not perfectly agree, the design authority promulgates an **order of precedence** that defines a hierarchy of authority in case of possible conflicts.

Obviously, any changes to the aircraft design will have an immediate impact on manufacturing operations, procurement from subcontractors, and requirements planning, so the body of engineering data is integrated with and fully accessible to data systems and databases used by the organizational units responsible for managing those interfaces.

Change management and configuration control

Aerospace technology advances inexorably over time, and aircraft design evolves continuously to reflect technological progress. New and better aircraft are designed, built, and introduced to the market. At the same time older aircraft are continuously modified to incorporate new technology.

For commercial airplane manufacturers, the impetus of product changes is often the competitive pressure to adapt to evolving market conditions and to gain benefits from new technology. Some changes are initiated because an airplane does not perform as expected. The incorporation of design changes to a modern large aircraft with millions of parts and integrated systems is a massively complex undertaking. Even simple changes can have significant engineering and production implications.

To manage this complexity, the aerospace industry has developed a disciplined and thorough change-management methodology. These management processes enable the mentality of continuous improvement and technological progress that is characteristic of the industry.

Design changes are initiated for many reasons, including improving safety, enhancing aircraft performance, reducing cost, complying with new regulatory requirements, satisfying new customer requests, phasing out obsolete parts and materials, and enabling more efficient servicing of the aircraft on the ground.

In the aerospace industry, engineering changes are assigned to one of three categories. The most significant is a **class 1 change**, in which the redesigned component of the aircraft is no longer interchangeable with the earlier design. Interchangeability is generally construed to mean that the form, fit, and function of the new parts are the same as the previous parts. The obvious downside of loss of interchangeability is that spare parts for the old design are no longer applicable to the new design, maintenance manuals must be revised, and in some cases the performance of the aircraft will be affected. **Class 2 changes** are minor redesigns that do not affect interchangeability. The third category consists of **record changes** that are commonly used to clean up minor errors in the documentation of earlier designs.

Illustrative of typical engineering changes to original baseline design were a number of technical modifications that Boeing made to the 787 Dreamliner in the early days of the program, briefly described next.

- Rain gutter: shortly after the introduction of the aircraft, airlines reported that rainwater was not being properly diverted over a passenger entry door. To address the complaints, Boeing initiated a design change to relocate the gutter to more effectively channel the water. As a result of the change the airlines had fewer water and maintenance issues, and passengers were able to enter and leave the aircraft on rainy days without getting wet. This was a significant enough design change to require certification work with the FAA.

- Incorrect shimming: Boeing found that during the manufacturing process shimming was performed incorrectly on a support structure in the aft fuselage. All 787s in production and in service were inspected, and engineers developed a solution and implemented procedures to prevent a recurrence. This process required FAA approval, which was achieved through a combination of testing and analysis.

- Side-of-body structure: during testing, Boeing engineers found the need to reinforce the side-of-body section of the airplane where the wing was joined to the fuselage. New fittings were installed at 34 stringer locations. Corrective action was implemented across the production system to solve the problem. This change was defined before the 787 was certified, so all testing and analysis was incorporated as part of the baseline design of the airplane.

- Elevator actuator assembly: engineers redesigned the assembly and issued revised drawings to split assembly of the actuator assembly into two parts. The change resulted in a better manufacturing process that avoided cost by improving access and reducing installation time. The new design was also less susceptible to damage. This was a significant enough change to require certification work with the FAA.

As noted earlier in this chapter, large aircraft are the sum of millions of parts, and because every individual part is integrated into the overall system, the act of changing any individual part can potentially have subsidiary consequences for the system as a whole.

For this reason, strict discipline is imposed to manage, control, and document the detailed design of aircraft. The management processes established to ensure this discipline are collectively called **configuration management**. An important tenet of configuration management is that any proposed changes to the existing design of the aircraft are thoroughly studied in advance to determine technical impact and implications for safety, cost, manufacturing processes, subcontractors, and postdelivery logistics. The results of these studies are then reviewed by a series of management boards, and planning is initiated to incorporate the design change into the manufacturing value chain and the maintenance network. Finally, the detailed design change is approved, documented, and released to all parties who will be involved in its incorporation. This process is called **change management**.

Configuration management involves managing changes across the life cycle of a product. Its importance is particularly felt in organizational units dealing with engineering, detailed design, production, and support services. It is the management discipline that applies technical and administrative direction to the development, production, and support life cycle of an aircraft or other controlled item. The discipline is applicable to hardware, software, processed materials, services, and related technical documentation.

Elements of Configuration Management

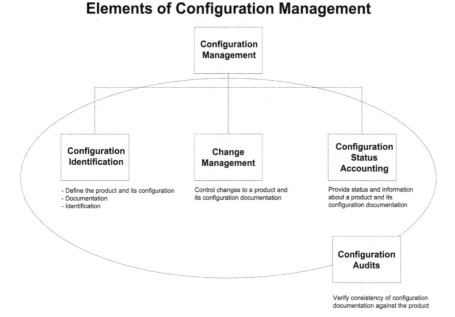

Figure 8.4 Conceptual outline of configuration management.

Configuration management consists of four major processes:

Configuration identification is the initial basis of the configuration management process. It involves defining and documenting the design baseline of the item or system to be controlled. The detailed baseline documentation includes all lower-level component parts, software, performance parameters, interfaces, purchased parts, and so on. Once an item is identified and defined it is referred to as a **configuration item (CI)**.

Change management involves the control of changes to a product and its configuration documentation during its life cycle. In this process, key responsibility resides with the **change control board (CCB)** and the configuration identification manager. The change control board, which is also sometimes referred to as a **configuration control board**, includes representation by the full range of stakeholders, including engineering authorities for diverse systems, customers, production control, product support, and supplier management. The CCB evaluates the changes in the context of issues such as safety, cost, performance, structural integrity, weight, and overall impact on all other subsystems. Configuration management is the gatekeeper for all design changes and maintains consistency between the changes and documentation.

Configuration status accounting maintains current and accurate information on products and processes for retrieval. This includes complete definition of the original design baseline, all past changes to the baseline, design

Top Level Configuration Management Process

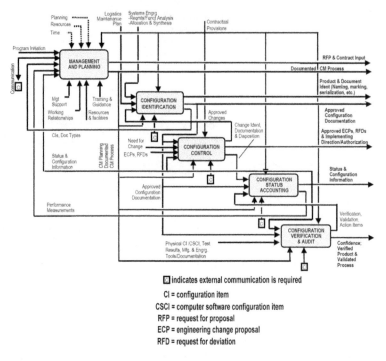

Figure 8.5 Configuration is a complex process requiring participation by many players.
Source: US DoD, MIL-HDBK 61B.

problems, production planning and life expectancy, changes planned for future incorporation, past rejected changes, and actions by certification authorities.

Configuration audit ensures that all the earlier processes have been performed correctly and integrated into the organization. Configuration audit is carried out continuously at different stages of the product life cycle. Audits performed before baseline establishment assure compliance with the requirements. A functional audit is carried out to verify the performances and functional characteristics required for configuration identification. A physical audit is carried out on as-built configuration identification to verify conformance to product configuration management documents.

The change management process

Of the four major components of configuration management, **change management** is generally considered to be the most complex and demanding. It involves relentless control over the minutiae of technical design, widespread coordination among diverse groups of stakeholders, analysis of multifaceted trade-offs, multiple levels of decision-making, and intricate implementation of new designs that affect production lines, subcontractors, maintenance operations, and certification authorities.

The conceptual basis of change management can be broken down into five fundamental steps:

1. **Initiation**. A good system is open to **engineering change requests (ECRs)** from almost anyone who works with or is affected by the existing design. This might be an assembly worker in the factory, a maintenance mechanic, an industrial engineer, or a representative of the customer. Anyone who has useful insight concerning how the design can be improved should be enabled to submit a change request. At a minimum, the request should include a statement of the problem and a recommended solution in general terms. An ECR is sometimes known simply as a **change request (CR)**.

2. **Evaluation**. Initial evaluation of change requests is performed by the design group responsible for the component that is the basis of the request. If the evaluation results in a preliminary conclusion that the request has merit, a more detailed summary of the problem is formulated, and a design solution is developed. This information is packaged into an **engineering change order (ECO)**. The ECO lists the items, assemblies, and documentation being changed and includes any updated drawings, CAD files, standard operating procedures (SOPs), or manufacturing work instructions (MWIs) required to make a decision about the change.

3. **Review**. The completed ECO is then distributed for review by all the organizational units affected by the potential change. Comments by the reviewers are solicited in matters such as technical feasibility, cost impact, effect upon production operations, implications for subcontractors and the entire supply chain, consequences for postdelivery logistical support, and reaction by customers.

4. **Approval**. The exact nature of the approval process depends upon the nature of the change, but all significant changes are formally presented to a **change control board (CCB)** for review and approval. The CCB is constituted by representatives of all the organizations that earlier submitted their individual comments on the ECO, and is generally chaired by a representative of the program manager. The CCB can either reject the ECO, approve it, recirculate it for further study and data, or direct that it be changed and resubmitted.

5. **Implementation**. After approval has been secured, the lead engineer and change analysts develop a plan to put the change into effect, and an **engineering change notice (ECN)**, is sent to affected individuals to let them know that the ECO has been approved and the change should now be implemented. Plan elements include detailed work statements

for each affected organization and implementation schedules for production teams and the supply chain, and a master plan that integrates all
requirements.

Because the process of studying and planning potential changes can be a major
draw on organizational resources, companies often follow a practice of sending change requests through a series of CCBs that have progressively more
authority. Lower-level CCBs perform preliminary reviews and are authorized
to reject undeserving CRs before excessive time and resources are expended.
Boeing, for example, customarily uses a three-tier system of CCBs for commercial aircraft design changes. The lowest level of these tiers, Change Control
Board 3, is convened after the lead engineer has gathered data from affected
organizations and supplier partners and initiated a change request. An impact
assessment review board is convened to ensure that all groups have been identified and asked for input. After all groups have weighed in, the change is
examined from various perspectives, and a decision whether to proceed with
the design change is made.

Change Control Board 2 comprises senior managers who review the implications of the proposal in the context of their areas of responsibility. These
managers are drawn from each engineering group expected to be impacted by
the change.

After passing through Change Control Board 2, the design solution is
then examined by a technical review board consisting of deputy chief project
engineers and other experienced technical specialists. This committee ensures
that the change is technically sound and is the best solution for the airplane.

Finally, the change reaches Change Control Board 1. At this review,
program leaders and the chief project engineer evaluate the change and make
the determination of whether to proceed. In some exceptional cases, a further
review by all of the program leaders may be required.

Under some circumstances the aircraft designer no longer has final design
authority. This is often the case when military aircraft are being designed and
built by a prime contractor for a government customer. Government procurement contracts typically include sections comprising a voluminous statement
of work and technical definition that specify the exact configuration to be
delivered by the contractor. Any significant departures from the contractual
technical definition can only occur if the contract is modified with the consent
of the customer.

The contractual document to effect configuration changes in the framework
of government contracts is the **engineering change proposal (ECP)**.
The ECP, which is submitted by the contractor, contains the same kind of
information included in the documents used by the manufacturer to manage
engineering changes for non-government contracts. The primary differences
are that the top-level change control boards are chaired by government
representatives who have final approval authority, and that the cost of changes
is generally paid by the government.

Typical Change Processing System

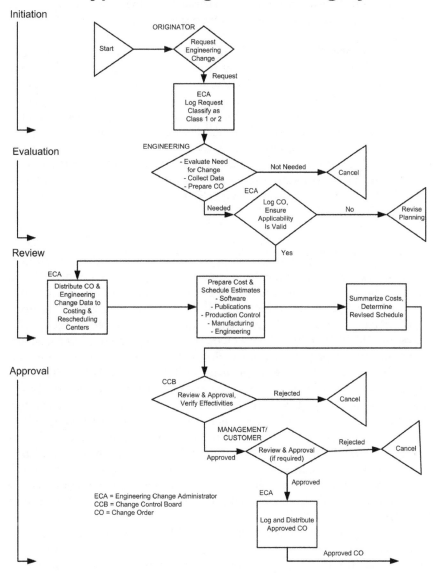

Figure 8.6 The major steps in a change control system.

Source: Adapted from Monahan, R 1995, *Engineering Documentation Control Practices and Procedures*, Marcel Dekker Inc, New York.

After the new engineering drawings are reviewed and approved, manufacturing engineers formulate production plans for technicians to initiate production of new parts and assembly into the aircraft.

After the release of the new engineering and planning drawings, technical teams perform follow-up validation to ensure that the data and instructions have been appropriately incorporated into systems pertaining to manufacturing and record-keeping.

Obtaining **certification** for a change is necessary when it entails a departure from the aircraft design that had received earlier certification from civil airworthiness authorities. If certification of the design change will be required, special engineering teams are tasked early in the change process to identify the documentation and perhaps testing required by the US Federal Aviation Administration for certification. The FAA analyzes data submitted by the manufacturer to ensure that all airworthiness requirements are met, and may dictate that testing be performed to generate additional information. In the case of aircraft for which certification is controlled by a civil airworthiness authority outside the USA, appropriate approval by the relevant national or regional authority is required.

Non-conforming material

Even in the best of companies, the manufacturing process is not perfect, and parts are produced that do not meet engineering specifications. When a non-conformance is detected at any point in the manufacturing process, a **non-conformance report (NCR)** is written to describe and record the specific problem. The NCR initiates a process that directs attention to the manufacturing or material error and determines what will happen to the defective part.

In the case of extremely minor faults detected on the factory floor, the NCR may be dispositioned by a liaison engineer based in the factory for the purpose of dealing with non-conformances that arise during manufacturing operations. If, for example, a shop-floor mechanic has inadvertently drilled an egg-shaped hole for a rivet, the liaison engineer might immediately disposition the NCR with direction that the hole be redrilled to the next larger size and that an appropriately larger rivet be used. If the non-conformance is more serious, or if the liaison engineer feels that the problem requires further technical study, the NCR is routed for study by a **material review board (MRB)**.

In its simplest form, membership of the MRB consists of the cognizant design engineer, a quality engineer, and a manufacturing engineer. The basic membership has the prerogative to request technical analysis or additional technical expertise from specialists. The MRB has four choices for disposition of the NCR:

- Use the part as-is.
- Scrap the part.

- Rework the part in accordance with specific guidance, so that it can be used.
- If the part is functionally usable and safe, attempt to obtain customer permission to use it by means of obtaining a contractual **deviation** or **waiver**.

The purpose of the NCR and MRB process is to ensure that defects are detected during production, bad parts are removed from the system, and parts that can be redeemed are correctly fixed and returned to production.

However, sometimes manufacturing mistakes or design shortcomings result in problems that cannot be easily remedied by reworking or replacing parts, and the only realistic course of action is to accept that the aircraft to be delivered will not conform to the design specifications. This might be the case, for example, if a door opening is assembled out of tolerance, and if the defect cannot be corrected because a large fuselage skin panel cannot be replaced without major rework and possible damage to the understructure. The consequence of the defect is that the standard interchangeable door will not fit the opening, so a standard door has to be slightly modified to fit the opening. Consequently, the special door will have a unique part number that must be reflected in the aircraft's configuration records and maintenance manuals. Further, if the door should have to be replaced in the future, standard spare interchangeable doors will not be usable.

Deviations and waivers are used to deal with this kind of departure from the aircraft design specification. A deviation is a short-term or temporary departure from an approved engineering standard, specification, drawing, or other engineering document. It is applicable for a specific small number of aircraft. It is used when no other solution is reasonably available. It does not result in any changes to the baseline design documentation.

A waiver is a long-term or permanent exemption from the requirements of a product design standard, a procedural or process standard, specification, drawing, or any other engineering document. Like a deviation, a waiver does not entail any changes to the aircraft design, but the configuration accounting records for the aircraft will include detailed notation of the exact ways in which the delivered aircraft does not conform to released engineering.

Although deviations and waivers serve the purpose of reconciling engineering configuration and records, the fact remains that the delivered aircraft does not conform to its design. Depending on the importance of the non-conformance, customers are likely to be unhappy, and the manufacturer and the customer commonly negotiate adjustments to price as compensation for the non-conformances. For US government customers, the Federal Acquisition Regulations require 'consideration' when the government accepts products affected by deviations or waivers. In extreme cases, in which for example aircraft fatigue life is reduced because of faulty assembly, the extent of this financial compensation can be significant.

Software

The aerospace and defense industries have historically been at the leading edge of incorporating advanced electronics, computers, and software into their products. Because of their technical intricacy, aircraft design and manufacturing have always entailed large-scale integration of complex programs, including increasingly complex software. Lockheed's F-35 fighter reportedly contains 8 million lines of on-board software code, all of which is fully integrated to operate critical systems such as flight control, engine control, navigation, communications, fire control systems, countermeasures, life support systems, and so on. Although many of the systems are largely autonomous, they invariably have interfaces with each other and must be integrated accordingly.

To some extent, the task of software design and integration in the aerospace industry is managed using methods and techniques utilized in other industries with complex, large-scale data management requirements. However, the aerospace industry remains distinct because of the scale and degree of complexity of its products, the exceptional downside consequences of software errors, and the magnitude of the task of managing configuration of critical software over long periods of time during which frequent design changes are implemented.

A few recent events have emphasized the vulnerability of modern aircraft to software problems. In May 2015 an Airbus A400M military transport crashed in Seville, Spain. The crash occurred during the aircraft's first flight, at the Airbus production facility at Seville. Subsequent accident investigation revealed that the cause was improper loading of software for the engine control units, contributing to a loss of engine power shortly after takeoff.

Far more dramatic were two crashes of new Boeing 737 MAX aircraft in October 2018 and March 2019 in Indonesia and Ethiopia. Investigation of the accidents revealed that recent redesign of the new aircraft model's flight control system had significantly contributed to the accidents. The specific problem related to a software subsystem known as the Maneuvering Characteristics Augmentation System (MCAS), which was programmed to direct the flight controls to push the nose of the aircraft downwards if the angle of climb was dangerously high. However, if the MCAS system erroneously guided the

Table 8.1 Aircraft design reflects the ubiquitous presence of software in modern life

Software content of successive US military aircraft

Aircraft	Lines of code
F-4	2,000
F-16D	236,000
C-17	2,000,000
B1B	1,200,000
F-22	7,000,000

Source: US Department of Defense.

aircraft downwards because of false readings from sensors, it was very difficult for pilots to manually overcome the erroneous software inputs to the flight control computer (FCC). In both crashes it was determined that sensors had provided bad data to MCAS, with the result that the FCC essentially over-rode manual efforts of the pilots to save the aircraft. Subsequent reviews of the Boeing software management practices and the FAA certification process revealed deficiencies by both parties. All 737 MAX aircraft were grounded for an extended period until the software problem was corrected and the revisions were certified by the FAA and its international counterparts.

Although safety-of-flight issues involving software occasionally arise, it is also true that the inherent safety of modern aircraft is immeasurably improved by avionics software, particularly flight control software, which is capable of detecting in-flight anomalies and taking immediate corrective action, often before problems are observed by human flight crews. The unfortunate 737 MAX experiences have emphasized to the industry and to its regulators that airborne software is particularly critical to flight safety, and requires meticulous testing and verification before it is certified.

In contrast to software-intensive systems used for most business applications and internet networks, aircraft design incorporates widespread software-embedded systems. **Embedded software** is used to control machines or devices that do not fit the retail consumer's common perception of computers. It is typically specialized for the particular hardware that it runs on and has time and memory constraints. Embedded software is generally the only software on the device that it controls, without a higher-level executive operating system. A distinctive characteristic of embedded software is that not all functions are initiated or controlled via a human interface, but through machine interfaces instead.

Software-embedded systems usually run continuously, commonly on custom-designed microprocessors that are part of specialized hardware, and the software must therefore operate in real time. In these systems, software in components is designed in accordance with requirements flowed down from system and subsystem levels. The requirements may be specified for individual software components, or for a group of components operating as a subsystem. In aerospace, embedded software, and its companion specialized hardware, are used in highly complex automation functions in military weapon systems and civil aircraft. Of course, simpler embedded software is used in the general economy for purposes as simple as controlling children's toys or household appliances. Embedded software is sometimes associated with **erasable programmable read-only memory (EPROMs)**, which are comparatively simple custom-designed microcircuits generally produced in relatively small production batches for specific applications. Likewise, individual EPROM manufacturers tend to use different programming processes. The end result is that EPROMs and embedded software are very efficient in performing the specialized tasks for which they are designed, but software maintenance becomes completely non-standardized, requiring specialized knowledge. As time passes, production of older devices cease and legacy software is no longer used on later systems. The older equipment and software remain in service because the cost of replacing them is prohibitive, with the result that the pool of human talent familiar with the legacy systems shrinks over time, exacerbating normal problems of software maintenance.

To deal with the problems caused by non-standard software across aircraft systems, and to make upgrades more manageable, industry and the US Department of Defense have launched initiatives to establish open systems and software in aircraft programs. The **Future Airborne Capability Environment (FACE)**, led by the US Navy, and the **Open Mission Systems (OMS)**, led by the US Air Force, have been developed with active industry participation. FACE is an open standard that ensures avionics software components within subsystems are portable and reusable between platforms. OMS is an open architecture for integrating subsystems such as payloads and sensors onto airborne platforms through the avionics service data bus. Another key element in the Air Force open architecture is the **Unmanned Aircraft Systems Control Initiative (UCI)**, the code that manages information passed between OMS-compliant subsystems on the avionics service bus. UCI was originally developed to standardize digital communications between ground stations and unmanned aircraft.

In spite of the best efforts by the aerospace industry and government customers to manage software, the scale and complexity of the task continue to pose serious challenges. The F-35 fighter, generally considered to be the aircraft with the most intricate software architecture to date, has repeatedly illustrated the difficulty of surmounting software problems. F-35 software design was inherently complex, because not only did it incorporate an extensive variety of inter-related embedded software subsystems, it was also created in three basic versions for application to three fundamentally different airframe variants: an advanced conventional fighter for the Air Force, a short takeoff and vertical landing version for the US Marines and international partners, and a large wing tailhook variant intended to land on US Navy aircraft carriers. The three configuration variants had much commonality, but had distinct differences in critical areas such as flight control systems, engine controls, and weapons management.

In 2018, as F-35 deliveries to customers were well underway after substantial delays partially attributable to software issues, the Pentagon's director of Operational Test and Evaluation, or OT&E, reported widespread deficiencies in the four major software release blocks at the time of the OT&E study:

- Block 2F for the Marine Corps F-35B, operational in 2015, was delivered with 'hundreds of deficiencies'.
- Block 3i for the Air Force F-35A, operational in 2016, was 'problematic' and performing poorly in development testing.
- Block 3F, which completed F-35 system development in 2017, was 'demonstrating poor performance'.
- Block 4, the first postservice-entry upgrade, was deemed too aggressive and underresourced.

The DoD joint-service program office responsible for managing all aspects of F-35 development, which had a somewhat contentious historical relationship with OT&E, acknowledged the software deficiencies, but had earlier taken the position that software perfection was unachievable. The joint program office declared that delivered aircraft would have no critical or safety-of-flight deficiencies, but that not all known software deficiencies would be corrected until after delivery, or perhaps would be left permanently unresolved if the operator did not consider them to be important. This position by the program office, which was taken primarily in the interest of meeting aircraft delivery schedules, elicited controversy from many quarters.

Software management remains a challenge for the aerospace industry, particularly in software-intensive defense programs. In 2018 the new US Air Force assistant secretary for acquisition proclaimed that his first priority would be reform of software management practices that had resulted in widespread delays and cost overruns of defense programs. He endorsed the use of **'agile'** software development featuring frequent releases of smaller software updates, as opposed to the current 'waterfall' model of infrequent major block updates. Although agile development has been used successfully for consumer and business requirements, it has not been widely applied to in-flight aerospace environments, where extensive, costly, and time-consuming testing and validation are required for even very small changes.

9 Management of aerospace programs

The aerospace industry has long been defined by the series of individual programs that it has created and managed. The programs have typically been ephemeral in nature, with well-defined beginnings and ends. Large programs have been technologically complex and intricately scheduled, and often the teams that planned and executed the programs were disbanded when the programs were completed.

Program life cycles

Aircraft programs have life cycles. During the limited period of its existence, a program passes through well-defined phases that overlap to some extent.

- The first phase includes **concept determination** of the new aircraft, including visualization of operational roles and desired performance parameters.
- The second phase is **system definition**, as specific design requirements are derived.
- The third phase is **system development**, which entails detailed design, development, configuration definition, qualification, and testing of the aircraft.
- The fourth phase is **system production and operations**, as the aircraft is produced and enters operational deployment, and as the network of maintenance and support ensures that it remains serviceable.
- Finally, in the fifth phase the aircraft reaches the end of its life, and **system disposal** occurs.

The origins of program management

Program management is often considered a creation of the aerospace industry. In fact, program management (or **project management**, an alternative term) has existed for millennia and has served most notably in monumental civil engineering projects.

Table 9.1 Life cycles of aircraft programs have historically been short, but have lengthened as programs have become more complex and costly

Postwar US military aircraft programs

Decade

1950s		1960s	1970s	1980s	1990s	2000s
XP-5Y	XF-Y	A-6	F-14	F-117	F22EMD	JSFEMD
A-20	F-8U	SR-71	S-8	F-20	YF-22	UCAV
XC-120	F-6M1	SC-4A	YA-99	X-29	YF-23	
F-4D	U-2	X-21	A-10	T-46	JSF X36	
F-3H	SY-3	X-19	F-15	T-45	JSF X37	
B-52	F-105	C-141	F-16	B-2	C-17	
A-3D	X-13	B-70	YF-17	V-22		
X-3	C-133	XC-142	B-1			
S-2F	F-107	F-111	YC-15			
X-2	B-58	A-7	YC_14			
F-10F	F-106	DV-10	AV-8B			
F-2Y	F-5D	X-22	F/A-18			
F-100	X-14	X-26B				
B-57	C-140	X-5A				
F-102	T-2	X-24				
R-3Y1	F-4					
F-104	A-5					
A-4D	T-39					
B-66	T-38					
F-11F	AQ-1					
C-130	X-15					
F-101	F-5A					
T-37	X-1B					

Source: RAND Corporation.

Unfortunately, there are very few surviving artifacts to provide insight into the program management techniques used for the creation of the Great Pyramid of Giza or the Great Wall of China or medieval cathedrals, but the programmatic nature of the undertakings themselves are recognizable: inherent technical complexity, intricate schedules, a vast workforce of diverse skills, and daunting logistical challenges. The historical record is more complete for comparatively recent programs such as the rebuilding of London after the great fire of 1666, construction of the canals at Suez and Panama, and the Transcontinental Railway.

The design and production of the earliest aircraft required an inherent program management instinct on the part of the entrepreneurs of the time. However, as the complexity and size of aircraft increased exponentially immediately following World War II, traditional management practices became inadequate to respond effectively to the new challenges of the industry.

Modern program management techniques in the aerospace industry trace their ancestry to the **Program Evaluation Review Technique (PERT)** developed in 1958 for the Polaris missile program by the Program Evaluation Branch of the Special Projects Office of the US Navy, helped by the Lockheed Missile Systems division and the consultant firm of Booz-Allen & Hamilton. The first PERT databases were designed so that they could be manipulated using the Naval Ordnance Research Calculator (NORC), a first-generation vacuum tube computer built by IBM for the United States Navy's Bureau of Ordnance, located at the Naval Proving Ground at Dahlgren, Virginia. At the time, NORC was considered to be the most powerful computer in existence.

The PERT methodology, which was simple in principle, involved identifying all the discrete tasks required for completion of the project, determining the interdependencies and sequences of these tasks, allocating span times and probabilities for accomplishment of each task, and continually managing and updating the details of the resulting network to ensure that everything stayed on schedule. The **Critical Path Method (CPM)** was similar to PERT, but focused on identifying and managing the longest chronological pathway through the PERT network, recognizing that this pathway would pace the time for completion of the program and was most critical.

PERT was an event-oriented, probabilistic technique to increase a program manager's knowledge and control in projects where time was a critical factor and time estimates were uncertain. PERT uses three time estimates for each activity: optimistic, pessimistic, and most likely. From these estimates, an expected time for each activity is calculated based on a beta probability distribution.

The US Department of Defense and the National Aeronautics and Space Administration quickly embraced the principles of PERT, and by 1962 DoD and NASA, with the collaboration of the aerospace industry, had published a manual formalizing PERT applications for government agencies and contractors.

Work breakdown structures

A fundamental element of PERT was the deconstruction of the overall program into discrete smaller tasks of manageable proportions. This process of deconstruction was soon formalized into a concept of **work breakdown structures (WBSs),** and in 1968 the DoD published *MIL-STD-881, Work Breakdown Structures for Defense Materiel Items*, which dictated the use of WBSs for management of all defense programs. *MIL-STD-881* was later revised and became *MIL-HDBK-881*.

Notably, WBS definition use was not limited to production tasks in the factory, but was applied to every element of programs, including design tasks,

PERT with Critical Path

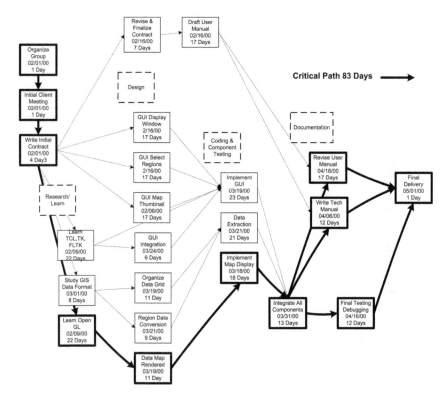

Figure 9.1 An example of a PERT chart for a software project.

Source: Tallyfy, Inc.

subcontracting, testing, personnel management, financial management, and so on.

A fundamental precept of the use of WBSs is that they must include every task that constitutes the program, so that each task is planned, integrated, and managed in the context of the overall program. The concept used to include lower-level tasks is the **WBS indenture system**, which shows successive levels of details as each WBS is broken down into its component parts. Commonly, the principal level 2 WBSs are broken down into many levels of progressively detailed WBS indentures. The complete set of WBSs with detailed indentures is sometimes known figuratively as the **WBS tree**.

Aircraft Systems Work Breakdown Structure

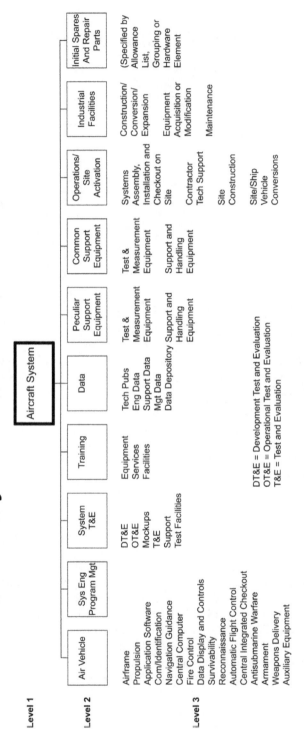

Figure 9.2 The first three levels of an aircraft WBS tree as defined by *MIL-HDBK-881.*

Source: US DoD *MIL-HDBK 881.*

Lower Level Work Breakdown Structure Indentures

Training Example

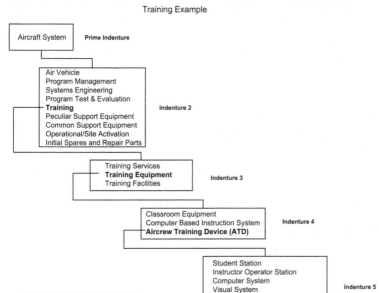

Figure 9.3 Lower-level WBS indentures defined by *MIL-HDBK-881*.

Source: US DoD *MIL-HDBK 881*.

Organization and responsibilities of program management

The concept of the **program manager** was created to deal with increasingly complex aerospace programs that became unmanageable within the framework of conventional organizations divided into discrete functional units. The role of the program manager is to coordinate and control the wide range of activities among the functional entities. As the title implies, the program manager's responsibility pertains to a single program. Often multiple programs and program managers coexist within a single company or agency.

The program manager, or **PM**, has responsibility for every aspect of the program under his or her jurisdiction. He or she is deeply involved in the initial planning and organizing process, including every aspect of the financial fundamentals of the program. The PM is responsible for monitoring and controlling every phase of execution of the program, including the management of design, production, the supply chain, international partnerships, and technical data. In the operational phase of the aircraft, the PM oversees the **integrated product support (IPS)** team that assures operational support. Throughout the life of the program, the PM works closely with contract managers to maintain close working relations with the customer and to ensure that commitments to the customer are met.

In spite of this daunting list of responsibilities, the program manager does not have direct organizational control over the functional departments that constitute the company. The production department, for example, is typically under the direct control of the production manager, who in turn reports to the general manager. However, the program management office is the organizational entity that determines what will be produced, at what cost, and to what schedule.

The organizational construct devised to depict the relationships between responsibilities of the functional organization and the program manager is the **matrix organization**. In a matrix organization, the separate functional units retain a traditional vertical hierarchical structure with 'solid line' reporting responsibilities among them. Program management has a horizontal purview crossing all the functional units, who report to the program manager with 'dotted line' responsibilities.

The **organizational breakdown structure (OBS)** is the organizational counterpart to the work breakdown structure. The program management team identifies members of the organization who will have direct responsibility for

Principal Responsibilities of Program Management

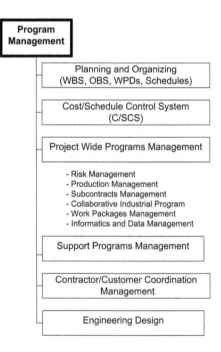

Figure 9.4 The broad spectrum of program management responsibilities.

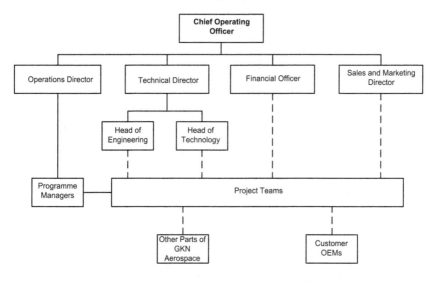

Figure 9.5 A simplified matrix organization including program management at GKN
   Aerospace Engineering Services, with solid line and dotted line reporting.

Source: GKN Aerospace Engineering Services.

the tasks specified in each WBS. The OBS also defines the organizational
framework for budgeting, cost allocation, cost reporting, and work performance reporting.

The matrix organization concept functions by means of **integrated product teams (IPTs)**, which are multidisciplinary groups composed of qualified
and empowered representatives with the authority and accountability to manage a specific WBS within a program. IPT members are drawn from functional
organizations but report to the program office.

Because the aerospace industry is a technology-intense environment, management of engineering design and technology is a significant component of
the program manager's responsibilities. As Chapter 8 showed, systems engineering shares many of its managerial concepts with program management.
Cross-functional integration is a basic tenet of both. Systems engineering
should be viewed as a major subdomain of program management. The overall
program manager has responsibility for executive functions such as program
planning and control that lie outside the technical jurisdiction of engineering.
However, in many areas, responsibility for program control and engineering
overlap. Examples are risk management, program reviews, and interfaces with
the customer on technical subjects.

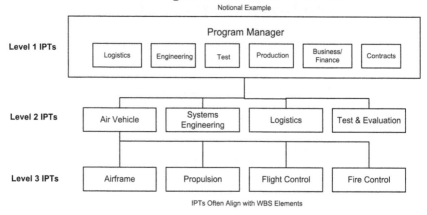

Figure 9.6 Integrated product teams at various levels of the WBS.

Source: General Dynamics.

Figure 9.7 Program management encompasses both systems engineering and program planning and control.

The integrated master plan

Of fundamental importance to any program is the **integrated master plan (IMP)**, which comprehensively depicts all the events that comprise the program, identifies the relationships among these events, assigns timing for the work and its completion, and allocates budget for discrete elements of work contained in the plan. Because timing is such an important aspect of the plan, it is represented in the form of a schedule with supporting documentation. The schedule itself is known as the **integrated master schedule (IMS)**.

Due to the inherent complexity of aircraft programs, each of the top-level events depicted in the IMP is deconstructed into greater detail focusing on accomplishment of the entire WBS tree. Thus, each of the events on the IMP top-level schedule has its own subsidiary plan and schedule, and the events on the subsidiary schedule are likely to have a third-level schedule, continuing until a complete waterfall of subsidiary schedules is created.

These integrated schedules tie together all program tasks, large and small, by showing their logical relationships and any constraints controlling the start or finish of each task. This process results in a hierarchy of related functional and layered schedules derived from the WBS that can be used for monitoring and controlling program progress. The schedule is also networked, which means that it depicts the interdependencies and sequencing of actions. It shows a specific sequence of events and specifies which activities must be completed before others are begun.

Orion Spacecraft Program

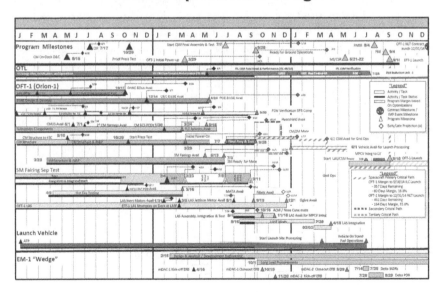

Figure 9.8 A Gantt chart depicting a segment of a master plan for a space program.

Note: this chart also depicts the critical path for the program.

Source: NASA.

Probably the most simplistic of the widely used program management tools is the **Gantt chart**, a scheduling technique developed by its namesake early in the last century. The original version of the charts showed only the tasks to be performed and the planned beginning and ending dates of each task. Modern software enhances Gantt charts by showing updated progress towards completion of individual tasks and by depicting dependencies among task, much like PERT charts.

Cost estimating

Because the program master plan is formulated in the earliest stages of the program, budgeting contained in the plan is based upon estimates of future cost.

Four principal cost estimating methods are commonly used for aerospace programs.

The **analogy method** compares a proposed system with a similar system for which cost data exists. The estimator makes a judgment of the differences between the new system and the old one, and adjusts the estimate to reflect the differences. It is a relatively simple estimating method, often used to cross-check other methods. An intrinsic weakness of the method is its dependence on subjective judgment.

The **parametric** or **statistical method** is similar to the analogy method in that it attempts to extrapolate historical data to apply to future programs, but is more granular in nature. It uses regression analysis of data from two or more similar systems to develop **cost estimating relationships (CERs)**, which are performance or design characteristics such as weight, speed, or payload. As with the analogy method, a critical consideration in parametric cost estimating is the similarity of the systems in the underlying database.

The **engineering method** entails a detailed effort to study every aspect of the projected new program and to assign them individual estimates, which

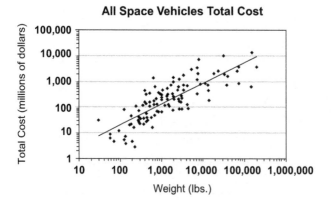

Figure 9.9 A NASA parametric correlation of weight and cost.

Source: NASA.

are added to reach an aggregate for the complete program. This method is predicated on the existence of sufficient program definition to enable discrete estimates of the program parts. Ideally the estimates can be developed based on the program WBSs and engineering design. The method is costly and time-consuming, and involves efforts by industrial engineers, cost analysts, subcontract managers, and accountants. It attempts to quantify detailed costs for labor, material, and overhead costs, including input from all functional areas that have a role in the future program.

The **actual cost method** projects future costs based on earlier experience on the same program. Actual costs recorded on the program for previous production work, similar tasks, or material purchases are used as the basis for projections of future cost. The cost data is manipulated to consider anticipated changes such as learning curve effects and cost discounts for material. Obviously, actual cost estimating cannot be used until the program has begun and some cost data is available from sources such as prototype production or early low-rate production. The actual cost method is generally considered to be the most accurate cost estimating method, but a major limitation on its usefulness is that it is unavailable for use until the program is already underway, when necessary data becomes available.

Budgeting

The budgeting process is a means for establishing and monitoring cost goals for every aspect of the program. Cost budgets and the program schedule are the major components of program baseline against which progress of the program is tracked.

As mentioned above, creating the WBS tree is an essential step in defining the project and establishing the baseline. The master schedule assigns time intervals, chronological order, and relationships to the specific tasks included in the WBS. The program budget is allocated across the scheduled activities and time periods, and becomes the integrated program baseline.

The WBS tree provides the fundamental framework for program planning and control. It is also the basis of control accounts, work packages, and planning packages, which are additional concepts used in program control.

A **control account**, also known as a **cost account** or **cost element**, is a discrete unit for purposes of monitoring cost and schedule performance. It can be a single WBS or group of WBSs. It is allocated a specified budget for completion and is included on the schedule with a start date and completion date.

The program manager uses control accounts to achieve several critical elements of program control.

- Accumulation and reporting of costs
- Variance analysis and reporting
- Assignment of responsibility to cost element managers
- Corrective action planning

An **element manager**, or **control account manager**, is assigned for every control account. He or she takes responsibility for ensuring that the task is performed on schedule and within the budgeted cost.

During the budgeting process the program manager allocates part of the total budget to a **management reserve** account prior to distributing budgets to the organizational units that will be accomplishing the work. The purpose of the management reserve is to enable the program manager to allocate additional budget as required in the future to deal with unforeseen problems that will inevitably cause budget overruns in specific cost accounts.

Because management reserve is not allocated at the beginning of the program, it is not included in the baseline against which schedule and budget variances are calculated. Management reserve funds remain at the program level until they are incrementally allocated to work units as required. Eventual allocations from management reserve are approved by the program manager. Documentation associated with management reserve transfers is maintained and reported by the program control function.

Program and schedule control

Program control encompasses all activities that the program manager undertakes to ensure that the actual program conforms to the developed plan, to include the implementation of necessary recovery action to get the program back on the plan if delays or disruptions occur. To control a program, the PM needs means to monitor program progress against the master plan. The program master schedule and budgeted cost define the baseline against which progress is measured. If there are indications that an activity is falling behind schedule or exceeding budget, the manager initiates corrective action to address the problem.

Schedule control involves identifying schedule variations and managing changes to the schedules in response to developments that unfold as the program proceeds. The schedule change control system defines procedures for tracking schedule performance and the authorization process for incorporating schedule adjustments, and is integrated into the program's overall change control system. Impact to schedule occurs for many reasons, including performance shortcoming, program changes, or replanning, and external factors such as funding changes or customer directions.

As program changes occur, potential impact to the schedule is assessed. In many cases, if performance shortcomings cause delays to occur to WBSs that are not in the critical path, there will be no impact to the top level of the master schedule. In this case, limited changes will be made to specific subsidiary schedules only. Large changes that affect the top-level master schedule are likely to result in changes throughout the entire family of subsidiary schedules.

The schedule change control system should routinely distribute information concerning schedule variations, schedule changes, explanations of causes for changes, and the development of corrective actions. Changes should be documented and made readily available to members of the program's management team, and to other programs.

Measuring cost performance

Earned value management (EVM) is a primary method commonly used to monitor program costs.

EVM integrates data pertaining to work scope, schedule, and cost goals, and measures progress against these parameters. The purpose of EVM is to provide accurate insight to enable monitoring of program execution. It provides a basis for management decision-making.

The fundamental benefits of EVM are:

* An indication of the status of program tasks in progress
* An evolving depiction of relationships among program cost, schedule, and physical progress
* A framework for systematic collection of data that is accurate, timely, and auditable
* A means for producing meaningful recurring reports to management

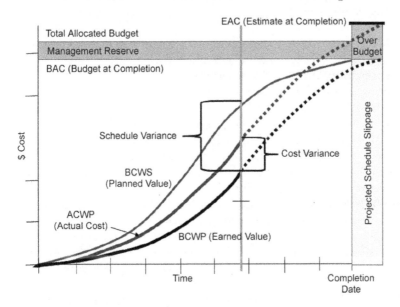

Earned Value Concept

ACWP = Actual Cost of Work Performed
BAC = Budget at Completion
BCWS = Budgeted Cost of Work Scheduled
BCWP = Budgeted Cost of Work Performed

Figure 9.10 A depiction of the relationships that comprise the earned value concept.

Source: Defense Acquisition University.

Earned value relates program planning to schedules and to actual performance. All work is planned, budgeted, and scheduled in time-phased **planned value** increments constituting a performance measurement baseline. As work is performed, it is 'earned' on the basis of either budgeted dollars or labor-hours. Planned value (**budgeted cost of work scheduled [BCWS]**) compared with earned value (**budgeted cost of work performed [BCWP]**) measures the dollar volume of work planned versus the equivalent dollar value of work accomplished. The difference is the **schedule variance**. Earned value (BCWP) compared with the **actual cost of the work performed (ACWP)** provides an objective measurement of cost performance. Any difference is called the **cost variance**. The three data points – BCWS, BCWP, and ACWP – provide the basic information needed to determine program status at a given time and to provide insight into relationships causing the variances.

Management of program risk and schedule risk

Risk is the potential that a program element will fail to be achieved as planned. Risks are as diverse as the program itself, and can fall in the domains of safety, technical execution, processes, cost, schedule shortfalls, or any number of external factors.

In the context of program management, individual risks can be considered to have three components:

* A **risk scenario**, which is identification of a potential occurrence that will have an adverse effect on the program if it occurs
* The **probability** that the adverse event will occur
* The **consequences** if the adverse event does occur

Cost risk involves the ability of the program to achieve its life cycle cost objectives. Two subcategories of risk affecting cost performance are the risk that the cost estimates and objectives are unrealistic or unattainable, and the risk that cost objectives will not be met because of failure to manage program schedule, performance, and cost incurred.

Schedule risk is associated with the adequacy of the time estimated and allocated for the development, production, implementation, and operation of the system. Two risk areas bearing on schedule risk are the risk that the schedule estimates and objectives are not realistically attainable, and the risk that program execution is poorly managed in the domains of cost, schedule, or performance.

Technical risk reflects the adequacy of the system attaining the level of performance necessary to meet technical requirements.

Process risk is associated with the ability of the design, test, and production processes to meet their commitments.

Programmatic risk or **exogenous risk** is the threat to the program from external factors over which the program manager has no control. Examples might be changes to the legal environment or changes in the international political context. Although these developments cannot be controlled, contingency actions to deal with them can be developed.

Risk management is a continuous process conducted by program managers throughout the life cycle of a system. It is an organized methodology for continuously identifying and quantifying uncertainties. It includes developing, planning, and implementing risk mitigation strategies, and monitoring implementation to ensure that risk is reduced.

The risk management process includes the following steps, performed on a continuous basis:

- Risk identification
- Risk analysis
- Risk mitigation planning
- Implementation of the risk mitigation plan
- Risk monitoring

Risk management is an essential requirement over the entire life of the program, but is especially important early in the program, at a time when programmatic details have not yet been completely finalized and when decision makers have greater flexibility to adjust program structure to minimize risks. Initial technical reviews should be performed at the outset of the program, as soon as performance requirements are developed, to ensure that critical performance risks, schedule risks, and life cycle cost risks are addressed, with mitigation actions incorporated into program planning and budget projections.

The **risk reporting matrix** is commonly used to present a simplified summary of program risks. It takes the form of a two-dimensional graph with Cartesian coordinates, with the x-axis representing the seriousness of the potential consequences of the risk scenario, and the y-axis representing the probability that the scenario will occur. Individual scenarios are plotted as points on the chart in positions depicting their assessed seriousness and probability. Scenarios that fall in the upper right quadrant (high probability and severe consequences) are managed most intensively. Scenarios that fall in the lower left quadrant (low probability and minimal consequences) are observed but receive less attention. The chart is traditionally color-coded with the danger zone in red and the relatively benign zone in green.

Program reviews

As described in Chapter 8, formal **program reviews** are useful management tools for integrating complex programs, and their use has become a formal element of systems engineering and program management. The US Department of Defense requires that a series of specific reviews be held over the period of military aircraft programs, and civil aircraft manufacturers have instituted similar reviews as part of their program management procedures. In commercial

The Risk Management Process

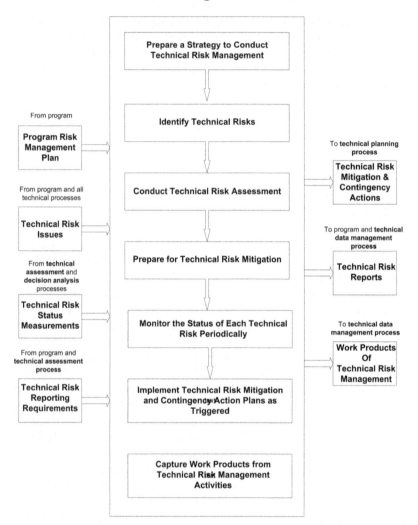

Figure 9.11 NASA's conceptualization of the process for managing technical risks.
Source: NASA.

aerospace, **gate reviews** are often held at critical junctures of aircraft programs, initially to determine if the program meets the business parameters to become a profitable undertaking, and later to verify that technical requirements have been addressed. For military aerospace programs, the government customer contractually compels the contractor to perform a series of formal reviews at milestones in the program to assure that all elements of the program

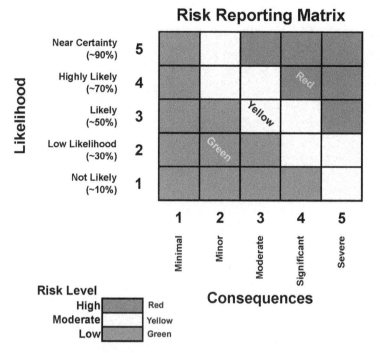

Figure 9.12 A standard risk–consequences matrix.

Figure 9.13 Boeing's Gate Review Process for introduction of new aircraft programs.
Source: Boeing.

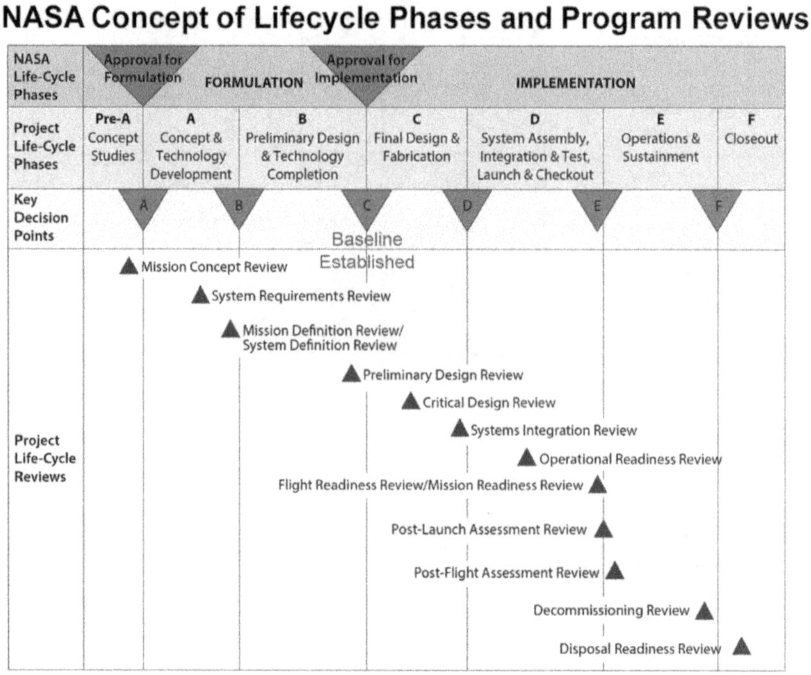

NASA Concept of Lifecycle Phases and Program Reviews

NASA Life-Cycle Phases	Approval for Formulation — FORMULATION — Approval for Implementation				IMPLEMENTATION		
Project Life-Cycle Phases	Pre-A Concept Studies	A Concept & Technology Development	B Preliminary Design & Technology Completion	C Final Design & Fabrication	D System Assembly, Integration & Test, Launch & Checkout	E Operations & Sustainment	F Closeout
Key Decision Points	A	B	C	D	E		F
Project Life-Cycle Reviews							

Baseline Established

▲ Mission Concept Review
▲ System Requirements Review
▲ Mission Definition Review/ System Definition Review
▲ Preliminary Design Review
▲ Critical Design Review
▲ Systems Integration Review
▲ Operational Readiness Review
Flight Readiness Review/Mission Readiness Review ▲
Post-Launch Assessment Review ▲
Post-Flight Assessment Review ▲
Decommissioning Review ▲
Disposal Readiness Review ▲

Figure 9.14 In actuality, the time span of operations in phase E typically exceeds the time of all the other phases combined. This is particularly true for commercial aircraft programs.

Source: NASA.

are on track and that contractual requirements are being met. Participants at the reviews represent all functional disciplines involved in the program.

Aerospace program management spans the entire life cycle of the aircraft, from the earliest of the conceptual phases until disposal after the aircraft is removed from service. The operational lifetime of most aircraft types extends for decades after production deliveries have ceased, and the accumulated costs of operation and maintenance almost always exceed the purchase cost of the system.

Integrated product support

The **integrated product support** concept recognizes the importance of product support to the success of any aerospace program, and requires representation by the product support organization in every phase of program management. Support considerations are weighed in the conceptual phase and throughout the design process. As the aircraft is being designed, engineers and maintenance specialists consider trade-offs concerning design features that will facilitate maintenance and reliability. Often improved maintenance characteristics entail penalties in terms of additional weight, power requirements, and manufacturing cost, and the program manager must consider the relative benefits or penalties and decide upon final configuration.

Installation of on-board systems diagnostics, for example, involves installation of additional subsystems that require processing capability, data connections to key aircraft systems, physical space to locate processing units, electrical connections to power the subsystems, and software integration with the overall aircraft avionics system and display panels. The extra cost, weight, and power is justified by the benefit to the aircraft operator, who becomes able to detect and diagnose systems anomalies in real time, and who can immediately take contingency action while the aircraft is in the air and can alert ground-based maintenance teams to prepare to fix the problem upon aircraft arrival.

Other typical maintenance trade-offs in the design process involve selection of materials used for airframe construction, location of maintenance access ports, paths of electrical wire harnesses, types of connectors for hydraulic lines, and so on. During design of the Boeing 787 and Airbus 350, for example, the weight and strength benefits of graphite composite structure were compared with the additional initial maintenance costs to operators, who would have to invest to establish widespread capability to repair the new materials.

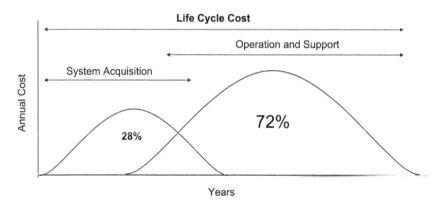

Aerospace System Life Cycle
Typical Pattern of Costs Incurred Over 30 Year Life Cycle

Figure 9.15 For a typical aircraft program, the cost of operation and maintenance far exceeds the purchase cost.

Source: US Office of the Secretary of Defense, Undersecretary for Logistics.

As aircraft design continues, product support continues to work with other key program elements to develop a complete maintenance infrastructure:

- Technical manuals for aircraft operation and maintenance
- Procurement of spare parts inventories, based upon expected failure rates and operational hours
- Preparation of maintenance facilities
- Training of technical maintenance personnel
- Depot support provisions for heavy overhaul
- Design of the network of support to be provided by subcontractors
- Design and installation of specialized test equipment
- Data collection systems

Experience has demonstrated repeatedly that the eventual quality of an integrated product support system is greatly improved if product support is addressed at the very beginning of a program, rather than added as an afterthought to a program that has already been launched.

There is no doubt that product support is an important consideration in the mind of the customer, who will have to ensure maintenance of the aircraft over many years of operation. Perceived quality of product support is often a discriminating factor during marketing campaigns. Several studies of life cycle cost have demonstrated that approximately 70% of an aircraft's cost to the owner is incurred after delivery.

10 Aerospace production management

The first airplanes had wooden structures of lightweight spruce and fir, constructed using boatbuilding technology. The modern terminology of aircraft structure reveals this heritage. Wings consist of spars and ribs. Fuselage compartments are separated by bulkheads, lateral movement is controlled by a rudder, and the theoretical horizontal centerline plane is referred to as the waterline.

The skins of these early aircraft were cloth, tailored to fit, laced to the structure, and painted with lacquer to add rigidity.

The introduction of metal airframes changed the nature of manufacturing processes and the skills required of production workers. As thin rolled aluminum alloys became available in the 1930s, aluminum skins replaced cloth, and wooden wing spars were replaced by aluminum tubes and beams. Skilled metalworkers replaced woodworkers on the shop floor. For production of all-metal heavy bombers and transport aircraft, the forming and fastening of sheet metal and frames came to resemble processes in the automobile industry, which was the principal repository of expertise in sheet metal forming and assembly at the time. Car manufacturers became involved in aircraft production, particularly during the industrial mobilization of World War II.

By the time the war ended, the aircraft industry had become large and well-financed, and its production technology had become specialized to the point that little manufacturing commonality with the automobile industry remained except in segments such as metal forming and hydraulic systems. During the same period, advancing aircraft design required materials, structures, and systems that were exceptionally strong, lightweight, could handle extreme environmental conditions, and were built to tolerances that far exceeded the standards of precision formerly demanded in manufacturing operations.

Aerospace manufacturing technologies

The special demands of the aerospace industry resulted in the development of specialized production technology to address the industry's needs. Eventually, many of the technologies spread throughout the general economy.

Numerically controlled machining

Computer-controlled milling machines, originally known as **numerically controlled (NC)** machines and later as **computerized numerically controlled (CNC)**, found their first widespread applications in the aerospace industry, where they replaced traditional human machinists working on hand-controlled machines. The clear value for aerospace production was that the machines were able to assure consistent and repeatable close-tolerance production of parts.

CNC machines have historically been controlled by computer programs written in **automatically programmed tool (APT)** language, which defines the tool path with respect to the geometry of the part being machined. Since modern aircraft structures are designed and defined in three-dimensional digital models such as CATIA, conversion language has been developed to greatly simplify the process of generating APT language from digital models.

Five-axis machining

Whereas traditional CNC machines move in three linear x, y, and z axes, cutters on five-axis machines move in all three linear axes plus two additional rotary axes. Five-axis machines are more expensive, but their additional versatility offers distinct advantages over conventional three-axis machining.

In the first part of the twentieth century, machine tool companies had recognized the conceptual benefits of five-axis machines and had experimented with impractical designs involving clumsy controls based on complex systems of levers and cams. The enabling technology that led to the introduction of practical five-axis machines was NC control. In 1958 the US Air Force awarded Cincinnati Milacron 'a contract to build and test an electric tracing of a 5-axis vertical mill to determine its feasibility'. The Cincinnati machine was a success, and the technology quickly spread throughout the aerospace industry and elsewhere.

The principal advantage of five-axis machining is the ability to machine the highly complex shapes and surface contours that are often characteristic of aircraft designs. Although three-axis machines were sometimes able to produce these shapes by means of multiple special fixtures or additional setups, the versatile movement capabilities of five-axis machines enable machining angles and arcs that allow complex parts to be completed with a single setup. Multiple setups are undesirable in machining operations, particularly when they involve large workpieces such as aircraft structure. Setups take substantial additional time and consume manpower, but more seriously they degrade the precision of the final product because precise alignment is partially lost with every additional setup when the 'zero' index location for the cutter is changed.

Composite materials

Composite materials are created as a combination of two or more dissimilar materials used together to create a new material with properties that neither of the constituent materials could achieve on their own. The concept is not new. Ancient Egyptians combined clay and straw to create bricks that supported heavy compression loads and were resistant to fracture.

Aerospace composites typically include individual plies of continuous, straight fibers such as carbon, glass, or aramid laminated in a host polymer matrix such as phenolic, polyester, or epoxy.

Composites used in aerospace have excellent specific strength and stiffness properties in relation to their weight. In addition, the laminated plies of composite materials enable the designer to tailor optimum mechanical properties by orientating the fiber direction with the primary load paths.

The use of composites in aircraft production became feasible with the invention of phenolic resins in 1909. The first aircraft with a composite primary structure was the de Havilland Mosquito fighter of World War II, which incorporated a bonded wooden ply-balsa-ply sandwich fuselage construction, resulting in an aircraft that was light, fast, and agile.

In contrast to metal structure, in which small cracks can quickly grow and result in catastrophic failure, the oriented plies of composites have the benefit of preventing crack growth, and for this reason composites are now exclusively used for components such as helicopter rotor blades, which historically were prone to abrupt failure due to metal fatigue, with disastrous consequences.

Originally aerospace composites were produced by hand layup methods, which involved wetting fabric with a liquid polymer, removing surplus liquid with a squeegee, and applying subsequent layers of fabric. Modern production methods involve the use of numerically controlled tape-laying machines, known as **automatic fiber placement (AFP)**. The AFP machines apply tape or cloth preimpregnated with polymer onto a mold that provides the desired curvature. The machine makes multiple passes, applying fabric at different orientations, rolling and cutting the fabric at each pass. After the layup process, the mold with the uncured composite is moved to an autoclave, where it is cooked under vacuum.

Initially, composites were used exclusively for skins and panels, with metallic supporting structure attached by means of mechanical fasteners. Advances in technology now enable cocured structures in which composite stiffeners and structural supports are joined under pressure to panels prior to curing, resulting in a monolithic final product that combines the panel and structure, eliminating the need for the additional time, work, and weight of adding fasteners.

Mechanical cutting of composites is problematic because it tends to cause delamination, generates heat, dulls tools, and produces noxious dust. A solution to these problems is **abrasive water jet (AWJ)** technology, in which small streams of water under extremely high pressure and mixed with tiny abrasive particles are used in lieu of mechanical cutters. The technology eliminates tool wear, requires very small cutting forces, and causes no thermal damage or delamination.

Because of their many attributes, the use of composite materials is expanding with every generation of new aircraft. However, their special properties

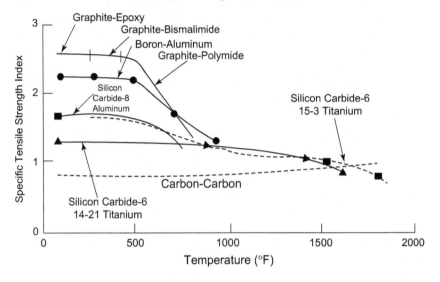

Figure 10.1 Advanced composite materials have clear advantages in many aerospace
applications.

Source: US Air Force.

impose some limitations on their applications. For example, they lose strength
at a much higher rate than conventional metals when temperatures rise,
and thus are sometimes not suitable for applications in high-temperature
environments.

Specialty metals and aluminum alloy structure

Because aircraft components must be light, strong, and resistant to extreme
temperatures, the steel alloys typically used for cars, trains, and ships are not
suitable. Jet engine hot section parts in particular require extreme temperature resistance, and consist of special alloys based on nickel, cobalt, or iron,
sometimes with components of titanium and chromium and even rare earth
elements such as yttrium. Special alloys of aluminum have been developed
for aerospace applications, assuring strength, corrosion protection, and fracture resistance, but sometimes requiring special machining and forming techniques. Titanium has been widely used for large high-load applications such
as landing gear and engine mounts, and has been formed into skin panels for
extremely high-speed aircraft such as the SR-71 high-altitude Mach 3 reconnaissance jet.

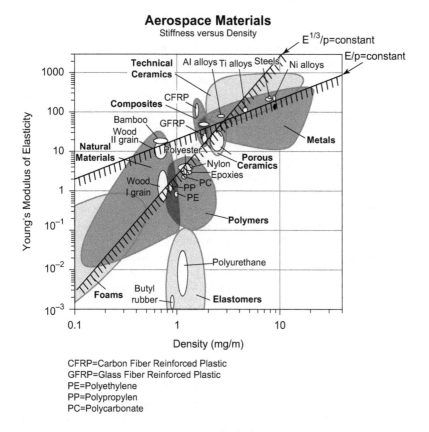

Figure 10.2 This chart indicates the wide variety of materials available to aerospace designers. Young's modulus is an indication of elasticity. Ideal materials would be plotted to the upper left quadrant. Note that both scales are logarithmic.

Source: Derived from Ashby, M 2005, *Materials Selection in Mechanical Design*, Elsevier-Butterworth Heinemann, Oxford.

Non-destructive testing

Because consequences of material failure in aircraft are potentially catastrophic, and because aircraft structure is designed with minimal margins of extra strength, the industry has a vital interest in detecting invisible flaws in its products. It has been a leader in the development of numerous technologies to test the integrity of structure without causing physical damage to the part being inspected.

• **Dye penetrant inspection** is used to detect tiny surface cracks and structural flaws in non-porous materials. Test objects are coated with a fluorescent dye which is allowed to settle into any eventual cracks. The object is cleaned, leaving just the dye which has penetrated the cracks. The object is then exposed to a black light, causing residual dye in any cracks to glow, revealing their presence.

- **Radiography** in aerospace uses X-rays for thin materials and gamma rays for thicker materials to reveal interior structure. As digital imaging has replaced traditional film the process has become faster and less cumbersome. Recent advances include 3-D computed tomography (CT) scanning, which captures multiple X-rays of a test object from different angles to build up a cross-section view of the object on a computer.
- **Ultrasonic testing** uses high-frequency sound waves to locate defects within material by analyzing the reflection of the waves. It is commonly used to detect defects in welds, fittings, joints, bolts, and adhesive bonding.
- **Eddy-current testing** induces an electromagnetic field in a conductive test object and measures the secondary magnetic field generated around the electric current to locate flaws. Eddy-current testing is widely used in aircraft maintenance to detect cracks caused by fatigue or corrosion.
- **Laser testing** includes techniques such as shearography, holography, and profilometry, using laser light to detect deformation on the surface of objects. It is particularly effective in detecting tiny flaws undetectable to other measuring systems.

Large-scale stretch forming of aluminum alloys

In contrast to automobile exterior panels that have traditionally been made by stamping sheet steel using male and female die sets, many large aircraft panels are shaped by a stretch forming process in which annealed aluminum sheets are pulled over a single male forming block. The process is feasible because of the relative softness of aluminum, which also has less springback after forming than steel. The annealed aluminum is typically heat treated after forming to increase hardness. The stretch forming process is slower than stamping, but enables production of large panels that would be difficult and impractical to make using stamping methods.

Photonic metrology

Since the early days of aircraft manufacturing, builders have confronted difficulties measuring structure. As successive generations of airframes inexorably grew larger, the problem became more acute. Traditional physical references such as templates or yardsticks were unwieldy and could not assure the accuracy required for the industry's close-tolerance designs, and engineers quickly began experimenting with light as a measuring tool. Initially, **theodolites** similar to surveyors' transits were used with some success. More recently, **laser trackers** coupled to computers generate a three-dimensional measurement of thousands of structural reference points in very short periods of time, assuring extreme accuracy and enabling a higher degree of automation in assembly operations.

Laser beam welding

Conventional electrowelding produces high coefficients of thermal expansion, resulting in volume shrinkage during solidification, often causing distorted weld joints or cracking. The conventional process is also prone to gas entrapment and embrittlement, causing weakness and irregular quality. These characteristics are unacceptable for the production of aerospace structure, which requires high precision and reliable strength.

A solution for these obstacles began to emerge by the mid-1960s as gas lasers were being used to weld experimentally. By the mid-1970s automated laser welders had emerged and were being used in aerospace production.

In laser beam welding, a laser beam is focused and directed through an optical lens to achieve high power density. The beam can produce precise, deep, and narrow welds with minimum local heat and negligible distortion of the final weld joint.

Laser welding systems are capable of delivering enormous amounts of energy very quickly and with pinpoint accuracy. The beams can be focused and reflected to target hard-to-access welds and can be sent down fiber-optic cables to provide additional control and versatility.

Metal bonding

Chemical bonding of aircraft structure has been an important production process from the early days of the industry, when hollow wooden wing spars were built by gluing together two hollowed-out halves using the animal-based hide glues employed in furniture making at the time. Later, as aluminum alloys became widely used for aircraft skins and understructure, the combination of adhesive bonds and rivets became common in aircraft design as a strategy to optimize weight savings, strength, and durability. Adhesive bonding of metal components spreads loads over larger areas than mechanical fastening with rivets.

Early metal bonding in the postwar aerospace industry generally utilized phenolic adhesives cured in ovens after application. The de Havilland Dove propeller airliner of 1945 and the de Havilland Comet jet transport of 1951 successfully incorporated this technology. In later aircraft, beginning with the Boeing 727 of 1963 and the Boeing 737 of 1967, hot cured epoxies replaced phenolics. Since then, virtually all Boeing and Airbus models have used epoxies, as have military and civil aircraft produced by other manufacturers.

A common application of adhesive bonding involves attachment of stringers to fuselage skins and wing skins to stiffen the structures. Adhesives are also widely used to manufacture stiff lightweight movable flight control surfaces such as elevators, ailerons, and spoilers, which are sometimes constructed of metal honeycomb core inside metal or composite skins. Numerous methods for application of adhesive have been developed, but commonly the adhesive is supplied as a film that is precisely cut and laid on metallic faying surfaces that have been chemically prepared to maximize bonding properties. The second faying surface is then positioned over the adhesive film, pressure is applied, and the assembly is baked in an oven under controlled conditions.

Precision casting

Investment casting using the lost wax method is known to have existed for thousands of years for jewelry making dating from the Mesopotamian and early Egyptian civilizations, but was not adopted for industrial applications in the West until the early 1900s. The aerospace industry during World War II created a demand for the manufacture of precision shapes in specialty alloys that could not be shaped by traditional methods, and precision investment casting was developed and refined for this purpose. The manufacturing process is relatively time-consuming and costly, but it produces results that would be difficult to achieve by other means. Desirable characteristics of the finished product include excellent surface finish, high dimensional accuracy, extreme intricacy of form, and absence of flash or parting lines. Notably, investment casting has come to be widely used in the production of jet engine compressor vanes of high precision and complex shapes using specialty alloys.

Chemical milling

Chemical milling is a process used in the aerospace industry to remove shallow layers of material from large aircraft components such as skin panels and airframe structural parts.

The concept of chemical milling is not new. Copper artifacts dating from 2300 BCE in Egypt were etched with citric acid, and medieval armor was often decorated with acid etching. The main industrial application of chemical machining developed after World War II. In 1953, North American Aviation used the process to etch aluminum components for rockets. The company named the process 'chemical milling' and patented it in 1956. A notable early application was for skin panels of the Apollo moon lander built in the 1960s.

A particularly useful attribute of chemical milling for aerospace manufacturing is that the process enables selective removal of material from specific areas of plates or sheets of aluminum until the remaining skins or walls are very thin. Conventional mechanical machining has historically been unable to mill aluminum below certain minimum thicknesses because the physical force of the cutter tends to tear the metal as it becomes very thin and because heat generated by the cutter distorts thin panels.

The chemical milling process entails coating the workpiece with precision-cut impervious masking material that leaves exposed only the areas where material will be removed. The piece is then immersed in a corrosive bath at a controlled temperature. After a specified period of time the piece is removed from the bath and immersed in a separate neutralizing tank, and the masking material is removed. Because the rate at which the corrosive process removes material is predictable and controllable, it is possible to produce dimensionally precise final results.

High-speed machining

In 1931 the German industrial conglomerate Friedrich Krupp AG was granted a German patent referring to a 'method of machining metal', based on metal cutting studies made by an inventor named Carl J Salomon, whose data supported the non-intuitive conclusion that at high cutting speeds, machining temperatures begin to descend rather than rise. Salomon's work became the basis of **high-speed machining (HSM)**, which later emerged as a major innovation in the industry.

In the late 1950s research into high-speed machining began to accelerate, as additional theoretical studies confirmed Salomon's findings and as technological advances enabled fabrication of machines with high-speed spindles. In 1979 the US Air Force funded a comprehensive research program in cooperation with General Electric to investigate the possibility of introducing high-speed machining into industrial applications.

Traditional conventional milling techniques had caused heat buildup that permanently distorted thin-walled parts, making them unusable for precision applications. Consequently, engineers had been compelled to design parts with

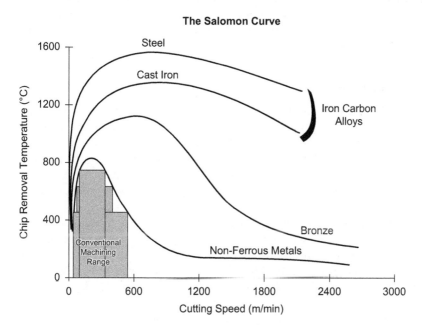

Figure 10.3 Eventually cutting temperatures fall as cutter speeds increase, enabling high-speed machining.

thicker walls that entailed weight and space penalties. High-speed milling of thin-walled parts is possible because the cutter loads are greatly reduced. Heat buildup and distortion are minimized.

The Air Force research yielded positive results, and in the 1980s Lockheed was an early adopter of HSM, quickly followed by others in aerospace manufacturing. Thereafter high-speed machining became a feasible alternative to conventional machining.

By the 1990s, high-speed machining had become a mainstream aerospace manufacturing process because it enabled higher productivity, better work quality, and ease of machining thin-walled structures.

As the terminology indicates, the distinguishing characteristic of high-speed machining is that the cutter moves at much higher speeds than in conventional machining. The cutting speed depends upon the rotational speed of the spindle, diameter of the cutter, number of flutes, and speed of feed. Typically, HSM operations have a reduced depth of cut but proceed at much faster feed rates, thus removing more material than conventional milling in the same time period, resulting in faster work. The resulting surface finish from HSM is smoother, and perhaps most importantly for aerospace production, the reduced depth of cut allows for milling of shapes with very thin walls.

The capability to machine thin walls has enabled engineers to redesign intricate structural assemblies composed of many smaller parts including sheet metal shapes, extrusions, and rivets, and to replace the assemblies with monolithic parts machined relatively quickly from a single plate or bar of aluminum. The resulting machined parts have closer tolerances that their assembled predecessors, require less time and labor to produce, and are less likely to have quality non-conformances.

Superplastic forming

In the early 1960s, researchers in the Soviet Union and the Massachusetts Institute of Technology described extraordinary formability of certain fine-grain aluminum alloys under controlled conditions. They noted that this property would potentially allow metals to be shaped using forming techniques borrowed from polymer and glass processing. Within 30 years this early research had evolved into proven manufacturing technology regularly used in the aerospace industry.

The **superplastic forming (SPF)** process is a forming technique useful for manufacturing structural components with a complex shape, especially for metal alloys such as titanium, magnesium, and aluminum. The value of the technology is that it permits metals to be shaped in extreme ways that would result in tearing and failure of the material if conventional forming methods were used.

Blow forming is an example of an SPF technique involving a single sheet of alloy laid on a female die that is then subjected to gas pressure, resulting in a formed part with the configuration of the die.

Common applications for titanium alloys in the aerospace industry are pylon panels, nacelle panels, engine parts, turbine vanes, and auxiliary power exhaust. Applications for aluminum alloys include lightly loaded or non-structural components, such as inlets, wing tips, access doors, and equipment covers.

The main advantage of the SPF process is its capacity to produce complex parts in one operation with an excellent surface finish. There is minimal residual stress and springback effect, increasing structural integrity. Consequently, in certain applications SPF reduces cost, saves weight, and enables shapes that were formerly not feasible.

Robotics

Aircraft assembly has historically been a domain of skilled craftsmen and women, performing precision tasks such as drilling, riveting, bonding, moving large structure, painting, inspecting, and so on. Although the industry began to use early robots for high-volume production of smaller machined parts, widespread use of robots in assembly operations was forestalled because of the diverse nature of the work, combined with relatively low rates of production.

However, the aerospace industry's extreme requirements for repeatability and precision in many ways align perfectly with the capability of robots, and industrial engineers have been successful in incrementally incorporating widespread use of robotics in aircraft production.

The most common application of robots is drilling holes in skin and supporting structure. A typical large aluminum skin panel requires thousands of precision holes to attach stringers and stiffening structure. Exact location of the holes is essential, as is close-tolerance drilling and alignment. Robots are able to produce consistent and fast results, automatically locating the hole positions and performing drilling, reaming, and countersink operations, followed by injection of sealant and installation of the rivet. Robots are faster than humans and produce consistent precise results each time.

Painting is another common task for robots in aerospace. The use of robots in painting operations removes humans from a toxic environment that is particularly dangerous in manual operations because it requires continuous movements on scaffolds high above ground. Robots with large work envelopes can reach to paint large surfaces, including entire aircraft, without scaffolding. Quality of robotic painting exceeds performance of even the most skilled human painters and is much faster.

Robots are also commonplace in non-destructive testing of structure, using ultrasonic and other imaging methods to inspect for delamination of composites and verify the integrity of rivets.

Managing the production system

The challenge of any factory operation is to successfully manage production technology, quality, resources, costs, and schedule.

Many of the manufacturing concepts that are now considered innovative modern factory management practices had in fact been recognized and incorporated into factory operations since the earliest days of mass production on assembly lines. As the US aerospace industry operated with an acute sense of urgency immediately prior to World War II, Boeing designed and built a flying prototype of the B-17 bomber in less than a year. The company's inexperienced workforce, half of whom were women, was able to deliver 15 of the aircraft per day.

After the war, as the sense of urgency diminished, efficiency declined. Much of the competitive pressure to control costs disappeared as the industry consolidated. Whereas the automobile industry continued Henry Ford's legacy as the archetype of large-scale mass production, the larger and more complex aircraft of the postwar era were produced in smaller quantities, at progressively lower rates, and with persistently high levels of hand craftsmanship.

Experiments with concepts of production improvement

In the commercial aerospace industry, the advent of Airbus Industrie in the 1970s ended this complacency. By the 1980s, US commercial aircraft makers were faced with an aggressive, competent, and well-funded international competitive threat. During this period Boeing and Douglas Aircraft embraced some of the popular management initiatives of the period, including **quality circles**, **productivity circles**, and **employee involvement** programs.

In the 1990s Boeing continued to experiment with other management trends of the period, including **continuous quality improvement**, **statistical process control**, **variability reduction**, and **hardware variability control**. In 1993 a group of Boeing managers undertook a 'Japan Study Tour' which involved visits to eight Japanese companies.

Thereafter, management expressed serious support for elements of the **lean** philosophy, including **just-in-time** production scheduling. Boeing hired several consultants to assess lean manufacturing, including Shingijutsu, a consulting agency founded by former Toyota managers who had worked with Taiichi Ohno, who had originally articulated the **Toyota Production System**, which was the basis of the lean manufacturing dogma.

In 1995 Shingijutsu led a group of Boeing managers to Japan to study the Toyota Production System, which Boeing fully embraced. In a long and close relationship with Shingijutsu, more than 1,000 Boeing managers participated in Shingijutsu-hosted training seminars addressing the Toyota system. By the year 2000, senior Boeing management had launched a mandatory enterprise-wide initiative to instill the precepts of lean manufacturing.

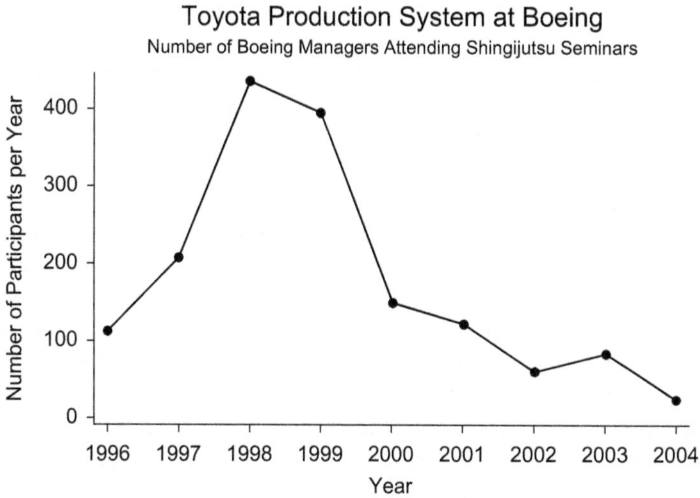

Toyota Production System at Boeing
Number of Boeing Managers Attending Shingijutsu Seminars

Figure 10.4 From 1996 through 2004 Boeing sent large numbers of managers for Toyota system training.

Source: Boeing.

Derived from concepts developed by Taiichi Ohno of Toyota, the so-called lean manufacturing principles are the theoretical basis for process improvements leading to increased efficiency in manufacturing.

Ohno identified seven types of waste found in any process:

- Transportation – unnecessary transport of parts under production
- Inventory – stacks of parts waiting to be completed or finished products waiting to be shipped
- Motion – unnecessary movement of people working on products
- Waiting – unnecessary waiting by people to begin the next step
- Overprocessing – extending the work with unnecessary extra steps
- Overproduction – producing more products than needed
- Defects – flawed products resulting from production errors

The Toyota system and the lean manufacturing concepts that followed are focused on getting the right things to the right place at the right time in the right quantity to achieve perfect workflow, while minimizing waste and being flexible and receptive to change. Application of the concepts can theoretically reduce the waste in production operations and business processes. The core philosophy is that cost and profits will grow if redundant or unnecessary operations and processes are reduced.

The concept of lean manufacturing is sometimes reduced to five simple sequential steps that repeat in a quest for continuous improvement:

1. **Identify value**, which is defined as any activity, outcome, or product beneficial to the final customer. Conversely, anything which the customer considers to be of no benefit has no value and should be removed from the process.
2. **Map the value stream**, which entails identifying and analyzing all of the activities in all the steps involved in creating the product. During this process the seven types of waste described previously by Taiichi Ohno are eliminated because they have no value.
3. **Create flow**, which includes organizing and charting the order in which activities will be performed, how they relate to each other, and how much time their performance will be allocated.
4. **Establish pull**, which means determining when the final product will be required, and from this exact time working backwards to determine when parts and components will be required for each of the intermediate manufacturing steps. The entire flow is then calibrated so that output from each stage of the production process arrives at the next step exactly when it is needed.
5. **Strive for perfection** as these improvements and efficiencies are introduced. The improvement process is continually repeated in a theoretical pursuit of perfection. In each cycle of the process, additional waste is removed and efficiency increases.

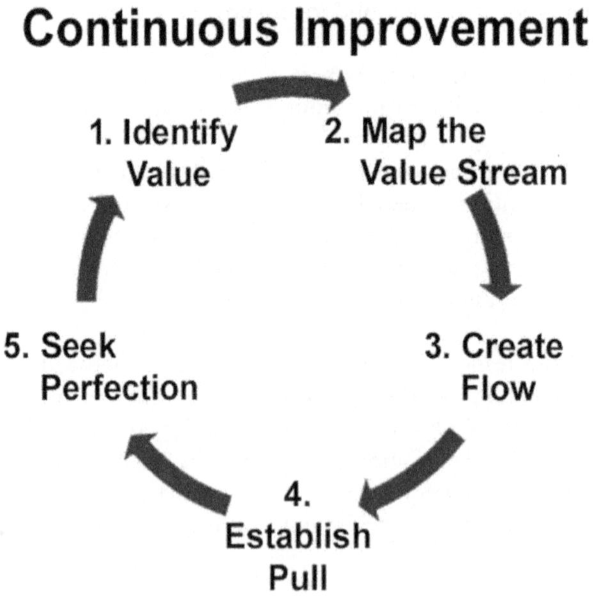

Figure 10.5 The search for perfection is a basic tenet of the Toyota system.

As part of its embrace of lean manufacturing, Boeing management aspired to redesign manufacturing flow in factory locations of its major commercial aircraft programs, culminating in the establishment of moving production lines for all aircraft assembly. The moving production line is a manufacturing technique widely used in the automobile industry, and was the basis for the Toyota system. Boeing identified a specific sequence of precursory steps to be accomplished to support attainment of the final objective of the moving lines. The Boeing initiatives corresponded in many respects with the tenets described previously.

1. Understand how value flows
2. Balance the line
3. Standardize work procedures
4. Put visual controls in place
5. Put everything at point of use
6. Establish feeder lines
7. Radically redesign products and processes
8. Convert to a pulse line
9. Convert to a moving line

In November 2000, the Long Beach final assembly line for the 717 airliner converted to pulse movements, and converted to a moving line in September 2001. In April 2001, 737 final assembly became a moving line, followed by 757 final assembly in August 2002.

Boeing declared impressive improvements in efficiency and reduction in production cycle time as a result of the conversion to moving assembly lines. Five years after the 737 production line at Renton, Washington, was completely reconfigured to incorporate lean manufacturing principles including a moving line, Boeing reported that factory cycle time was 46% less, stores inventory was 59% less, work-in-progress inventory was 55% less, and the overall factory footprint had been reduced by 21%. Perhaps most indicative of the improvements, flow time in final assembly had been reduced to 11 days from the former span of 22 days.

In recent decades the aerospace industry has demonstrated remarkable focus on its efforts to increase productivity, reduce cost, shorten schedules, and improve quality. Each company's experience has been unique, but in some ways Boeing's journey is representative:

1978
  • Fabrication Division Productivity Circles
1980
  • Productivity Circles
  • 757 Productivity Program
1984
  • Visit by Joseph Juran, early proponent of Quality Improvement and Quality Circles
  • Quality Improvement Circles formed

1986
- Total Quality Process at Boeing Commercial
- Managing Quality seminars
- Visit by Edwards Deming, proponent of 'Statistical Product Quality Administration' in postwar Japanese manufacturing

1990–1991
- Study trips to Japan by management
- Continuous Quality Improvement as a management system

1992
- World Class Competitiveness training
- 5S implementation
- Work Management/Process Management initiatives
- Just-in-time implementation at Boeing Arnprior site in Canada

1993
- Fabrication Division just-in-time pilot program
- Rapid just-in-time implementation workshops
- Propulsion Systems Division just-in-time pilot program

1995
- Manufacturing leadership summit
- Tour by Boeing Manufacturing Business Unit to North American manufacturers
- Visit to Boeing by James Womack, co-author of the best-selling book *The Machine That Changed the World*
- Boeing Wichita just-in-time start-up
- First Shingijutsu Japan Kaizen seminar

1997
- Boeing Military Aircraft and Missiles lean kickoff

1998
- Development of lean plan for Delta IV rocket production
- Boeing Space and Communications lean kickoff

2000
- Long Beach initiation of 717 final assembly pulsed line
- Implementation of nine tactics for lean manufacturing
- Implementation of Six Sigma program enterprise-wide

2001
- Moving lines implemented for 717 and 737 final assembly
- Disparate production efficiency teams merged into Six Sigma group

2002
- Moving line implemented for 757 final assembly

2003
- Lean manufacturing initiatives implemented at 26 Boeing Defense and Space sites

A cynical observer might surmise that Boeing's production management initiatives for this period of several decades were a smorgasbord of most of the popular management fads of the moment, hyped by management consulting firms in fashion at the time. Certainly, there was an element of experimentation in Boeing's experience, driven by general management awareness that the company's manufacturing systems had grown inefficient and needed to be restructured. The same management techniques and mind-sets with which Boeing experimented were widely implemented throughout the aerospace industry at the time. The techniques were invariably based on a valid core insight that could be utilized to the benefit of the company. At a minimum, the constant experimentation served the useful purpose of unsettling the inefficient status quo, and eventually led to manufacturing systems that were unquestionably better and more efficient than their predecessors of the 1980s.

At the same time that Boeing was striving to increase productivity, Airbus was testing many of the same management concepts, often with a slightly different European élan. Airbus fully embraced the tenets of lean manufacturing, but their mentor from the automobile industry was Porsche, which operates a lean consulting business unit. Porsche's lean expertise derives from its experience as it approached financial collapse in the early 1990s, at which time it hired a team of Toyota-trained consultants to completely redesign its production methods and supply chain management.

In many ways the Airbus industrial structure lends itself naturally to the tenets of lean manufacturing. It is a decentralized industrial network resulting from the partitioning of production tasks mandated by the national governments that have provided launch funding for successive Airbus models. As per lean manufacturing precepts, large structural components are assembled in various locations throughout Europe, stuffed with wiring, tubes, and mechanical, electrical, and hydraulic subsystems, and are shipped to final assembly lines for completion in relatively short span times. However, like any lean system, it is subject to serious dislocation if any single supplier or interface fails.

In the case of the A380, major disruption and delay were encountered on the final assembly line when workers discovered that wiring harnesses installed in structural components could not connect because of length mismatches. The mismatches, which were attributed to differences in CAD software used by designers at different Airbus factories, caused miles of wiring to be removed from the stuffed structure, to be replaced by new harnesses incorporating design changes. The production disarray was in many ways similar to the disruptions shortly thereafter that beset Boeing 787 assembly because of failures of critical suppliers.

In spite of occasional painful learning experiences on the 787 and A380, both Boeing and Airbus claim spectacular improvements in production performance as a result of lean implementation, citing greatly reduced flow times in final assembly, reduction in manhours, lower cost, and improved quality.

Work breakdown structure

An essential aspect of managing production activities is the breakdown and identification of the individual manufacturing tasks that, when combined,

The Boeing and Airbus Lean Production Houses
Borrowing Concepts from the Toyota Manufacturing System

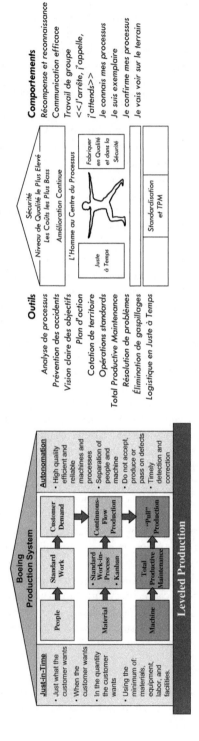

Figure 10.6 Airbus and Boeing simultaneously embraced the values of the Toyota Production System.

Source: Airbus and Boeing.

yield the complete finished product. In the aerospace industry, the **work breakdown structure (WBS)** is the methodology used to identify all of the tasks required to create the aircraft, and to show the relationships among these individual tasks. The WBS concept was discussed in detail in Chapter 9.

The origin of the WBS methodology dates from 1957, when the US Navy was attempting to solve problems in management of the Polaris missile program. The Navy developed the basic WBS concept and by 1962 had expanded the concept with NASA support. In 1968 the Department of Defense published *The Work Breakdown Structures for Defense Materiel Items* (*MIL-STD-881*), which established work breakdown structures as a standard across the DoD and mandated their use on certain complex defense contracts. Utilization of the WBS concept is now standard through the aerospace and defense industry.

The benefits of the WBS concept are obvious:

- It identifies and provides a visual representation of all parts of a project.
- Used as a scheduling tool, it presents a view of status of tasks.
- It defines specific and measurable outcomes.
- It breaks the work into manageable segments.
- It can be used as a basis for estimating costs and allocating resources.
- It reduces the possibility of omissions or redundancies of tasks.

The aerospace and defense industries use a standard numbering system to identify aircraft structure and components. The entire aircraft is designated as 1.0, and subsidiary tasks and material are designated by adding additional digits and decimal points to the number as the tasks become smaller. The numbering system is referred to as the **WBS tree** because the top-level tasks are broken into smaller lower-level tasks, which in turn are broken into still smaller tasks, and so on.

Each progression downwards to smaller tasks is called an **indenture**. A sixth indenture WBS would probably include small subassemblies, whereas a second indenture would include large structural pieces.

The WBS concept is fundamental to aircraft production, but has additional importance in the era of lean manufacturing because of the moving line concept characteristic of lean factories. Line balancing is essential to assure that the time required for processing and assembly tasks at each individual workstation is approximately the same. If WBSs can be grouped so that all the station times are equal, the line will be in balance and production will flow smoothly. When workstation times are unequal, the slowest station will determine the overall production rate of the line. In a continuing effort to achieve perfect balance of the line, industrial engineers selectively move small WBSs between workstations.

The tasks identified at individual WBSs are often scheduled using Gantt charts, a formal scheduling technique developed in the early twentieth century by Henry L Gantt at the Frankford US Army Arsenal during World War I.

Typical Aircraft Work Breakdown Structure Numbering System

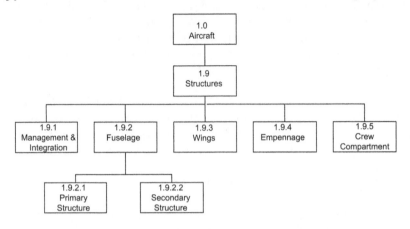

Figure 10.7 The WBS system deconstructs the aircraft into manageable subunits.

Source: US DoD *MIL-HDBK 881.*

It is a simple method of scheduling discrete tasks, depicting their span time, and showing their chronological relationship to one another. Over the years enhancements to the basic technique have been developed to show relationships, dependencies, and constraints affecting individual tasks, and Gantt charts remain widely used in the modern era by scheduling software that monitors progress and allocates resources among activities. Additional critical information can be included by overlaying critical path lines and showing the extent of completion of individual task bars.

Depending on the desired level of scheduling detail, Gantt charts can range from very simple to very complex. A summary chart might only show the top-level indentures, for example, whereas a chart for daily status control might depict the complete lower-level indentures.

Monitoring production cost and schedule

Earned value management (EVM) is a convergence of program management and cost accounting that provides visibility into the cost impact of departures from the schedule. The concepts of EVM have been recognized by industrial managers since at least early in the twentieth century, and by the 1960s the US Air Force and Department of Defense had formalized the concepts as part of their methodology for managing defense contracts. In 1998, the National Defense Industrial Association (NDIA) obtained acceptance of the earned value management system by the American National Standards Institute as standard ANSI/EIA-748.

F-35 Manufacturing Sequence Flow

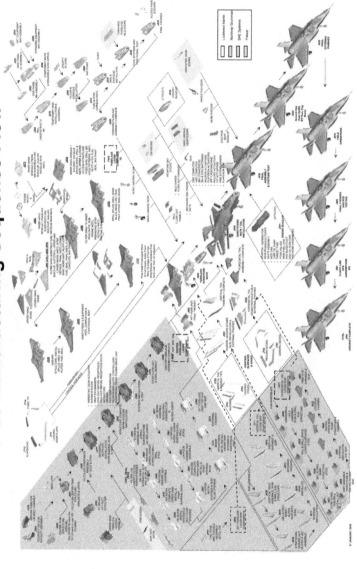

Figure 10.8 The WBS indenture system enables a degree of clarity into the production flow of the F-35. This depicts the conventional take-off and landing (CTOL) version. The SWBS acronym indicates stuffed WBS.

Source: Office of Assistant Secretary of the Navy for Research, Development, and Acquisition.

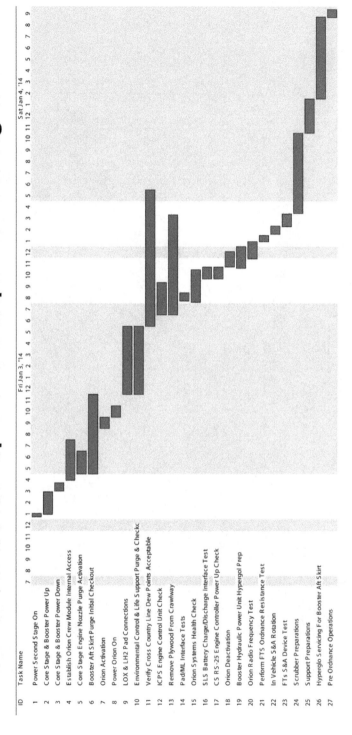

Figure 10.9 A fragment of a detailed Gantt chart used for a NASA program.

Source: NASA.

The baseline of EVM methodology consists of two components:

- The **master production schedule**, which shows the start and completion dates for each WBS or manufacturing task
- The **standard cost**, which is a budgeted amount for the completion of the task, based upon an initial estimate of the time required

The combination of the production schedule and the standard cost for each task is the **planned value**, and the estimated cost to complete the entire job is the **budget at completion**.

As work proceeds, status of actual production progress versus the master schedule is monitored. Physical progress towards completion of the task is considered **earned value**. The difference between earned value and the schedule is called **schedule variance**.

The costs incurred during production activity for each individual task are called **actual costs**. The difference between actual cost and standard cost is the **cost variance**.

Continually during the production process, as current schedule variance and cost variance data become available, managers can assess status and develop new **cost-to-complete (CTC)** estimates. The sum of past incurred costs plus the CTC becomes an updated projection of total cost at completion.

Managing the production process

The first formal step in the production process is the issuance by the Program Office of a **program directive** announcing the critical parameters of the program, including the essential performance and schedule requirements. The directive assigns specific responsibilities for various parts of the program and is distributed widely among the organization.

Upon receipt of the directive, Engineering begins work on design of the product. As the design begins to emerge, the Program Office develops a **make-or-buy plan** for all parts, material, and services that will be required to manufacture the product. As the make-or-buy plan takes shape, it is transmitted to Procurement, which will have responsibility for buying the purchased parts, material, and services. At the same time, Engineering furnishes Procurement with technical definition of the items to be bought. Procurement then establishes a **procurement plan** and begins buying activities by either negotiating prices or conducting competitive selection among suppliers, followed by issuing **purchase orders** to suppliers. The purchase orders include contractual terms, pricing, schedules, statements of work, and a technical data package.

Engineering transmits the technical definition package to Industrial Engineering. Following the guidance of the make-or-buy plan, Industrial Engineering begins work on detailed **shop floor instructions** that provide detailed step-by-step guidance for making each part of the product that will be produced in-house.

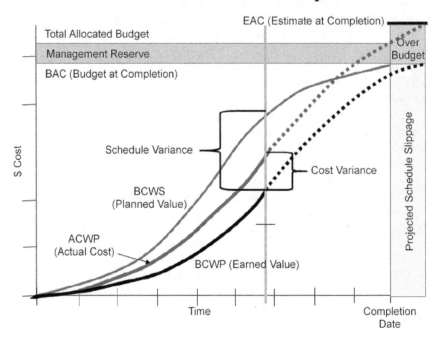

Earned Value Concept

ACWP = Actual Cost of Work Performed
BAC = Budget at Completion
BCWS = Budgeted Cost of Work Scheduled
BCWP = Budgeted Cost of Work Performed

Figure 10.10 Earned value management enables correlation of costs, schedule, budgets, and physical progress.

Source: Project Management Institute.

As Industrial Engineering prepares shop floor planning, it develops estimates of manhours required for each discrete manufacturing task. These estimates, known as **standard hours**, will be used as a standard for performance of the factory workforce. The standard hours estimates are transmitted to Cost Accounting.

Working in close collaboration with the Program Office, Engineering, Industrial Engineering, Procurement, and other critical functions, Production Control establishes a **master schedule** for production tasks.

Related to this effort, Industrial Engineering also creates **tooling designs** for the manufacturing operations, and designs the **factory lay-out**. The tool designs are sent to the Tooling department for fabrication, and the lay-out plans are sent to Facilities, which begins work preparing the physical manufacturing space. Industrial Engineering also develops a **manpower estimate** for the work to be performed and passes this estimate to Human Resources, which takes action to assure that sufficient manpower will be available, establishes a **hiring plan** if necessary, develops a **training plan**, and writes **syllabi** for training courses. Workers who have completed training and have received **certification** report to the factory for job assignments.

The Tooling department, after receiving designs from Industrial Engineering, fabricates **control tools** and **production tools**. After acceptance by Quality Assurance, the tools are transferred to the factory floor in accordance with the lay-out plan. Tooling also provides software customized for operation of numerically controlled machines involved in production.

As Quality Assurance receives released engineering and shop floor planning, it begins development of a **quality plan** to define overall quality processes for the program, including points for in-process inspections, first article inspections, and acceptance inspections.

Meanwhile, suppliers who have received purchase orders have begun work, and ship their completed parts and material either to the buyer's warehouse or directly to the assembly line in the factory. The warehouse, which has received a **kitting plan** from Industrial Engineering, assembles kits of parts and hardware for individual production units and transfers them to the factory.

As trained manpower, material, tooling, shop floor instructions, and the schedule become available in the factory, Production Control begins to release **shop orders** that launch discrete manufacturing tasks in the factory. The ongoing flow of incomplete tasks in the factory is known as **work-in-process (WIP)**.

As work proceeds in the factory, labor hours spent on each manufacturing task are recorded. The records of these hours, known as **actual hours**, are transmitted to Cost Accounting, where they are compared with standard hours, and positive or negative variances are calculated. Cost records and variances are reported regularly to the Program Office.

As individual production items are completed, they undergo final acceptance inspection by Quality Assurance. If the customer has a quality representative at the factory, the production item may also undergo a customer inspection and acceptance process. After acceptance is complete, the item is formally delivered to the customer.

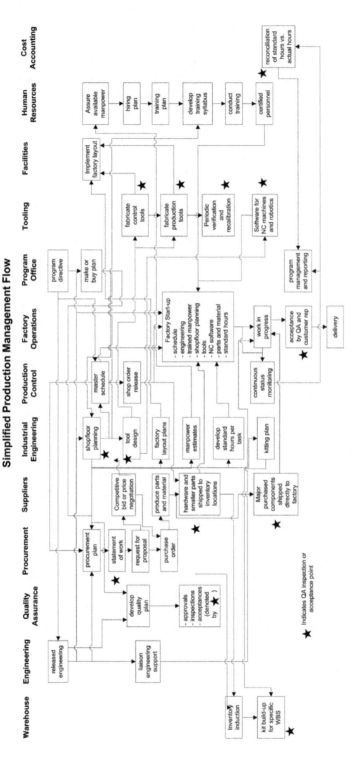

Figure 10.11 Production management is a highly structured and disciplined process.

Conclusion

Aerospace production technology has advanced exponentially during more than a century of the industry's existence, and techniques for managing production have evolved accordingly. In spite of these changes, the fundamental constants remain, and today's managers strive towards many of the same objectives as their predecessors at the beginning of the last century: efficiency, cost control, repeatability, visibility, quality, and overall customer satisfaction. In the years to come the industry will continue to experiment with new technologies and management methods, but these constant objectives will certainly remain.

11 Management of aerospace quality assurance

Cost of quality

In most industries the cost of quality is a financial optimization concept that balances the cost of making a high-quality product versus the cost of poor quality that can result in consequences such as irritated customers. The cost of low quality in aerospace is far higher than in typical industries. Consequences of mistakes in design or manufacturing are potentially catastrophic in terms of human mortality and financial loss.

Aerospace is among a small group of industries (including, for example, nuclear-power generation, manufacturers of medical devices, pharmaceuticals, and submarines) that strive to build the highest quality product possible, regardless of the cost.

Cost of Quality – Traditional Industry

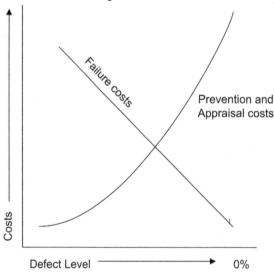

Figure 11.1 For traditional industries, cost of quality is a simple economic calculation.

A fundamental concept of the aerospace industry is that product quality is assured by designing and building quality into the product in the first place, rather than depending on inspection to catch substandard products. In other words, primary responsibility for a quality product belongs to production workers, supply-chain managers, and senior management, rather than quality-control inspectors.

A corollary of this philosophy is that the only cost-effective strategy for improving the quality of the product is to raise the standard of production work in the factory rather than intensify inspection and surveillance. This is accomplished by eliminating significant variations in the production process and by establishing production processes that are capable of producing within required specifications.

This mentality has been repeatedly demonstrated in the modern aerospace industry. In 2019 Boeing's commercial aircraft production unit announced that it intended to eliminate 450 jobs for quality inspectors despite increasing production rates. The initiative, called 'Quality Transformation' by Boeing, involved changing the design of parts to make them easier to build correctly, adjusting the sequence of work to make assembly simpler, and adding tools and automation to ease the jobs of assembly workers. These built-in efficiencies and fail-safe features in the factory were intended to raise the level of production quality and reduce the number of inspections required.

The new features included, for example:

- Wirelessly connected torque wrenches that automatically verified the torque values and sequence of operations during tightening of fittings on hydraulic lines
- Redesign of electrical connectors that prevented misaligned connections of wire harnesses

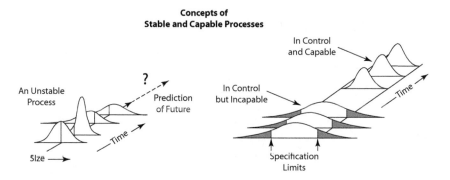

Figure 11.2 Effective manufacturing processes produce results with minimal variation and within specifications.

Source: Defense Manufacturing Management Guide.

- Robot drilling machines that automatically recorded hole locations and dimensions
- Replacement of manual feeler gauges with electronic gap-measuring tools that automatically recorded data as they measured gaps

FAA regulatory requirements for inspection of airplane-manufacturing work have not changed to accommodate initiatives that replace manual inspection by automatic data recording and task control on the factory floor. Manufacturers

Cost of Quality – Aerospace Industry

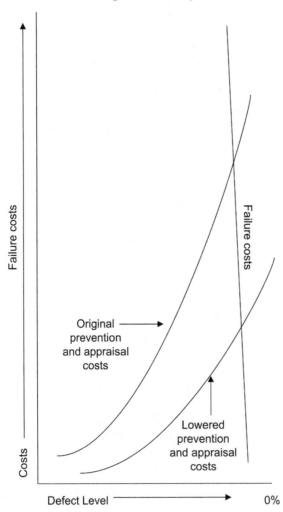

Figure 11.3 In the aerospace industry poor quality has extreme economic and moral costs.

Table 11.1 NASA's series of failures seriously impaired its reputation for excellence

NASA mission losses caused by parts failures 2009–2015

Mission	Orbiting Carbon Observatrory[1]	Glory[2]	Orbital ATK Commercial Resupply[3]	SpaceX Commercial Resupply[4]	Soil Moisture Active Passive[6]
Date	24 Feb 2009	4 Mar 2011	28 Oct 2014	28 June 2015	7 July 2015
Failed part	Payload fairing	Payload fairing	Liquid oxygen turbopump	Support strut	Radar power supply
Cost	$209 million	$388 million	$51 million	$118 million[5]	$550 million

Source: NASA Office of Inspector General evaluation of reported mishaps.
Notes:
[1] Mission was to provide space-based observations of atmospheric carbon dioxide.
[2] Mission was to collect data on human-caused aerosols in Earth's atmosphere.
[3] Lost about 5,000 lb. of supplies, science experiments, crew provisions, and spare parts.
[4] Lost more than 5,300 lb. of hardware, including an International Docking Adapter, crew supplies, and critical materials to support research investigations.
[5] Only includes cost of cargo and excludes NASA's launch vehicle costs.
[6] Mission had reduced capability to provide measurements of Earth's soil moisture and freeze/thaw state.

remain fully responsible for conducting inspections and verifying compliance to standards, but are permitted to change methods to accomplish this verification.

As an illustration of consequences of poor quality, the National Aeronautics and Space Administration (NASA) lost investments in equipment of more than $1 billion from 2009 to 2015 because of a series of five separate mission failures attributable to bad parts. This series of quality shortcomings undermined NASA's reputation as a quality leader in the industry and resulted in a series of government investigations and audits that found an erosion of the agency's culture of excellence.

Historically, the industry's method of assuring the quality of its products has been to establish written procedures governing every aspect of work performed, to rigorously enforce compliance with the procedures, and to frequently inspect and test the product during its production process and at time of delivery. The procedures also dictate measures for accountability, traceability, and documentation of critical parts.

Evolution of modern aerospace quality standards

Earlier in the history of the industry, quality standards had primarily been dictated by customers, particularly the US Department of Defense (DoD). Principal US military specifications were *MIL-Q-9858, Quality Program Requirements*, pertaining to supplier quality and dating from the 1950s, and *MIL-I-45208A, Military Specification: Inspection System Requirements*, pertaining to inspection practices. In the absence of an internationally recognized industry standard, individual firms began to implement the DoD standards and to mutually recognize the standards of other firms that had also embraced the same requirements. However, individual firms often superimposed their own tailored quality requirements on the DoD standards, with the result that a cacophony of similar but slightly different standards emerged in the industry, burdening the firms with additional time, effort, and cost as they did business with one another.

To address this problem of non-productive duplication of effort, the International Organization for Standardization (ISO), a Geneva-based international standard-setting body composed of representatives from various national standards organizations, published in 1987 the **ISO 9000** standard, named *Quality Management Systems*. ISO 9000 encompasses a family of quality systems and includes **ISO 9001**, which addresses requirements that must be met by organizations attempting to meet the standard.

In support of this international initiative towards standardization, in 1995 the Defense Department canceled MIL-Q-9858 and designated ISO 9001 as the quality system of choice for its suppliers, replacing MIL-Q-9858. Thereafter, the major aerospace companies began requiring their suppliers to institute quality programs in compliance with ISO 9001.

As the industry implemented ISO 9001 many of the leading firms found that the standard did not completely address requirements demanded by their customers and regulators, including DoD, NASA, FAA, and commercial entities. To deal with the shortcomings they added their own supplements, such as Boeing's D1-9000 or the automotive Q standard. As this collection of dissimilar addenda to ISO 9001 grew, industry suppliers found themselves again confronted with a body of dissimilar standards that defeated the fundamental objective of the standardization movement.

To address the inadequacies of ISO 9001 for aerospace, the principal American aerospace corporations created the American Aerospace Quality Group (AAQG) and began collaborating to develop a new standard. Participants in this collaboration effort included Allied-Signal, Allison Engine Company, Boeing, General Electric Aircraft Engines, Lockheed Martin. McDonnell Douglas, Northrop Grumman, Pratt & Whitney, Rockwell Collins, Sikorsky Aircraft, and Hamilton Sundstrand. The product of this effort was *AS 9000, Aerospace Basic Quality System Standard*. The new standard, which was eventually released in 1997 under the auspices of the Society of Automotive Engineers (SAE), was based on ISO 9000 and was largely modeled after Boeing's D1-9000 standard. It contained dozens of additional standards of particular pertinence to the aerospace industry. AS 9000 quickly became the de facto quality standard for the industry in the United States. In an initiative to establish AS 9000 as an international standard, in 1998 SAE founded the International Aerospace Quality Group (IAQG) as an internal working group.

The product of this international collaboration effort was **AS 9100**, formally named *Quality Management Systems – Requirements for Aviation, Space and Defense Organizations*, which replaced AS 9000. The original version was simultaneously released in October 1999 by the Society of Automotive Engineers in the United States and by the European Association of Aerospace Industries.

IAQG eventually became an independent association registered under Belgian law in 2013. The entity is sponsored by SAE of the United States, the Aerospace and Defence Industries Association of Europe (ASD), and the Society of Japanese Aerospace Companies (SJAC). To reflect its international sponsorship, IAQG consists of three components:

- American Aerospace Quality Group (AAQG), encompassing North, Central, and South America
- European Aerospace Quality Group (EAQG), encompassing Europe, the Middle East, Russia, and Africa
- Asia-Pacific Aerospace Quality Group (APAQG), encompassing Asia and Oceania

Today the AS 9100 standard has gained worldwide recognition, and is known as EN 9100 in Europe and JISQ 9100 in Japan. It has become the operative standard for major aeronautics manufacturers including Airbus, Boeing, General Electric Aero Engines, and Rolls-Royce.

The pertinent international quality standards currently applicable to the aerospace industry are:

- *AS/EN 9110 Quality Management Systems – Requirements for Aviation Maintenance Organizations*
- *AS/EN 9120 Quality Management Systems – Requirements for Aviation, Space and Defense Distributors*
- *ISO 9000 Quality Management Systems – Fundamentals and Vocabulary*
- *ISO 9001 Quality management systems – Requirements*
- *ISO 90042 Managing for the Sustained Success of an Organization – A Quality Management Approach*
- *ISO 10007 Quality management systems – Guidelines for Configuration Management*
- *ISO 19011 Guidelines for Quality and/or Environmental Management Systems Auditing*

Of these, the standard of most relevance to the aerospace industry is AS 9100, which over the period of its existence has been revised, strengthened, and expanded several times. Revision D to AS 9100 and its equivalents was released in 2016.

All of the International Aerospace Quality Group's international standards are available through the organization's website at: www.sae.org/iaqg/.

Overview of the AS 9100/EN 9100/JISQ 9100 International Quality Standard

As noted previously, the three standards are effectively identical, and are issued by the three standards bodies with jurisdiction over three geographical areas. The standards bodies are, respectively, American Aerospace Quality Group

(AAQG), European Aerospace Quality Group (EAQG), and Asia-Pacific Aerospace Quality Group (APAQG). For purposes of simplicity in this chapter, the three standards will collectively be referred to as AS 9100.

The many additional requirements that AS 9100 imposes on the ISO 9001 framework reflect the specialized nature of the aerospace industry and its exceptional emphasis on control and record-keeping. Examples of these additional requirements include:

- Control and retention of records created by suppliers
- Maintenance of configuration management throughout the design verification and validation process
- Design review authorization for progression to next stage
- Control of testing processes and records of results
- Approval by customers and regulatory authorities of design changes
- Rights of access by organizations, customers, and regulatory authorities to supplier facilities and records as applicable
- Requirements for suppliers to flow down requirements to subtier suppliers
- Evidence of completion of all production and inspection and verification operations
- Provision for tooling, utilities, and removal of foreign objects
- First article inspection
- Control of equipment, tooling, and software programs
- Planning for critical items and process control of key characteristics
- Positive recall processes for non-conforming product
- Documentation of inspection plans, instructions, measuring instruments, and records to provide evidence of product qualification
- Documentation requirements for product at time of delivery
- Processes for approval of personnel who disposition non-conforming product
- Restrictions on use-as-is or repair dispositions
- Requirements for scrap marking and disposal
- Timely reporting of non-conforming product to other parties
- Flow down of corrective action to suppliers
- Determination of whether additional non-conformities exist based on causes found

For individual firms, the framework for managing quality internally is the **quality management system (QMS)**. The QMS is highly structured and is customized to reflect the specific needs and operating environment of each firm. It is defined in a formalized document known as a **quality manual**. The creation and documentation of a QMS is a principal requirement of AS 9100.

The main elements of the QMS are:

- Identification of the processes required for the quality management system, with a description of how the processes will be applied throughout the organization

- Definition of the sequence and interaction of these processes
- Determination of criteria and methods to ensure that the operation and control of these processes will be effective
- Establishment of controls to ensure the availability of resources and information necessary to support the operation and monitoring of these processes
- Creation of procedures to ensure that the processes will be monitored, measured, and analyzed
- Implementation of actions necessary to achieve planned results and continual improvement of the processes

In addition to providing a system for control of the company's internal processes, the QMS must also ensure control over any process that is outsourced to suppliers by defining procedures for supplier quality management.

An essential element of the QMS is thorough documentation, consisting of at least the following components:

- Statements of the company's quality policy and quality objectives
- The company's customized quality manual, which describes the scope of the quality management system, enumerates the documented procedures encompassed by the system, and describes the interaction between the system processes
- A list of documents, including procedures and records determined by the organization to be necessary to ensure the effective planning, operation, and control of its processes

Because control of documents is so essential to the effectiveness of any quality system, the QMS invariably includes detailed procedures stipulating how documents will be managed and controlled. Document control procedures include the following elements:

- Approval of documents for adequacy prior to issue
- Systematic review and update of documents, with current revision status affixed
- Measures to ensure that applicable documents are available at points of use
- Identification and distribution of documents of external origin determined to be necessary for the quality management system
- Systematic cancelation and deletion of obsolete documents

Records serve the important purpose of providing evidence of conformity to requirements and of the effective operation of the quality management system. In the event that quality non-conformities are eventually detected, historical records also provide a means of tracing procedural failings. Control of records is an important part of document control. Record control involves establishing a documented procedure for the identification, storage, protection,

Quality Management System

AS 9100 Process Flow Chart

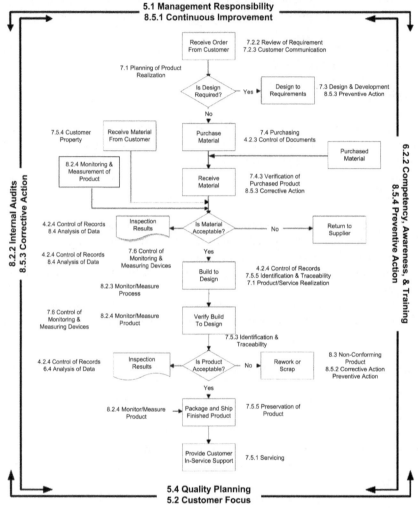

Reference Numbers Refer to AS 9100 Chapters and Sections

Figure 11.4 This generic chart depicts processes and controls of a quality system following the AS 9100 standard. Quality systems for individual organizations will vary to reflect the individual nature of their business.

retrieval, retention and disposition of records, including records that are created by suppliers.

Obviously, no quality system can be effective unless it has the active support of management of the enterprise. In recognition of this reality, the AS 9100

Hierarchy of Quality Documentation

QMS=Quality Management System

Figure 11.5 Documentation is a fundamental element of every quality management system.

standard requires senior management to demonstrate their commitment to the development and implementation of the quality management system through specific actions, including:

- Communicating to the organization the importance of meeting customer requirements and complying with statutory and regulatory obligations
- Defining responsibilities and authorities within the organization and clearly communicating this information to management and the workforce
- Establishing the **quality policy**. Senior management is responsible for establishing a quality policy that is appropriate for the purpose of the organization and includes mechanisms to ensure compliance. The quality policy provides a framework for establishing and reviewing quality objectives. It should be communicated and understood within the organization and continuously reviewed for suitability to reflect the changing needs of the organization.
- Ensuring that **quality objectives** are established and disseminated throughout the organization. The objectives should be tailored for each level and function of the organization to correspond with the specific responsibilities of organizational units. The quality objectives should be measurable and should align with the quality policy.

- Conducting **management reviews**. At regular intervals, senior management should review the organization's quality management system to assess its continued effectiveness. Opportunities for improvement should be solicited and assessed. The agenda for reviews should include:
  - Results of audits
  - Customer feedback
  - Process performance and product conformity
  - Status of preventive and corrective actions
  - Follow-up actions from previous management reviews
  - Changes that could affect the quality management system
  - Recommendations for improvement
  - Resources needed
- Ensuring the availability of resources adequate to implement the quality system
- Designating a manager with responsibility and authority to:
  - Ensure that processes needed for the quality management system are established, implemented, and maintained
  - Report to top management on the performance of the quality management system and any need for improvement
  - Ensure the promotion of awareness of customer requirements throughout the organization
  - Operate with unrestricted access to top management to resolve quality management issues
  - Communicate and conduct business with external parties on matters relating to the quality management system

The quality management system requires **resources** in order to function. It is the responsibility of senior management to ensure that resources of appropriate quantity and quality are made available to perform the task.

The principal resources required are:

- **People**, in sufficient quantity and with appropriate education, training, skills, and experience
- **Infrastructure**, such as buildings, workspace, and associated utilities; process equipment and software; and supporting services such as transport, communication, or information systems. These resources must be supported, maintained, and updated as necessary to respond to product requirements
- **Work environment** suitable for performing the job

Product realization is the term used to describe the work of the organization to develop, manufacture, and deliver the finished goods or services. In many ways this is the core function of the enterprise, and the organization must plan and develop processes to govern these activities. Planning of product

Table 11.2 FAA requirements for suitably trained technicians are reflected in AS9100. This example shows requirements for non-destructive inspection (NDI) technicians

Minimum classroom training and experience requirements non-destructive inspection

NDI method	Levels			
	Classroom instructions (hr)		*Experience (hr/mo)*	
	Level I	*Level II*	*Level I*	*Level II*
Eddy-current	40	40	480/3 mo	1,440/9 mo
Ultrasonic	40	40	480/3 mo	1,440/9 mo
Magnetic particle	16	16	160/1 mo	480/3 mo
Penetrant	16	16	160/1 mo	480/3 mo
Radiography	40	40	480/3 mo	1440/9 mo
Thermography/infrared	40	40	210 hr	1260 hr
Other	40	40	480/3 mo	1440/9 mo

Source: FAA Advisory Circular 65-31B.

realization should align with the requirements of the other processes of the quality management system. The organization should create a **quality plan** that identifies and defines essential elements to be addressed:

- Quality objectives and requirements for the product, including:
  - Safety
  - Reliability, availability, and maintainability
  - Producibility and access for inspection
  - Suitability of parts and materials
  - Selection and development of embedded software
  - Recycling or final disposal of the product at the end of its life
- The need to establish processes and documents, and to provide resources specific to the product
- Required verification, validation, monitoring, measurement, inspection, and test activities specific to the product and the criteria for product acceptance
- Records needed to provide evidence that the realization processes and resulting product meet requirements
- Configuration management appropriate to the product
- Resources to support the use and maintenance of the product

The organization should establish a **risk management** process addressing the accomplishment of applicable requirements, including:

- Assignment of responsibilities for risk management
- Definition of likelihood and consequences of known risk factors
- Identification, assessment, and communication of risks throughout product realization
- Identification of action to mitigate
- Identification of known risks considered to be acceptable

A **configuration management** process should be implemented, including:

- Configuration management planning
- Configuration identification
- Change control
- Configuration status accounting
- Configuration audits

A process for control of **work transfers** should be established to plan and control temporary or permanent transfers of work, such as from one internal facility to another, from the internal facility to a supplier, or from one supplier to another. The process should provide for verification of the quality of the product after the transfer.

During every aspect of the product realization process, the organization should remain cognizant of **customer requirements**, including the requirements for delivery and postdelivery activities such as the fulfillment of warranty provisions, contractual obligations such as maintenance services, and supplementary services such as recycling or final disposal. In addition to customer requirements, requirements by government agencies and regulatory authorities should be understood and disseminated within the organization.

A **requirements review** related to the product should be conducted before the organization commits to supply a product to the customer. This review should verify that:

- Product requirements are defined
- Changes to earlier contracts or orders are resolved
- The organization is able to meet the defined requirements
- Special requirements of the product are identified
- Risks have been identified

Results of the review should be documented and records should be maintained. If customer requirements are vague or undefined, the organization should document its internal interpretation of the requirements and should present that interpretation to the customer for formal confirmation.

In the earliest stages of **design and development planning** the organization should define:

- Specific stages of the design and development process
- Review, verification, and validation actions appropriate for each design and development step
- Assignment of organizational responsibilities and authorities for design and development

To facilitate management control, the design and development effort should be divided into incremental activities. For each activity, the individual tasks, necessary resources, responsibilities, design content, input and output data, and planning constraints should be defined. Design and development planning should consider activities required to produce, inspect, test, and maintain the product. Interfaces between different organizational groups should be coordinated to ensure effective communication and unambiguous assignment of responsibility. As design and development progress, planning should be updated and communicated within the organization.

Inputs relating to product requirements should be determined during the design process and records should be kept. Inputs typically include functional and performance requirements, applicable statutory and regulatory requirements, and information derived from previous similar designs.

The format of the outputs of design and development should be structured to enable verification against the design and development input. All output should be reviewed and approved by appropriate levels of management prior to release. Design and development outputs should:

- Meet the input requirements for design and development
- Provide appropriate information for purchasing, production, and service provision
- Contain or reference product acceptance criteria
- Specify the characteristics of the product that are essential for its safe and proper use
- Specify any critical items, including any key characteristics, and specific actions to be taken for these items

Data requirements to enable the product to be identified, manufactured, inspected, used, and maintained should be defined. Data requirements typically include engineering drawings, digital datasets, parts lists, technical specifications, material specifications, and process specifications.

Design and development reviews should be held at appropriate milestones as activities advance, and formal records should be kept. The agendas should include:

- Evaluation of the current status of the design and development effort towards meeting requirements
- Identification of problems and proposed recovery plans
- Formal management authorization to advance to the next stage

As the design and development efforts approach completion, a **design and development verification** should take place to confirm that the design and development outputs have met the design and development input requirements. Records of the results of the verification should be kept.

A scheduled **Design and Development Validation** should be performed to ensure that the resulting product is capable of meeting the requirements for the specified application or intended use. If possible, validation should take place prior to delivery. Records should be kept.

Changes that occur during the design and development process should be rigorously controlled and recorded. No changes should be implemented until they have been reviewed and approved in compliance with formal procedures. All changes should be controlled in compliance with the configuration management process.

The purpose of the **purchasing process** is to ensure that purchased items conform to specifications and requirements. Not all purchased items are equally critical to the integrity of the final product, and the type and extent of control applied to the supplier should be commensurate with the importance of the purchased item. Critical items should be managed intensively. The organization is responsible for the conformity of all purchased items, including items from suppliers designated by the customer. The organization should establish criteria for selection and evaluation of suppliers in order to enable choice of suppliers based on their ability to supply product in accordance with the organization's requirements. The basis for each individual supplier selection should be documented and records should be kept. As part of its supplier selection process, the organization should:

- Maintain a register of suppliers, indicating whether they have been approved or disapproved, and noting the scope and type of any approvals
- Periodically review supplier performance, with the objective of determining the level of controls to be implemented for individual suppliers
- Define the corrective actions to be taken when suppliers fail to meet requirements
- Ensure that customer-approved special process sources are used by the internal organization and all suppliers, when required
- Clearly define the process, responsibilities, and authority for approvals of supplier status, and delineate how suppliers may be utilized depending on their specific approved status
- Evaluate and manage risk when suppliers are selected and when they deliver product

Comprehensive and precise **purchasing information** should be developed to describe the product to be purchased. This information should include:

- Requirements for approval of product, procedures, processes, and equipment
- Requirements for the qualification of personnel
- Quality management system requirements
- Identification and revision status of specifications, drawings, process requirements, inspection and verification instructions, and other relevant technical data

Supplier Management Process
Representative Quality Manual Depiction

Forecast Planning, Supplier Selection & Procurement

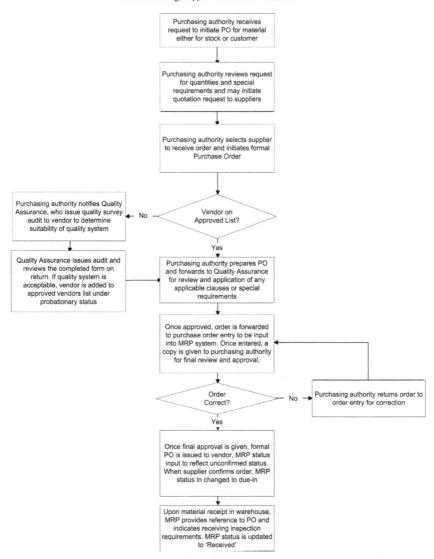

Figure 11.6 A typical process for selecting and managing suppliers in compliance with AS 9100.

- Requirements for design, test, inspection, verification, use of statistical techniques for product acceptance and related instructions for acceptance by the organization, and treatment of critical items
- Requirements for test specimens for design approval, inspection, verification, and auditing
- Requirements regarding the need for the supplier to:
  - Notify the organization of non-conforming product
  - Obtain organization approval for disposition of non-conforming product
  - Notify the organization of changes in product or process, changes of suppliers, and changes of manufacturing facility
  - Flow down to the supply chain the applicable requirements including customer requirements
- Records retention requirements
- Right of access to the supplier's records and physical facilities by the procuring organization, the final customer, and regulatory authorities

A system of **verification** is necessary to ensure that purchased items meet specified purchase requirements. To accomplish this, the organization should implement measures including systematic **inspection** and other appropriate actions. Regardless of previous inspections and verifications performed at other points in the supply chain, the buyer has ultimate responsibility for the quality of the product and should not rely entirely on reports from external entities. Verification activities may include:

- Review of objective evidence of the conformity of the product from the supplier, such as accompanying documentation, certificates of conformity, test records, statistical records, and process control records
- Inspection and audit at the supplier's premises
- Review of the required documentation
- Receiving inspection
- Supplier certification or delegation of verification to the supplier

Sometimes purchased items are conditionally released for production use before all required verification activities have been completed. In this case, the unverified items must be clearly identified and records should be kept to allow recall and replacement if the subsequent verification process determines that the items do not comply with requirements.

Sometimes the buyer delegates verification to the supplier. In this case the requirements for **delegation** should be defined and a register of delegations should be maintained. If the buyer or its customer intends to perform verification at the supplier's premises, the buyer's purchasing documents should communicate in advance the intended verification arrangements.

The organization should plan and perform production and services under **controlled conditions**. The elements that provide the constraints for this control include:

- Information that describes the characteristics of the product, such as drawings, parts lists, materials, and process specifications
- Work instructions, as necessary, including process flow charts, inspection documents, and production documents such as manufacturing plans, travelers, routers, work orders, and process cards
- The use of defined equipment and media such as software and product-specific tools, including jigs, fixtures, and molds
- The use of monitoring and measuring equipment
- The implementation of product release, delivery, and postdelivery activities
- Accountability for all product during production
- Evidence that all production and inspection operations have been completed as planned, or have acquired another status that is documented and authorized
- Provision for the prevention, detection, and removal of foreign objects
- Monitoring and control of utilities and supplies such as water, compressed air, electricity, and chemical products
- Criteria for workmanship, such as written standards, representative samples, and illustrations

Effective control should be incorporated into the planning process, to include:

- Establishing, implementing, and maintaining appropriate processes to manage **critical items**
- Designing, manufacturing, and using tooling to measure variable data
- Identifying in-process inspection or verification points when adequate verification of conformance cannot be performed at later stages of realization
- Special processes

First article inspection, also known as **production process verification**, is a procedure in which a representative item from the first production run of a new part or assembly is intensely inspected to verify that the production processes, production documentation, and tooling are effective in producing parts and assemblies that meet requirements. A new first article inspection should be performed each time significant design or production changes affecting the production article occur.

A procedure for **control of production process changes** should be established by the enterprise. Changes affecting processes, production equipment, tools, or software programs should be controlled and documented, and personnel authorized to approve changes to production processes should be designated.

A procedure should be implemented to ensure that production equipment, manufacturing software, and tools are validated prior to release for production.

Requirements should be defined for storage of production equipment and tooling.

Postdelivery support procedures should include:

- Collection and analysis of in-service data
- Actions to be taken, including investigation and reporting, when problems are detected after delivery
- Control and updating of technical documentation
- Approval, control, and use of repair processes
- Controls required for off-site activities

A procedure for **identification and traceability** should be established, enabling identification of the product by suitable means throughout product realization, and any departures from design configuration should be recorded. If traceability is a requirement, the unique identification of the product should be tracked and records kept. In the design of some systems, the configuration management subsystem is the means by which identification and traceability are maintained.

The organization has responsibility for management and protection of **customer property** while it is under the organization's control. Procedures should be implemented to identify, verify, protect, and safeguard customer property provided for use or incorporation into the product. Intellectual property and personal data should be considered to be elements of customer property.

During internal processing and delivery to the intended destination, the product should be appropriately preserved, including identification marking, handling, packaging, storage, and protection. Depending on applicable product specifications and statutory and regulatory requirements, **preservation of the product** also includes:

- Cleaning
- Prevention, detection, and removal of foreign objects
- Special handling for sensitive products
- Marking and labeling, including safety warnings
- Shelf-life control and stock rotation
- Special handling for hazardous materials

In order to determine the conformity of the product, the organization should define necessary monitoring and measurement to be undertaken and should identify the equipment necessary to perform the tasks. A register of the **monitoring and measuring equipment** should be maintained, and the processes necessary for their **calibration and verification** should be defined, including details of equipment type, unique identification, location, frequency of checks, check methods, and acceptance criteria. Monitoring and measuring equipment includes test hardware, test software, automated test equipment (ATE) and plotters used to produce inspection data. It may also include customer-supplied equipment. Processes governing the use of monitoring and measurement equipment should be established. To ensure valid results, measuring equipment should:

- Be calibrated or verified prior to use or at specified intervals, and records should be kept
- Be adjusted as necessary to ensure accuracy
- Be marked with identification sufficient to determine its calibration status
- Be safeguarded from unauthorized adjustments
- Be protected from damage

A process should be established for the recall of monitoring and measuring equipment requiring calibration or verification. If the equipment is found not to conform to requirements the organization should assess and record the validity of the previous measuring results. Calibration records should be kept.

A plan for **monitoring, measurement, analysis, and improvement** is an important part of any quality management system. The processes included in the plan should produce the following results:

- Demonstrate conformity to product requirements
- Ensure conformity of the quality management system
- Continually improve the effectiveness of the quality management system

The plan should designate the applicable methods to be used, including statistical techniques. Depending on circumstances, nature of the product, and specified requirements, statistical techniques can be used to support:

- Design verification, including reliability, maintainability, and safety
- Process control
- Selection and inspection of key characteristics
- Process capability measurements
- Statistical process control
- Design of experiment
- Inspection
- Failure-mode, effect, and criticality analysis

An important indication of the performance of the quality management system is customer perception as to whether the organization has met customer requirements. The organization should develop methods for obtaining and using information pertaining to **customer satisfaction**. Information to be used for the evaluation of customer satisfaction should include product non-conformity rates, on-time delivery performance, customer complaints, corrective action requests, and survey results. A customer-satisfaction plan should be developed to address deficiencies identified by these evaluations and to assess the effectiveness of the results.

Control of Monitoring and Measurement Equipment
Representative Quality Manual Depiction

Control of Monitoring and Measurement Equipment

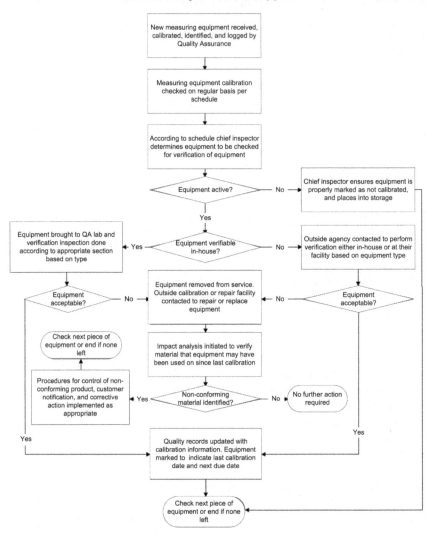

Figure 11.7 A typical process for control of monitoring and measurement equipment in compliance with AS 9100.

Internal audits should be conducted at planned intervals to determine if the actual activities of the enterprise comply with its quality management system and with the AS 9100 standard. The audit program should direct attention to areas to be audited in proportion to the importance of the processes and areas. The audit plan should also consider the results of previous audits. The audit criteria, scope, frequency, and methods should be defined. Impartiality of the audit process is essential, and selection of auditors and implementation of audits should be handled in a way to ensure objectivity. Responsibilities and requirements for planning and conducting audits, establishing records, and reporting results should be defined in accordance with an established procedure. Every audit should result in a formal written record. Following the audit, corrective action should be taken promptly and follow-up verification should be planned.

Monitoring and measurement of processes of the quality management system should take place continuously, and the organization should develop suitable methods for performing the task. The purpose of the methods is to demonstrate the ability of the processes to achieve planned results. When analysis indicates that planned results are not achieved, corrective action should be taken. If process non-conformities are discovered, the organization should:

- Take appropriate action to correct the non-conforming process
- Evaluate whether the process non-conformity has resulted in product non-conformity
- Determine if the process non-conformity is limited to a specific case or whether it could have affected other processes or products
- Identify and control any non-conforming product

To verify that product requirements have been met, procedures should be established for **monitoring and measurement of the product**. This should be performed continuously throughout the product realization process in accordance with the planned arrangements. Evidence and records of conformity with the acceptance criteria should be maintained. Exact documented requirements for product acceptance should include:

- Criteria for acceptance and/or rejection
- Definition of the point in the sequence where measurement and testing operations are to be performed, and required records of the measurement results
- Any specific measurement instruments required and any specific instructions associated with their use

Critical items, including key characteristics, should be identified by the organization, and procedures should be established to ensure that they are controlled and monitored in accordance with the established processes. If sampling is used as a means of product acceptance, the sampling plan should comply with recognized statistical principles that are appropriate for the circumstances.

Product Verification
Example of an Airbus Production Flight Test Profile

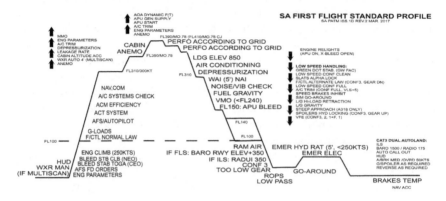

Figure 11.8 Flight tests are a unique aerospace verification process. This test profile is from Airbus.

Source: Airbus.

The rigor of the sampling plan should correspond to the criticality of the product and to the process capability. If items are released for production prior to completion of all required measurement and monitoring activities, they should be identified and recorded to allow recall and replacement if it is subsequently found that the product does not meet requirements. Records should identify the person authorizing the release of products for delivery to the customer. The product should not be released to the customer unless all defined requirements are met, except in exceptional circumstances that are well documented and approved by management. Records should provide evidence that the product meets the defined requirements. All documents necessary to demonstrate verification of the product should be present at delivery.

A process for **control of non-conforming product** should ensure that product that does not conform to product requirements is identified and controlled to prevent its unintended use or delivery. Controls and related responsibilities and authorities for dealing with non-conforming product should be specified in a documented procedure. Responsibility and authority for the review and disposition of non-conforming product should be defined in the organization's documented procedures.

The organization should address non-conforming product in the following ways:

- By taking action to eliminate the detected non-conformity
- By authorizing its use, release, or acceptance under concession by a relevant authority and, where applicable, by the customer

- By taking action to preclude its original intended use or application
- By taking action appropriate to the effects, or potential effects, of the non-conformity when non-conforming product is detected after delivery or use has started

Notification of non-conforming product should be provided in a timely manner to suppliers, internal organizations, customers, distributors, and regulatory authorities, as appropriate. Prompt action is important in order to contain the effect of the non-conformity on other processes or products.

Only an authorized representative of the organization responsible for design of the product should be able to approve a disposition of **use-as-is** or repair. If the non-conformity results in a departure from the contract requirements, the organization should not use dispositions of use-as-is or repair unless specifically authorized by the customer. If an item is dispositioned for scrap it should be conspicuously and permanently marked accordingly.

The process for disposition of non-conformances

If an item fails inspection, it enters a very specific process to determine how it will be handled, known as the **disposition of non-conformances** process. Outcomes of the process vary depending upon the nature and seriousness of the non-conformance.

- The first step in the process occurs when production presents the item to a quality inspector.
- Upon examination, the inspector has two alternatives. The part can be accepted to be delivered or continue in the production flow, or it can be rejected.
- In the event of rejection, the inspector prepares a **non-conformance report (NCR)** that details the nature of the discrepancy that caused the rejection.
- The non-conformance report is passed to a liaison engineer, who is a specialized member of the Engineering department stationed on the factory floor for the purpose of dealing with production problems as they arise. When the liaison engineer receives the NCR and studies the circumstances of the non-conformance, he or she has several choices:
  - The item can be judged to be irreparably defective, in which case it is condemned and the NCR disposition notes that the part must be scrapped.
  - Alternatively, the production defect may be minor in nature, and the engineer may declare a **use-as-is disposition**. At that point the item reenters the production flow.
  - Another alternative is that the engineer may determine that the part can be used if it undergoes a relatively simple **standard rework** procedure.

- The final alternative is that the liaison engineer may decide that determination of disposition of the non-conformance requires further technical analysis and expertise. In this case the NCR is elevated to the **material review board (MRB)** for further study.

The material review board, which consists of representatives from Engineering, Quality Assurance, Contracts, and the Program Office, calls upon specialized expertise to study the non-conformance, and may initiate further special testing as required. When sufficient analytical data is available, the MRB can choose among three alternative courses for disposition of the item:

- The MRB can rule to condemn the item, in which case the factory is directed to scrap it.
- A second alternative is to fix the item to restore it to conformity by means of a special rework. In this case, Industrial Engineering is directed to write shop-floor instructions to accomplish the rework. The instructions are passed to the factory, where the rework is performed, and the item reenters the production flow.
- In a third alternative, the MRB determines that there is no way the item can be reworked to make it comply with design engineering, but the board believes that the item can be used in the assembly of the final product without compromising the integrity, performance, or safety of the final product. In this case, the MRB sometimes takes the course of directing the Contracts department to contact the customer with a request for a contractual deviation or waiver. If the customer refuses to grant the request, the item is scrapped. If the request is approved, contractual language authorizing the deviation or waiver is prepared, and the factory is authorized to use the item. Almost always, deviations and waivers entail a financial penalty paid by the manufacturer to the customer. For this reason, they are rarely requested unless the value of the non-conforming item is sufficiently high to justify the cost and complications of the procedure. The subject of deviations and waivers is discussed further in Chapter 8.

Continual improvement

The **continual improvement** of the effectiveness of the quality management system should be established as an organizational objective to be accomplished through the use of the quality policy, quality objectives, audit results, analysis of data, corrective and preventive actions, and management review. Implementation of improvement activities should be monitored and evaluated for effectiveness. Potential opportunities for continual improvement initiatives can result from lessons learned, resolution of past problems, and benchmarking of best practices.

Collection and **analysis of data** is essential to demonstrate the suitability and effectiveness of the quality management system. It enables the organization

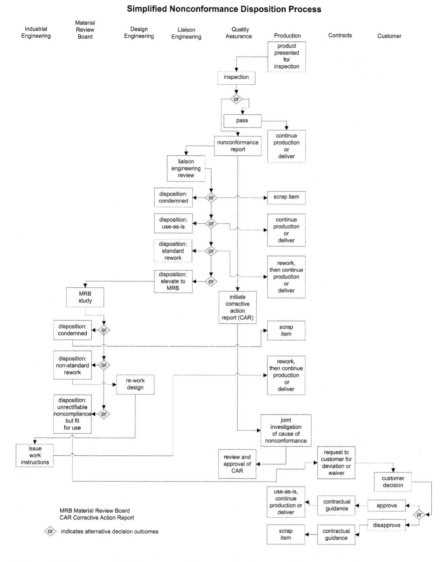

Figure 11.9 An example of a process for control of non-conforming product.

to identify where continual improvement of the quality management system can be made. Data collected should include results of monitoring and measurement and information from other relevant sources. The analysis of data should provide insight relating to:

- Customer satisfaction
- Conformity to product requirements

- Characteristics and trends of processes and products, including opportunities for preventive action

A process of **corrective action** should be institutionalized to eliminate causes of non-conformities in order to prevent recurrence. Documented procedures should be established to define requirements for:

- Reviewing non-conformities and related customer reports of dissatisfaction
- Determining the causes of non-conformities
- Evaluating the need for action to prevent recurrences
- Determining and implementing action needed
- Recording results of action taken
- Reviewing the effectiveness of the corrective action taken
- Flowing down corrective action requirements to suppliers responsible for non-conformities
- Determining if additional non-conforming product exists based on the causes of the non-conformities, warranting further action

A program of **preventive action** should be established to eliminate potential causes of non-conformities in order to prevent their occurrence. A documented procedure should be established to define requirements for:

- Determining potential non-conformities and their causes
- Evaluating the need for action to prevent occurrence of non-conformities
- Determining and implementing action needed
- Records of results of action taken
- Reviewing the effectiveness of the preventive action taken

Applying the AS 9100 standard to the individual enterprise

AS 9100 and its international equivalents do an excellent job of outlining requirements for a quality management system, but they do not provide the detailed procedures that must be established to manage quality in the organization. As the standards clearly recognize, every aerospace enterprise is unique, with different product categories, supply chains, manufacturing processes, distribution networks, engineering methods, geographic dispersion, customer involvement, corporate organization, and so on.

Consequently, each firm is faced with the task of dissecting the AS/EN/ JISQ 9100 standard paragraph by paragraph, comparing the dictates of the standards versus the firm's current procedures, and adjusting those procedures to comply with the standard if they do not already do so.

Certainly, the processes and the organizational structure of the quality management system are essential, but an equally essential factor is compliance with processes that have been implemented. Compliance remains a continuing challenge for management and the entire organization.

After an organization implements a quality management system in conformance with the standard, the system must be certified by an authorized third party before the company can formally qualify as AS 9100-compliant by prospective customers, regulators, and business partners. The **certification** must be issued by a certification body accredited by the International Aerospace Quality Group (IAQG) or the Americas Aerospace Quality Group (AAQG). Numerous independent private entities have received accreditation as certification bodies and are in the business of conducting audits and certifying companies.

12 Management of the aerospace supply chain

Graphics depicting aerospace supply chains are minor works of industrial art, showing the multitude of companies and countries that provide the many parts of a modern airplane. Perhaps no other industry encompasses such diversity among its suppliers and the technologies they provide.

Boeing 787 Work Sharing Partners

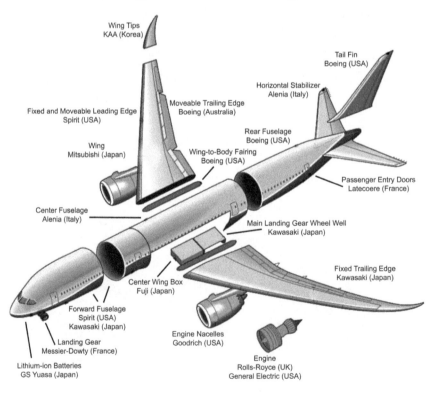

Figure 12.1 The complex supply chain of the Boeing 787.

Table 12.1 Boeing estimates that its vast supply chain consists of
5,400 supplier factories with 500,000 employees

Parts counts for commercial aircraft

Aircraft	Quantity of parts
737	400,000
767	3.1 million
787	2.3 million
777	3 million
747–8	6 million

Source: Boeing.

Modern aircraft have lots of parts. According to Boeing and Airbus, the 747-8 consists of six million parts and the A380 has four million. It is a daunting task to design, integrate, purchase, stock, and assemble each individual part, which has to be available at the right time and in the right place to support factory operations.

The companies with overall responsibility for designing, assembling, and delivering aircraft, known as **original equipment manufacturers (OEMs)**, typically buy more than 70% of the value of their aircraft from suppliers. The entire body of suppliers in the aggregate is known as the **supply chain**, or sometimes as the **value chain** or **extended enterprise**.

The concept of the extended enterprise is especially pertinent as firms have become more specialized and interdependent, trade has become more global, and information technology has enabled a more complete integration of the many entities involved in creation of the final product. By outsourcing design and production activities that had previously been performed internally, OEMs have been able to concentrate their resources on their unique core competencies. How an extended enterprise is organized and structured is called **enterprise architecture**.

Early in any new aircraft program, the OEM is confronted with literally millions of decisions concerning which parts of the airplane should be manufactured internally and which should be bought from outside sources. These **make-or-buy** decisions form the nucleus of the company's **program acquisition strategy**, which identifies the principal considerations as the decisions are made and attempts to reconcile them into a coherent plan of action that maximizes the company's interests. The strategy normally addresses certain specific key elements important to the program's success:

- Business strategy
- Contracting strategy
- Major subcontracts
- Incentives and penalties
- Technical data management
- Sustainment

Supply-chain tiers

Although all suppliers are important, a hierarchy exists to group them into tiers that reflect the nature and the complexity of the products they provide.

At the top of this hierarchy are the OEMs. They have overall financial responsibility for the aircraft program and are ultimately responsible for converting the millions of individual parts into flyable aircraft.

Immediately below the OEMs are the first-tier suppliers, who provide major aircraft subsystems and large structural components such as landing gear systems, wings, fuselage sections, cockpit avionics, and so on. The products from the first-tier suppliers are delivered directly to the OEM's assembly line.

The second-tier suppliers make parts and subassemblies such as wheels, doors, hydraulic actuators, light assemblies, and antennae. Shipments from second-tier suppliers sometimes go directly to the OEM, but more commonly are directed to first-tier suppliers.

The third tier delivers what are known as **build-to-print** or **make-to-print** products. They make items that are precisely defined by engineering drawings, datasets, and technical specifications furnished by their higher-tier customers. Examples might be skin panels, spars, wire harnesses, hydraulic tube assemblies, and brackets.

And the fourth tier, the foundation, furnishes raw materials, castings, forgings, extrusions, standard hardware, standard electrical components, commercial off-the-shelf components, and so on.

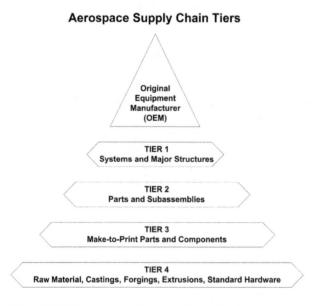

Aerospace Supply Chain Tiers

Original
Equipment
Manufacturer
(OEM)

TIER 1
Systems and Major Structures

TIER 2
Parts and Subassemblies

TIER 3
Make-to-Print Parts and Components

TIER 4
Raw Material, Castings, Forgings, Extrusions, Standard Hardware

Figure 12.2 The aerospace hierarchy of supplier tiers.

For the most part, suppliers can be classified neatly into appropriate tiers based upon the physical properties of the material they provide. However, this hierarchical orderliness becomes less tidy upon examination of the flows of material among members of the different tiers.

In the postwar period, when aircraft designs were less intricate and involved fewer parts, it was common for the overwhelming majority of parts to be delivered directly to the OEM. At that time, many of the major aircraft companies operated large integrated manufacturing facilities that were capable of performing the entire spectrum of production operations required to build aircraft. The companies would receive plates or sheets of aluminum, cut them to rough shapes, heat-treat them, perform machining or metal-forming operations, chemically anodize the parts, and apply surface coatings. The parts would be assembled into subassemblies that would in turn be assembled into major components, which would finally be assembled into a complete aircraft structure. Throughout the process, the structure would be stuffed with hardware, wiring harnesses, and equipment for hydraulic, electrical, and mechanical systems.

Over time the OEMs came to realize that most of the simpler manufacturing tasks could be done just as well, and often cheaper, by smaller specialized subcontractors. And, as aircraft became larger and more complex, the challenge of building parts and subassemblies in-house became a management distraction from the primary focus of the OEM, which was designing, integrating, and delivering the aircraft. As the myriad factors affecting their make-or-buy equations evolved, the OEMs elected to make less and buy more.

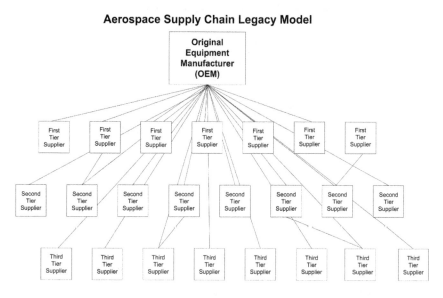

Figure 12.3 A conceptual representation of the traditional supply-chain model.

This new simplified subcontracting model in the aerospace industry was partly modeled on Toyota's supply chain in the automobile industry, which has been much admired by students of management. Toyota outsourced approximately 70% of its manufacturing work to a trusted group of partner firms, enabling Toyota to shorten development cycles for new cars. A fundamental aspect of the Toyota supply-chain model was that the company maintained tight control over the overall design and engineering of its vehicles and only outsourced to suppliers who had proven their ability to perform within the parameters demanded by the OEM.

The concept of utilizing smaller specialized production facilities is known in the terminology of today's management theory as **focused factories**. Aerospace OEMs have recognized the benefits of the practice when used by subcontractors, and have begun to apply the concept to some of their own in-house manufacturing work by grouping certain types of similar manufacturing tasks into smaller semi-autonomous focused factories under their own purview.

In recent aerospace supply chains, the role of the OEM is typically limited to the production tasks for which the OEM has unique specialized capability or strategic interest, and far fewer subcontractors deliver their parts and material directly to the OEM. Instead, most subcontractors at each tier deliver their products to other subcontractors in the tier above themselves. Eventually the limited group of tier 1 suppliers delivers major structure and subsystems to the OEM, who integrates, assembles, and delivers the completed aircraft.

This simplified supply chain structure that reduces the network of material shipment channels going directly to the OEM is often called the **tier 1** model.

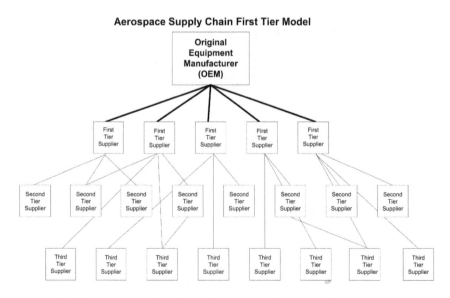

Aerospace Supply Chain First Tier Model

Figure 12.4 The tier 1 model reduces the number of suppliers shipping directly to the OEM.

Under this concept, the OEM concentrates attention on managing the smaller number of tier 1 suppliers, who in turn concentrate on managing their own suppliers, and so on.

A characteristic of the tier 1 model is that suppliers in the top tier often are risk-sharing partners in the overall program. The supplier of wings, for example, might have responsibility for designing the wing structure, based on parameters provided by the OEM concerning aerodynamic shape, weight, required strength, forces necessary for control surfaces, and interfaces with other parts of the aircraft. The tier 1 supplier makes the necessary financial investment to design the structure, produce prototype articles for testing, build production tooling, and support the cost of work-in-process in the factory. The supplier's investment is at risk if the overall program is not a financial success. If the program succeeds and has a long production run, the supplier is likely to enjoy an extended period of production work with reliable revenue.

Management of the extended enterprise

An aspect of the tier 1 model is that it requires a greater degree of integration and cooperation among the entire network of suppliers. Because the OEM is no longer the single gatekeeper for flows of information and material, information is distributed widely throughout the network in a standardized format, using common software and data systems. In theory the tier 1 model promotes a more collaborative environment among suppliers and the OEM. The idea of enhanced collaboration among the entire value chain has received increased attention within the aerospace industry and among students of management, and has come to be known as the **extended-enterprise** concept. The notion of enhanced collaboration and cooperation among the supplier network is intuitively appealing, but initiatives to implement the concept have encountered some difficulties attributable to the sheer complexity and scale of supplier relationships within the network. Another limit on the spirit of collaboration is the inherent self-interest of the multitude of firms within the network, which are sometimes reluctant to freely share information because they are competitors.

For their most recent programs, the OEMs of large civil aircraft have aggressively pursued the tier 1 model. Airbus reports that its new A350 program encompasses less than 100 major suppliers, and that 80% of the aircraft value is outsourced.

The Boeing 787 program is a recent example of the tier 1 concept carried to its limits. Overall the program has been a notable success, but was afflicted by a number of early production problems, many attributed to the structure and management of the program's supply chain. Because of the exceptional extent to which the 787 program relied upon outsourcing of major aircraft components to risk-sharing partners, Boeing's experience has been extensively studied by management experts to assess the successes, failures, and corrective strategies of the program in general and its supply chain in particular.

Table 12.2 Theoretical benefits of the extended enterprise concept

Comparison of supply chains, value chains, and the extended enterprise

Business factor	Supply chains/value chains	Extended enterprise
Environment	More stable and static	Dynamic and changing
Focus	Tends to be industry-centric	Finds partners who bring part of the business solution
Value-creation approach	Leverages own competencies, more self-sustaining	Leverages the competencies of all members
Relationship type	Teaming approach with some aspects of partner-like behavior	Strong collaborative behavior with very solid partnering behavior
Infrastructure thrust	Cost-driven	Value-driven
Profit focus	Increasing own profit is the default	Increasing profits system-wide
Knowledge	Shared carefully but tends to look internally	Shared widely over the system
Orientation	Tends to emphasize workflows	Complete business solution, long term planning

Source: Davis, E and Spekman, R 2004, *The Extended Enterprise*, Prentice Hall, Upper Saddle River.

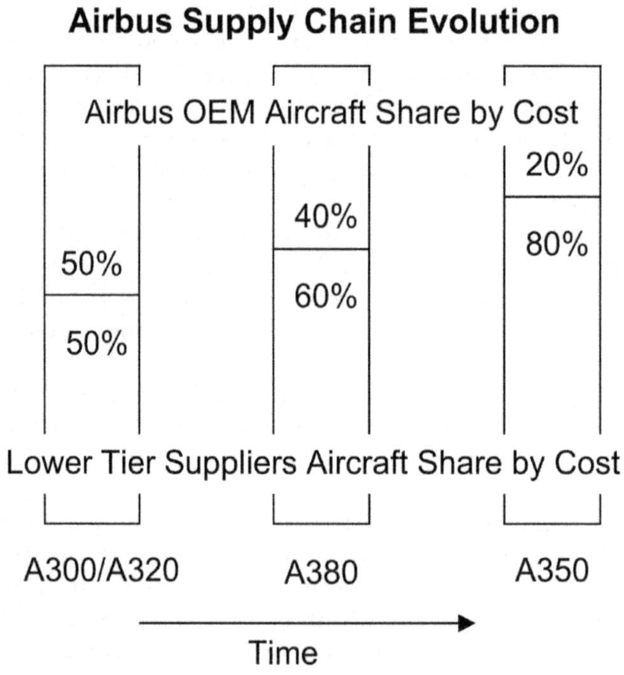

Figure 12.5 Evolution to the tier 1 model at Airbus.
Source: Airbus.

At the outset of the 787 program Boeing already had an extensive domestic and international network of major subcontractors. On earlier programs, the company had generally bought subsystems, parts, and subassemblies from the suppliers under fixed-price contracts. Many suppliers at different tiers had shipped directly to Boeing, where much of the component assembly was performed prior to final assembly of the aircraft, which spanned weeks or even months. It was a classic example of a legacy supply chain.

The 787 program was structured so that only a small number of tier 1 subcontractors producing major structural components, subsystems, and aircraft sections shipped directly to Boeing. The structure typically included preinstalled wiring harnesses, hydraulic lines, and various electrical, mechanical, and hydraulic components. Thus, when the structure arrived at the Boeing factory, the final assembly task was simplified because much installation work had been performed by suppliers. The scheduled span time for this streamlined final assembly was reduced to a few days. Under this new framework, Boeing business relationships with many of the tier 1 suppliers were no longer fixed-price contracts, but took the form of risk-sharing contracts under which they invested their own funds during the start-up and development phase, but could expect to benefit from a long industrial partnership if the aircraft became a success in the market.

At the outset of the program, Boeing worked intensively with its existing supplier network to discuss potential work packages and contractual terms for the new aircraft industrial plan. Eventually a relatively small number of risk-sharing partners was enlisted, including international participants from Japan, Italy, the UK, Australia, Korea, France, Sweden, and Canada. Major domestic suppliers were located in Kansas, Oklahoma, South Carolina, Ohio, and California. The overall work-sharing arrangement is shown in Figure 12.1.

The geographic dispersal of manufacturing operations posed daunting challenges. The large aircraft sections were often too big for transportation by

Table 12.3 Differences between the traditional supply chain of the 737 program and the tier 1 concept of the 787 program

Comparison of 737 and 787 supply-chain concepts		
	737 program	*787 program*
Sourcing strategy	Outsource 35–50%	Outsource 70%
Supplier relationship	Traditional supplier relationship (purely contract-based)	Strategic partnerships with tier 1 suppliers
Supplier responsibilities	Develop and produced **parts** for Boeing	Develop and produce **entire sections** for Boeing
Number of suppliers	Thousands of suppliers delivering directly to Boeing	Approximately 50 tier 1 strategic partners
Supply contracts	Fixed-price contracts with delay penalty	Risk-sharing contracts
Assembly operations	30 days for final assembly at Boeing	3-day assembly of complete sections at Boeing

Source: *Seattle Post-Intelligencer.*

highway or other conventional shipment modes, so Boeing and the suppliers worked to develop specialized transport systems, often involving ships, railcars, and specialized air freight. In this aspect of the program Boeing could refer to the prior experiences of Airbus, which for years had been shipping oversize aircraft sections among its plants in European countries.

Airbus A320 Industrial Geography

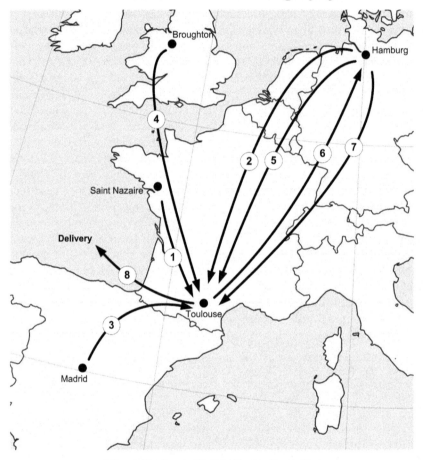

1. Forward fuselage built in Saint Nazaire, flown to Toulouse
2. Aft fuselage built in Hamburg, flown to Toulouse
3. Tail section built in Madrid, flown to Toulouse
4. Wings built in Broughton, flown to Toulouse
5. Unfinished aircraft ferry flight to Hamburg for installation of cabin interior
7. Return ferry flight to Toulouse for painting and final checks
8. Delivery flight to customer

Figure 12.6 At the same time Boeing was struggling with the geographical complexities of the 787 program, Airbus was dealing with international challenges of its own.

Source: Airbus data.

In addition to contractual and logistical issues, suppliers were challenged by technical issues resulting from the advanced design of the 787. In order to reduce weight and add strength, Boeing designers had largely replaced the conventional riveted aluminum structure with molded graphite composite shapes. Whereas Boeing's previous aircraft, the 777, contained 12% of composite structure by weight, the 787 was approximately 50% composite. At the inception of the program most of the suppliers had production experience with composites, but they were unaccustomed to working with the 787 process specifications and the very large dimensions of the structure. The aircraft also had an unconventional electric system that introduced additional unfamiliar practices. And, as they prepared for production start-up, suppliers were engaged in installation and testing of unfamiliar new tools, equipment, and chemical processes.

Although the aircraft's design innovations and technical risks warranted more intense direct involvement and monitoring by the OEM in the supply chain, the tier 1 structure resulted in more delegation of detailed engineering and procurement to subcontractors, some of whom were not independently capable of performing their assigned tasks.

Production start-ups of large new aircraft programs are formidable undertakings fraught with risks, and the 787 program was no exception. Almost immediately the program fell behind schedule as subcontractors encountered technical difficulties and cascading parts shortages, and several of the key

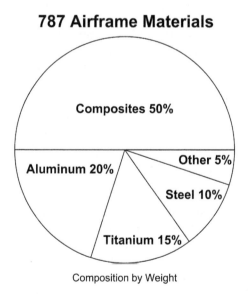

787 Airframe Materials

Composites 50%

Aluminum 20%

Other 5%

Steel 10%

Titanium 15%

Composition by Weight

Figure 12.7 The 787 design incorporated a high percentage of advanced materials. In contrast, the earlier 777 model was only 12% composite.

Source: *The Seattle Times.*

second-tier suppliers failed to adequately manage their third- and fourth-tier suppliers. In response, Boeing dispatched teams of engineers and technical specialists to subcontractors throughout the supply chain to resolve technical problems and coordinate corrective action across the supplier network. The recovery effort resulted in substantial unplanned costs and production delays. To partially reduce assembly delays, the incomplete structure was shipped by subcontractors to Boeing, where random unplanned extra tasks had to be performed in awkward production sequence, further disrupting factory flow.

A notable disruption of the 787 supply chain involved the failure of Vought Aircraft Industries, a tier 1 supplier based near Charleston, South Carolina, with responsibility for delivery of aft fuselage sections built of graphite composite materials. From the early stages of the production program Vought began to experience technical difficulties requiring major additional financial investments. Vought's owner, the private equity capital firm Carlyle Group, was unwilling to spend the money. Boeing was forced into a choice of either allowing Vought to collapse or buying the Charleston facilities from Carlyle in order to rescue the program. Boeing paid $1 billion to acquire the Vought factory, which became Boeing Charleston. Thus, a former major tier 1 supplier became an integral part of the OEM, instantly reducing the scope of the external supply chain.

Other significant disruptions to the supply chain occurred when a small manufacturer of critical fasteners fell behind schedule, and when Alenia in Italy experienced schedule and quality problems with its work share. Technical problems with the aircraft's electrical system and advanced lithium-ion batteries resulted in further program delays. Overall the program fell approximately three years behind its original schedule, resulting in large additional costs and negative cash flow to Boeing and its partners and straining relationships with the airlines whose flight operations were impacted by the late aircraft deliveries.

By the time 787 deliveries began in 2011 Boeing had an order backlog of approximately 800 aircraft, and by the end of 2012 the company was delivering at the rate of 11 aircraft per month. The program soon resolved its major supply-chain issues and overcame its early financial problems.

Supply-chain data networks

As supply chains become increasingly decentralized, information networks to share data and monitor status of subcontractors throughout the chain have become increasingly important. To manage this task, both Airbus and Boeing use specialized data systems based upon proprietary third-party software. The Boeing system is a licensed application of the Exostar value chain management system. Airbus's Extended Enterprise system is an integrated framework partially built upon several commercially developed modules. Numerous other commercial supplier risk and performance management software platforms are available to perform similar functions.

The various integrated management systems are different in many aspects, but have common fundamental features:

- Distribution and control of integrated work packages
- Standardized systems for sharing engineering data, software, and technical specifications
- Standardized engineering change management channels and processes
- Provisions for collaboration and sharing during technical design process
- Detailed and standardized schedule data, including real-time updates and recovery plans
- Creation of individualized risk profiles and performance metrics for each supplier
- Cost and financial data

Rethinking the tier 1 trend

A non-intuitive characteristic of the aerospace industry supply chain is that lower-tiered suppliers have historically recorded significantly higher profit margins than the OEMs. Observers have offered various explanations for this relationship, including the theory that OEMs are under more direct pricing pressure and risk than are lower-tier suppliers, and that OEMs have not been effective at aggressively implementing cost controls spanning multiple layers of procurement within the supply chain.

Partly in reaction to this disparity in profit rate, in 2012 Boeing announced its 'Partnering for Success' initiative, which applied pressure on suppliers to discount their prices by 15% and directly threatened to exclude suppliers who declined to participate in the initiative by banishing them to a 'no-fly list'. In a noteworthy example of consequences of the policy, long-standing 777 landing-gear manufacturer United Technologies Aerospace Systems (UTAS) declined to bid to provide gear for the new 777X model, declaring that Boeing's pricing pressure would make the subcontract unprofitable. Boeing instead awarded

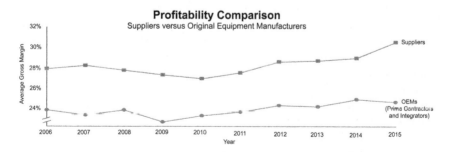

Figure 12.8 Gross margins are higher for suppliers than for OEMs.

Source: S&P Capital IQ.

the contract to a relatively small competitor, Héroux-Devtek, headquartered in Quebec.

In a further departure from its unsatisfactory experience with the tier 1 model on the 787 program, Boeing subsequently announced that it intended to move in the opposite direction by increasing the company's vertical integration. The vertical-integration strategy was specifically intended to raise program profits, and included plans for Boeing to participate in follow-on support business after aircraft delivery.

Boeing began to acquire several aerostructure facilities, built a large-scale factory for the production of composite wings, and established a center of excellence for propulsion technology. The company also continued to explore expanded capability in design and production of complete engine nacelles and thrust-reversers, which are key elements of future aircraft designs with high-bypass-ratio engines. These components have steady aftermarket revenue streams. At approximately the same time Airbus announced its intent to produce the same components for its A320neo. Boeing also considered adding the capability to make engine pylons, which Airbus produced internally for its products.

As part of its extreme tier 1 focus at the launch of the 787 program Boeing had abandoned much of its aircraft systems capability, but subsequently reversed direction after experiencing production and financial problems on the program. It regained prime responsibility for flight-control integration for the 777X, resumed actuator production, and reclaimed responsibility for design and aftermarket servicing of the 777X's landing gear after outsourcing it on the 787. Boeing considered the prospect of adding flight-control computer capability, following Airbus's initiative on the A380 program. The company also became more involved in the design of electrical power distribution.

In 2017 Boeing announced the establishment of an avionics center of excellence, indicating an intent to increase its presence in that subsector. Tangential activities will perhaps include increased involvement in the 'common-core' data network that is the infrastructure for data exchange throughout aircraft systems.

Cabin interiors are a significant element of aircraft cost and offer opportunities for aftermarket business as airlines periodically update cabins overextended lives of aircraft. In 2011 Boeing opened an Interiors Responsibility Center in Charleston, South Carolina, to expand manufacturing capability in that area. In 2018 it announced a joint venture with automotive interiors specialist Adient to produce aircraft seats. These initiatives expanded Boeing's experience as a supplier of interior panels, luggage bins, and crew rest compartments. While Boeing was expanding into this specialty, Airbus was experiencing significant disruption to deliveries of its new A350 model after Zodiac, its supplier of aircraft interiors, fell behind schedule and was acquired by Safran after encountering financial difficulties.

Certainly, the aerospace industry will continue to experiment with alternative structures for its supply chain. The implications in terms of investment, risk, reliability, span of control, and profit are immense. OEMs must weigh important trade-offs as they attempt to balance competing priorities. Without a doubt the industry will continue to expand its systems and networks for sharing data among suppliers and OEMs as they collectively attempt to better manage complex challenges.

Management of subcontracts

An essential element of any major aircraft program is subcontracts, which are numerous, intricate, diverse, and of critical importance. The discipline for managing suppliers and subcontracts is prescribed by the **subcontract management program**. The subcontract management program encompasses procurement and subcontract planning, supplier selection, contract development and award, and continuous monitoring and verification of contractually required subcontractor activities to assure that program requirements and contractual terms are met.

The subcontracting strategy of a program takes into consideration the objectives of the acquisition, affordability, constraints, availability of resources and technologies, acquisition methods, types of contracts, terms and conditions of the contracts, management considerations, risk, and the logistics considerations for the resulting products or services. Depending upon circumstances and the judgment of management, the source selection method of procurement for various types of goods and services will be either **competitive** or **non-competitive**.

Competitive procurement

In a competitive procurement, two or more potential suppliers are invited to respond to a **request for proposal (RFP)**. Their proposals are evaluated during **source selection**, and the contract is awarded to the contractor whose proposal is deemed most advantageous to the customer.

Preparation of the RFP involves the development of solicitation documents, evaluation criteria, and a source-selection approach. Depending on the nature of the item to be bought and the number of qualified sources for the item, the buyer may decide to open the competition to all or to invite a limited number of competitors. Full and open competition allows any qualified company to submit a proposal. This alternative is often chosen for build-to-print parts, standard hardware, and raw material, which are typically market segments characterized by many suppliers of relatively small size.

In cases of purchase of sophisticated subsystems and components, where the population of qualified suppliers is small and well known, the buyer may want to limit the number of competitors by extending invitations to compete. Often these procurements require the supplier to develop an original design in response to technical requirements furnished by the buyer. The prospective supplier is provided with data including performance requirements of the system, limits governing weight and space, and power available to the system.

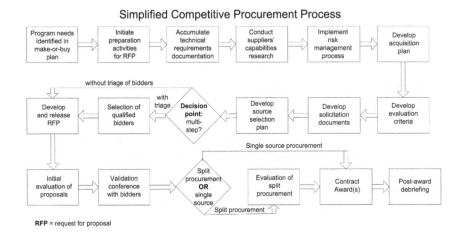

Figure 12.9 Competitive procurement steps.

Another alternative, less commonly used, is to conduct a multistep competitive procurement using competitive prototyping as a means to further evaluate the solutions offered by prospective subcontractors. A further alternative is a phased competition, in which the competition advances through several stages, with the number of competitors being reduced at the conclusion of each stage, until a final winner is selected.

The sequential steps in a representative competitive procurement are illustrated in Figure 12.9.

Non-competitive procurement

OEMs dislike **non-competitive**, or **sole-source**, procurement because it deprives them of the leverage that derives from having several subcontractors competing for the same business. It is used when a unique system or service is available from a single source. Occasionally, engines and electronic systems are purchased sole-source. More often, sole-source procurement is used with suppliers who are already under contract to the buyer, as in the case of incremental redesigns of structural components for derivative designs of existing aircraft models. Often the justification for sole-source awards is that the contractor has proprietary rights to products. Sole-source awards generally take less time than competitive RFP and source selection processes.

RFP development process

Development of the RFP is a crucial step early in the procurement process. The RFP preparation is generally led by the program's purchasing team,

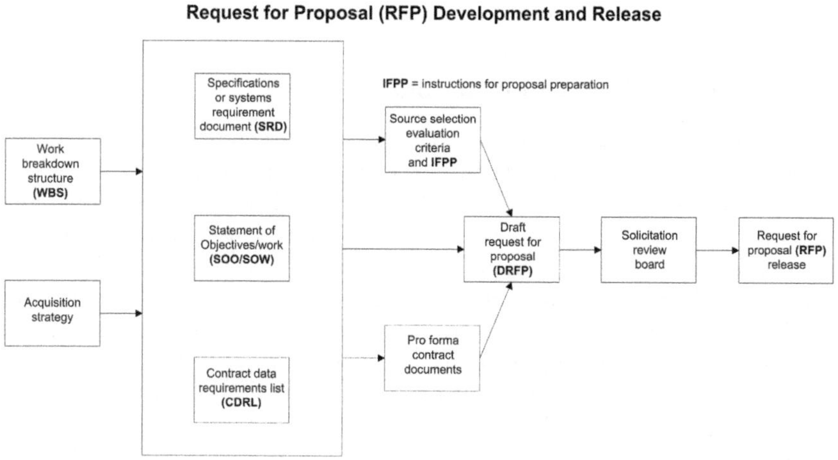

Request for Proposal (RFP) Development and Release

Figure 12.10 Preparation of the request for proposal.

comprised of subject–matter experts including systems engineers. The program acquisition strategy provides the basis for the development of the RFP. The **work breakdown structure (WBS)** provides the definition of the production program and is the basis for defining tasks to be subcontracted. Depending on the nature of the product to be procured, the technical content of the RFP can include specifications, a **system requirements document (SRD)**, the **statement of objectives (SOO)**, the **statement of work (SOW)**, and the **contract data requirements list (CDRL)**.

The steps for development and release of the RFP are shown next.

The subcontract management plan

Planning is an indispensable requirement for managing subcontracts, and the principal planning tool is the **subcontract management plan (SMP)**. It identifies management and surveillance responsibilities and specifies the methods to be used throughout the program to ensure subcontractor and subtier supplier compliance with program requirements. The SMP delineates the processes for managing and integrating program activities and provides methods and guidance for selection and management of subcontractors using proven processes and methods that increase the likelihood of successful program execution.

The span covered by the SMP begins at the preproposal stage and continues through subcontract execution, performance management, and closeout. Subcontractor and subtier supplier verification methods typically include scheduling of reviews and status reporting meetings, evaluation of deliverables, monitoring of contractor-supplied metrics and databases, and surveys of facilities. The SMP specifies surveillance milestones, reporting requirements, and detailed risk mitigation plans in the case of problems during execution. The SMP is continually updated throughout the program.

Management and control of suppliers

The OEM performs surveillance and management control of subcontractor and subtier suppliers so that program progress can be monitored and assessed, enabling timely corrective action when warranted. The purpose of the monitoring and control system is to ensure that subcontracted items obtained from first-tier and all lower-tier suppliers meet contract requirements, including quality specifications and delivery schedules. At the outset of the program, the OEM stipulates methods, milestones, and success criteria for subcontractor monitoring and control, and identifies the methodology to be used for each type of monitoring activity, such as lot sampling, site surveys, statistical analysis, and scheduled delivery performance records.

An important aspect of subcontracting is the concept of comprehensive and specific flowdown of critical program management and technical requirements to suppliers in every tier. The contractual language flowed down includes mandatory requirements governing risk, protection of data, financial reporting, legal requirements, schedule, quality standards and systems, status reporting, and standard contractual terms and conditions. Examples are:

- Manufacturing requirements
- Inspection and testing
- Material specifications and standards
- Control of critical components
- Special qualifications, approvals, or certifications
- Non-destructive tests
- Control of hardware and software documentation and changes
- Applicable product and process specifications
- Reliability and maintainability standards and metrics
- Safety factors
- Preservation, packaging, marking, and packing
- Product storage and handling
- Contractor source quality control
- Shipping instructions
- Age control and shelf life
- Contractor-furnished equipment
- Data retention
- Control of tools and test equipment
- Non-conforming products
- Control of manufacturing methods, materials, and processes
- Applicable workmanship standards
- Reviews and audits
- Identification of hardware and software deliverables
- Statistical process control program

Prior to engaging in a subcontract with a supplier, the OEM or upper-tier supplier performs due diligence to verify the supplier's capability to perform. This process includes review of the supplier's past performance history, financial stability, technical and managerial qualifications of the workforce, physical facilities, and security practices. Emphasis is placed on engineering, manufacturing and integration operations, supplier management, mission assurance, quality assurance, and program management processes. Part of this due diligence normally includes surveys of subcontractors' facilities and meetings with management. Results of the due diligence are documented, serve as a basis for possible corrective action upon receipt of the subcontract, and remain available for review by the OEM.

Aerospace suppliers are expected to have quality management systems formally certified to comply with the AS 9100 standard, as described in Chapter 11. In addition, certain types of hardware and software, such as autopilots, flight controls, engine controls, and some test equipment, require airworthiness certification by the FAA, international airworthiness authorities, or military customers.

Normally OEMs establish formal systems to rate suppliers based upon the quality of performance for each type of goods and services being purchased. The system compiles past performance data dealing with subcontractor quality, cost, schedule, and technical performance and trends. The data is continuously updated to identify performance trends. Suppliers whose performance is unsatisfactory are given special attention by upper-tier subcontract managers, who work with the supplier to identify the cause of the problems and develop corrective action plans.

Because upper-tier buyers have responsibility for the performance of their suppliers, they generally establish a program of surveillance and periodic audits at the subtier subcontractor's site to ensure conformance to contract requirements, including the following:

- Product inspection
- Special manufacturing processes
- Controls for inspection and test equipment
- Configuration management procedures for engineering drawings and computer software
- Subtier supplier quality management program
- Controls and corrective action processes for nonconforming products
- Shipping documentation
- Qualification and acceptance tests
- Timely notification to management of discrepancies or deficiencies

Safety is a primordial consideration in aviation, and aircraft designers designate certain parts and systems as critical. Because these are elements of the aircraft that are essential to sustain flight, they are tracked and recorded in detail throughout the production process and afterwards. The OEM is responsible for identifying and controlling **critical items**. Detailed procedures governing the manufacture, inspection, and control of critical items are documented as a part of the total quality-control program. Subcontracts for critical items specify special transportation, handling, and storage requirements and the subcontractor is required to document in detail the methods and processes that will be used.

Almost every deliverable from subcontractors is subject to delivery inspection. For larger subcontracts, the upper-tier buyer will often perform a **source inspection** at the seller's facility, done either by the buyer's resident quality assurance representative or by a buyer's inspector who makes periodic visits to the facility. If source inspection is not practical, **delivery inspection** is performed when the item is received at the upper-tier buyer's facility. These inspections are intended to verify that the subcontractor's product complies with the requirements of the purchase document, including compliance with the latest applicable engineering changes and specifications.

Customer-furnished equipment

In some cases, parts or subsystems to be installed on aircraft are purchased by the customer and provided to the OEM as **customer-furnished equipment (CFE)**. Often the justification for CFE is that the product is of a specialized nature of which the customer has special knowledge or preferences, such as aircraft interior furnishings or entertainment systems. Frequently, engines are purchased directly by the customer and furnished as CFE because the customer prefers to negotiate and contract directly with the engine manufacturer. In the case of military aircraft, the equivalent of CFE is **government-furnished equipment (GFE)**. GFE may be provided in the case of items such as armament, which is subject to burdensome security controls. In cases in which the government customer is using common equipment such as radios across multiple types of aircraft, it may procure the equipment directly and furnish it to aircraft prime contractors as GFE.

When CFE is shipped to the OEM's assembly line, it is held in a quarantined storage area apart from standard inventory. Customarily the OEM is contractually required to manage and protect the CFE inventory while it is at the OEM's facility.

Although the customer is responsible for most aspects of CFE, the OEM retains responsibility for verifying that the CFE is certified for use on the aircraft and that it functions properly when installed.

Addressing the threat of counterfeit parts and material

In recent years the prevalence of counterfeit parts in the aerospace supply chain has increased, according to studies by the Department of Defense, the Federal Aviation Administration, and the Aerospace Industries Association. Parts are considered to be counterfeit if they are sold in the aerospace supply chain without legitimate approval by civil or military airworthiness authorities.

AS5553 Concept
Control of Counterfeit Parts

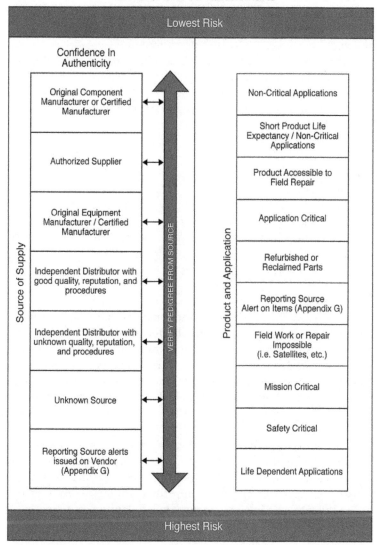

Figure 12.11 A depiction of the Aerospace Standard AS 5553 'Concept for Controlling Counterfeit Parts'.

Source: SAE International.

The unapproved parts typically have false paperwork that disguises their provenance and provides bogus evidence of approval by airworthiness authorities.

The problem includes mechanical parts, electronic parts, and materials. Examples of mechanical parts are bolts, nuts, and rivets. Electronic parts include resistors, capacitors, and integrated circuits. Materials have included steel and titanium, and chemicals used in the fabrication of composites. Counterfeit electronic parts in particular have been detected in high numbers and are of special concern.

To address this threat, the FAA and DoD have implemented procedures to control the risk, and have imposed the adoption of AS 5553, a formal standard published by the Society of Automotive Engineers (SAE) for the purpose of avoiding, detecting, mitigating, and disposing of counterfeit parts, particularly electronic items.

AS 5553 standardizes practices to:

- Maximize availability of authentic parts
- Procure parts from reliable sources
- Assure authenticity and conformance of procured parts
- Control parts identified as counterfeit
- Report counterfeit parts to other potential users and government investigative authorities

Conclusion

It is difficult to overstate the importance of the supply chain for the aerospace industry. As noted at the beginning of this chapter, modern aircraft consist of millions of parts, most of which are supplied by subcontractors, who produce approximately two-thirds of the value the aircraft. The task of identifying, selecting, and establishing contracts with these individual contractors is daunting. The task of coordinating production schedules, monitoring status, controlling configuration, assuring quality, and managing costs is a challenge to management.

Because of the enormous financial risks and rewards at stake in the supply chain, OEMs will continue to refine their management techniques in the domain and will certainly experiment with new structural concepts that offer the possibility of increased profits and competitive advantage. And, as they have learned in the past, painful consequences will follow any missteps.

13 Aerospace marketing

Phases in the marketing and sales process

Distilled into its simplest elements, management of the sales process consists of a few simple steps:

1. Identify an opportunity and formulate an objective.
2. Understand the customer's process of selection and procurement.
3. Establish a strategy.
4. Execute the strategy while continuously measuring and monitoring progress.

International aerospace marketing is inherently difficult to manage because every sales campaign is different. Standardized metrics for measuring sales progress are often not effective because customers impose individualized processes for competitive selection, contracting, and procurement. Because customers follow different procurement roadmaps, they use different milestones.

Some customers establish a detailed, clearly defined acquisition process, supplemented with detailed schedules for key competitive milestones and contractual events. The US Department of Defense, for example, publishes volumes of detailed procedures governing how its equipment acquisition selection process works, and DoD program managers for individual acquisition programs customarily provide all competitors with program schedules covering all significant milestones. Consequently, marketing managers experienced in working with the DoD have an easy job of identifying major milestones in their marketing campaigns and establishing dates for completion of the milestones. They know which individual offices of the DoD or the military branches will have responsibility for which task, and they know the procedures that the customer will follow to complete the milestone. It is relatively easy to put together a detailed marketing plan that corresponds to the known DoD requirements, schedule milestones, and evaluation processes. Once the plan is established, the sales campaign can be managed by continually monitoring actual progress compared to the marketing plan, taking corrective action whenever serious departures from the plan become apparent.

The marketing manager's job is not so straightforward when the customer has not publicly disclosed information about her acquisition process. It may be necessary to begin campaigns with no detailed knowledge about how the customer will evaluate competitors, which customer officials will make key decisions, and what schedule the customer will follow. Under these circumstances, it is difficult to prepare a meaningful marketing plan against which to measure accomplishments.

In any case, the job of the marketing manager is to properly allocate marketing resources; apply discipline to the sales process by means of realistic plans and schedules; monitor marketing performance by tracking status of plans and schedules; and intervene as appropriate when the marketing effort appears to be in trouble.

For management purposes, marketing campaigns are customarily divided into discrete phases that transpire more or less sequentially. Each of the individual phases represents an identifiable step in the marketing process, with the occurrence of characteristic events in the customer's acquisition process. Although these defining events are determined by the customer, they generally require corresponding activity on the part of the seller.

As a marketing campaign advances from one phase to the next, formal management reviews are generally held to evaluate progress of the marketing campaign, to authorize action recommended by the marketing department, and to approve budget required to support marketing activities through the next phase.

Phases are defined differently by individual companies, but a typical sequence might be as follows:

Phase A – Prospecting, information gathering, and general customer development.

Phase B – Recognition of a definable sales opportunity; definition of the requirement in more detail; formulation of a preliminary concept of a suitable offering; and projection of resources required to pursue the opportunity.

Phase C – Development of a sales strategy, creation of an internal program capture team, and internal definition of a suitable program to offer the customer, including an engineering element, a financial element, a product support element, an offset element, and so on.

Phase D – Formal offer of a contractual proposal to the customer.

Phase E – Approval of negotiating positions and a final contractual settlement.

Phase F – Development and approval of a **keep-it-sold (KIS)** plan, if the marketing campaign has led to a sale.

Phase G – Development and circulation of an internal critique of the marketing campaign, including lessons learned, whether or not the marketing campaign was successful.

Milestone reviews

As the marketing campaign proceeds in a more or less linear fashion through these successive phases, the company becomes progressively enmeshed in marketing activities, with increasing commitments in terms of time and resources devoted to the campaign. As resources are required, management should continuously review the status of the campaign and progressively commitment to provide resources. These management reviews, sometimes called **campaign milestone reviews**, are customarily established as the campaign advances from one phase to the next. The purpose of the reviews is to give management sufficient information upon which to base an intelligent decision to authorize the expenditure of the resources required to sustain the campaign through its next phase. For marketing campaigns of financial or strategic importance, the management review should be chaired by the general manager of the business unit.

Here are examples of the relationships of typical campaign milestone reviews to campaign phases:

The **First Campaign Milestone Review** takes place as the campaign passes from phase A to phase B. The general prospecting and information-gathering activities in phase A have led the marketing team to believe that an active marketing campaign is warranted. The purpose of this milestone review is to give Marketing a forum in which to justify their recommendation that resources be made available to support activities required in phase B. A major purpose of the review is the **qualification** of the customer as a viable and creditworthy buyer. Accordingly, the material presented and discussed at the milestone review includes the following subjects:

- A detailed description of the customer's perceived requirement
- Key background information about the customer, including historical context, key decision-makers, and financial factors
- A critical evaluation of the customer's overall qualifications to buy, particularly focusing on his ability to operate the equipment in a safe and profitable manner, his ability to pay, and the seriousness of his intent to buy
- A preliminary synopsis of the technical product that will be required to satisfy the requirement
- An estimated value of the sale
- A preliminary projection of the schedule of major events in the customer's schedule for making the purchase
- An assessment of how the selling company's capabilities and market presence fit with the customer's perceived requirement
- A preliminary assessment of significant capital investment that will be required if the campaign leads to a sale
- A listing and assessment of expected competitors
- An estimate of budget required to sustain the marketing campaign through the upcoming phase

- Initial estimates of probability that the purchase will actually occur $(\mathbf{P}_{go})$ and that the company will win the competition $(\mathbf{P}_{win})$

From a budgetary point of view, this transition from phase A to phase B is particularly significant, because it marks the transition of the campaign from the general market development budget to an individual campaign budget, as described earlier in this chapter. A major conclusion of the first milestone review is that the opportunity under study has matured to the point that it can be recognized as a bona fide marketing campaign, with its own discrete budget and resources. If this conclusion is not reached, the sales prospect remains in the category of a longer-range developmental opportunity.

The **Second Campaign Milestone Review** occurs as the campaign makes the transition from phase B to phase C. As the campaign enters phase C, activities that took place during phase B should have enabled the marketing team to acquire a more profound insight into the customer and the factors that can be expected to affect the outcome of the competition. Because phase C will be largely devoted to establishing and executing a comprehensive campaign strategy, the second milestone review gives management an opportunity to evaluate the strategy.

The principal elements presented in this review are:

- A synopsis of circumstances that have changed since the first milestone review
- A detailed assessment of the customer's requirements
- A technical description of the product that the company should offer in response to the requirement
- A summary of the customer's procurement process and acquisition plan, including schedule and contracting characteristics, in as much detail as possible
- A detailed overview of the marketing strategy
- Identification of key customer decision-makers, and a plan for contact
- An overview of the business case for the program, including expectation of a winning sales price, investment required, time-phased cash flow, earnings, and the other key financial metrics
- Time-phased projection of the budget that will be required to support the marketing campaign until its conclusion
- Identification of the capture team and leader
- Speculation concerning the offerings and marketing strategies of competitors
- Updated estimates of $(\mathbf{P}_{go})$ and $(\mathbf{P}_{win})$

The marketing strategy will include elements such as identification of the customer's highest priorities and principal objectives, followed by specific plans of action to convince customer decision-makers that the seller's offering satisfies these objectives.

A critical part of the strategy involves analyzing the decision-making process within the customer's organization. A common practice is to assemble a working group of people with special knowledge of the customer, and to define the identity of all the individual executives within the customer's organization who will have authority to make specific decisions. This working group should also identify key individuals who are external to the customer, but who have the capability to affect the customer's decision. The most important advisors to these decision-makers are also identified. As the working group identifies decisions that are critical to making a sale, a strategy is developed to influence key decision-makers in a favorable direction.

The capture team to be introduced in the second milestone review is a group representing functional disciplines such as marketing, contracts, engineering, manufacturing, estimating, offset management, and program management. These team members have responsibility for ensuring that their departments provide the support necessary to carry out the marketing strategy.

The **Third Campaign Milestone Review** is principally a senior management evaluation and approval of the formal priced proposal that will be offered to the customer, to begin phase D of the campaign. The review begins with a summary of significant changes that are known to have occurred since the second milestone review.

The focus of the review is on the content of the proposal: engineering configuration, pricing, contractual terms, delivery schedules, logistics support package, and industrial offsets if they are involved. Of particular interest to management will be the cost estimates that were used as the basis for the pricing, and the program financial projections in standard metrics such as cash flow, rate of return, net profit, and company investment. Program risks should be identified, their magnitude should be estimated, and the downside projected negative impact on the program should be depicted.

At this review, the agenda should once again include a detailed overview of the customer's anticipated schedule and process for aircraft or equipment selection and contract execution. The marketing team should give an explanation of its latest assessment of P_{go} and P_{win}, and should give an overview of expected competitor strategies and offerings.

The **Fourth Campaign Milestone Review** occurs if the customer extends an invitation to negotiate a contract based upon the formal priced proposal submitted earlier. Procedurally, this step is the beginning of phase E.

An invitation for face-to-face discussions of the proposal is generally a positive development. In the most favorable scenario, the customer finds the offering to be attractive and wants to conduct negotiations with the intent of moving promptly to a signed contract. In the least favorable scenario, the customer has no immediate intent to purchase, but simply wants to gather information pertaining to pricing and other elements of the proposal.

However, anytime a negotiating team is sent to a customer to discuss a proposal, the team should have clearly defined limits to its negotiating position, and the limits should be approved in advance by management. If the members of the capture team have gained an effective understanding of the customer, they should be able to anticipate the contractual concessions that the customer will seek. It is generally assumed that the customer will negotiate for a lower price. Other possible concessions will depend upon the customer's unique circumstances, but might involve special contractual terms and conditions, a customized configuration, special postdelivery support, or favorable offset arrangements. Limits for the negotiating team must be established for all elements of the proposal that will be under discussion.

The presentation at this review should include a summary of expected customer issues at the negotiation, an overview of the customer's anticipated negotiating strategy, and a scenario of the path that the negotiations will follow. All of these factors are key pieces of information necessary to enable management to make an informed decision concerning an appropriate **Best and Final Offer (BAFO)** that the negotiating team will be authorized to work towards.

Obviously, it is difficult to accurately predict how major negotiations will unfold. Almost invariably, the customer will steer negotiations in a direction not anticipated by the offering company, and the negotiating team will have to request additional management approval for new negotiating limits in some area of the proposal. Approval for new negotiating limits, which often result from late-night telephone discussions between management and the negotiating team located in a hotel room near the customer's offices, are construed as a supplement to the fourth milestone review.

Once the proposal is formally presented to the customer, leadership in the business acquisition process transfers from the marketing department to the contracts department.

There are three main possible outcomes from the negotiations:

1. The customer buys the seller's product.
2. The customer buys the competitor's product, or spends the budget to buy an unrelated system.
3. The customer decides to buy nothing, or to postpone the decision.

Whichever of these three outcomes occur, the **Fifth Campaign Milestone Review** is scheduled immediately after negotiations are completed or broken off. The purpose of the fifth milestone review is to obtain management approval for postnegotiation marketing action in the campaign. The period following negotiations is a particularly critical juncture in the marketing process, and the marketing team should ensure that internal decisions are made quickly at this point.

If the outcome of negotiations is the first alternative, and the customer elects to buy the seller's product, note that the milestone review should take place directly after the agreement to buy, and should not be delayed until the contract signature, which often follows the agreement by several months as financing, board of directors ratification, issuance of export licenses, and government regulatory approvals are finalized by the customer. In the case of government customers, delays may be even longer as various ministerial approvals and sometimes parliamentary ratification are obtained.

A significant percentage of sales agreements in the aerospace industry fail to convert into paid sales orders. If the negotiations culminate in an agreement to purchase the product, various forces will continue to work diligently to void the selection before the contract is awarded. These forces include competitors, who will make desperate last-ditch offers and who possibly will file lawsuits protesting improper influence; government officials who have vested interests in alternative outcomes; industry interests who stand to benefit from selection of other competitors; and various other parties who are unhappy with the outcome.

If negotiations resulted in a sales agreement, the primary purpose of the fifth milestone review is to approve a plan to ensure that the sales agreement does not unravel before the final contract signature and financial guarantees are in place. This is the **keep-it-sold** plan. Keep-it-sold activity is phase F of the campaign.

The KIS plan should include anticipation of how competitors and other adversaries will attempt to void the sales selection. In response to each of these possible adversarial actions, counterstrategies should be developed to protect the sales agreement.

The best strategy for protecting a sales agreement is to move aggressively to convince supporters and doubters that the seller will deliver an outstanding product and will comply with all aspects of the deal. Incorporated in the KIS plan should be a specific plan of action to immediately take visible, concrete steps to establish credibility concerning the company's commitment to the program. This action should include regular visits to the customer by senior executives of the selling company.

If, unfortunately, the negotiations resulted in alternative 2, a sales agreement with a competitor, the fifth milestone review has a completely different character and objective. Unless the marketing team believes that the campaign has been definitively and irrevocably lost, they will use the fifth milestone review to justify a recommendation to develop a **spoiling strategy** intended to derail the competitor's sales agreement prior to actual contract award. The spoiling strategy will strive to draw attention to all the weak or questionable aspects of the competitor's offer, and will undermine the perception of the competitor's ability to perform.

The tenor of the spoiling strategy must be determined by the circumstances of the sale. If the losing company has a long-term relationship with the customer, and expects to obtain significant future business from him, any spoiling action should be sufficiently discrete to avoid antagonizing the customer. If, on the other hand, the losing competitor feels that he has nothing to lose by directly and publicly questioning the selection decision, the spoiling strategy can be brutal and direct.

If the marketing team recommends a spoiling strategy during their fifth milestone review, their presentation to management will provide justification for that strategy and a tentative outline of specific approaches that should be considered. If management endorses the recommendation to mount a spoiling strategy, the campaign will be declared to have regressed to phase C, where the detailed new strategy will be developed. Thereafter, the campaign will undergo milestone reviews as it passes quickly through phases D and E as new unsolicited proposals to the customer are developed and defined.

In the case of the third possible alternative outcome of negotiations, in which the customer decides to do nothing or postpones the decision, the marketing team must evaluate the significance of the customer's action. If a future sale still appears to be likely, the team probably will attempt to reopen negotiations based upon the proposal that has been submitted. If, however, it seems that the customer has a serious problem with the proposal or the program concept upon which it was based, the seller should question the fundamental soundness of his marketing strategy, and should consider revising it. Under these circumstances, the marketing team would return the campaign to phase C, and would later develop a revised proposal based on a new strategy as the campaign passes again through phases D and E.

The **Sixth Campaign Milestone Review** is the presentation to management of a frank internal after-the-fact critique of the marketing campaign. This review should be held as soon as the competition is considered to be definitively won or lost.

The emphasis of the sixth milestone review is on finding ways to improve future results. An impartial senior manager should be temporarily assigned responsibility for compiling a report, and all parts of the company that were directly or indirectly involved in the marketing campaign should be invited to contribute comments and suggestions. The report should include:

- Identification of actions and strategies that were effective
- Identification of actions and strategies that were ineffective or counterproductive
- Reconstruction of the customer's decision-making process
- Review of competitor's actions, and analysis of their effectiveness
- After-the-fact speculation concerning alternative outcomes that might have resulted if alternative courses of action had been followed
- Specific suggestions concerning how procedures or management processes should be changed to improve future chances of success

After the critique is presented to senior management at the sixth milestone review, it should be presented and discussed in a bigger group of marketing specialists and representatives of other functions normally involved in marketing and sales activity. The purpose of the critique is to disseminate lessons learned widely throughout the company. Copies of the report should be distributed, and a master library of critiques from successive marketing campaigns should be maintained for reference.

The Marketing and Sales Process – Phases and Milestone Reviews

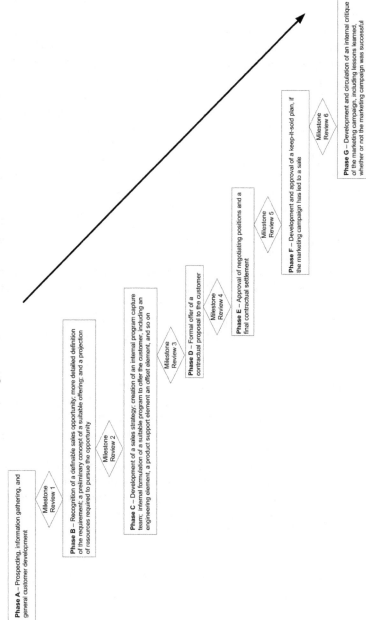

Phase A – Prospecting, information gathering, and general customer development

Milestone Review 1

Phase B – Recognition of a definable sales opportunity; more detailed definition of the requirement; a preliminary concept of a suitable offering; and a projection of resources required to pursue the opportunity

Milestone Review 2

Phase C – Development of a sales strategy; creation of an internal program capture team; internal formulation of a suitable program to offer the customer, including an engineering element, a product support element an offset element, and so on

Milestone Review 3

Phase D – Formal offer of a contractual proposal to the customer

Milestone Review 4

Phase E – Approval of negotiating positions and a final contractual settlement

Milestone Review 5

Phase F – Development and approval of a keep-it-sold plan, if the marketing campaign has led to a sale

Milestone Review 6

Phase G – Development and circulation of an internal critique of the marketing campaign, including lessons learned, whether or not the marketing campaign was successful

Figure 13.1 All marketing campaigns are different but generally proceed through similar phases.

Operations analysis

In the aerospace and aviation industries, **operations analysis**, as the words imply, is the application of quantitative analytical techniques to the operations of aircraft and equipment.

Aircraft operations in both civil and military service are complex, involving many variables that have a bearing upon costs, efficiency, and the ability of the aircraft to perform specific missions. The job of the analyst is to identify the variables, quantify them, consolidate them into an abstract model of cost or performance, and use the model to predict performance or to recommend mixes of variables that will result in optimal outcomes for the operator.

This is of fundamental importance during marketing campaigns. In theory, aircraft customers want to buy the aircraft that will provide them with optimal outcomes. At the top level, airlines want to maximize their earnings and air forces want to field the most formidable national defense. The purpose of operations analysis is to convince the customer that the seller's aircraft will enable them to achieve these desired outcomes.

The problem and the opportunity are that customers often do not have a precise definition of their desired outcome. An airline operator, for example, might be searching for the aircraft that can enable profit maximization on a specific route. A reliable projection of passenger volume and ticket price, combined with knowledge of the cost of ownership and operating costs of alternative aircraft, should provide sufficient information for the operator to create a simple analytical model to indicate which aircraft will deliver best results.

However, the model can become infinitely more complex if other variables are introduced:

- If the new aircraft is from a different manufacturer than existing aircraft in the operator's fleet, the operator faces cost penalties because pilots qualified for one type cannot be easily reassigned to fly the other type.
- Aircraft of optimal efficiency for a specific route may be unsuitable as substitute aircraft for other routes.
- If an aircraft type with a lower reliability rate is used, the purchase of additional aircraft may be necessary to assure service on the route.
- Better cargo-carrying capacity of one of the alternatives may outweigh the marginal passenger-carrying capacity of the other alternative.
- Faster projected turnaround times on the ground of one alternative may enable the operator to use their limited airport gates more efficiently, or to fly additional flights.
- Differences in the maximum range may allow desirable future expansion to possible longer routes and new markets, and so on.

In the case of combat aircraft, the variables and the relationships among them are even more complex. Analysis of a fighter aircraft might consider factors such as sustained turn rates, rates of climb, range, armaments load, pilot workload, radar cross-section, radar capability, survivability, maintainability, interoperability, and any number of other variables.

Operations analysis, colloquially called **ops analysis**, has many applications, both for the aircraft operator and the manufacturer. Both parties have an interest in understanding factors that determine the effectiveness of aircraft in the marketplace, and both utilize ops analysis to gain insight.

Because of its capability to relate customer desires, hardware, and the business case, ops analysis is of particular interest for strategic planners within the aviation industry. It is uniquely useful for identifying target markets, calibrating market size, evaluating alternative aircraft configuration to serve the markets (including competitor aircraft), and assessing economic factors relating to hypothetical new product lines. When management decisions concerning strategic planning are made, ops analysis can be used as a tool to justify and explain the decisions to stockholders, governments, creditors, and the media.

Apart from marketing applications, ops analysis is used in an important way during the design process for new aircraft. As the customer defines operational needs and missions, it is the job of analysts to define operational characteristics of the aircraft. For example, if a detailed survey of a specific market segment for passenger transport aircraft identifies a variety of size and range requirements, operations analysts can reach theoretical conclusions concerning optimal payload and range capabilities that should be designed into an aircraft targeted at the market segment. It then becomes the job of the design engineers to translate the required capabilities into detailed aircraft design.

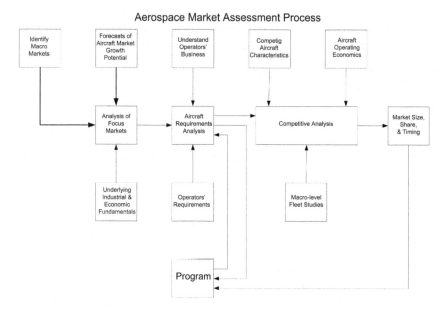

Figure 13.2 Reliable market assessments are based upon systematic gathering of relevant data, analysis of the data, and formulation of logical conclusions.

Logically, one would assume that the operator would understand his own business better than anyone else. This is not necessarily the case. The experience, competence, and management capability of operators vary enormously. As in other business sectors, aviation operators span the entire continuum from the highly knowledgeable to the complete neophytes. Often unsophisticated customers rely upon aircraft manufacturers to provide guidance and recommendations pertaining to the appropriate utilization of aircraft and equipment. In contrast, technically sophisticated customers typically have highly specific ideas concerning the operational characteristics of the aircraft they desire.

The nature of the technical dialogue between the marketing team and the customer is affected by the level of technical sophistication of the customer. In the case of customers without extensive analytical experience, the analysts on the marketing team often provide the customer with tutorials that show how analytical methods can be applied to the customer's operational needs. Needless to say, customers are generally shrewd enough to recognize that analytical methods can be manipulated to produce outcomes favorable to the individual sellers. Although customers do not blindly accept the conclusions of operations analysis performed by the marketing team, they are usually interested in understanding the factors and variables used in the analysis.

Apart from its role as a common language between customers and sellers, ops analysis is of fundamental importance to both the customer and the marketer, for several reasons:

- It provides quantitative identification of missions, objectives, economic factors, and operational environments of the customer.
- As operational factors and variables are defined, ops analysis enables technical definition of specific customer requirements.
- Ops analysis provides a bridge between technologies and market requirements, and provides a means for illustrating relationships between the two.
- Of particular interest to the marketer is that ops analysis provides a quantifiable means for marketing teams to support sales efforts for existing products to domestic and international customers.
- Ops analysis enables the seller and the customer to compare the operational qualities of competing aircraft.

The nature of the operations analysis process varies, depending upon the nature of the customer, the product, and the objective of the analysis. However, the process normally passes through a sequence of standard stages that yield a final conclusion concerning the suitability of the product for the customer's operations. Like all theoretical analysis, it is limited by the quality of the raw data, the validity of the underlying hypotheses, and the robustness of the analytical model. The fundamental process is similar for both civil and military operators, although the nature of their equipment and their operations obviously differ enormously.

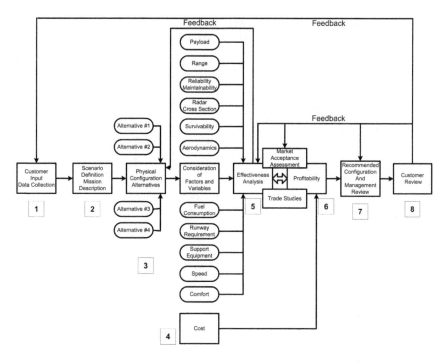

Figure 13.3 The nature of analysis varies according to circumstances and objectives, but the process generally involves identifying requirements and alternatives, evaluating factors, assessing effectiveness, and identifying an optimal outcome.

1. Almost all ops analysis begins with **customer input**, which often takes the form of meetings with the customer to discuss operational needs and desires. During these discussions, the analysts attempt to reach an understanding of the customer's immediate requirements and longer-term objectives. For use in subsequent studies, the analysts attempt to elicit as much detailed technical information as possible, including customer expectations concerning costs and budgets.
2. After gathering initial information, the analysts and marketers develop a specific description of the customer's **operating scenarios and missions**. This describes the job the customer wants to accomplish, the time available, the prevailing environmental conditions, anticipated enemy capabilities, ground facilities available, etc.
3. When the operating scenarios are understood, the analysts work with engineering project offices and design engineers to develop **physical configuration alternatives**. These alternatives are different engineering concepts that would theoretically enable the customer to attain objectives. The alternatives could include, for example, designs for aircraft layouts for two engines versus four engines, or aluminum structure versus composite

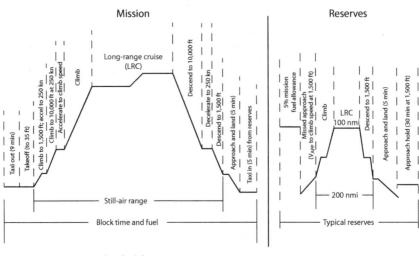

Mission Profile

Typical Mission Rules

- Standard day
- Fuel density 6.7 lbs per US gallon
- Nominal performance
- Passengers at 200 lbs (90kg) passenger and baggage

Figure 13.4 Data elements relating to operating scenarios are ascent profiles, required fuel reserves, cruise altitude, distance, and taxi time.

Source: Boeing.

structure, or twin aisle versus single aisle. If a major new design is not envisioned, the alternatives may be more modest, involving competitive avionics equipment or minor airframe modifications.

4. When the alternatives are defined, their specifications are routed to technical offices that specialize in operational characteristics of the aircraft or equipment under consideration. Within these offices, **evaluation of factors and variables** pertaining to each of the alternatives is performed, assuming that each of the designs will be used for the operational scenarios defined earlier. Depending on the nature of the scenarios, evaluations include flight characteristics, weapons effectiveness, interoperability, survivability, stealth characteristics, range, takeoff and landing constraints, payload, ground handling constraints, loading and unloading characteristics, reliability, maintainability, operating costs, expected sales price, and any number of other factors.

5. Upon completion of their analysis, the technical specialists forward their evaluation to the operational analysts, who perform **effectiveness analysis**. This analysis is generally based upon a computer model that calculates final scores for each of the alternatives by ascribing weighted coefficients

to each of the operational variables. Obviously, the validity of the overall outcome is entirely dependent upon the formulas used to calculate the scores.

6. As effectiveness analysis is being performed, financial analysts are calculating the projected **profitability** of each of the alternative configurations. Profitability assessments consider factors such as projections of development costs, sales price, manufacturing cost, risk, sales quantities, and investment required.

   During the overall operations analysis process, there typically exists an inherent conflict between objectives involving effectiveness and profitability. Effectiveness generally entails higher levels of investment, technological risk, customized engineering, and various expensive improvements. Maximum profitability, on the other hand, often implies less investment and lower levels of technological risk.

   The process of evaluation and analysis recognizes these inherent conflicts and includes an iterative mechanism for resolution. As the physical design alternatives of new aircraft emerge, **trade studies** are conducted by engineers, financial managers, marketers, ops analysts, and maintenance specialists. Because aircraft design always involves compromise among conflicting priorities, the trade studies are intended to evaluate the overall effect if marginal capability of one type is sacrificed in order to boost capability of another type. The entire design concept is based on resolution and optimization of these trade-offs, such as size versus cost, speed versus efficiency, big wing (more lift, more internal fuel) versus small wing (less drag, less weight), and so on. Many aspects of the trade studies are performed by the ops analysts. These trade-offs relate to systems engineering, which was discussed in Chapter 8.

   Because changes of this sort will affect customer acceptance of the product, marketing specialists are involved to provide their judgment as part of **market acceptance assessments**. At the culmination of the trade studies, the result is the selection of an aircraft configuration that is theoretically the best combination of effectiveness and projected profitability.

7. After the thorough iterative process of optimizing performance, cost, and anticipated customer acceptance, the recommended configuration is formally defined, and is submitted for **management review**.

8. Following acceptance by management, the configuration is formally presented for **customer review** and further discussion. If the customer has an active requirement to acquire aircraft, the marketing team's objective is to elicit a request for further information, eventually leading to contracting activity.

Operations analysis is commonly used in the marketing battleground between competitors. Analysis is an effective tool for sellers to demonstrate the superiority of their products to customers. The analysis is tailored to meet fit the circumstances, but certain types of comparisons have become industry standards.

Cost per passenger mile is a relatively simple metric of primary interest to passenger airlines. For cargo airlines, the equivalent metric is cost per revenue ton. The math is more complex than it appears at first glance, because the calculations consider factors such as flight profiles, distances, load factors, and other variables. Sometimes the calculations are based only on direct operating costs, which primarily include fuel and maintenance costs. For other purposes, total operating costs, which include additional factors such as cost of ownership, crew salaries, insurance, overhead, etc., are included.

A commercial airline's calculation of the value of an aircraft is straightforward. Financial analysts calculate the cost per flight hour of aircraft utilization, based upon the airline's internal costs and aircraft operating costs specified by the manufacturer. These cost calculations include cost of ownership of the aircraft, which relates directly to the purchase price. The analysts then calculate the revenue the aircraft will generate, based on projections of quantities of passengers flown, multiplied by ticket prices, multiplied by the number of times the aircraft will provide service over the route. If the difference between revenues and costs is sufficient to meet the airline's standards for profitability and return on investment, the aircraft is theoretically a good investment. However, the airline financial analysts can be expected to perform the same financial analysis of all competing aircraft. When the analysis is complete, the aircraft that will theoretically generate the highest profit has a competitive advantage.

Because time has a dramatic impact on airline economics, **route block times** are routinely used as a basis for estimating aircraft schedules and revenues to be earned. The block times are developed by applying aircraft flight capabilities to the specific routes to be flown. The final results depend upon factors such as rates of climb, cruise speed, takeoff and landing distances, noise footprint, avionics equipment, and ground-handling characteristics.

For transport aircraft, perhaps the most basic of all analysis is the **payload and range graph**. For fixed atmospheric conditions, it depicts the relationship between payload that the aircraft can carry and the distance that it can be carried. Greater payload entails shorter range. These graphs are often used for comparisons between competitive aircraft.

Maintenance costs are generally considered to be an element of direct operating costs. For civil operators, they have a significant impact upon profitability. For military users, they represent a major component of operating costs over the lifetime of any aircraft. To some extent, maintenance costs can be extrapolated from accumulated data from aircraft in service. However, these costs vary significantly depending upon the age of the aircraft, the quality of the maintenance it receives, and the conditions under which it operates. Aircraft operated in the salt air of coastal environments, or in desert areas where sand infiltration is a problem, tend to experience higher maintenance costs than aircraft operating in benign environments such as inland areas of Western Europe.

Cargo capacity is a primary consideration for freighter aircraft and military transports, but is also important for passenger airlines, which earn important

Table 13.1 This worksheet depicts the relationships between investment costs, direct operating costs, and fixed operating costs

Estimated operating costs worksheet

A. Investment cost
- Basic aircraft $_____
- Options $_____
- Initial spares $_____

Total investment cost $_____

B. Direct operating costs
1. Fuel at $_____per gallon times ____G/FH $_____
   Oil at 1.5% of fuel cost $_____
2. Aircraft maintenance at $ ____per manhour times $_____
   ____MMH/FH
3. Reserve for major dynamics overhaul and repair $_____
4. Reserve for engine and APU overhaul and repair $_____
5. Reserve for airframe consumable spares $_____
6. Reserve for airframe reparable spares $_____
7. Reserve for rotor blades $_____

Total direct hourly costs $ per flight hour

C. Fixed annual operating costs
1. Depreciation: total investment cost minus residual value $_____
   divided by years of service
2. Interest on investment $_____
3. Hull insurance $_____
4. Liability insurance $_____
5. Flight crew salaries and costs $_____
6. Maintenance overhead $_____
7. General and administrative overhead $_____
8. Non-revenue flights $_____

Total fixed annual costs $ per year

Total hourly operating costs
- Total direct cost per hour $ per flight hour
- Total fixed cost per hour (total annual fixed costs $ per flight hour
  divided by flight hours per year)

Total cost per flight hour $ per flight hour

---

revenue from freight carried in the lower cargo hold. Air freight is transported in a vast variety of physical shapes and sizes, including many standard and non-standard container types, open pallets of various shapes, unpalletized crates, and roll-on-roll-off vehicles. Cargo analysis attempts to show how the dimensions and weight limits of the cargo bay can best accommodate the variety of expected freight.

Passenger cabin dimensions, directly related to passenger comfort, are of fundamental interest to airlines. Historically, airlines have considered dual-aisle widebody aircraft to be more appealing to passengers than narrower single-aisle layouts. Internal space is appealing because it permits greater headroom, accommodates greater storage area, and conveys an overall impression of spaciousness.

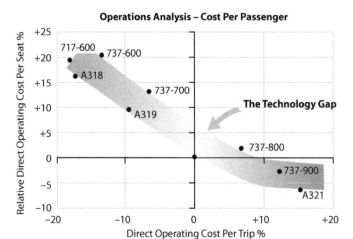

Figure 13.5 Operations analysis in its most elemental form: Airbus claims its planes are more efficient than Boeing's. Boeing, of course, has analysis to prove otherwise.

Source: Airbus.

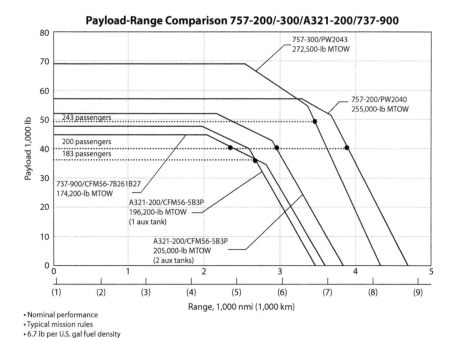

Figure 13.6 Payload-range analysis is a staple of transport aircraft analysis.

Source: Boeing.

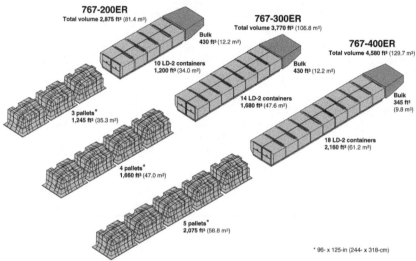

Figure 13.7 For passenger transports, the size of the lower cargo hold matters.

Source: Boeing.

Crew training and cross-training are important to airlines that operate mixed fleets of aircraft that require air crews to be transferred from one type to another. Because flight training is expensive, and because crews occupied in training are unavailable to generate revenue, airlines prefer to minimize training time. The major civil aircraft manufacturers commonly promote their 'families of aircraft' with common cockpit designs that facilitate cross-training of crews between types.

Mission radius is a standard basis of analysis for military aircraft. The aircraft is given a specific configuration of weapons load or cargo, and is assumed to fly a combat mission of a specific profile in terms of speed, altitude, loiter times, and so on. Based on these parameters, the maximum mission radius can be defined and used for comparison with competitors.

Maneuvering capability and general flight performance are of particular interest to military operators, for whom speed and agility are often associated with lethality or survivability. Analysts and engineers apply aircraft characteristics to fixed scenarios to calculate maximum speeds, turn rates, rates of climb, g-forces, and so on. The results of the calculations can be used to predict survivability or capability to perform specific missions.

Table 13.2 Analysis of training time for pilot transition between aircraft types can build an economic argument in support of aircraft that require shortest transition periods

Comparative pilot transition times Boeing 757 versus Airbus A321

Number of days required for transition between other airplanes and the 757 or A321-200

Current fleet	757	A321
L-1011	21 days typical	25 days typical
DC-10		
A300		
A310		
747-100/-200/-300		
767-200ER/-300ER	4 hours	25 days typical
767-400	2–4 days	
777	14 days typical	25 days typical
747-400		
737-300 through -900		
A330	21 days typical	8 days
A340		9 days

Source: Boeing.

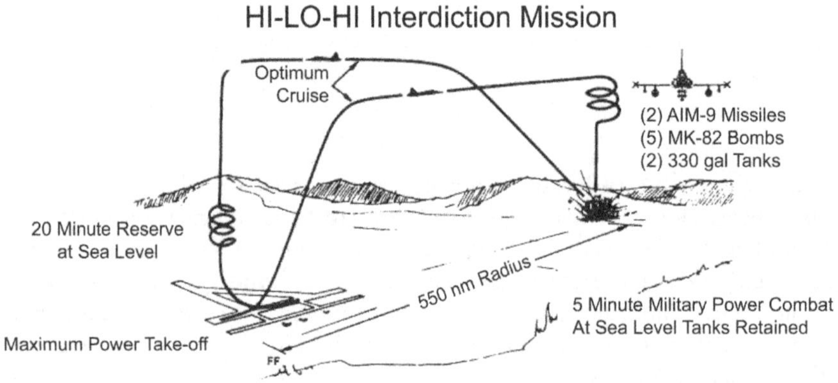

HI-LO-HI Interdiction Mission

Figure 13.8 Typical radius analysis depicts round-trip distances over which military aircraft can perform specific missions. This particular analysis pertains to the Northrop F-20.

Source: Northrop.

Operations analysis is an indispensable part of the aerospace marketing process. It provides operators, manufacturers, and designers with a common vernacular to discuss requirements, capabilities, efficiencies, and costs. For the seller, it offers a means of understanding the customer's needs, and furnishes a way of communicating how those needs can be met by the product being offered. It is the common international language of the aerospace marketplace.

Turn Performance at 15,000 ft (4572 m)
Utilizing Maximum Afterburner Power

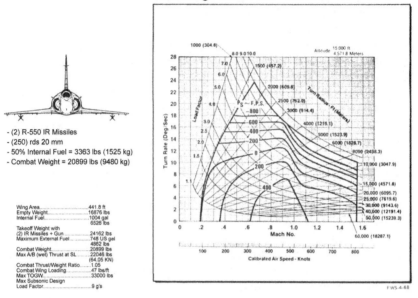

Figure 13.9 An example of maneuverability capabilities of a fighter aircraft.

Source: Dassault Aviation.

C-130J Performance Improvements
International Configuration

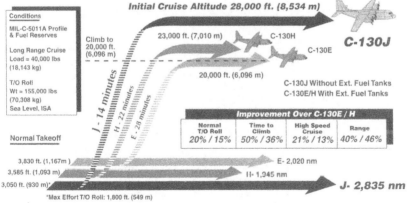

Figure 13.10 Basic analysis of flight performance depicts takeoff distances, time-to-climb, and cruising altitude.

Source: Lockheed Martin.

Market-based pricing strategies

Simply put, market-based pricing strategies ignore cost factors and strive to sell product for the highest price that market circumstances will permit. In the aerospace industry, this type of pricing is sometimes referred to as **commercial pricing**. Aerospace sales to national governments, in contrast, are often required by law to be cost-based, in order to protect governments from abuses that sometimes result from market-based pricing strategies.

Many observers of the aerospace industry believe that pricing of commercial aircraft follows an evolution that is in concert with the life cycle of the product itself. In the initial **launch** phase of a new aircraft, the manufacturer tends to offer an aggressively low price in order to garner sufficient orders to reach critical mass to launch the program. In the face of enormous start-up investments, the builder also wants to maximize early orders to get positive cash flow. The second phase, **demand growth**, allows the seller to raise prices as the marketplace accepts the new aircraft and demand strengthens as airlines vie to acquire the new model. The third phase, **consolidation**, allows sellers to maintain firm pricing as the aircraft becomes commonly established among operational fleets. In the final phase, **oldie-but-goodie**, the aircraft remains capable of rendering credible service, but is eclipsed by newer models. Affordable pricing is its primary means of competing against more modern challengers.

Within the broad category of market-based pricing, a number of distinct subcategories of pricing strategies are frequently applied. Although these strategies are dissimilar, it is important to recognize that they share a common

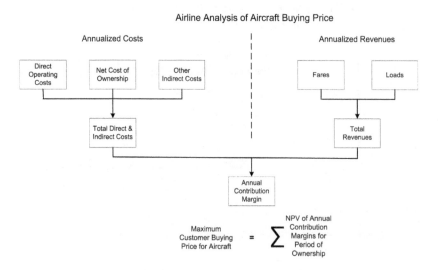

Figure 13.11 The rational commercial operator will only buy if the price is low enough to enable a profit. If competing aircraft are available, the customer will buy the one that yields the largest projected profit.

characteristic: they are primarily oriented to the **demand side** of the market, and they consider factors such as activities of competitors, expected behavior of customers, market share, and so on.

Market penetration. Market share is a very important consideration in the aerospace industry. The industry is characterized by exceptionally high capital-investment requirements, perhaps greater than any other industry. In order to amortize this capital investment, long production runs at reasonably high rates are required. The small number of oligopolists fight for market share in order to generate production volume necessary to enable amortization of capital investment and low production costs.

In addition, manufacturers are faced with enormous fixed costs of supporting their aircraft and equipment after delivery. By their very nature, aircraft are expected to be geographically dispersed, and manufacturers are obligated to sustain facilities worldwide to provide immediate support in terms of technical services and spare parts. Cost of these facilities vary according to the number of aircraft to be supported, but the basic infrastructure, and its associated cost, has to be maintained whether the worldwide fleet of aircraft is small or large.

Aircraft operators have compelling reasons to maintain loyalty to a single aircraft manufacturer rather than operate mixed fleets of aircraft from several suppliers. Operational costs are lower for single-source fleets because cockpits and controls are similar, resulting in lower pilot-training costs and flexibility in assigning pilots to fly multiple aircraft types. Ground operations are cheaper because much ground-support equipment is common. Spare-parts inventories are lower because aircraft from the same vendor tend to utilize common parts and systems.

Consequently, aircraft suppliers attempting to penetrate a new market, or sell to a new customer, face formidable barriers to entry. Often their single most powerful tool against these barriers is pricing. At some price point, the customer's economics will favor purchasing dissimilar aircraft from a new supplier, regardless of negative considerations involving support and operating costs.

This is the logic of pricing for market penetration. The seller prices his aircraft or equipment at a level, often below short-term cost, that enables selling in a market that would otherwise be closed. The objective is to eventually raise production rates and deployment efficiencies to the point where the seller can compete on equal terms with existing suppliers.

Airbus Industrie is a textbook example of effective application of pricing for market penetration. Entering a 1970s airliner market dominated by Boeing and McDonnell Douglas, Airbus had no choice but to compete on the basis of pricing. Supported heavily by financial assistance from European national governments, the producer gradually clawed its way toward a significant market share, and after more than 20 years achieved market parity with Boeing. Airbus did not publish consolidated profit-and-loss statements during the early decades of its existence, so no definitive public information about profitability is available. However, most knowledgeable observers believe that Airbus's financial losses in the 1970s, 1980s, and 1990s were large. Regardless, the Airbus strategy to gain market share was ultimately successful.

Monopoly pricing. This type of pricing, also relatively rare in the aerospace industry, involves companies that are the sole suppliers of a specialized type of equipment and who take advantage of the lack of effective competition to price their products so that they earn exceptional profits. For years, customers and competitors were heard to complain that Boeing's pricing on the 747 was monopolistic because of the lack of any effective competition for very large civil transports. Generally, the rare perceptions of monopolistic pricing occur in smaller, more specialized segments of the industry, where the volume of business is inadequate to support multiple suppliers. Sometimes, suppliers of specialized radio-frequency antennas are accused of monopoly pricing, for example.

According to economists, true monopolistic power does not exist unless barriers to entry effectively prevent other competitors from entering the market. In fact, the perception of monopolistic profits often is an incentive to other firms to compete. Airbus's introduction of the A380 super widebody is a perfect example of a strategy to counter monopoly pricing by a competitor.

Matching competitor pricing. Economists describe markets characterized by a small number of large sellers as oligopolistic markets. A common practice in oligopolistic markets is price matching. The few firms involved want to avoid aggressive price competition that will reduce profits for all, and they tend to offer list prices that are in the same range for similar products.

However, when one or more of the oligopolistic firms becomes dissatisfied with its market share and chooses a strategy to increase market share, or when the size of the overall market is in decline, price competition becomes more severe. Although price competition among oligopolists is good for the customer, it does not necessarily yield the desired outcome to the original price-cutting supplier. Typically, the other oligopolists, remaining true to the past practices of their industry, match the price cuts of the original firm, eliminating any competitive advantage, and reducing profits for all sellers.

Responding to customer affordability. At the outset of a planned competitive procurement, customers sometimes announce the quantity of aircraft they intend to buy and the budget that has been approved for the procurement. Often this procedure is a calculated bluff by commercial operators who are seeking to reduce costs, but sometimes, particularly when government procurements are involved, the budgetary limit is real and non-negotiable.

When the customer has directly or indirectly communicated the maximum price he or she is willing to pay, the supplier has several possible courses of action. One choice is to meet the customer's price, regardless of whether the price enables a normal profit. A second choice is to withdraw from the competition, if a sale at the customer's price would be a money-losing proposition with no compelling strategic value. Or, third, the seller can remain in the competition at a price higher than stipulated by the customer, with the hope that the customer will eventually find a way to increase the available budget to cover the higher price offered by the supplier.

Buying-in. For reasons discussed previously, it is often problematic for aerospace customers to abandon traditional suppliers, even if later developments make other competitors more attractive. Because sellers recognize this, they sometimes offer extremely aggressive pricing to win initial competitions in programs that are expected to have subsequent follow-on buys. The concept is that profits foregone or losses incurred on the initial program can be recaptured by means of higher prices on subsequent rounds of procurement. Intentional use of this pricing strategy is illegal under some circumstances, such as when selling to the US government. In general customers are understandably unhappy if they suspect their supplier has an explicit plan to raise prices after an initial commitment is obtained.

Pricing to maximize spares and maintenance revenue. This strategy, sometimes known as the **give-away-the-razor-but-sell-the-blades** strategy, considers product pricing in the context of the long-term revenue stream that will result from selling spare parts and postdelivery support for in-service aircraft and installed equipment.

The volume of business resulting from postdelivery support is substantial. The US Department of Defense, in studies involving life-cycle costing, estimates that the cost of operating and maintaining military aircraft will be from three to seven times the initial purchase price of the aircraft. Much of this cost results from spare parts and technical services provided by the original manufacturer.

The relationship between the initial sales price and future spares and maintenance revenue varies greatly among types of equipment. Jet engines, which last many years and require many spare parts and maintenance actions, offer prime examples of how the pricing strategy can work effectively, and jet-engine manufacturers are known for heavily discounting their products in order to assure future lucrative streams of revenue from support business. The same is true of manufacturers of helicopter dynamic components such as transmissions, rotor hubs, and swashplates, which require relatively frequent overhauls. On the other hand, major commercial aircraft manufacturers have historically been less likely to be heavily involved in postdelivery support. Airframe structure can last indefinitely without replacement, and often aftermarket maintenance, repair, and overhaul specialist companies (MROs) capture much of the maintenance business. The equipment items that require replacement or overhaul are generally provided by subcontractors who compete for the repair and replacement business themselves. Consequently, the expectation of future support business has not been a major consideration in the pricing strategy of many aircraft original-equipment manufacturers. However, as will be discussed in Chapter 14, OEMs are becoming more active in the MRO business, with uncertain implications for the future.

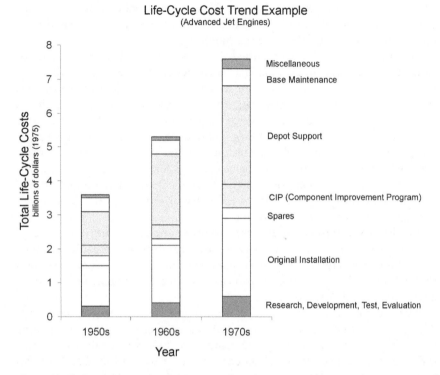

Figure 13.12 For many equipment items such as jet engines, the cost of spare parts and maintenance over a lifetime will exceed the initial purchase price. This reality is an incentive for sellers to price their product low in order to profit from support business.

Source: Institute for Defense Analyses.

Cost-based pricing strategies

In a competitive marketplace, price is determined by the interplay of supply and demand. Cost has a bearing on the supply side of the market. In the long run, the price at which suppliers are willing to offer their products will depend upon their investments and cost of manufacturing.

The ability of the seller to reduce prices by reducing costs is in large part dependent upon the time horizon. When an imminent sale of an existing product is at hand, costs are generally known and are difficult to reduce in the short term. The seller might choose to reduce prices, but realistically will not be able to implement immediate cost reductions of any significance. In contrast, at the beginning of a new program in which all design and manufacturing decisions remain to be made, the manufacturer has a great deal of freedom to select design characteristics and manufacturing plans that will have a profound impact on cost.

However, as noted in the example of Airbus list pricing earlier in this chapter, supply-side factors rarely determine the final selling price. If demand is weak, the manufacturer may be faced with a choice of temporarily lowering price below the breakeven point, or not making a sale.

A predictable characteristic of aerospace costs is that manufacturing hours per unit tend to decrease over time as the cumulative quantity of aircraft manufactured increases. This phenomenon, which has been widely studied and is discussed in more detail in Chapter 7, is the **learning curve** effect. A theoretical effect of this phenomenon is that, to the extent that pricing is based upon costs, early buyers will pay more than later buyers. In fact, because declining-cost tendencies related to learning curves can be offset by inflation over the long term, cost-based aerospace prices have historically risen over time.

One important segment of the aerospace market in which cost-based pricing is regularly used is defense contracting in NATO countries. In most major defense contracts, the government customer makes separate incremental payments for non-recurring costs such as engineering research and development and manufacturing tooling. Because of technological uncertainties, costs for R&D are notoriously difficult to accurately predict, and thus are customarily paid for by the customer on a cost-reimbursement basis rather than as a fixed price. Later, as aircraft or systems enter full-scale production, the government customer, who owns much of the technology and production tooling, exercises a contractual right to limit the manufacturer's profits to a reasonable level.

Defense contractors in NATO countries are normally required to maintain meticulous cost records that are periodically audited by government officials. These records form the basis for cost-based pricing.

Relationship marketing

Person-to-person buying and selling deals are sometimes divided into the two general categories of **transaction marketing** and **relationship marketing**.

Table 13.3 Relationship marketing prevails in the aerospace industry, with profound implications upon behavior of marketing professionals

Time, account behavior, and marketing approach	
Relationship marketing (Long-time horizon)	*Transaction marketing (Short-term horizon)*
Typified by lost-for-good customers	Typified by always-a-share customers
High switching costs	Lower switching costs
Substantial investment actions, especially in procedures and lasting assets	Smaller investment actions
High perceived exposure	Lower perceived exposure
Focus on a technology or on a vendor	Focus on a product or on a person
High importance: strategic, operational, and personal	Lower importance

Source: Bund Jackson, B 1985, *Winning and Keeping Industrial Customers*, Lexington Books, Lanham.

Some sales are single transactions in which the buyer and seller never expect to deal with each other again. However, many sales occur in the context of long-standing relationships between buyers and sellers. Customers prefer suppliers who are known to them, whom they trust, and who have a proven record of credibility and performance. In the aerospace industry, where both the customer and the supplier are mutually subject to complex circumstances, a knowledgeable long-term relationship between buyer and seller is especially crucial.

According to studies of conventional marketing, personal contact between the seller and the buyer is particularly important if the product is expensive, is technically complex, and if the number of customers is relatively small. Certainly, these conditions apply to most segments of the aerospace industry.

Relationships and trust are developed over time, and are more important in some cultures than in others. But even in the modern business environment, where reorganizations, management mobility, and changes in ownership are common, and where business people are accustomed to relatively short-term

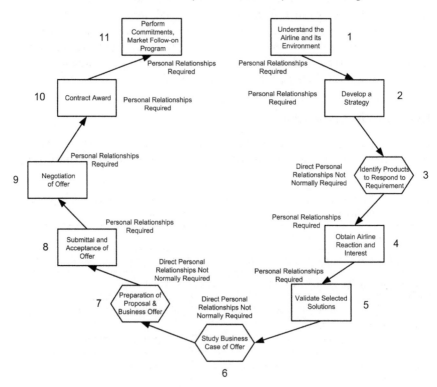

Figure 13.13 The importance of relationships in aerospace marketing.

personal relationships, long-term relationships are especially valuable in industries in which trust and credibility are essential.

The process of developing relationships involves more than simply arranging periodic meetings. Effective relationships are based on mutual trust and credibility. From the customer's perspective, a valuable contribution of the marketing manager is detailed knowledge of the product. He or she is expected to communicate to the customer all necessary technical information about the product itself, the capabilities of the product, and operational experience with the product. In addition, the seller is expected to provide useful knowledge about the business operations and program management of his or her company, including possible delivery schedules, configuration changes, financing arrangements, and so on. He or she is also expected to serve as a communications conduit between the customer and all parts of the selling company, including senior management.

Well-executed relationship marketing can be extremely effective in the aerospace industry, where customers become committed to expensive, complex systems and expect first-class support and service over the long term.

14 Aerospace maintenance, repair, and overhaul

Aircraft maintenance, repair, and overhaul (MRO) is an essential part of the aircraft life cycle, spanning the entire period of operational service. MRO activity includes routine scheduled maintenance as well as unscheduled or unplanned maintenance due to damage, component and engine failures, and mandatory modifications. It also includes upgrades to the aircraft performed at the discretion of the aircraft owner, with the approval of airworthiness authorities.

Logistics, which is often considered part of the MRO sector, covers the management, storage, and control of aircraft parts and material necessary to perform MRO operations. It is generally construed to include packing, preservation, and shipment of parts.

Maintenance technical documentation

Maintenance of aircraft is performed in accordance with procedures and intervals delineated in maintenance manuals and technical specifications, usually provided by the aircraft manufacturer. In the case of civil aircraft in the USA these manuals must be designated and marked as **'approved data'** verified by the Federal Aviation Administration (FAA). In the FAA document control system, the manuals are classified as **'instructions for continued airworthiness' (ICA)**. In Europe practices are virtually identical, and the European Aviation Safety Agency (EASA) uses the same terminology of ICA. Initial maintenance manuals are approved during the process of issuing the original airworthiness type certification of the aircraft.

As aircraft enter service, the original ICA data is supplemented and updated in several ways:

Airworthiness directives (ADs) are issued when the FAA becomes aware of an unsafe condition affecting an aircraft, engine, component, or any part. The ADs notify aircraft owners and operators of the danger and require immediate special inspections, repairs, or modifications to correct the unsafe condition.

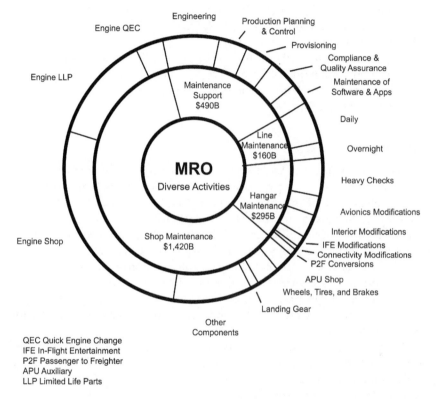

Maintenance, Engineering, Parts, Upgrades
Market Segments

Projected Total Revenue 20 Years 2018-2037
$2,365 billion

Engineering

Engine QEC

Production Planning & Control

Provisioning

Compliance & Quality Assurance

Engine LLP

Maintenance of Software & Apps

Maintenance Support $490B

Daily

Line Maintenance $160B

Overnight

MRO

Diverse Activities

Heavy Checks

Hangar Maintenance $295B

Avionics Modifications

Interior Modifications

Engine Shop

Shop Maintenance $1,420B

IFE Modifications
Connectivity Modifications
P2F Conversions

APU Shop

Wheels, Tires, and Brakes

Landing Gear

Other Components

QEC Quick Engine Change
IFE In-Flight Entertainment
P2F Passenger to Freighter
APU Auxiliary
LLP Limited Life Parts

Figure 14.1 MRO has many facets. Boeing estimates that the sector will generate $2.365 trillion within the next 20 years.

Source: Boeing.

Service bulletins (SBs) are notices to aircraft operators from a manufacturer notifying them of updated maintenance information or product modifications. **Alert service bulletins** are issued by the manufacturer when a condition exists that the manufacturer considers to be a safety-related matter as opposed to just a product improvement. These alert SBs usually result in the FAA issuing an AD. The AD will reference the alert service bulletin as the method of compliance with the airworthiness directive. If a service bulletin is not an alert service bulletin or a bulletin referenced in an AD, it becomes optional and incorporation by the operator is voluntary.

Manuals and technical updates for military aircraft vary internationally. For the US Air Force, as a typical example, manuals are initially prepared by the aircraft manufacturer in a format specified by the Air Force. When the aircraft enters service, responsibility for the manuals transfers to the US Air Force Material Command, which issues updates and revisions thereafter. The equivalent of service bulletins is the **technical order (TO)**, which contains routine update information. The equivalent of a civil airworthiness directive is the **time compliance technical order (TCTO)**, which has safety implications and must be implemented immediately.

In the case of both civil and military maintenance manuals and technical data of all sorts, publications for modern aircraft have become overwhelmingly digital in format. For older aircraft, printed manuals are rapidly being converted to digital media.

Software

On-board software is an increasingly important aspect of design and operation of modern aircraft. In particular, the prevalence of **loadable software**, which is intended to be progressively updated as a routine maintenance operation, has expanded exponentially. The International Air Transport Association (IATA) estimates that the Boeing 787 has more than 500 loadable software applications, installed in more than 800 locations on the aircraft.

Aircraft loadable software should be controlled and managed through a single control point to ensure standardization of the upgrade processes and to enable effective configuration control. Sometimes these control points are in-house engineering or avionics offices, and can also be specialized certified firms working under contract.

OEMs or vendors notify operators of software upgrades through various channels such as service bulletins, engineering orders, service letters, vendor notifications, and OEM-specific communications. Safety-critical updates are transmitted through airworthiness directives or alert service bulletins.

When software upgrade notifications are received, they are generally registered through the operator's technical library and processed to the relevant engineering department to assess applicability, validity, and compliance requirements.

Software upgrades follow the standard engineering change management and configuration control process, and if eventually approved are released as change notices that specify aircraft effectivity and implementation schedules. The actual installation of software is typically performed during line maintenance.

Material inventory management and classifications

In order to enable the tasks of maintaining and modifying aircraft, inventories of parts and materials necessary to perform the work must be stocked and managed to make them readily accessible to MRO operators. Parts and material are grouped into a few major categories, and are managed differently according to their categorization.

Rotables are parts that can be repeatedly overhauled and returned to serviceable condition. An example is hydraulic pumps. When rotables are removed from the aircraft they will eventually be sent to an overhaul source, so after removal they are placed in a separate inventory of unserviceable rotables until they are once again returned to serviceable condition.

Repairables are parts and components that can possibly be restored to serviceable condition after removal, but will possibly be scrapped depending on condition. Examples are cabin-floor panels and windows.

Expendables are items such as rivets and O-rings. They are used once and discarded in future maintenance operations.

Consumables are items such as paint and lubricants that are intended to be progressively used during maintenance.

A separate categorization of aircraft spares inventory involves the distinction between **line replaceable units (LRUs)** and **shop replaceable units (SRUs)**. Components, which are generally rotables, are customarily classified as either LRUs or SRUs. As the terminology implies, LRUs can be quickly removed and replaced on the flight line, expediting maintenance during operations and returning the aircraft to flight status. SRUs are generally subcomponents of LRUs, and must be removed from the LRU and replaced in specialist backshops. Taking an example of an LRU such as a flight control computer, an SRU might be an internal circuit board. This subject is addressed in more detail later in the section on component repair.

Table 14.1 The four basic categories of aircraft parts and material inventory

Rotables, repairables, expendables, and consumables	
Rotables	Complex components
	Normally unlimited number of repair cycles
	Normally no scrap expected
	Controlled by individual serial number
	Exchanged during maintenance
Repairables	Components that can be technically and economically repaired
	Under normal conditions, serial number control is not necessary
	Limited repair cycles, with possibility of scrap
Expendables	Scrapped after removal if inspection determination is unserviceable
	100% replacement items
	Not economically repairable
	Standard parts and hardware
Consumables	Any material used only once
	Raw materials
	Paints, oils, lubricants, and chemical products
	Items that cannot be removed intact after installation

The supply chain for parts and material varies according to the nature of the maintenance work performed, and is also discussed later.

Line maintenance

Line maintenance includes frequent, regular checks after every flight to ensure that aircraft are fit for flight. As required, it also includes troubleshooting, defect rectification, and component replacement. As aircraft problems occur, technicians diagnose and correct issues. Line-maintenance activity can be grouped into three categories:

- Transit checks, which are performed after each landing, prior to the next take-off
- Routine daily and weekly checks
- A-checks, which are conducted at intervals of eight to ten weeks, and include changing filters, lubricating where required, checking fluid levels, and performing a detailed inspection of all emergency equipment. Typically, an A-Check on a Boeing 737, as an example, can be completed overnight on the flight ramp.

Approximately 90% of line maintenance is performed by operators themselves, who often view it as critical to on-time performance. It is generally subcontracted to an outside provider only at sites where the number of an operator's daily flights is too low to justify the expense of a dedicated maintenance team.

The two primary cost elements of line maintenance are labor and material. Labor accounts for approximately 85% of the total, reflecting the labor-intensive nature of the tasks. This cost includes direct labor required to inspect, troubleshoot, and remove and replace LRUs and engines as required. Labor cost also includes general and administrative overhead and employee benefits. Over 98% of line-maintenance technicians in the USA are FAA-certificated because certification is a requirement to perform inspections, sign aircraft logbooks, and release aircraft for flight following maintenance actions.

Material, which accounts for the remaining 15% of cost, is primarily expendables and consumables, such as fasteners, brackets, paints, solvents, and the like. Line-maintenance activities include removal and replacement of expensive LRUs such as avionics, hydraulic components, and electrical systems. However, these items are normally issued from depot inventories and are not charged against line-maintenance budgets.

Airframe heavy maintenance

Airframe heavy maintenance, performed in enclosed hangars and sometimes called depot maintenance, is the inspection, maintenance, and repair of the aircraft airframe, performed at specified time intervals. These intervals are based upon the guidelines of the aircraft manufacturer, but are subject to approval by official airworthiness authorities such as the FAA and EASA. It is the aircraft owner's responsibility to establish heavy-maintenance schedules that meet safety and operational requirements that comply with national and international regulations. Scheduled inspections typically take place at intervals defined by fixed numbers of flight hours. There are three levels of inspection for commercial jet aircraft, usually termed A-, C-, and D-checks. A-checks are handled as part of line maintenance, and were discussed previously. C- and D-checks are included as part of heavy maintenance. (B-checks existed formerly but have largely disappeared as their requirements have been met through other arrangements.)

C-checks take place at intervals of approximately 3,000 flight hours, and include structural inspection, removal of some secondary structure to facilitate inspection, flight control verification and rerigging, and repainting as necessary.

The D-check is performed approximately every six years, and is a complete overhaul. The aircraft is extensively dismantled to allow technicians access to inspect the structure. The interior fittings of the cabin are removed. Engines are removed. The aircraft is placed on jacks, and the landing gear is detached and sent for overhaul. Numerous systems are removed, tested, overhauled if necessary, and replaced. Total costs are typically in the millions of dollars.

Performance of a complete C-check takes several weeks, and a D-check often takes months. In order to avoid this aircraft downtime and the loss of revenue it entails, MROs have developed a system of phased checks, in which smaller parts of the complete task are performed incrementally in shorter periods of time, including overnight periods when the aircraft is scheduled to be out of service. These phased checks cumulatively accomplish many of the requirements of the conventional C- and D-checks, with less overall schedule downtime.

Four types of firms perform airframe heavy maintenance:

Original equipment manufacturers. The involvement of the big OEMs in airframe heavy maintenance has historically been limited to less than 10% of the business. More recently, however, the OEMs have recognized MRO as a profitable and expanding market segment where their capabilities and resources offer a competitive advantage. Both Boeing and Airbus have aggressively entered the market. In contrast to the historical lack of interest by the large aircraft OEMs, the two major regional jet manufacturers, Embraer and Bombardier, operate several heavy-maintenance facilities in the USA. Business and general aviation (BGA) OEMs such as Cessna, Hawker Beech, Gulfstream, Dassault, Embraer, and Bombardier are actively involved in the market. Most of their customers do not have sufficient scale to establish independent heavy-maintenance capability.

Operators. Despite a continuing trend of airlines to outsource heavy maintenance, a few major operators with in-house airframe maintenance capability still perform their own checks. Notable in this group are British Airways, American Airlines, and Japan Airlines.

Independents. Maintenance firms unrelated to either OEMs or airlines usually have the lowest labor costs among the competitors and are significant players in the heavy-maintenance market. The largest companies in this category include ST Aerospace, SR Technics, ATS, AAR, and Timco.

Airline third parties. Specialized maintenance subsidiaries of airlines contribute earnings for their parent companies by performing airframe MRO work for other airlines. Important companies in this category are Lufthansa Technik, Air France Industries/KLM Engineering, Ameco Beijing, and Singapore Airlines Engineering Company.

Historically, aircraft operators have performed more than half of the heavy maintenance for their own fleets, splitting the rest between independents and airline third parties, with a small percentage going to OEMs. This allocation is changing, however, as airlines continue to outsource maintenance work and as OEMs expand their share of the sector.

A noteworthy characteristic of heavy maintenance is that a significant share of the business is performed outside the home geographical region of the airline. Large aircraft can be easily moved to overseas facilities offering attractive pricing and technical expertise.

The three primary cost elements in airframe heavy maintenance are material, labor, and repair/specialty services.

Direct and indirect labor is the largest component of heavy maintenance cost, accounting for 70%. In 2009 the FAA reported that there were 221,578 technicians engaged in airframe heavy maintenance worldwide, of whom nearly 30% were certified by the FAA or international airworthiness authorities as mechanics or repairmen. In the USA in that year there were 101,946 technicians, of whom 55,132 were FAA-certificated as mechanics or repairmen. For an independent airframe heavy-maintenance facility, typically more than half of the technicians are FAA-certificated. At airline MROs more than 90% of technicians are FAA-certificated. This gives airlines flexibility to utilize hangar technicians to perform line maintenance activities if required.

Material is the second largest cost category at 20% of the total, and as with line maintenance, includes consumables such as solvents, hardware such as fasteners and standard parts, and airframe parts. As with line maintenance, aircraft LRUs and systems are provided from the operator's inventory and are not charged as material costs.

Outside repairs and services, usually specialized in nature, account for approximately 10% of the cost. Examples are specialized inspection, chemical processes, seat repairs, and fuel-tank inspection.

The three principal supply channels for parts and services for aircraft heavy maintenance are parts suppliers, distributors, and repair/specialty service suppliers.

Direct sources of parts are OEMs, Part Manufacturer Approval (PMA) holders and hardware manufacturers, and surplus dealers. Of these, OEMs provide

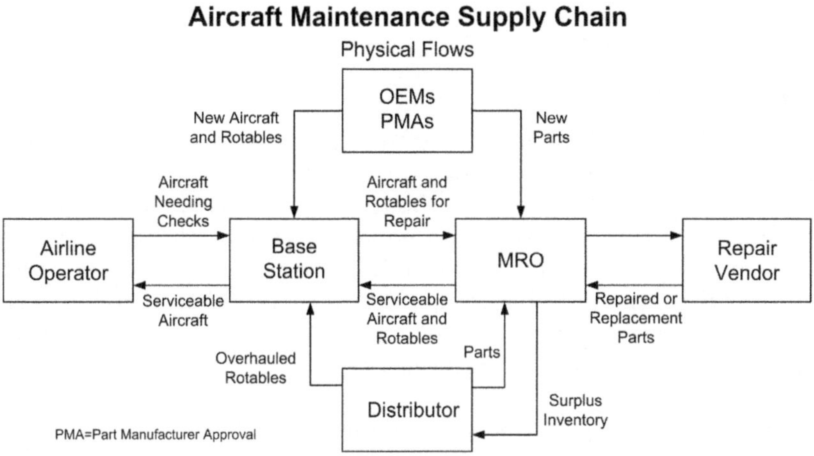

Aircraft Maintenance Supply Chain

Physical Flows

Figure 14.2 Principal sources of serviceable parts for heavy airframe maintenance are OEMs, PMAs, distributors, and specialized repair shops.

most airframe parts. PMAs are not the original manufacturer of the aircraft or components, but have been approved by the FAA or international airworthiness authorities to make replacement parts. The PMA market is small and is mostly involved with seats, galleys, toilets, and cabin furnishings. Companies such as HEICO, Wencor, and Regent are major presences in this segment. Standard hardware, particularly fasteners, are routinely replaced during MRO activities. These items are categorized as standard parts, which are parts or material that conform to an established industry- or government-published specification. The FAA's acceptance of a standard part as an approved part is based on the certification that the part has been designed and produced in accordance with an independently established set of specifications and criteria. The third direct source, surplus dealers, is a minor source of material for most aircraft, but becomes important in support of older aircraft no longer in production. Surplus dealers have recently received attention as bogus non-certified parts have entered the supply chain through this channel. The subject of bogus parts is discussed in Chapter 12.

Distributors commonly serve as intermediaries between parts suppliers and heavy-maintenance facilities. Over 60% of distributors are based in the USA. Airframe heavy MRO providers typically work with three to four major distributors for major items, but often use many smaller distributors for standard hardware and consumables. As an indication of the strategic movement of OEMs into the MRO sector, Boeing has purchased Aviall, the largest worldwide distributor.

Specialty services often perform maintenance and repair of interior furnishings such as seats, galleys, and toilets. Sometimes they are small machine shops that repair airframe parts. In all cases they are required to have appropriate FAA certification.

Engine overhaul

Off-wing engine overhaul involves disassembling the engine, performing inspections, and replacing or repairing parts as necessary. The engine is then reassembled and tested before being reinstalled on the aircraft. For engines of commercial transports, overhaul is performed on an as-needed basis, except for the replacement of life-limited parts (LLP), which occurs at fixed intervals dictated by the civil aviation authority. For engines of business and general aviation aircraft, overhaul is performed at specified time intervals according to guidelines established by the engine manufacturer and approved by the airworthiness authority.

Firms performing engine overhauls are grouped into four categories:

OEMs have by far the largest share of the engine MRO services market. OEMs for air-transport-class engines include GE, Pratt & Whitney, Rolls-Royce, Safran, CFM International, and International Aero Engines. OEMs involved in the business and general aviation market include Pratt & Whitney Canada, Honeywell, Williams International, GE, and Turbomeca.

A few large **operators** have in-house engine overhaul capability. This group includes United Airlines, American Airlines, Japan Airlines, and Iberia.

Independent Engine MRO Providers are firms other than OEMs or operators. Examples are Standard Aero, MTU, SR Technics, Aerothrust, Dallas Airmotive, Vector Aerospace, Aveos, Timco, Pacific Gas Turbine, and ST Aerospace.

Airline third-party providers are partially or fully owned by airlines. In addition to conducting engine overhauls for their owners, they perform work for third-party customers. Examples are Delta TechOps, Air France Industries, and Lufthansa Technik.

Almost half of engine overhaul work is performed by OEMs, followed by operators, who have roughly a quarter of the market. The remainder of the market is shared approximately equally between independents and airline third parties.

The largest cost component of engine overhaul is material and parts, accounting for more than 60% of the total, in contrast to airframe maintenance, where labor is the most significant cost. Most parts come from the OEM, although secondary sources are PMAs and used parts in serviceable condition. Labor accounts for more than 20% of overhaul cost. According to FAA data from 2009, worldwide 217,376 technicians worked in engine overhaul, of whom 26% were certified by airworthiness authorities. In the USA in that year there were 95,272 technicians in the business, of whom 54% were FAA certified.

As with the airframe maintenance operations, the sources of supply to engine overhaul facilities are engine OEMs, PMA holders, and surplus dealers. Approximately 60% of engine OEMs are based in North America including GE, Pratt & Whitney, Honeywell, and Williams International. Virtually the entire remaining 40% are based in Europe, including Rolls-Royce and Safran. A small number of large PMA holders based in the USA control half the PMA market. These suppliers include HEICO, Chromalloy, BELAC, and Wencor. The remainder of the PMA market is distributed among hundreds of smaller, lower-tier suppliers. Surplus dealers of engine parts include OEMs as well as numerous smaller entities.

Component maintenance

Aircraft components include systems for aircraft control and navigation, communications, control surface movement, cabin air conditioning, electrical power, braking, and so on. Large transport aircraft have hundreds of such components from dozens of manufacturers, and the component MRO market is fragmented to a high degree.

As mentioned previously, components are customarily classified as either **line replaceable units (LRUs)** or **shop replaceable units (SRUs)**, depending upon whether they are removable on the flight line or must be disassembled in specialist backshops.

Wheels and brakes are usually the biggest items of component maintenance spending on aircraft, accounting for 15 to 20%. They are high-maintenance equipment due to the trauma to which they are exposed during repeated landings.

Flight deck avionics constitute the second-largest component MRO category, including cockpit displays, communications equipment, navigations systems, and autopilots. Collectively the group includes numerous LRUs and accounts for roughly 15% of component maintenance costs for commercial transports.

The third-largest category is maintenance of auxiliary power units (APUs), the small gas turbine-powered generators that provide electric power, engine starting capability, and cabin temperature control on the ground.

Other significant categories are fuel systems (8%), flight controls (8%), thrust reversers (5%), hydraulics (4%), electrical systems (4%), and landing gear (4%).

As with heavy airframe maintenance and engine overhaul, component maintenance is performed by OEMs, operators, airline third parties, and independents.

Component OEMs perform basic repair activities, refurbish parts, and sell new parts and components. Major OEMs include: Honeywell, Goodrich, Hamilton Sundstrand, Rockwell Collins, Thales, Safran, Parker Aerospace, GE Aviation, Eaton Aerospace, Meggitt, Woodward, Zodiac, Liebherr, and B/E Aerospace. Customarily, OEMs perform maintenance only on their own equipment.

Airline operators with significant in-house component maintenance capability include United Airlines, American Airlines, Delta Airlines, British Airways, Air France/KLM, Japan Airlines, and Lufthansa.

Airline third parties active in component repair include Delta TechOps, Lufthansa Technik, Air France/KLM Engineering, Singapore Airlines Engineering Company, United Services, and HAECO.

Many independent FAA-certified component repair firms serve the global market, of which the largest are SR Technics, ST Aerospace, Aveos, Triumph, AAR, Aviall, and NORDAM.

Component OEMs have the largest portion of this market with approximately 35% of the total, and their share rises to approximately half for APUs and avionics. Operators perform about 30% of the work, with airline third parties and independents accounting for the remainder.

Because of the relative ease and speed of packaging and shipping components internationally, the repair market is global. The USA has the largest share of component OEMs and unsurprisingly is the biggest presence in the component repair market. Europe ranks second.

Military MRO

Concepts used by military organizations to maintain, repair, and overhaul their aircraft are very similar to practices in the commercial sector. Flight-line operations generally take place at military bases, and heavy maintenance is conducted at depots or contractor facilities. Normally military entities maintain their own extensive inventories of spares rather than rely on supply from OEMs.

Within the US Air Force, flight-line maintenance is performed at individual operating bases but heavy maintenance is performed at contractor sites or at three depots called **air logistics complexes** located in Utah, Oklahoma, and Georgia. The three depots, which are part of the US Air Force Materiel Command, are also the principal Air Force repositories of parts and material.

The US Air Force uses a concept of **Integrated Product Support (IPS)** to manage and support its aircraft in service. IPS consists of the following 12 elements.

1. **Product Support Management**: plan, manage, and fund weapon system product support.
2. **Design Interface**: integrate reliability, availability, maintainability, etc. into the aircraft design process.
3. **Sustain Engineering**: provide continuing engineering and technical support following introduction of the aircraft in service.
4. **Planning and Management**: identify, plan, provide resources, and implement maintenance concepts and requirements.
5. **Manpower and Personnel**: acquire trained and qualified personnel to assure support of aircraft.
6. **Supply Support**: assure availability of parts and material.

7. **Support Equipment**: acquire and maintain ground support equipment.
8. **Technical Data**: conduct the process of acquiring and managing data to support the aircraft.
9. **Training and Training Support**: plan and implement training of personnel.
10. **Computer Resources Support**: identify, acquire, and manage facilities, hardware, software, documentation, and manpower to provide computer support.
11. **Facilities and Infrastructure**: provide and manage appropriate facilities and infrastructure.
12. **Packaging, Handling, Storage, and Transportation (PHST)**: manage inventory of parts and material.

Management and implications of MRO data

Modern digitized aircraft produce vast amounts of data, much of which is related to maintenance requirements and operational characteristics of the aircraft while in service. To facilitate and improve maintenance, all new transport aircraft are equipped with **aircraft health monitoring (AHM)** systems that continually capture data pertaining to parameters of operation of equipment while in flight. Sometimes this data is broadcast in real time directly to ground stations.

The volume of this data is increasing exponentially as sensors, processors, and communications systems improve. The AHM system of the Boeing 767, for example, monitors 10,000 operational parameters, whereas the newer Airbus 320 system monitors 15,000 and the Boeing 787 monitors 100,000. On a single typical flight, a Boeing 777 generates less than a single megabyte of transmissible AHM data. The 787 generates approximately 23 megabytes.

The availability of this data presents almost limitless possibilities for increased efficiency and cost savings. The respected consulting firm ICF International has estimated that future exploitation of data generated and received by aircraft in flight can reduce global airline costs by $5 billion per year through improvements such as:

* Improved dispatch reliability
* Reduction of erroneous fault diagnoses
* Inventory reduction due to more accurate anticipation of material requirements
* Improved labor productivity
* Continuous speed and altitude optimization in flight
* Expedited turnaround times
* In-flight routing optimization

However, the industry has begun to consider other aspects of the new plethora of data. Because the data clearly has value that in some cases remains to be discovered by imaginative entrepreneurs, the important question of ownership of the data arises. Ownership is ambiguous, and can reasonably be claimed to some extent by the airlines themselves, the MRO operators, and the OEMs. Certainly, in the future a more specific legal framework governing aircraft-generated data will evolve.

Another important legal issue involves liability for erroneous data. Limits have not yet been established to the degree to which users can prudently rely upon the accuracy of the millions of bytes of data produced by aircraft, but in the domain of aircraft maintenance any decision based upon false information can have serious negative consequences. And, as the troves of data are eventually used for secondary applications beyond the purposes for which they were originally intended, questions and controversies will inevitably arise concerning the extent to which the original sources of the data are responsible.

15 Environmental challenges and the aerospace industry

In this age of environmental consciousness, the aerospace industry is on the defensive. It builds machines that consume vast amounts of fossil fuels, emit untold tons of atmospheric pollutants, and broadcast noise at levels harmful to human beings.

It may be hyperbolic to portray environmental concerns as an existential challenge facing the industry. Nevertheless, in an epoch in which citizens and their governments agonize over global climate change, automobile miles per gallon, depletion of natural resources, and urban noise pollution, industry leaders have recognized that they must move aggressively to address the legitimate environmental concerns of the public and their customers.

In general, the aerospace industry has accepted responsibility for its share of the problem and has mobilized its considerable technological resources to devise solutions. Progress has unquestionably been made, and continuing innovations bring promise of further improvement in the future, but technological constraints are daunting.

Context of the problem

Currently, aviation generates a significant but small percentage of total global emissions, generally measured in the neighborhood of 2%.

Furthermore, air travel is a relatively benign mode of travel in terms of fuel consumed per passenger per mile traveled. For most of its history, commercial aviation's fuel consumption per passenger mile had been well above other common travel modes, but by the 1990s new technologies in aircraft and their engines had reduced consumption to the point that flying consumed less fuel than traveling in automobiles or public busses.

Environmental issues have become emotionally charged and politically controversial, and disagreements on the subject are rife. However, there is no disagreement that aircraft produce several pollutants, particularly carbon dioxide (CO_2), generic nitrogen oxide pollutants (NOx), and noise, that are potentially harmful to people and the environment. Scientists generally acknowledge that they do not fully understand the extraordinarily complex

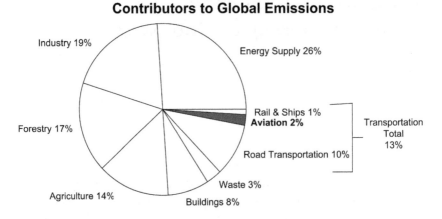

Figure 15.1 Air transportation currently contributes a minor share of greenhouse gasses.
Source: National Business Aviation Association.

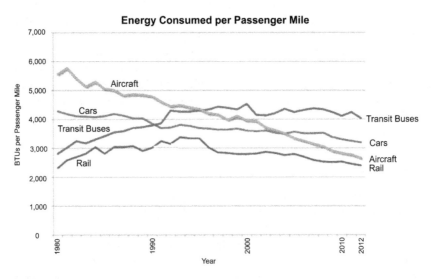

Figure 15.2 Improved comparative energy efficiency of air travel.
Source: Federal Aviation Administration (FAA).

processes through which atmospheric pollutants cause climate change, but the body of knowledge on the subject has increased profoundly in recent decades, and extensive study and research have yielded a broad consensus concerning the role of aircraft emissions in the creation of greenhouse gasses and other pollutants.

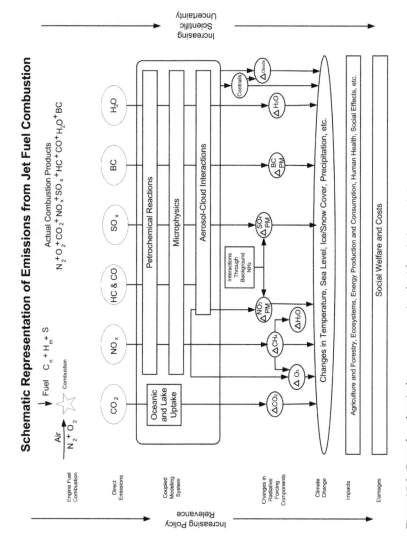

Figure 15.3 Complex chemical processes associated with aviation emissions.

Source: Federal Aviation Administration (FAA).

Contrails

A current controversial topic attracting the interest of climate scientists is the possible effect of contrails upon climate. Contrails, which are condensation trails produced by jet aircraft, normally form only above altitudes of about 8 km, where temperatures are typically below −40°C. In that temperature range, ice crystals form spontaneously because water vapor from combustion sublimates directly into ice. Contrails can also be triggered by changes in air pressure at wingtip vortices or as air passes over the wing surface.

The controversy surrounds the question of whether contrails affect surface temperatures, and if so, how much and in which direction. One hypothesis is that contrails cause sunlight to be reflected back into space, thus lowering average daytime temperatures. Experiments have indicated that solar radiation at the surface of the earth is reduced by 3 to 5% when sunlight passes through a contrail. On the other hand, cirrus clouds, which are similar to contrails, are known to have a warming effect on the global climate because they block longer-wave heat radiation attempting to leave the earth. But other experiments indicate that ice crystals in contrails are smaller than in cirrus clouds, with the effect that contrails would be much less efficient at blocking heat escaping from the surface.

The controversy over the climatic effects of contrails remains unresolved, with some scientists maintaining that contrails have the same warming effects as cirrus clouds, and other scientists concluding that contrails have a net cooling effect on the planet. The subject continues to be studied.

Climate accords

Landmark international accords in the past few years portend dramatic changes to the aerospace and aviation industries. The 2015 Paris Agreement, in particular, was an indication that the international community recognized climate change as a serious threat to human society and was prepared to act aggressively to deal with the threat.

The Paris Agreement content was negotiated by representatives of 196 state entities at the 21st Conference of the parties of the United Nations Framework Convention on Climate Change (UNFCCC). By the end of 2018, 195 UNFCCC members had signed the agreement and 183 had ratified it. The Paris Agreement's long-term goal is to limit global temperatures to a level 2°C above preindustrial levels.

The Intergovernmental Panel on Climate Change (IPCC) has announced that achieving the 2°C target will entail stabilizing atmospheric CO_2 at approximately 400 parts per million (ppm). The 400 ppm target is somewhat controversial, with various studies concluding that 450 ppm, 550 ppm, or other concentrations would accomplish the 2°C target.

Reaching the target would entail a level of international cooperation that has never before been possible, and would involve drastic changes in the way energy is produced and consumed in economies throughout the world.

Although it is not certain that the 2°C objective can be met, climate scientists have performed meaningful analysis by overlaying graphical plots of projected increases in CO_2 emissions from the air-transport sector and projected best-case decreases in CO_2 emissions for the rest of the economy. One such graph is shown in Figure 15.4, depicting emissions from 15 major EU economies. The alarming conclusion is that by the year 2050, CO_2 originating from transport aircraft will be roughly equivalent to the amount of CO_2 produced by all other parts of the economy combined.

This conclusion is highly controversial, and at best should be considered to be an extreme worst-case scenario. However, it has the useful effect of focusing attention on the unavoidable issue of aircraft emissions.

This analysis has been received with some skepticism because of underlying assumptions that are possibly unrealistic. The studies, conducted in the UK, assume that all goals for the reduction of emissions in the general economy will be accomplished by measures such as nationalization of the rail network, exponential expansion of the nuclear-power network, and fundamental changes in the role of automobiles.

In response to an increased general awareness of the potential risks to the environment posed by aviation, in 2001 the Advisory Council for Aviation Research and Innovation in Europe (ACARE) was launched. ACARE is

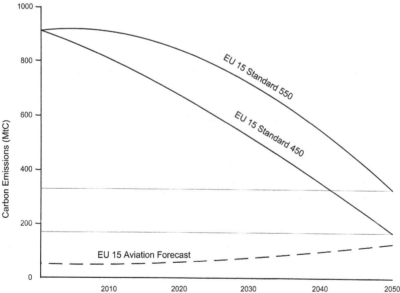

Figure 15.4 This chart demonstrates that projected aircraft emissions trends are moving contrary to aspirational environmental goals of the European Union.

Source: Tyndall Centre for Climate Change Research.

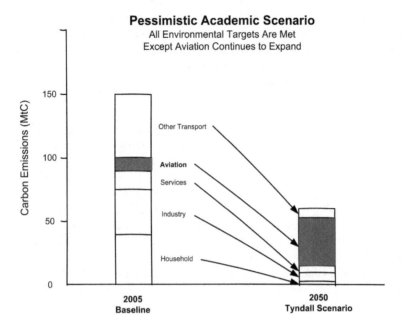

Figure 15.5 Other data developed by the same researchers as Figure 15.4 show dramatically
rising shares of greenhouse-gas emissions from aviation.

Source: Tyndall Centre for Climate Change Research.

sponsored by the European Commission and includes membership by representatives of European governments, the European Commission, and stakeholders such as manufacturing industry, airlines, airports, service providers,
regulators, research establishments, and academia.

ACARE has promulgated an agenda of goals relating to aircraft emissions,
to be accomplished by 2050, using the year 2000 as a baseline reference:

- A 75% reduction in CO_2 emissions per passenger kilometer
- A 90% reduction in NOx emissions
- A 65% reduction in perceived noise emission of flying aircraft

These are extremely aggressive goals, considered by many experts to be unrealistic. Historical data shows that over a period of approximately 30 years from
the mid-1960s to the mid-1990s, the aerospace industry was able to reduce
fuel consumption of its commercial transports by roughly 50%, as measured
by fuel burn per passenger per mile. Aircraft manufacturers continue to work
relentlessly to reduce fuel consumption, and the FAA projects that fuel usage
per passenger mile will decrease at an average annual rate of 1.39% between
now and the year 2050. Even if this exceptional rate of improvement can be

Table 15.1 Goals established by NASA for emissions reduction

NASA subsonic transport aviation improvement goals			
Technology benefits	*Technology generations*		
	Near-term (N+1) 2015–2025	*Mid-term (N+2)* 2025–2035	*Far-term (N+3)* beyond 2035
NOx emissions (takeoff and landing) (below CAEP 6)	70–75%	80%	>80%
NOx emissions (cruise) (relative to 2005 best-in-class)	65–75%	80%	0.20 > 80%
Aircraft fuel / energy consumption (relative to 2005 best-in-class)	40–50%	50–60%	60–80%
Noise (cumulative below Stage 4)	22–32 dB	32–42 dB	42–52 dB

Note: CAEP = ICAO Committee on Aviation Environmental Protection Standards.
Source: US National Aeronautics and Space Administration (NASA).

achieved in the decades to come it will be insufficient to meet the ACARE targets. However, the aerospace industry, aircraft operators, and the jet-fuels industry clearly recognize that their future existence is threatened by environmental issues, and they are allocating vast resources to develop technically innovative solutions to the problem.

Carbon dioxide (CO_2) has only been viewed as a pollutant since the 1960s, when scientific consensus began to emerge recognizing it as the dominant greenhouse gas responsible for global warming. As a consequence of the widespread understanding of the role of CO_2 in climate change, the aerospace industry has justifiably been a target of proponents of CO_2 reduction worldwide.

For a given fuel type, the amount of CO_2 emitted is directly proportional to the mass of fuel burned. Thus, the aerospace industry's historical trend of producing increasingly more fuel-efficient aircraft also results in reduced CO_2 emissions, although the absolute amount of the emissions remains significant.

Oxides of nitrogen (NOx) have various effects upon atmospheric chemistry and air quality, impacting human health in different ways. The importance of NOx as an atmospheric pollutant and the role of aircraft as a contributing factor remain subjects of study. NOx is produced by aircraft when nitrogen oxidizes at high temperatures in jet engines. In contrast to CO_2 emissions, which are directly proportional to the amount of fuel burned, the quantity of NOx emissions depends to a large extent on the design and operating characteristics of the engine. Only a small proportion of the nitrogen in the air entering the engine is converted to NOx. In general, the amount of NOx produced increases as the combustion temperature and pressure rise. This scientific reality exacerbates the problem for aircraft designers, because modern jet engines operate at increasingly high temperatures and high pressures in order to achieve higher levels of fuel efficiency.

International regulatory standards for aircraft-engine NOx emissions have been established by the International Civil Aviation Organization (ICAO)

Historical Data of Aircraft Fuel Burn

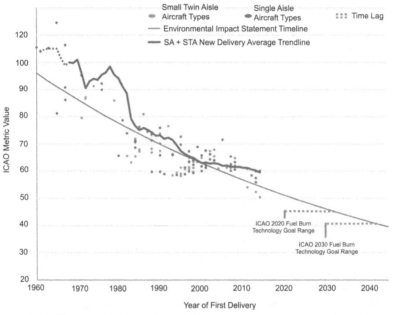

(The **ICAO Metric Value** is a calculated index of the rate of fuel burn per revenue tonne kilometre performed.)

Figure 15.6 Aviation fuel consumption and emissions have decreased steadily, but at historical rates insufficient to meet recent aggressive environmental goals.

Source: Wickrama, U, Henderson, S, Vedantham, A, et al. 1999, 'Aircraft Emissions: Current Inventories and Future Scenarios' *Aviation and the Global Atmosphere. Intergovernmental Panel on Climate Change*, Cambridge University Press, Cambridge.

Committee on Aviation Environmental Protection, or CAEP. The current working standard is CAEP/6, which imposes a decrease of approximately 40% from the original NOx limits set in the 1980s. According to ICAO, modern jet engines are generally in compliance with this standard. The US Environmental Protection Agency has adopted ICAO's certification standards as national regulations. The FAA, in turn, enforces these standards through engine certification. However, separate NOx targets for 2020 promulgated by ACARE (mentioned earlier in this chapter) entail an 80% reduction relative to the year 2000, and are thus much more aggressive. A third NOx target proposed by the National Aeronautics and Space Administration (NASA) in the USA, known as N+2, falls between the ICAO goals and the ACARE goals. The future technical advances required to meet both the ACARE and NASA targets would have to significantly exceed the rate of technical progress achieved over the last 30 years. Achieving the goals will be a daunting task for all concerned.

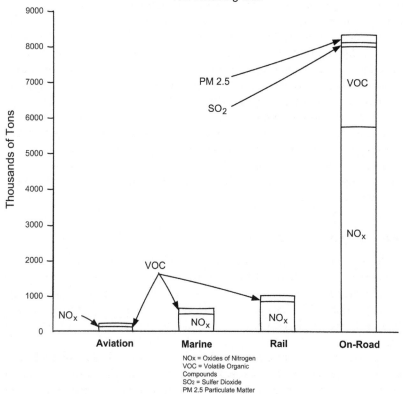

Figure 15.7 Currently aviation remains a minor producer of all types of harmful gasses.

Source: Federal Aviation Administration (FAA).

Table 15.2 Even in major American metropolitan areas with busy airports, emissions from aircraft remain a relatively small percentage of the total

Aircraft emissions contribution to US metropolitan areas

Percentage of total emissions

Metropolitan area	NOx (%)	VOC (%)	$PM_{2.5}$ (%)
Washington, DC	1.22	0.57	0.21
Philadelphia	0.64	0.35	0.20
New York	1.40	0.42	0.41
Denver	1.42	0.54	0.31
San Francisco	1.57	0.63	0.29
Dallas	1.76	0.58	0.23
Minneapolis	1.07	0.59	0.39
Chicago	1.27	0.49	0.36

Source: Federal Aviation Administration (FAA).

Aircraft noise

Noise generated by aircraft has come to be recognized as an important environmental concern, particularly when the aircraft are close to the ground, and especially around airports. Aircraft noise emanates from a number of sources, and historically engine noise such as jet exhaust and moving turbine blades have been the principal culprit. Modern jet engines, however, are much quieter than the first turbojets, and thrust-related noise has dropped by around 20 effective perceived noise in decibels (EPNdB), which is equivalent to a hundredfold reduction in sound power, and a fourfold reduction in perceived level. As engines have become quieter, other sources of aircraft noise have become proportionally more significant, particularly when engine power is reduced on approach to landing. These 'airframe-noise' contributions arise because of unsteady airflows, mainly around the landing gear and the wing high-lift devices such as flaps.

Increasing trends in air travel

Ironically, a major aspect of the environmental challenge confronting the aerospace industry is a direct result of the growing popularity of commercial air travel. Even though fuel consumption per passenger mile continues downward, the number of aircraft continues to increase as more passengers travel. Credible estimates indicate a 5% annual increase in air travel over the next 20 years.

As a consequence of more travelers and more aircraft, aircraft fuel consumption is projected to rise inexorably over the decades to come, in spite of increased efficiency of newer aircraft and improved aircraft operating practices

Historical Evolution of Aircraft Noise Levels

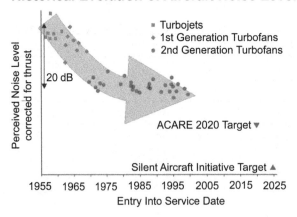

Figure 15.8 Aircraft noise has declined remarkably but has begun to plateau.

Source: Hall, C 2009, 'Low Noise Engine Design for the Silent Aircraft Initiative', *Aeronautical Journal.*

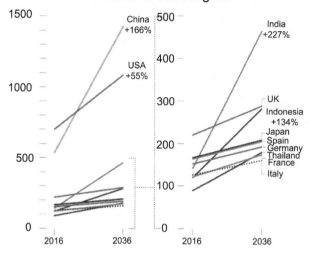

Top Ten Air Passenger Growth Markets
Millions of Passengers

Figure 15.9 The worldwide growth in air transportation.

Source: International Air Transport Association (IATA).

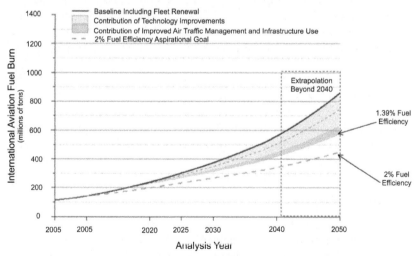

Fuel Burn Trends of International Aviation 2005–2050

Dotted Line in Technology Sliver Represents the 'Low Aircraft Technology Scenario'

Figure 15.10 Increased aircraft efficiency is not projected to offset fuel burned by increased aircraft use.

Source: International Civil Aviation Organization (ICAO).

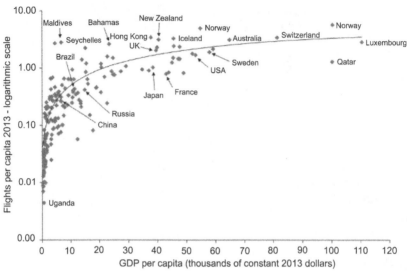

Figure 15.11 The very strong link between wealth and flying.

Source: International Civil Aviation Organization (ICAO).

that will also reduce consumption. Even if average fuel burn by aircraft per passenger mile decreases annually by 1.39% through 2050, as estimated by FAA analysis, aggregate aircraft fuel use will nonetheless triple during the same period because of the projected steep increase in the number of passenger miles flown.

Data and analyses that forecast this increase in air travel are robust. A very strong correlation exists between income and the amount of air travel. If international economies continue to grow, it appears almost certain that the extent of air travel will continue to increase. Air travel has also been shown to correlate strongly with the urbanization of populations, which is a continuing trend worldwide.

Alternative fuels

Faced with the inevitability of public and legislative pressure to reduce their environmental emissions, aircraft operators, jet-engine manufacturers, the FAA, and worldwide aviation authorities have publicly embraced a transition to alternative fuels. According to the FAA, development and deployment of sustainable alternative aviation fuels enable environmental improvements, energy security, and economic stability for aviation. The government and industry are cooperating through forums such as the Commercial Aviation

Alternative Fuels Initiative (CAAFI). New technical certification standards for alternative jet fuels have been established by the American Society for Testing and Materials (ASTM), and aircraft flight tests using alternative fuels are being conducted to confirm their suitability and environmental benefits. To date, ASTM has approved three categories of alternative jet fuels for blending with standard petroleum-based jet fuel. They include fuels from biomass, coal, or natural gas known as Fischer–Tropsch (FT); fuel from fats, plant oils, and greases known as Hydroprocessed Esters and Fatty Acids (HEFA); and fuel from fermented sugars known as Synthesized Iso-Paraffins (SIP). Fuels from other sources are undergoing certification, including fuels derived from municipal waste.

As ASTM approval and FAA certification for new fuels are granted, an industry to produce the fuels has come into existence and is rapidly growing, thus providing airlines with assured sources of supply.

Table 15.3 The steadily expanding alternative fuel industry

US synthetic jet fuel or biodiesel production facilities

Operational or planned

Project	Location	Feedstock	Technology	Capacity (million gallons per year)	Operation year (anticipated)
Fulcrum Sierra Biofuels	Storey County, NV	Municipal solid waste (MSW)	Gasification, FT	10	(2019)
Emerald Biofuels	Gulf Coast	Fats, oils, greases	HEFA	88	2017
Red Rock Biofuels	Lakeview, OR	Woody biomass	Gasification, micro-channel FT	16	2017
AltAir Fuels	Los Angeles, CA	Fats, oils, greases	HEFA	40	2016
REG Synthetic Fuels	Geismar, LA	Fats, oils, greases	HEFA	75	2014
Diamond Green Diesel	Norco, LA	Fats, oils, greases	HEFA	150	2013
SG Preston	South Point, OH	Fats, oils, greases	HEFA	120	(2020)
SG Preston	Logansport, IN	Fats, oils, greases	HEFA	120	(2020)

Notes:
All fuels are total gallons of production for combined jet and diesel.
FT = Fischer–Tropsch process.
HEFA = Hydrogenated Esters and Fatty Acids.
Source: US Department of Energy.

The vision of routine commercial flights operating with biofuels in their tanks has advanced from concept to reality as thousands of passenger-carrying flights have been completed without incident using the new fuels. Perhaps most impressive of these scheduled flights are the daily KLM flight from Los Angeles to Amsterdam of a Boeing 747-400 burning reprocessed waste vegetable oil, and the regular direct trans-Pacific Singapore Airlines flight from Singapore to San Francisco of an Airbus A350-900 using HEFA biofuel.

Alternative fuels do not result in a significant reduction in emissions during the combustion phase when the engine is in operation. This is because strict fuel specifications require alternative aviation fuels to have 'drop-in' characteristics that are essentially identical to fossil fuels during combustion. The benefit of sustainable alternative fuels is that they reduce aviation greenhouse-gas emissions during the production phase compared with production of petroleum-based fossil fuels. In the case of sustainable alternative fuels, the production phase includes the cultivation or acquisition of renewable biological material, known as feedstock, and the process of conversion of the feedstock into fuels. Thus, comparisons of alternative fuels to petroleum-based fuels are based upon the complete life cycle of the fuels. This basis is known as 'well-to-wake', or WTW.

Life-cycle analysis of alternative fuels attempts to measure the extent to which their production and use would reduce carbon emissions on a life-cycle basis compared with conventional jet fuel. The analysis takes into account all emissions released during the process of producing fuel. The measurements begin, depending on the nature of the fuel, from an oil well, planting of oil seed crops, or conversion of municipal solid waste. Added to these production-cycle emissions are the gasses emitted during combustion aboard the aircraft.

Although biomass-derived alternative jet fuels do not result in lower emissions during the combustion process, they have the potential to reduce life-cycle emissions compared to conventional jet fuel, since biomass-based hydrocarbons absorb CO_2 from the atmosphere during their growth, which is not the case with traditional fossil fuels. The absorption of CO_2 by the biomass is counted as a credit that is considered to partially offset the combustion CO_2 at the end of the life cycle. This biomass credit is the primary difference between biofuels and fossil fuels in terms of their carbon emissions.

However, like petroleum-based fuels, biofuels also generate emissions during their production processes, associated with acquiring a feedstock, transporting the feedstock, converting the feedstock to fuel, and transporting the fuel. Availability of farmland resources necessary to produce crop-based biofuels is also a potentially problematic consideration.

Many different types of alternative fuels are theoretically available, derived through different production processes and feedstock. These differing variables for each fuel type inevitably have an impact upon the practical feasibility of

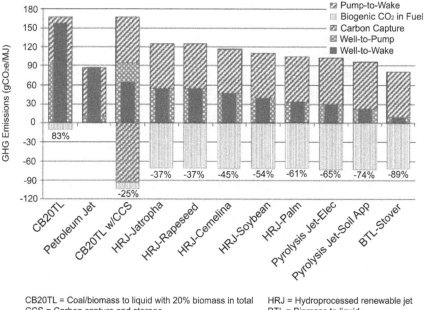

Figure 15.12 Biofuels can result in dramatic reductions in life-cycle emissions.

Source: National Academies of Sciences, Engineer, and Medicine 2016, *Commercial Aircraft Propulsion and Energy Systems Research: Reducing Global Carbon Emissions*, The National Academies Press, Washington DC.

producing the individual types in large-scale industrial operations. For biofuels originating from agricultural crops, for example, a significant potential downside is that emissions are typically generated by the direct or indirect conversion of land necessary to cultivate the crops. Agriculturally sourced biofuels also potentially compete for resources with food production. Consequently, alternative fuels produced from wastes are a particularly attractive possibility because they offer the potential to utilize a feedstock that is accessible without generating additional greenhouse gasses to produce it.

According to the European Aviation Safety Agency, aviation emissions may potentially be reduced by as much as 80% through the use of alternative fuels, depending on the feedstock type, the nature of the land used for cultivation, and the production processes. Likewise, the US Department of Energy estimates that WTW emissions of alternative fuels can be 85% less than petroleum fuels using currently available technology.

Land Use Requirements
Replacement of Petroleum Aviation Fuel by Biofuels

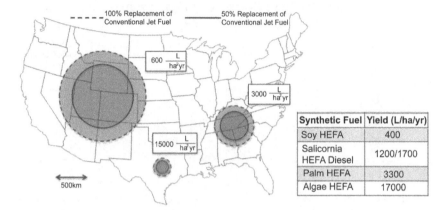

Synthetic Fuel	Yield (L/ha/yr)
Soy HEFA	400
Salicornia HEFA Diesel	1200/1700
Palm HEFA	3300
Algae HEFA	17000

Land Surface Necessary to Replace Conventional Jet Fuel with 50/50 Biofuel Blend or 100% Biofuel
(assumes US domestic jet fuel usage of 1.4 bpd, per EIA estimate 2009)

bpd = barrels per day
EIA = US Energy Information Administration
HEFA = Hydroprocessed Esters and Fatty Acids

Figure 15.13 Large-scale production of biofuels would occupy vast areas of land.

Source: Federal Aviation Administration (FAA).

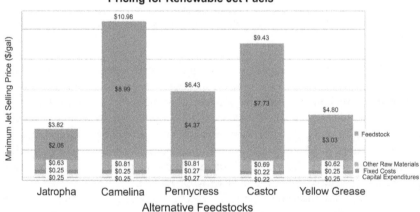

Figure 15.14 Biofuels remain more expensive than petroleum-based fuel, but costs are decreasing.

Source: Tao, L, Milbrandt, A, Zhang, Y, and Wang, W, 2017, 'Techno-economics and Resource Analysis of Hydroprocessed Renewable Jet Fuel', *Biotechnology for Biofuels*.

Of course, cost is a major factor in the feasibility of alternative fuels for aviation. As the alternative fuel industry remains in its infancy, potential producers are dealing with incomplete knowledge of science, technology, and economic factors associated with acquiring feedstocks and producing fuels. Small batches of many different types of fuels have been produced in laboratories or experimental facilities, but it remains difficult and unreliable to extrapolate these small-scale results to the massive industrial scale necessary to supply the worldwide aviation industry. Even as a few larger-scale processing plants have begun operation as proof of concept of the technology, many questions remain concerning availability and costs of feedstocks needed to provide the enormous quantities of jet fuel required by the aviation industry.

An additional benefit from the use of alternative fuels could be improved air quality. Depending on types of feedstocks and production methods, alternative fuels may contain reduced aromatics and sulfur, with the result that soot and sulfur oxides emissions are reduced when combustion of the final product takes place.

Biojet Fuel Production Facilities
North and South America 2015

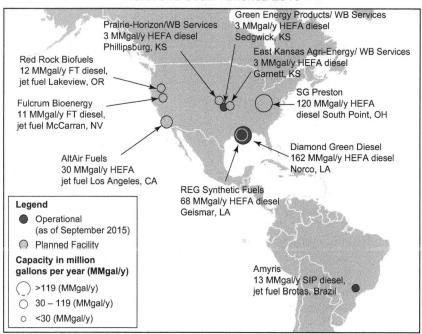

Figure 15.15 The infant alternative fuel industry in the Americas.

Source: US Energy Information Administration (EIA).

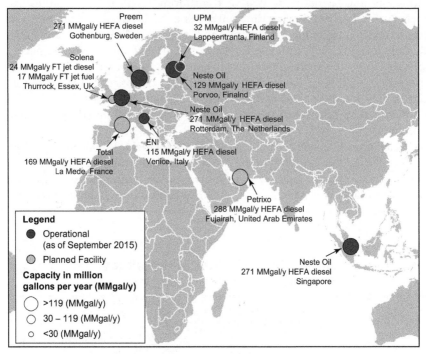

Figure 15.16 The infant alternative fuel industry in Europe and Asia.

Source: US Energy Information Administration (EIA).

Soundwaves

The second principal form of objectionable emissions from airplanes takes the form of soundwaves. Noise is produced by aircraft in flight and sometimes on the ground. Sources of aircraft noise fall into two general categories.

- Aerodynamic noise, produced when air meets the moving surfaces of the aircraft, including propellers, and is diverted to move around it. Aerodynamic noise is particularly apparent on the ground and when aircraft are flying at low altitudes at relatively high speeds. Noise of this type emanates notably from control surfaces and landing gear.
- Mechanical noise, primarily produced by rotation of the engine parts, especially when fan blades reach supersonic speeds. (In a sense, noise created by movement of gasses by fan blades can technically also be considered to be aerodynamic noise.)

For purposes of managing aircraft noise, a property of special interest is loudness. Generally, loudness correlates with pressure variations, as expressed by a unit of measurement known as a pascal, abbreviated as Pa. However, pascals are cumbersome to use in calculations because of the extremely wide range of values, so the unit of measurement most commonly used is the decibel (dB), which uses a logarithmic scale with a much narrower range. A particularly pertinent aspect of the decibel scale is that it gives a much better approximation of human perception of relative loudness than the pascal scale. This is because the response of the human ear to changes in loudness levels is more or less logarithmic in nature, which corresponds to the decibel scale.

Although excessive loudness may be the most objectionable characteristic of aircraft noise, other characteristics are also obnoxious to humans. Effective perceived noise, or EPNdB, is a measure of human annoyance to aircraft noise which has special spectral characteristics and persistence of sounds. In addition to human response to spectral shape, it accounts for intensity, tonal content, and duration of noise from an aircraft. EPNdB is calculated based on these measured variables and decibel levels.

Numerous studies have confirmed that excessive noise is detrimental to human health. The impact of aircraft noise was the subject of a 2006 large-scale statistical analysis by Bernhard Greiser for the Umweltbundesamt, Germany's central environmental office. The health data of more than 800,000 residents around the Cologne airport were analyzed for health effects correlating with aircraft noise. The results were then corrected for other noise influences in the residential areas, and for socioeconomic factors, to reduce possible skewing of the data. The German study concluded that excessive aircraft noise is significantly detrimental to health. For example, a daytime average sound level of 60 dB increased coronary heart disease by 61% in men and 80% in women. Likewise, a night-time average sound level of 55 dB increased the risk of heart attacks by 66% in men and 139% in women.

Other studies have shown that possible consequences include sleep disturbance and hearing impairment, as well as workplace accidents caused by stress. Memory and recall can also be affected.

Because of the undesirable effects of excessive aircraft noise, limits on noise emissions have been proposed by various national and international agencies, notably including the Advisory Council for Aeronautics Research in Europe (ACARE) and the National Aeronautics and Space Administration (NASA) of the USA. Noise targets published by the agencies differ somewhat in format, timing, and value, but are similar in that they promote drastic reductions in aircraft noise by the middle of this century.

Beginning in 1972, the International Civil Aviation Organization (ICAO) has established noise limits for aircraft of its member nations. The limits, identified by the 'chapters' of the international agreements of which they are part, have been continuously tightened over the years. As more recent aircraft designs have resulted in quieter aircraft, the ICAO standards have generally

Table 15.4 Aircraft noise reduction targets in Europe and the USA

Category	ACARE		NASA	
	Vision 2020	*FlightPath 2050*	*N+2 (2025)*	*N+3 (2030–2035)*
Noise	50%	65%	42 EPNdB	71 EPNdB
	Relative to year-2000 aircraft		Cumulative, relative to Stage 4	

Source: ACARE and NASA.

been met. The standards will certainly continue to become more rigorous as they eventually converge with the long-term NASA and ACARE targets.

Technical causes of aircraft noise are generally understood by design engineers, who have reduced noise levels by approximately 80% since the 1950s. However, due to trade-offs that are inevitably part of aircraft design, changes to reduce noise potentially entail degradation of other aspects of performance. Much of the noise reduction in recent decades is attributable to jet-noise reduction, a characteristic of high-bypass-ratio engines, which have also yielded greatly improved fuel efficiency. High-bypass-ratio engines, however, have increased fan diameters and large nacelles, which increase aircraft weight and aerodynamic drag. Thus, at some theoretical point the noise reduction and efficiency benefits of increasing bypass ratios will be offset by penalties imposed by larger nacelles. Numerous noise reduction opportunities involving airframe aerodynamic design also involve difficult trade-off decisions. For example, the noise from wing leading-edge slats

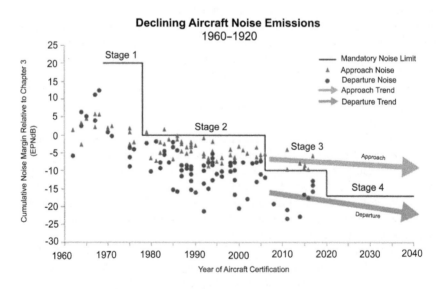

Figure 15.17 International standards progressively mandate quieter aircraft.

Source: National Aeronautics and Space Administration (NASA).

separated by gaps is significantly higher than a 'drooped leading edge' design, which performs the same purpose as slats but has historically been less aerodynamically efficient, resulting in higher fuel consumption. Likewise, airframe noise can be reduced very effectively by reducing landing speed. However, slower landing speed requires a larger wing, which entails substantial weight and drag penalties. Another comparatively simple but effective technical solution for noise reduction involves the installation of aerodynamic fairings around landing gear components. The landing gear has historically not been designed with aerodynamic shape as a priority and consequently generates inordinate turbulence and commensurate noise. The noise problem is particularly problematic because, obviously, the landing gear is deployed when the aircraft is close to the ground. Testing by NASA and Boeing indicates that landing-gear noise can be greatly attenuated by means of relatively simple fairings that divert air to minimize turbulence.

Jet-exhaust noise is caused by the violent turbulent mixing of the exhaust gasses with the atmosphere and is exacerbated by the shearing action caused by the difference in the relative speeds between the exhaust jet and the atmosphere. With past jet-engine designs, turbulence created at the engine exhaust exit caused a high-frequency noise unpleasant to humans. Low-frequency noise is created further downstream. At the same time, a shock wave is formed when the exhaust velocity exceeds the speed of sound. Recently developed technology to diminish exhaust noise involves incorporating serrated edges, called **chevrons**, on the engine exhaust nozzle and the back end of the engine nacelle. The chevrons have the effect of partially dispersing the concentrated exhaust flow, thus reducing the violent mixture with the atmosphere.

Noise Reduction Technology
Chevrons on Engine Exhaust and Nacelle

Figure 15.18 Chevrons reduce noise by altering aerodynamic flows.

Source: National Aeronautics and Space Administration (NASA).

Emissions trading systems

As governments worldwide consider the imposition of draconian plans to reduce greenhouse-gas emissions in order to achieve targets associated with strategies to reverse global-warming trends, aircraft manufacturers and operators find themselves in uniquely challenging circumstances.

As discussed earlier in this chapter, the aircraft industry faces two fundamental realities as it confronts environmental issues:

- Although fuel consumption per passenger mile is decreasing consistently and significantly, the annual number of passenger miles traveled is increasing at an even higher rate as worldwide income levels rise. Thus, the total quantity of fuel consumed by commercial aviation is rising rather than falling.
- Weight is a primordial consideration for aircraft design and operation, and so far, no practical power sources have been developed that have the **energy density** of hydrocarbons that emit CO_2 when burned. Unlike other transport vehicles that can, for example, carry heavy batteries and stop periodically to recharge, intercontinental aircraft flying across oceans or mountain chains require a fuel that is light and powerful. No realistic substitute for hydrocarbons currently exists.

Faced with this fact of life, aircraft operators are confronted with the likelihood that they will be unable to meet future government-mandated emissions limits, and in order to continue operating, may have to find recourse through official **emissions trading systems (ETS)**. Emissions trading systems are sometimes referred to as **cap-and-trade** schemes.

In the aftermath of the Paris Agreement of 2015 and the United Nations Framework Convention on Climate Change, numerous emissions trading systems were developed nationally and regionally. The 'cap-and-trade' principle of a typical ETS works as follows.

A cap is set on the total amount of certain greenhouse gasses that can be emitted by installations covered by the system. The cap is reduced over time to achieve the objective of overall reduced emissions. Within the cap, companies receive or buy emission allowances that they can trade with one another as needed. In some systems, they can also buy limited amounts of international credits from other emission-saving projects around the world. Because the total number of allowances is limited, there is reasonable assurance that they will have a value.

By far the largest emissions trading system currently in operation is that established by the European Union, known as the **EU-ETS**. It governs the emissions of all 28 EU countries plus Iceland, Liechtenstein, and Norway, and covers around 45% of the EU's greenhouse-gas emissions. National or regional systems also operate in China, South Korea, Canada, Japan, New Zealand, Switzerland, and the USA.

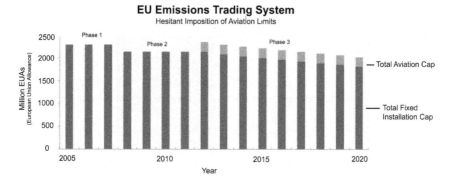

Figure 15.19 The EU-ETS has struggled to deal with aviation emissions.

Source: European Commission.

When the EU-ETS was initially established it did not include an emissions cap for the aviation sector, but the system was modified by EU legislation in 2008 to provide for the inclusion of aviation emissions beginning in 2012. The new rules applied to European airlines and all international carriers flying in European airspace, requiring them to buy credits.

Implementation of the EU-ETS provisions to include the aviation sector has been chaotic. Foreign airlines and their governments objected to the EU rules, protesting that they were essentially a tax that violated national sovereignty. China threatened to cancel planned purchases of Airbus aircraft.

The EU authorities immediately backtracked in an adjustment euphemistically referred to as 'Stop-the-Clock', and agreed to exempt international flights until 2017 in order to give ICAO time to formulate an international agreement that would accomplish the objectives of the EU-ETS. However, by 2017 no ICAO agreement had been implemented, and the EU indefinitely suspended the ETS requirement that credits be purchased for all international flights entering and leaving the EU.

In fact, in 2016 ICAO member states adopted an emissions trading system known as the Carbon Offsetting and Reduction Scheme for International Aviation, or CORSIA, which does not become mandatory until 2027. CORSIA imposes less aggressive limits than the EU-ETS, and has been criticized by environmental campaigners and some members of the European Parliament. Airlines generally support CORSIA because they prefer a single worldwide scheme rather than a disparate body of conflicting national regulations.

In the final analysis, CORSIA is often regarded as an imperfect regime by the diverse parties interested in aviation emissions, including environmentalists, airlines, the aerospace industry, air travelers, and others. However, it does offer a partial resolution of the greenhouse-gas emissions problem, for which no other workable solution has yet been developed.

Aircraft operational efficiency improvements

An important avenue for reduction of aviation emissions is the possibility of fuel savings resulting from improvements in aircraft operating efficiency. Large volumes of fuel are unnecessarily burned because of outdated aircraft operating practices. These operational inefficiencies include long wait times on taxiways with engines running, circling airports because of air traffic congestion at destinations, and following indirect routes in flight because of antiquated air traffic control systems.

Airlines have long been painfully aware of additional costs incurred by these operational inefficiencies and have attempted to enlist support for infrastructure changes necessary to reduce the problem. The recent international consciousness of greenhouse gasses produced by aircraft has added extra urgency to the quest for a solution.

Because of the highly regulated nature of the aviation industry, government commitment is indispensable to implement major changes in regulations and operational practices pertaining to aircraft movements. In the USA, the air traffic control system operated by the Federal Aviation Administration is essentially a technological legacy dating from the period following World War II. The system is highly reliable but is limited by the capabilities of its obsolete equipment.

To address the inadequacies of the system, in 2007 the FAA launched the Next Generation Air Transportation System, known as NextGen. Estimates of the cost of NextGen have increased since implementation began, but it now appears that more than $30 billion will be spent on the project before installation is complete in 2030, by which time the new system is projected to save 2.8 billion gallons of jet fuel that would otherwise have been unnecessarily burned.

The NextGen system encompasses numerous subsystems, several of which rely upon satellite technology. In the context of reduction of emissions, some capabilities are especially pertinent:

- More precise control of aircraft traffic, enabling aircraft to be grouped more closely together, thus reducing wait times in the air and on the ground
- Guidance of aircraft along smooth trajectories to their destinations rather than following zigzag paths to intermediate ground beacons, as is current practice
- Improved guidance of aircraft during their ascent and descent phases, notably enabling them to follow a consistent glide slope to landing, thus avoiding the current inefficient stair-step procedure of descending to a fixed altitude and flying level until instructed to descend to the next fixed altitude
- An improved instrument landing system that will reduce delays in bad visibility

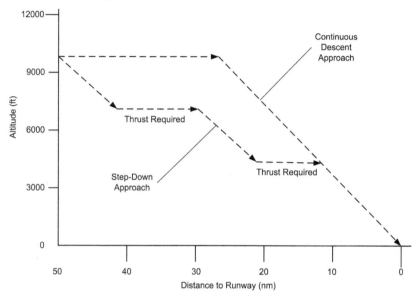

Figure 15.20 Continuous descent approach is an example of fuel savings through efficient
air traffic management.

Source: Eurocontrol.

Other technology to reduce operational inefficiencies involves reducing the amount of fuel unnecessarily burned by aircraft operating their main engines as they slowly transit taxiways. A project initiated by Airbus and Safran aims to install small electric motors connected to the landing gear wheels of the Airbus A320. Electrical power to the motors will be provided by the aircraft's auxiliary power unit, thus enabling the aircraft to propel itself along the taxiway while the main engines are shut down. The companies have announced that they intend to have the first unit installed and in service by 2020, and that they anticipate that the system will reduce average fuel consumption by 4%, with a commensurate reduction in emissions.

Operational inefficiencies have been a long standing characteristic of commercial aviation, resulting in unnecessary consumption of significant amounts of fuel and emission of greenhouse gasses. The steadily increasing quantity of commercial aircraft in service has exacerbated the problem as airspace and airports have become more congested. The good news is that existing technology can be used to reduce or eliminate many of these inefficiencies, and that the diverse stakeholders in the international aviation community are working together to implement modern systems that will help solve many of the problems.

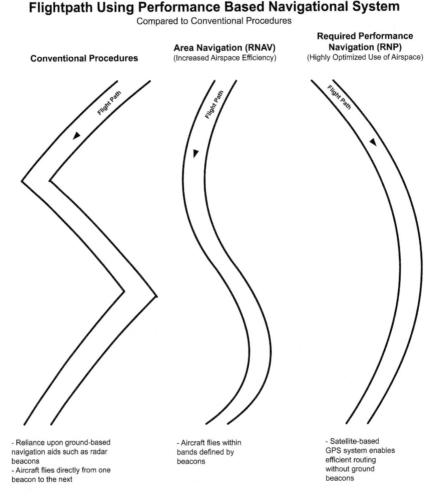

Flightpath Using Performance Based Navigational System
Compared to Conventional Procedures

Conventional Procedures

Area Navigation (RNAV)
(Increased Airspace Efficiency)

Required Performance Navigation (RNP)
(Highly Optimized Use of Airspace)

- Reliance upon ground-based navigation aids such as radar beacons
- Aircraft flies directly from one beacon to the next

- Aircraft flies within bands defined by beacons

- Satellite-based GPS system enables efficient routing without ground beacons

Waypoint: A predetermined geographical point that is most often used to indicate a change in direction, speed, or altitude along the desired path.

Figure 15.21 Fuel consumption declines if flight paths are smooth rather than zigzags.

Source: US Government Accountability Office.

Aeronautical design efficiency improvements

Over time, the aerospace industry has made remarkable technological progress to reduce the fuel consumption, atmospheric emissions, and noise of its products. However, aircraft improvements have been incremental, as designers have incorporated marginal aerodynamic improvements and have progressively improved engine power and fuel efficiency. The basic 'tube-and-wing' layout

Blended Wing Body Conceptualization

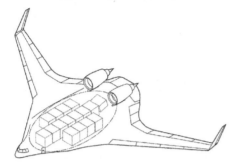

Figure 15.22 The blended wing body configuration is a departure from the shape of aircraft since the 1930s.

Source: National Aeronautics and Space Administration (NASA).

of commercial aircraft has not fundamentally changed since the 1920s, and the configuration of today's jet engines is remarkably similar to those of the 1960s.

In recognition of the urgency of the planet's environmental issues, aircraft designers have begun to seriously consider transformative technologies and new design concepts that depart radically from tradition. New concepts that are receiving widespread serious attention are new aerodynamic aircraft shapes and propulsion systems involving electrical power or hybrid fuel–electric technology.

Known in the popular media as flying wings, aircraft designs based on blended wing and body, or BWB, have been the subject of experimentation since World War II. The primary basis of their appeal as potential commercial transports is that they theoretically have inherently more efficient aerodynamic design and thus offer reduced fuel consumption and lower operating costs. For military applications, a compelling attribute is that the shape has a reduced radar cross-section, enabling stealth characteristics that increase prospects of survival in combat. The B-2 bomber of the US Air Force is a BWB design in service since 1997.

Flying properties of BWB aircraft are reasonably well understood, but continue to be studied by major aircraft manufacturers and NASA. Northrop Grumman has long been interested in the concept, and is the prime contractor for the B-2. McDonnell Douglas and later Boeing have worked with NASA to explore BWB technology, including designing and extensive flight testing of the X 48, a reduced scale, remotely piloted demonstrator. Lockheed has collaborated with the US Air Force and NASA to explore BWB concepts for military-airlifter and in-flight-refueling aircraft.

Like all aircraft design concepts, the BWB entails numerous trade-offs, but studies have reached the unanimous conclusion that the BWB has aerodynamic characteristics that allow significant improvements in operational efficiency when compared with conventional tube-and-wing layouts. The design allows lower weight, greater lift, and reduced drag. The exact extent of efficiency improvements depends upon the specifics of the design, but fuel consumption reduction in excess of 20% is widely projected. As a bonus, the design also reduces perceived noise on the ground.

Table 15.5 Aerodynamic attributes of the blended wing body shape

Aerodynamic efficiency of blended wing configuration

Wetted area comparison

	Conventional layout (ft²)	*Blended wing body (ft²)*
Fuselage	23,000	22,000
Wing	12,000	6,000
Propulsion	4,000	1,200
Empennage	5,000	500
Total	44,000	29,700

Note: Blended wing body has 33% less wetted area than conventional configuration.
Source: Liebeck, R 2006, 'Blended Wing Body Subsonic Transport Subsonic Transport Then, Now & Beyond', International Council of Aeronautical Sciences.

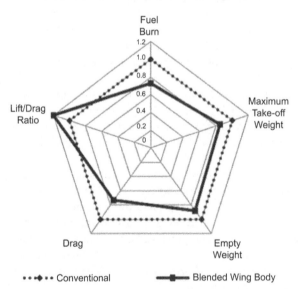

Figure 15.23 The blended wing body shape is aerodynamically superior but is not perfect.

Source: Marino, M and Sabatini, R 2015, 'Blended Wing Body Aircraft Compared to Current Airliners', in proceedings of International Symposium on Sustainable Aviation, Istanbul, Turkey.

Numerous important design issues have to be addressed before the BWB is ready to be introduced for commercial use. For example, limits on the thickness of the wing means that small versions would not have sufficient overhead clearance to enable passengers to stand, so the BWB layout will probably be limited to larger passenger aircraft. Additionally, the relatively flat shape of a wing is structurally less well suited to changes in pressurization than is the round shape of a traditional fuselage, so new internal structural design concepts would have to be used. Also, new flight control systems and software would have to be perfected. Other potential obstacles, such as possible passenger resistance to a strange new design, remain to be addressed.

One particularly intriguing possibility of the BWB is potential to fly with engines that consume liquid-hydrogen fuel. Because combustion of hydrogen releases zero CO_2 into the atmosphere, it has long been viewed as the ultimate sustainable aviation fuel, but the possibility of its use confronts a nearly insurmountable obstacle: hydrogen is not heavy, but its energy per unit volume is one-quarter that of standard jet fuel. In other words, it requires tanks four times as large to achieve the same payload and range. However, the much increased

Interior Layout Comparison
Conventional Boeing 767 and BWB Concept

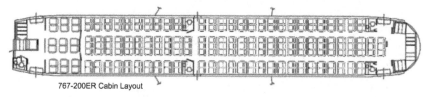

767-200ER Cabin Layout

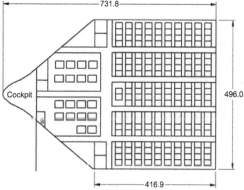

	Boeing 767 ft^2	BWB 216 ft^2
Seating Area	1367.1	1380
Aisle	358.4	367.5
Galley	74.6	74.7
Lavatory	62.2	62.7
Cockpit	78.7	76.9
Wardrobe	8.2	8.4
Cabin Crew Seats	15.0	15.6
Total Cabin Area	1964.2	1985.8
# of Exits	6	6
# of Middle Seats	30	98
# of Aisles	2	4

BWB 216 Cabin Layout and Associated Area Data

Figure 15.24 The new external shape results in a different interior layout.

Source: National Aeronautics and Space Administration (NASA).

internal volume of the BWB offers the possibility of greatly enlarged fuel tanks, although probably not by a multiple of four. Another negative factor is that aviation enthusiasts familiar with films of the Hindenburg disaster may not relish the prospect of boarding an aircraft that is essentially a flying hydrogen tank. In 2011 Boeing was granted a US patent for an original design involving the installation of a hydrogen fuel tank in a BWB aircraft.

As any child knows, toy airplanes powered by electricity fly very well. What captures the imagination of adult aircraft design engineers is the challenge of developing a full-scale electric transport aircraft that releases zero atmospheric emissions.

So far, the daunting obstacle facing designers of electric aircraft is that, as mentioned earlier in this chapter, the energy density of batteries is much less than the energy density of jet fuel or gasoline. For an equivalent weight of its power supply, the range of an electric aircraft would be much less than an airplane powered by hydrocarbon-based fuel.

Nonetheless, aircraft powered by electric motors have inherent efficiency advantages. The motors themselves tend to be lightweight, and they can easily be made in a range of sizes. It is comparatively easy to mount multiple small motors at various aircraft locations in what is known as distributed electric propulsion. Distributed propulsion can yield greater aerodynamic efficiency than a smaller number of larger conventional engines.

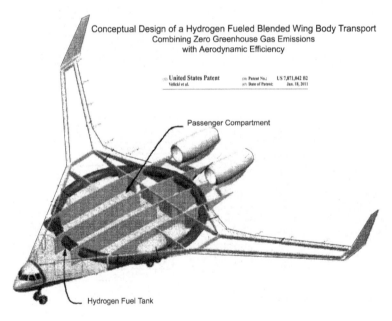

Figure 15.25 Boeing's concept of a hydrogen-powered blended wing body transport.

Source: Boeing, US Patent Office.

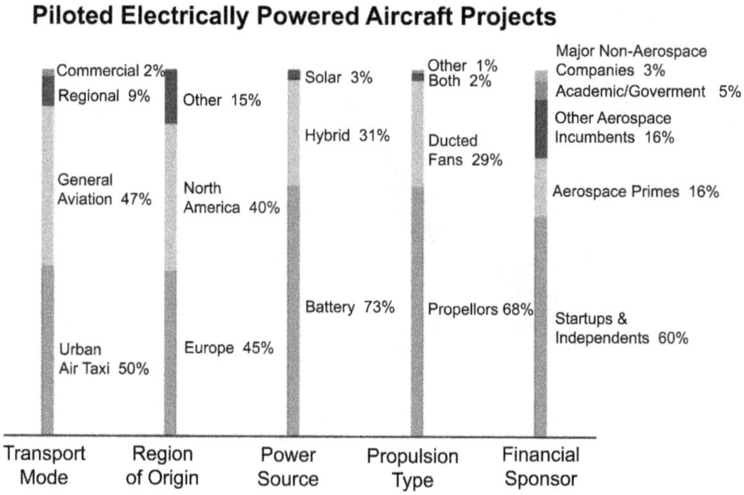

Piloted Electrically Powered Aircraft Projects

Commercial 2%

Regional 9%

Other 15%

Solar 3%

Other 1%
Both 2%

Major Non-Aerospace
Companies 3%
Academic/Goverment 5%

Hybrid 31%

Ducted
Fans 29%

Other Aerospace
Incumbents 16%

General
Aviation 47%

North
America 40%

Aerospace Primes 16%

Battery 73%

Propellors 68%

Startups &
Independents 60%

Urban
Air Taxi 50%

Europe 45%

Transport Mode	Region of Origin	Power Source	Propulsion Type	Financial Sponsor

Figure 15.26 Electrically powered aircraft are the focus of widespread research and development.

Source: *Aviation Week and Space Technology.*

Recent demonstration flights by prototype aircraft have confirmed the theoretical possibilities of electric propulsion. In 2016 the Swiss–built Solar Impulse completed a manned circumnavigation of the globe, powered exclusively by batteries and solar panels. Although the trip consisted of 17 relatively short segments interspersed with maintenance stops, its longest single leg was a 5-day flight across the Pacific Ocean from Japan to Hawaii. The aircraft had an average airspeed of 75 km per hour, weighed 2.3 tons, and had a payload of a single pilot. In 2018 an experimental remotely piloted solar-powered aircraft by Airbus stayed aloft for a continuous period of almost 26 days. It weighed 75 kg.

Capitalizing on continuous improvements in battery technology and the efficiencies of distributed propulsion, numerous entrepreneurs and a few established aircraft companies, including Boeing and Airbus, are attempting to develop electric aircraft suitable for commercial operations.

Because of limitations imposed by battery capabilities, virtually all aircraft powered entirely by electricity are short-range machines of relatively small size. However, serious well-funded research in the domain of turboelectric and hybrid fuel–electric propulsion seems to indicate that they possibly can be used effectively in larger, longer-range aircraft. NASA is actively working with private-sector companies to develop the technology.

Turboelectric systems encompass a fuel-powered turbine engine driving an electrical generator, which in turn provides power to electric motors driving fans. The relatively small size and weight of the electric motors allows them to

NASA Sceptor Distributed Electric Propulsion Concept

Multiple Small Electric Motors Driving High Lift Props

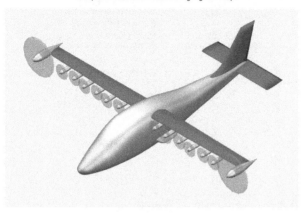

Figure 15.27 A NASA electric aircraft design.

Source: National Aeronautics and Space Administration (NASA).

Zunum Hybrid Regional Jet

Figure 15.28 Hybrid aircraft such as this Zunum design combine electric fans, batteries, and a turbine-powered electric generator.

Source: Zunum Aero (James Provost, illustrator).

be located to maximize aerodynamic efficiency, often employing distributed propulsion concepts.

A partially turboelectric concept developed by NASA has high-power generators integrated with each of the two wing-mounted turbofan engines. In addition to producing thrust, the engines generate megawatts of electricity that is routed to the tail of the airplane, where an electric motor and aft fan provide thrust and reduce drag by reenergizing the low momentum boundary layer air flow.

Fuel–electric hybrid aircraft systems exist in several variations. One configuration alternative uses onboard batteries to drive a motor that is attached to the aircraft's principal turbofan engine, augmenting the shaft speed during the cruise phase of the flight. This approach reduces the amount of jet fuel required to produce thrust from the engine, thereby reducing emissions.

A particularly aggressive hybrid development is a joint program announced by Airbus, Siemens, and Rolls-Royce. Using a four-engine BAe 146 test airframe, the partners intend to remove two of the turbojets and replace them with electrically powered fans. The fans will receive power from an onboard generator driven by a separate modified fuel-powered Rolls-Royce turboprop engine installed inside the fuselage. Batteries housed in the cargo hold will produce 2 MW of power for takeoff and cruise, further reducing fuel consumption. The partners project that the prototype will be flying by 2020 and that a certificated production version of a 50–100 seat aircraft using the technology will be available to enter service with regional airlines by 2035.

Index